AN INTRODUCTION TO
DIGITAL
MULTIMEDIA

T. M. SAVAGE

K. E. VOGEL

Both of University of New Hampshire at Manchester

JONES AND BARTLETT PUBLISHERS
Sudbury, Massachusetts
BOSTON   TORONTO   LONDON   SINGAPORE

World Headquarters

Jones and Bartlett Publishers
40 Tall Pine Drive
Sudbury, MA 01776
978-443-5000
info@jbpub.com
www.jbpub.com

Jones and Bartlett Publishers
Canada
6339 Ormindale Way
Mississauga, Ontario L5V 1J2
Canada

Jones and Bartlett Publishers
International
Barb House, Barb Mews
London W6 7PA
United Kingdom

Jones and Bartlett's books and products are available through most bookstores and online booksellers. To contact Jones and Bartlett Publishers directly, call 800-832-0034, fax 978-443-8000, or visit our website www.jbpub.com.

Substantial discounts on bulk quantities of Jones and Bartlett's publications are available to corporations, professional associations, and other qualified organizations. For details and specific discount information, contact the special sales department at Jones and Bartlett via the above contact information or send an email to specialsales@jbpub.com.

Production Credits
Acquisitions Editor: Timothy Anderson
Production Director: Amy Rose
Associate Production Editor: Melissa Elmore
Senior Marketing Manager: Andrea DeFronzo
V.P., Manufacturing and Inventory Control: Therese Connell
Composition: Northeast Compositors, Inc.
Cover Design: Kristin E. Ohlin
Cover Image: © Tischenko Irina/ShutterStock, Inc.
Printing and Binding: Malloy, Inc.
Cover Printing: Malloy, Inc.

Library of Congress Cataloging-in-Publication Data
Savage, Terry M.
  An introduction to digital multimedia / Terry M. Savage, Karla E. Vogel.
      p. cm.
  Includes bibliographical references and index.
  ISBN-13: 978-0-7637-5052-7 (pbk.)
  ISBN-10: 0-7637-5052-2 (pbk.)
  1. Multimedia systems. 2. Digital media. I. Vogel, Karla E. II. Title.
  QA76.575.S29 2008
  006.7--dc22
                        2008013119

6048
Printed in the United States of America
12 11 10 09 08   10 9 8 7 6 5 4 3 2 1

Preface

Digital multimedia, or "new media" as it is sometimes called, has created a revolution in communications, commerce, and entertainment. *An Introduction to Digital Multimedia* was written with the belief that effective use of modern multimedia requires a new combination of knowledge and skills—some centered on the keyboard and others oriented to concepts and context.

First, multimedia development requires practical skills in the use of specific software and hardware: operating systems, media editing programs, authoring applications, and software utilities. Because they vary with specific applications and continually evolve with each new release, these essential skills are best developed through software-specific texts and workbooks. Second is the understanding of the fundamental concepts that guide efficient and effective use of software and hardware: the defining properties and the uses of digital data, the various categories and purposes of software, and the components and functions of hardware systems. These are presented in this text through chapters that cover each of the major areas of multimedia development. Finally, there is vision, the understanding of the actual and potential uses of multimedia. Although the most abstract and elusive of the three areas, this is also the most basic: every multimedia product, from the simplest individual creation to multi-million dollar productions by skilled teams of professionals, implements some kind of vision. This book seeks to inform and deepen that vision by introducing readers to the history and legacy of the multimedia pioneers, by revealing the continuing revolutionary potential of computers themselves, and by encouraging reflection on the essential features of traditional analog media and their dramatic extension and transformation by digital technology.

An Introduction to Digital Multimedia can be used in several ways. It serves as a general survey of the essentials of the field for any interested reader. It may also be used as the primary resource for a variety of college courses in digital media. The text contains all that is needed for a first course in computing, including introductions to the fundamentals of computer hardware, software, and digital data. Courses with computer science or computer information systems prerequisites may use these chapters for a brief review or to begin discussions of individual media. Courses and workshops that focus on practical production skills may choose to focus on the media and authoring chapters.

For a full course in multimedia, we suggest using *An Introduction to Digital Multimedia* in conjunction with one or more of the many excellent texts and workbooks on specific media editing and authoring programs. In this way, the computer skills taught in the lab will be reinforced and deepened through an understanding of:

- The historical origins of multimedia
- The nature of digital data
- Fundamentals of computer hardware and software
- Defining features, uses, and practical development considerations for each of the major media: text, graphics, sound, video, and animation
- Authoring software and the authoring process
- Multimedia development: stages, tasks, and participants

Digital multimedia is a new form of literacy and a powerful tool of creative expression available to nearly everyone. Whatever you choose to do with this exciting medium, we hope that the chapters that follow will make your experiences with multimedia richer and more satisfying. We also hope that you will add your own vision to the dreams of the pioneers in the field as you discover new uses for the extraordinary tools of the digital age. Above all, *An Introduction to Digital Multimedia* is an invitation to join the multimedia revolution.

Instructor Resources

- Answers to Exercises
- PowerPoint Lecture Slides

Acknowledgments

We want to express appreciation to our spouses, Jane and Marty, for their support throughout the process of producing this book. Their patience and encouragement made this project possible.

Thank you to the reviewers for their feedback: Dr. Chareen Snelson, Boise State University; Dr. Amir Hussain, University of Stirling; Jim Mahoney, Marlboro College.

Special thanks also go to the entire editorial and production team at Jones and Bartlett. Their wonderfully efficient guidance and support was critical in transforming our manuscript into a finished product.

We especially want to acknowledge and express appreciation to the students in our multimedia classes at UNHM. Their "beta" testing of each chapter and their suggestions for additions and improvements over the past four years have been invaluable.

We dedicate this book to them, and to the students yet to come, in the hope that it will contribute to their knowledge and talents as they shape the exciting new world of interactive multimedia.

Table of Contents

Chapter 1

The Multimedia Revolution

Topics you will explore include:

"Any sufficiently advanced technology is indistinguishable from magic."

Arthur C. Clarke

Multimedia computing has produced a revolution. We shop, study, research, play, and communicate differently because of it. Like other advanced technologies, multimedia is, as Clarke would say, magical.

How else should we describe a little box, which gets smaller but more powerful each year, and which pours forth an endless stream of words and sounds of pictures and movies? The multimedia computer captures all manner of worldly experience and even presents us with worlds of its own.

As dramatic as the impact of multimedia has been, its story is far from finished. We have good reason to anticipate ever more powerful multimedia systems. Multimedia is not only advanced; it is advancing. The revolution will continue.

Revolutions displace traditional beliefs and practices. They also create entirely new activities and products. The industrial revolution displaced traditional craftsmanship; goods that had been produced by hand in small shops were now made in factories by machines. It also produced new materials and products—steel, plastic, automobiles, and airplanes—that radically changed the ways in which people conducted their lives. The multimedia revolution is also displacing tradition and ushering in new products and activities. In this chapter we explore the nature of contemporary multimedia as well as the innovations of the pioneers whose visions shaped its evolution.

After completing this chapter, you should understand:

- The defining elements of modern multimedia, including its different forms.
  - Non-interactive
  - Interactive
    - Basic
    - Hypermedia
    - Adaptive
    - Immersive
- Key contributions to the development of multimedia by:
  - Vannevar Bush
  - Alan Turing
  - Douglas Engelbart
  - Theodore Nelson
  - Alan Kay
  - Steve Jobs
  - Tim Berners-Lee
- The potential of digital multimedia.

1.1 Multimedia Defined

Contemporary **multimedia** is defined as the development, integration, and delivery of any combination of text, graphics, animation, sound, or video through a computer.

The key term in this definition, the one that transforms tradition and produces "new media," is "computer." The digital computer displaced traditional techniques for creating and editing all forms of media. Word-processing displaced the typewriter, the CD transformed sound and music production, and digital cameras and editing software are replacing film and the darkroom. The reason for this transformation is simple: computers can now create media that rival the quality of traditional products and they can do so more efficiently and more economically. Analog media, like traditional craftsmanship, will continue to exist, but their dominance in the marketplace is at an end. Most media professionals are building their careers with digital technology.

> The term "computer" derives from the human calculators who performed complex mathematical operations before these functions were completely automated. For many years, most people thought computers would only be used for calculation and sorting data.

The multimedia revolution is not just about performing traditional tasks in new ways. It is also about creating new approaches to communication, commerce, education, and entertainment. Cell phones become text messengers, cameras, and video displays. E-commerce gives shoppers instant access to countless products and services complete with pictures, demos, reviews, and price comparisons. Classrooms lose their walls as digital media—graphics, animation, sound, and video—stream through electronic networks. New forms of entertainment, such as podcasts, video games, online poker tournaments, and interactive film, have transformed that industry as well. In these cases, and in many more, digital multimedia is changing the world by making it possible for users to interact with information in new ways.

So important are these new forms of interactivity that multimedia applications are often differentiated based on the degree and quality of interaction they support. Some applications are designed to allow little or no interactivity; others encourage as much interaction as possible.

In **non-interactive multimedia**, the user has no control over the flow of information. The developer establishes a sequence of media elements and determines the manner in which they will be presented. An information kiosk at a museum might regularly repeat a series of slides describing the day's events. Such applications are often a simple and effective way to draw attention to announcements, products, or services without requiring any action of the part of the viewer. Digitally animated films, such as *Toy Story* or *Shrek*, are much more sophisticated and are engaging examples of non-interactive multimedia. The greatest promise and power of multimedia, however, lies in its ability to transform passive recipients of information into active agents.

In **interactive multimedia**, users are able to control the flow of information. There are several types of interactive multimedia. The first provides **basic interactivity**. Basic interactions include menu selections, buttons to advance screens, VCR-like controls, clickable objects, links, and text boxes for questions or responses. **Hypermedia** is a more advanced form of interactive media in which the developer provides a structure of related information and the means for a user to access that information. An online anatomy tutorial, for example, organizes information based on physiological relationships and may enhance a user's understanding through hyperlinks to related text, drawings, animations, or video.

Still more advanced forms of interactive multimedia adapt the presentation of information to the needs or interests of users. Such applications range from relatively simple merchandizing programs that offer suggestions for purchases based on past interactions to advanced tutorials that adjust lessons based on student performance. These applications embody aspects of intelligence and decision-making and are described as **adaptive multimedia** or **intellimedia**. The range of these forms of multimedia is likely to expand significantly with continued development in another major area of computer research—artificial intelligence.

Another powerful form of multimedia interactivity is found in advanced simulations and games that create their own **virtual reality**. Virtual realities are not simply responsive to users; they are *immersive*. An **immersive multimedia** application draws its users into an alternate world, engaging them intellectually, emotionally, and even viscerally. Advanced flight simulators so thoroughly immerse pilots in a world of virtual flight that they routinely serve as substitutes for training in actual aircraft. Video games can draw players into other worlds for hours or even days on end.

Multimedia will continue to shape our world, and each of us can benefit from knowing more about what it is, where it came from, how it works, and where it is likely to go. Individual involvement in the creation of multimedia will vary widely. For some, multimedia production may mean little more than attaching photos to email. Others will create presentations or build their own websites. Yet others will become specialists in one of the many areas of professional multimedia development. All will find that advancing digital technology continually puts more power in their hands—power to shape media to their own purposes.

Using this power effectively requires an understanding of the basic concepts that underlie multimedia hardware and software. It also requires a basic knowledge of the practices and principles of a wide range of media. Multimedia is, first and foremost, interdisciplinary. By definition, it draws on the multiple traditions, talents, and perspectives of text, graphics, sound, video, and animation. To use these varied resources effectively, multimedia developers need an awareness of the traditions and best practices of each. In chapters to come, we will explore each of these topics.

Taking advantage of the power of multimedia also means looking to the future and actively considering the new possibilities of digital technology. To try to envision the future, it helps to revisit the visionaries of the past. These were the pioneering theorists who glimpsed the promise of multimedia long before there were multimedia computers. Their stories will help us understand the reasons for many of the features of multimedia computers—hyperlinks, mice, windows, graphical user interfaces—and also the reasons to expect more innovations in the future.

1.2 Origins of Multimedia

In a sense, multimedia can be traced to the beginnings of civilization. Early humans had a clear appreciation of the value of reinforcing their messages with different kinds of sensations. Cave paintings at Lascaux in southern France were given an air of mystery through the psychological and sensory effects of the passageways—deep, dark, and cold—which led the visitor away from an ordinary world to an otherworldly realm (Packer and Jordan 2001, xx–xxi).

Early theatrical performances greatly extended this interest in multi-sensory experience. Ancient Greek actors performed to the accompaniment of music and the chanting and singing of a chorus. Elaborately painted stage scenery, apparently with convincing three-dimensional effects, and stage props (furniture, weapons, even chariots) formed a backdrop for performances. The Greeks also made use of various machines to heighten the intensity of the dramatic performance. One (the *keraunoskopeion*) simulated lightening; another (the *bronteion*) produced the rumble of thunder.

Multimedia further evolved as new technologies arose to represent various forms of sensory experience. By the early twentieth century, it was possible to add sound to previously silent films, and movies became multimedia. As new capabilities were added later in the century (including color, stereo, and surround sound), and as filmmakers learned to exploit the potential of their tools (close-ups, fades, flash-backs, cut-aways, and special effects), the movie developed a formidable expressive power.

By the mid-twentieth century, the pace of technological development increased dramatically. A very different kind of machine emerged, and a few individuals began to glimpse the possibility of using it to dramatically extend the scope of multimedia.

Vannevar Bush and the Memex Machines

Few men were as well poised as **Vannevar Bush** (1890–1974) to understand the revolutionary potential of the emerging technologies. Bush was the director of the (U.S.) Office of Scientific Research and Development during World War II and oversaw the work of some six thousand scientists on projects ranging from radar to the atomic bomb. He was also an experienced and talented scientist in his own right, having developed, among other things, the Differential Analyzer, a massive electro-mechanical, analog computer for solving differential equations.

In 1945, Bush wrote "As We May Think." In this now-classic article, he proposed the creation of a new kind of machine to make the work of scientists more efficient and to make more effective use of the huge and "growing mountain of research" (88). The machine would accomplish this by overcoming human weaknesses and building on human strengths. Bush's hypothetical machine was called Memex and multimedia was central to its design.

Memex I

One important human limitation is memory. We are limited in how much we can remember and our memories are neither completely reliable nor permanent. In Bush's first vision, **Memex** (or "memory extender") would solve these problems with microfilm. He envisioned a complete *Encyclopedia Britannica* stored in the space of a matchbox. Many other texts, photos, and handwritten notes would readily fit in the space of his desk-like machine. The capacity of Memex would be huge—one could add five thousand pages a day and it would still take hundreds of years to fill the machine. The contents of the Memex would be completely accurate and they would last forever.

Another human limitation is data recording. This is often a slow and laborious process. Bush proposed several multimedia devices to aid in collecting and recording data for the Memex. These included a "vocoder," which would produce written input from the spoken word, and a "Cyclops Camera" to be worn on the forehead and controlled by a wire running to a hand (Figure 1.1). The camera would allow a researcher to immediately photograph anything of interest. Pictures would be rapidly developed using a dry-photography technique and could also be connected to the written record in the machine.

Figure 1.1 Sketch of Cyclops Camera.

Time-consuming repetitive thought processes, such as arithmetical calculations, also limit human intellectual productivity. Bush's machine would take over these tasks by automatically performing mathematical calculations and carrying out simple forms of logical reasoning. Memex I would not be capable of "mature thought"; however, by freeing its user of the burdens of calculations and simple inferences, it could make more time available for creative, original thinking.

In a number of ways, then, Bush believed that his machine could compensate for the limitations of human intellect. Memex could also revolutionize the way information was stored and accessed by taking advantage of a human strength.

The human mind, he argued, operates by association: "With one item in its grasp, it snaps instantly to the next that is suggested by the association of thoughts, in accordance with some intricate web of trails carried by the cells of the brain" (Nyce and Kahn 1991, 101). Traditional systems of organizing information rely on alphabetical or numerical lists. These have nothing to do with the way information is generated or used in the mind. As a result, it is often difficult to find related facts and beliefs. Bush's Memex, in contrast, would organize its information based on associations, or as we actually think.

To form an association between two items of knowledge (facts, beliefs, theories, etc.), the Memex user would simply display them together and tap a key. The items would

Figure 1.2 Visionary Sketch of Memex (Note mechanical details).

then be joined. Repeating this process with other items would produce a **"trail"** of associations that could then be preserved, copied, shared, modified, and linked to other trails. The next time a particular item was accessed, all of its connections to related information would also be available. The pattern of associations Bush had in mind would be vast and complex. In fact, he described Memex as "an enlarged intimate supplement" to its user's memory, one that "stores all his books, records, and communications, and which is mechanized so that it may be consulted with exceeding speed and flexibility" (Nyce and Kahn 1991, 102) (Figure 1.2).

"As We May Think" also covered some of the operational details of the Memex—levers to advance pages, keys to return to the first page, the ability to annotate sources, the advantages of vacuum tubes over mechanical switches, and so on. In general, however, his article was a kind of "imagineering" in which new conceptual possibilities rather than blueprints for actual machines were his concern. He had ignored, as he said, all sorts of "technical difficulties" but he insisted that he also had ignored "means as yet unknown" that would dramatically accelerate progress toward the actual construction of a Memex. Between 1945 and 1959, a number of such advances did occur and these occasioned another article by Bush called "Memex II."

Memex II

Memex II was very similar to the original Memex. Bush still emphasized the importance of association as a means of indexing knowledge, and he still thought of his machine as a device to assist individuals in accessing and manipulating different forms of information. Technical developments suggested, however, that the original dream was much closer to realization and that it could be extended in various ways. Many innovations had impressed Bush, but the most significant were magnetic tape, the transistor, and the digital computer.

Magnetic tape was a more suitable storage medium than the dry photography of Memex I. It could be written to, or erased, almost instantaneously and it could hold more information. Magnetic tape also had greater multimedia capability—in addition to recording text or still images, it could hold "scenes, speech, and music" as well as movies and television.

Memex I aided its owner by storing and retrieving information by association and by automatically performing repetitive, time-consuming mental tasks. Memex II envisioned an extension of these benefits with large, professionally-maintained associational databases. These databases could be purchased on tape or even delivered remotely via facsimile transmission. Bush's "trails" of associations would now be more sophisticated (color-coded to reflect their age, for instance) and reinforced by repetition, much as the mind can reinforce its memories.

More significant, however, were the ways in which an improved Memex might be combined with a digital computer. The Memex could efficiently organize enormous amounts of information, and it could perform basic logical operations on that information. To realize its full potential, however, Bush believed that "Memex needs to graduate from its slavish following of discreet trails . . . and to incorporate a better way in which to examine and compare the information it holds" (Nyce and Kahn 1991, 180). The computer seemed to Bush to offer the possibility of such a "better way." Memex II could be used in many different disciplines. As an example, Bush sketched a system in which this new, hybrid machine would use evaluation functions to continually revise its recommendations for medical diagnoses and treatment plans to physicians. His machine would learn from experience, effectively incorporate incomplete or even contradictory information, and thus even demonstrate a form of judgment. Doctors could use Memex to supplement their own memories of particular cases and to receive diagnostic advice based on the machine's database of previous cases and treatments.

Bush stressed that such machines would always be subordinate to their human owners and he thought that there would be areas of human creative endeavor that "will always be barred to the machine" (Nyce and Kahn 1991, 183). But he also recognized the significance of early work in artificial intelligence (AI) and he even anticipated, at least in general outline, such future AI initiatives as expert systems.

> **AI and Expert Systems**
>
> **Artificial intelligence** is a field of computer science dedicated to developing computer systems that behave as if they have human intelligence. **Expert systems** were AI initiatives of the 1970s and 80s. These systems incorporated the knowledge of content experts such as physicians or engineers. One of the first, *Mycin*, aided in the diagnosis of blood diseases.

Bush's work is remarkable for its early insights into the ways in which multimedia machines might improve the collection and use of information. He knew that advancing technology provided an opportunity to shape new tools to serve human needs and his work remains a model of the creative possibilities of "imagineering." The revolution Bush foresaw continues, and it continues for a reason that he glimpsed but did not fully articulate. The machine that he saw as a useful addition to his Memex came to dominate all information systems and, for that matter, virtually every aspect of modern life. The source of the extraordinary development, and continuing potential, of the digital computer is to be found powerfully expressed in the work of another twentieth century theoretician, the British mathematician Alan Turing.

Alan Turing and the Universal Machine

Alan Turing (1912–1954) was an important contributor to the development of the modern computer. Turing made practical contributions to computing, including work on a special-purpose computational machine, the "Colossus," used to break the German Enigma code in World War II. His most significant contribution was theoretical, however. He made it in 1936, well before there were any digital computers at all. In that year, Turing published a paper with the formidable title, "On Computable Numbers with an Application to the Entscheidungsproblem." The paper was concerned with the problem of proving whether or not there could be an effective procedure (that is, a step-by-step process) to answer all questions of mathematics.

He concluded that there would always be mathematical problems that could not possibly be solved. In order to demonstrate this, Turing needed a clear definition of "effective procedure." He found his definition in the operation of a kind of abstract machine, which has come to be known as a "Turing machine."

A Turing machine is an imaginary device with three main components: first, an infinitely long tape consisting of a single row of squares; second, a read/write head that can move along the tape one square at a time; and third, a set of instructions. The machine can read and write a number of symbols and can be changed from one to another "state." What the machine does at any particular time is determined by the state it is in, the contents of the tape, and the rules it is given to follow. Once set in motion, the machine scans the square above its read/write head, compares the contents of the square to its instructions, performs the relevant operation (writing, erasing, leaving blank) and moves left or right to start the process once again on another square. When the machine reaches a state in which no more instructions apply, it halts. The marks remaining on the tape then represent the response to the task at hand.

Turing's analysis suggested that "Turing machine computable" and "effective procedure" mean the same thing; any time we have an effective procedure we can always design a specific Turing machine to carry it out. If we know how to calculate the area of a sphere, we can create (at least in our imagination) a Turing machine to perform this task. If we know how to plot the trajectory of an artillery shell, we can create another Turing machine that will carry out this task, and so on. Every effective procedure will have a corresponding Turing machine.

Such single-purpose machines were, however, only part of Turing's analysis. He also demonstrated that it was possible to build *one* machine that could imitate any and every single-purpose machine. This new machine, the so-called universal Turing machine, stood ready to carry out (at least in theory) any conceivable effective procedure.

> An *effective* procedure is a step-by-step process guaranteed to produce a particular result. For instance, the rules of long division provide an effective procedure for calculating the result of dividing one number by another. If we follow each step properly, we are guaranteed a correct answer.

The universal Turing machine differs from a simple Turing machine in that it is able to accept a description of another machine and imitate the latter's behavior. The universal Turing machine, in short, is universal because it can imitate *any* Turing machine. If we can build a machine to add and another to alphabetize lists, we can also build a third that can perform both tasks. In fact, the third can perform the tasks done by any Turing machine at all. This means that there is a single machine that can carry out *any* effective procedure.

Turing showed how such a universal machine could be built—how data and instructions could be given to it, how the machine might process the data, and how it could then return an answer. The modern electronic computer is a practical embodiment of Turing's universal machine. The programs we install on our computers in effect turn them into a variety of special-purpose machines—machines to solve equations, process words, edit photos, compose songs, create video, and so on. Our computers have important limitations, of course: they always seem to need more memory, processing speed, and bandwidth. But the question naturally arises: What might we do with a computer if we could have all the computational power we might want?

Turing's central contribution was to answer this question. His answer was that such a computer could perform *any* information-processing task for which we (or the computer itself) can devise a set of rules.

The radical implications of his answer were not lost on Turing himself. Later he would argue that computers would one day think for themselves and that the answers to any question posed to them would be indistinguishable from the answers of human beings. He even proposed an exercise, the so-called "**Turing Test**," that he thought would prove this.

Multi-sensory experience would also eventually be possible for Turing's machines. He envisioned such future creations moving about, gaining their experience from direct interaction with the world, and learning in much the same way as humans learn. This dream, of course, presupposes a very sophisticated form of multimedia computing and one that many would reject for a variety of reasons. Objections aside, however, Turing's enduring legacy was his demonstration of the remarkable power and versatility of the computer—if we can think of a way to do it, a computer *can* do it. Computationally, there is every reason to dream and there is no end to the magic.

1.3 Second-Generation Innovators

Bush and Turing belonged to a generation of theorists with the imagination and foresight to predict what they could not yet actually do. By the 1960s, the evolution of digital computers led a new generation of theorists to propose innovative practical uses for these new machines.

Douglas Engelbart: New Forms of Human-Machine Interaction

Like Bush, **Douglas Engelbart** was convinced that computers could be used to improve human problem solving. In "Augmenting Human Intellect: A Conceptual Approach," 1962, he proposed the immediate development of practical devices to increase "the intellectual power of society's problem solvers" (Packer and Jordan 2001, 90). Engelbart fully understood the wide-ranging potential of computers and immediately proposed applications beyond their customary mathematical and sorting operations. In fact, he argued that anyone who uses any form of symbol ("the English language, pictographs, formal logic or mathematics") "should be able to benefit significantly" (69). Among the innovations he proposed in his article were word-processing ("think of it as a high-speed electric typewriter with some special features" [74]) and computer-aided architectural design.

Engelbart insisted that there was no need to wait for an improved understanding of the human mind or for more powerful computers: progress on augmentation systems could be made immediately. He then acted on his own advice. With funding from Advanced Research Projects Agency (ARPA), he established a team of researchers at the

Stanford Research Institute, and by 1968 he was able to demonstrate (at the Fall Joint Computer Conference in San Francisco) several significant innovations in human-computer interactivity. These included the mouse (Figure 1.3), windows for text editing, and electronic mail. These components were integrated into a system that he called the NLS, or oNLine-System. Engelbart had pointed the way to a new, intuitive interface with computers and to new ways in which computers could be used to communicate with others.

Figure 1.3 Engelbart's Mouse.

Theodore Nelson: Hypertext and Hypermedia

Ted Nelson was a pioneering theorist of early computer communications. He coined the terms *hypertext* and *hypermedia* in 1963 to represent his vision of a new form of information storage and retrieval. **Hypertext** is interactive text that is linked to other information. Engelbart's mouse might now be used to click on a word, causing the computer to transport the user to another screen of text containing a definition, explanation, or other related information. **Hypermedia** extends this interactivity to other media, such as images, sounds, or animations.

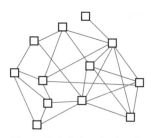

Nelson's vision was directly and deeply influenced by Vannevar Bush's 1945 article, "As We May Think" and by Douglas Engelbart's explorations of interactive computing. Like Bush, Nelson emphasized the associational qualities of human thought, but he also carried this vision further than Bush. For Nelson, knowledge was intrinsically unstructured, "a vasty cross-tangle of ideas and evidential materials, not a pyramid of truth" (Packer and Jordan 2001, 157) (Figure 1.4). "Professionalism," he suggested, "has created a world-wide cult of mutual incomprehensibility and disconnected special goals. Now we need to get everybody back together again" (161).

Figure 1.4 Nelson's sketch of a "cross tangle of ideas."

The computer, he argued, would be central to this task. Engelbart's NLS, with its keyboards, screens, mouse, and network connections, impressed Nelson as a "wonder and a glory" (162). NLS showed how the computer could revolutionize the creation and transmission of knowledge. Nelson began to plan a vast knowledge resource that would create "a community of common access to a shared heritage" (161). He called his proposed worldwide, cultural resource "**Xanadu**" after the "magic place of literary memory" (155) described in a poem by Samuel Taylor Coleridge. No longer focused on the needs of scientists and other specialists, the Xanadu project would create a dynamic, ever-expanding, hypertext library available to everyone. Xanadu would also support collaborative editing, track text changes throughout the revision process, and provide a means of crediting authors and distributing royalties. While Xanadu itself has not been completed, it serves as a model of the form Bush's original dream might take in an age of universal Internet access.

In Nelson's vision, hypertext and hypermedia would transform the uses of machines, placing them in the service of humans the world over. As he expressed it in 1974: "Now that we *have* all these wonderful devices, it should be the goal of society to put them in the service of truth and learning" (161).

Alan Kay: The GUI and the Multimedia Computer

Among the members of the enthusiastic audience for Engelbart's 1968 presentation was **Alan Kay**. Kay was introduced to the field of interactive computer graphics as a graduate student at the University of Utah. His doctoral dissertation dealt with a personal information device very similar to the modern laptop computer.

In the early 1970s, Kay joined Xerox PARC (the Palo Alto Research Center) and founded the Learning Research Group. Here he combined his interest in computer technology with explorations of various learning theories. His goal was to design a computer to support the ways in which people actually perceive, learn, and create. He named his proposed machine the "**Dynabook**" and he thought of it as a "personal computer" (Figure 1.5). But "personal" did not mean "personally owned" for Kay— it meant "intimate," closely tied to the mind and interests of its user. And the users were not going to be computer specialists—anyone should be able to use the Dynabook. This meant that Kay needed to find an intuitive, natural way for people to interact with computers.

Kay's solution is known as a **GUI** (pronounced "gooey") or Graphical User Interface. A GUI uses graphic symbols to represent the components and processes of computers—a picture of a typed page to represent a text file, a folder to represent a directory, and so on. These elements are selected and used with a combination

Figure 1.5 Sketch of Proposed Dynabook.

of input devices such as a mouse and keyboard. Today the graphical user interface is nearly universal and is often taken for granted, as if it was the inevitable result of advancing technology. In fact, Kay produced the GUI by adapting technology to the insights of various learning theorists including Jean Piaget, Seymour Papert, and Jerome Bruner. The interface Kay designed was intuitive because it grew out of basic principles of human learning.

The Dynabook was also intended to support a wide range of creative activities. Kay envisioned the computer as a powerful aid to writing, painting, and music composition. His research group designed programs to support each of these areas, allowing the machine to display graphics and play music as well as process numbers and text. In fact, the Dynabook was to be a full-blown multimedia computer—he called it a "**meta-medium**," a machine that could embody any medium. The Dynabook would also be "**modeless**." Users would be able to move seamlessly between different media, not thinking of themselves as confined to writing, painting, or animating mode. They could switch instantly to a different medium and activity by simply clicking on another window.

The Dynabook became the model for intuitive, accessible multimedia computing, and although it was never put into production, it greatly influenced the first commercial GUI computer, the Xerox Alto produced in 1973.

Steve Jobs: The Multimedia Hardware Revolution

> Imagine having your own self-contained knowledge manipulator in a portable package the size and shape of an ordinary notebook. Suppose it had enough power to outrace your senses of sight and hearing, enough capacity to store for later retrieval thousands of page-equivalents of reference materials, poems, letters, recipes, records, drawings, animations, musical scores, waveforms, dynamic simulations, and anything else you would like to remember and change (Kay and Goldberg 2003, 394).

For the population at large, the vision Kay presented of a new form of multimedia computer was, in 1977, little more than an enticing dream. Steve Jobs and the Apple computer would change that.

Steve Jobs and Steve Wozniak founded Apple in 1976. In 1979, Jobs visited Xerox PARC and was immediately "saturated," as he would later say, by the idea of the graphical user interface. Jobs saw in the GUI a potential revolution, one that "empowered people to use the computer without having to understand arcane computer commands" (Jobs, 1995). By 1984, this "humanistic" idea had been given technical expression in the Apple Macintosh.

The Macintosh was conceived and marketed as a direct challenge to the IBM personal computer. In the 1980s, IBM used the Microsoft DOS operating system. Computer users typed cryptic commands to instruct the machines to perform such tasks as loading programs, saving files, or accessing storage devices. This "command line" interface required users to learn the language of the computer, a language that few found intuitive.

The GUI, as it was further developed and refined at Apple, allowed users to control the computer through icons with familiar human associations—desktops, file folders, trashcans, and the like. These graphical symbols were only one aspect of Apple's multimedia vision. The Mac was also the first mass-produced personal computer with built-in sound support. In fact, the first Macintosh actually introduced itself to the audience by speaking.

Job's vision of "communication appliances" that could serve the needs of a wide range of people could now be put into practice. Musicians, graphical artists, publishers, scientists, and engineers soon were using Macs.

Millions of Macs would eventually be sold. The GUI and multimedia functionality had become mass-market innovations. In 1985, Microsoft announced Windows 1.0, a graphical user interface added to the DOS operating system. The release of Windows led to an extended legal controversy between Apple and Microsoft, with Apple alleging infringement of its rights to the GUI. Apple would ultimately fail to prevent the proliferation of the Windows operating system, ironically fulfilling Job's own ambitions for the Macintosh:

> Macintosh was basically this relatively small company . . . taking on the goliath, IBM, and saying 'Wait a minute, your way is wrong . . . . and we are going to show you the right way to do it and here it is. It's called Macintosh and it is so much better. It is going to beat you and you're going to do it.' (Jobs 1995)

And so they did. Today we need no longer speak of "multimedia computers" for the simple reason that computing routinely incorporates all media.

Tim Berners-Lee: From Hypertext to the World Wide Web

In the 1980s, the British engineer **Tim Berners-Lee** began actively exploring the practical application of hypertext and hypermedia. Berners-Lee worked at CERN, the European particle physics laboratory at Geneva, Switzerland. CERN, like most large organizations, was structured hierarchically, but it actually functioned, as Berners-Lee saw it, as "a multiply connected 'web' whose interconnections evolve with time" (Packer and Jordan 2001, 192). Communication crossed departments and the most productive thinking often occurred in informal settings such as hallways. This fluid structure, with its unconstrained flow of information among researchers, was an important source of the creative environment of the lab. When combined with a high turnover rate, however, it could also be a source of frustration—information was sometimes lost and only recovered "after a detective investigation in an emergency" (192).

Berners-Lee noted that the needed information often existed; it simply could not be located. Like Bush and Nelson before him, he was struck by the inadequacy of conventional modes of storing and accessing information. Hierarchical patterns, such as tree structures, simply could not accommodate the multiple interconnections that often accompanied the lab's research findings. A new structure was required, one that would "not place its own restraints on the information" (193).

The solution he proposed was a "'web' of notes with links (like references) between them . . . ." (193). The items to be linked he termed "nodes." Nodes could be virtually anything: any form of text, graphics, or other media. Borrowing a term from Ted Nelson, Berners-Lee spoke of his proposed system as "hypermedia."

In the late 1980s, various commercial products, such as Apple Computer's Hypercard, made it possible to create hypermedia applications on individual computers (Figure 1.6). Berners-Lee had broader objectives in mind, however. The first of these was "remote access across networks"—hypermedia resources should be broadly distributed. Since different systems were used on the network at CERN (Unix, Macintosh, etc.), "heterogeneity" was another requirement: the same hypermedia resources should be accessible regardless of computer platform. "Private links" were another specification: "One must be able to add one's own private links to and from public information. One must also be able to annotate links, as well as nodes, privately"(Berners-Lee 2001, 198–9). Finally, in keeping with his conception of a flexible web of information, Berners-Lee insisted upon "non-centralization." "Information systems," he insisted, "start small and grow. They also start isolated and then merge. A new system must allow existing systems to be linked together without requiring any central control or coordination" (198).

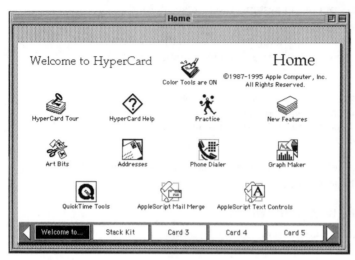

Figure 1.6 HyperCard.

Berners-Lee had identified the essential conditions for the emergence of a revolutionary form of information system—a system accessible from any computer, anywhere; a system to which anyone could add information at any time; a system that could incorporate and interrelate multiple media; and a system that could take on a life of its own, developing organically without any central guidance or control exercised over servers, documents, or links.

With the response at CERN less than enthusiastic, Berners-Lee developed the essential elements of what would become the World Wide Web on his own. In 1990, he developed the software needed for *servers* (the computers that store and distribute information). He also created the first *browser* programs to be used on the individual machines connected to the server (*clients*). In the following year, he began distributing his software to scientists over the Internet. These first programs were written for a specific computer called the Next. This was the machine used by Berners-Lee and many of his colleagues at CERN. In 1993, graduate students at the University of Illinois developed Mosaic, a version of the browser for use on the Macintosh and the PC. Mosaic opened the Web to millions of computer users the world over. The explosive growth of the Web was underway.

The Web made a dramatic contribution to the development of multimedia computing. In the 1980s, the arrival of CD-ROMs had offered the first practical solution to the problem of storing and delivering large multimedia files. CD-ROMs could hold the information of hundreds of floppy disks. They could be reproduced inexpensively and shipped easily. They were limited, however, in two critical respects—they were expensive to master and they needed to be formatted differently for different computer platforms. The Web immediately addressed the issue of cross-platform compatibility; all computers connected to the network could (with appropriate software) read the same information. It also dealt with expense, as multimedia websites could be inexpensively created and distributed nearly instantaneously.

Multimedia computing soon became a worldwide phenomenon with endless possibilities.

1.4 Legacy of the Multimedia Pioneers

The multimedia revolution was born in Bush's recognition that something was bound to come of the dramatic technical innovations of the twentieth century. Microfilm, magnetic storage, vacuum tubes, and transistors would lead to new tools that would transform our understanding of the world. His Memex promised to both empower and change us, altering what we could do, and how we think.

Bush also understood that the tools that shape understanding could, in turn, be shaped *by* understanding. His enduring legacy is the inspiration he provided to others to actively design new technologies to meet human needs and interests.

The machine that would eventually make Bush's vision possible was the digital computer. In Alan Turing's pioneering theoretical work, the defining feature of this fundamentally new kind of device was made clear—the computer was a *universal* machine. This meant, among other things, that the computer was a device of unprecedented flexibility.

Douglas Engelbart used this flexibility to develop novel forms of human-computer interactivity. His mouse, windows, and electronic mail made computers more accessible and useful, furthering his goal of "augmenting human intellect" and improving communication. Drawing on Engelbart's vision, Alan Kay developed the GUI and the first multimedia computer. Steve Jobs and Apple Computer made Kay's vision a practical reality by creating the Macintosh.

Theodore Nelson further developed Bush's early vision of associational indexing in the form of hypertext and hypermedia. Nelson's work was, in turn, given powerful expression in Tim Berners-Lee's development of the foundations for the World Wide Web.

1.5 Multimedia Today

Many elements of the visionary proposals of Bush and his successors are now practical realities. Links, sophisticated associational searches, mice, windows, GUIs, and the ready integration of all media—text, graphics, audio, video, and animation—are defining features of a fundamentally new form of communication. The revolution that the multimedia pioneers foresaw is far from complete, however. They knew that human ingenuity could actively shape an emerging technology. They glimpsed new possibilities as they considered the fundamental properties of computers, information, and people and they developed machines and systems to match this potential. As they well understood, however, a universal machine has unlimited possibilities, possibilities to be further defined by a new generation of multimedia innovators. Perhaps their greatest legacy is the inspiration they provide to continue the "imagineering." There are also specific reasons, inherent in contemporary social and technological changes, to anticipate a further development of the potential of digital multimedia. These include:

- A continuing technical revolution in hardware and software. Refinements in existing technologies and the development of new modes of computing will continue to increase computing power while lowering costs. Greater computing power will continue to spread to an ever-wider array of users.

- Continued integration of computers in other devices. "Smart" products of all kinds will lead to refinements in sensors and processing that will improve our understanding and control of existing media and lead to the creation of others. Multimedia will include new interactive possibilities with text, images, video and animation and with the devices that produce them. New possibilities, including smell and tactile experience, will eventually be added to the multimedia experience.
- The "digital merger" of disparate technologies and industries. The merger of film, television, radio, telephone, and the Internet is driving a growing appetite for multimedia communication. No longer is a phone simply an instrument for conveying sound; no longer is catalog shopping a simple engagement with a printed page. As technologies and industries are joined, they generate a corresponding merger and integration of media.
- The expansion of creative opportunity. The most important source of the continuing revolution in multimedia is the creative potential generated by the worldwide distribution of computing power to an ever-wider array of individuals. The great revolutions of the past developed in circumstances that created a synergy of disparate visions and experiences. Digital communications have dramatically increased both the speed and the reach of interpersonal contact across all cultures, while simultaneously providing a common tool of virtually unlimited flexibility.

In the following chapters, we will explore the fundamental concepts and the practical tools needed to participate in the ongoing magic of the multimedia revolution. As we use those tools, we should remember the dreams of those who helped to shape them. We, too, have the power to shape tools to our purposes, to improve traditional modes of communication, and to create entirely new ones.

Key Terms

Adaptive Multimedia	Jobs
Artificial Intelligence	Kay
Basic Interactivity	Memex
Berners-Lee	Metamedium
Bush	Modeless
Dynabook	Multimedia
Engelbart	Nelson
Expert Systems	Non-interactive Multimedia
GUI	Trails
Hypermedia	Turing
Hypertext	Turing Test
Immersive Multimedia	Universal Turing machine
Interactive Multimedia	Virtual Reality
Intellimedia	Xanadu

References

Berners-Lee, Tim. 2001. Information management: A proposal. In *Multimedia*, edited by Randall Packer and Ken Jordan. New York: W. W. Norton.

Bush, Vannevar. 1991. As We May Think. In *From Memex to Hypertext*, edited by James Nyce and Paul Kahn. Boston: Academic Press. First published in *Atlantic Monthly* 176(1):641–649.

———. 1991. Memex II. In *From Memex to Hypertext*, edited by James Nyce and Paul Kahn. Boston: Academic Press.

Engelbart, Douglas. 2001. Augmenting human intellect: A conceptual approach. In *Multimedia*, edited by Randall Packer and Ken Jordan. New York: W. W. Norton.

Jobs, Steve. 1995. Interview by Daniel Morrow, April 20. http://americanhistory.si.edu/collections/comphist/sj1.html

Kay, Alan. 2001. User interface: A personal view. In *Multimedia*, edited by Randall Packer and Ken Jordan. New York: W. W. Norton.

Kay, Alan, and Adele Goldberg. 2003. Personal dynamic media. In *The new media reader*, edited by Noah Wardrip-Friun and Nick Montfort. Boston: MIT Press.

Nelson, T. 2001. Computer lib/Dream machines. In *Multimedia*, edited by Randall Packer and Ken Jordan. New York: W. W. Norton.

Packer, Randall, and Ken Jordan. 2001. *Multimedia*. New York: W. W. Norton.

Turing, Alan. 1936. On computable numbers, with an application to the Entscheidungsproblem. *Proceedings of the London Mathematical Society* 2, 42:230–265.

Review Questions

1. What is contemporary multimedia?
2. Why are media professionals building their careers with digital technology?
3. What is the essential difference between interactive and non-interactive multimedia? Give an example of each type.
4. Why is hypermedia a more advanced form of interactive multimedia?
5. What are two features of adaptive multimedia?
6. Why is virtual reality called immersive multimedia?
7. Why is multimedia interdisciplinary?
8. Why did Bush propose his Memex I and II?
9. What are the distinctive features of Memex I and II?
10. How is the simple Turing machine different from a universal Turing machine?
11. What did Theodore Nelson hope to achieve with his Xanadu proposal?
12. What did Alan Kay mean by "personal computer"?
13. Why was the Macintosh a turning point in multimedia computing?
14. Why was Tim Berners-Lee's development of the World Wide Web significant in the evolution of multimedia?
15. Why is "imagineering" significant to multimedia?

Discussion Questions

1. What is a revolution? In what ways has computing generated a multimedia revolution?
2. In what ways is multimedia central to the theoretical design of Vannevar Bush's Memex systems?
3. Discuss the relevance of Turing's Universal Machine to the future of multimedia technology.
4. Explain the significance of the Turing Test.
5. Explain the similarities between Bush, Nelson, and Lee in their approach to managing information.
6. Identify the pioneers in multimedia computing and list the main contributions of each.
7. Compare and contrast the visions of the multimedia pioneers and the realities of multimedia computing today. Which of their dreams has been realized? Which remain unfulfilled? Which aspects of modern multimedia did they fail to anticipate?
8. Research current developments in virtual reality or video games and report how they are extending the potential of multimedia.

Chapter 2

Digital Data

Topics you will explore include:

- Elements of Digital Media
  - Symbol
  - Data
  - Information
- Digital Codes
  - Bits
  - Bytes
  - Effective and Efficient Codes
- Files
  - Size
  - Format
  - Compatibility and Conversion
  - Maintenance
- Digitization
  - Sampling
  - Quantization
  - Sample Resolution
  - Sample Rate
- File Compression
- Advantages of Digital Information
- Challenges of Digital Information

The language of modern multimedia is digital. Most multimedia products—presentations, websites, tutorials, games, and films—are created and delivered using digital computers. Multimedia developers encounter a varied, and constantly changing, array of digital codes—ASCII, RTF, TIFF, JPEG, PDF, MP3, .MOV, and so on. Understanding their nature, purposes, advantages, and limitations is essential for effective work in all areas of digital media.

This chapter presents the elements of digital encoding and explores the basic techniques and issues common to the digital representation of various media. After completing this chapter you should understand:

- Relationships between *symbol*, *data*, and *information*
- Main differences between analog and digital data
- Use of bits to encode digital data and the meaning of effective and efficient codes
- Essentials of files—formats, compression, and conversion
- Digitization—sampling, quantization, sample resolution, and sample rate
- Description-based and command-based media
- Key advantages and challenges of digital information

2.1 Symbols, Data, and Information

Multimedia applications include many different types of information. Information begins with data, and data is encoded using symbols.

Symbols are representations, or "stand-ins," for something else. Groups of letters often serve as symbols of words, as they do on this page. What letters and other symbols represent is determined by the **convention** that governs their use. The convention of *roman numerals*, for example, uses letters to represent numbers rather than words—IX stands for 9. Agreed upon conventions facilitate communication by defining the meaning and use of symbols.

Symbols organized and understood according to a convention are used to represent data. **Data** are the givens of experience—measurements, observations, facts, beliefs, and the like. A listing of twenty-four numbers (30.12, 30.05, 29.99, etc.) summarizing hourly barometric pressure readings is data.

This listing of data is not yet information. **Information** is data made useful, data interpreted and applied to produce understanding. The amount of information conveyed through data is dependent on the knowledge of the recipient. The casual observer may see the numbers above and understand that the barometric pressure is dropping. The meteorologist prepares for the approaching storm. Multimedia developers carefully consider the knowledge and skills of their intended audiences. Only in this way can they assure that the data presented in their applications will become meaningful information.

Data: Digital and Analog

Data is either digital or analog. **Digital data** consists of separate, discrete units. A digital clock presents the time as a sequence of distinct numbers. **Analog data** varies continuously. An analog clock presents time through the continuous movements of its hands (Figure 2.1).

Traditionally, images and sounds were created and delivered in analog form. Paintings and photographs were comprised of continuous areas of color, and music was produced through analog motions of strings, reeds, and other devices. But analog media cannot be directly created, edited, or distributed by a digital computer. To take advantage of the power of the computer, multimedia data must be digital.

Figure 2.1 Data—Analog and digital.

2.2 Digital Data: Bits, Bytes, and Codes

Digital information starts with digital data, and digital data starts with digits. A *digit* can be any one of the ten symbols, 0–9. Most people are very familiar with this "base-10" system—it's the one they use in their everyday lives. Some of the first digital computers also made use of all ten digital symbols.

Modern computers are electronic and many of their components (such as transistors) are especially well suited to represent one of two different states (high/low voltage, magnetized/non-magnetized, etc.). As a result, the "language" of these machines uses only two of the ten available digits: *0* and *1*. The symbols *0* and *1* are the two elements of a *binary* system ("binary" means having two parts). Each is a *binary digit* or, for short, a **bit**.

Bits are the symbols used to encode modern digital data. **Digital encoding** is the process of assigning bits to a data item. The number of bits a coding system requires depends upon the number of distinct data items to be represented. Each item must be given a unique symbolic representation, that is, a unique arrangement of bits. More bits make it possible to generate a larger number of distinct combinations.

If only two data items need to be encoded, such as a "yes" or "no," a single bit suffices. The bit can take on one of two values and a convention could be adopted in which a 1 designates "yes" and a 0 designates "no." One-bit encoding has obvious limitations. For instance, a one-bit digital code for temperature could only represent two readings of a thermometer. *0* might stand for a temperature of zero degrees Celsius, and *1* might designate one hundred degrees Celsius. This coding scheme could then alert us to the likely freezing or boiling of water but it could not tell us anything about other temperatures.

Adding another bit to the code produces four distinct combinations: 11, 10, 01, and 00. These combinations still employ just the two symbols, *0* and *1*, but now more than one symbol is used to represent the data item. Using a two-bit code, the four possibilities A, B, C, or D for a multiple-choice question could now be represented. But a two-bit coding system would still be inadequate for most uses of temperature readings. Just four temperatures, for example 0, 33, 67, and 100 degrees Celsius, could now be represented—still not enough to allow us to choose between a t-shirt and a parka as we leave for work in the morning.

A three-bit code produces eight distinct three-bit combinations: 111, 110, 101, 100, 011, 010, 001, and 000. In general, the number of distinct bit combinations that can be produced is given by the formula, 2^n, where *n* is the number of bits used in the code. A four-bit code can thus represent 2^4 or 16 distinct data items. Each additional bit adds a power of two and thus doubles the number of unique encodings.

Four-bit codes are known as "nibbles."

Eight-bit codes allow for 256 distinct data items (2^8). This is more than adequate to represent the variety of symbols in most uses of the printed English language (the letters of the alphabet, numerals, punctuation marks, mathematical and scientific symbols, etc.). It is also adequate for some uses of sound and graphics (256 different amplitude values for sound samples or 256 colors in pictures). Computers also usually process data either in 8-bit format or in a format that is a multiple of eight bits, for example 16, 32, or 64 bits. This eight-bit unit is so commonly used in computing that it has a name of its own—a **byte**.

Effective and Efficient Codes

An **effective code** is one that can represent each desired data item with a unique combination of symbols. The days of the week can be effectively encoded using three bits; the 12 months of the year would require four.

In addition to effectively identifying individual data items with unique codes, a coding scheme should also be efficient. An **efficient code** is one that does not waste processing, storage, or transmission resources. Longer encodings use more bits and consume more processing time, storage space, and transmission bandwidth. Efficient codes conserve these resources. For example, if the goal is to represent each degree of temperature between the freezing and the boiling point of water on a Celsius scale (0–100 degrees), six-bit codes are not enough (64 possibilities) and eight-bit codes are too much (256 possibilities). Seven-bit codes (128 possibilities) provide the closest match and the most efficient encoding.

A basic concern in all multimedia development is assuring that the digital encoding being used can effectively and efficiently represent the required range of media data. As the range or quality of media expands, developers often need to adopt more flexible coding options. For example, the original formulation of the text code known as **ASCII** (American Standard Code for Information Interchange) used just seven bits. This was adequate for the representation of the letters, numbers, and other symbols used in computer-generated text at the time. Later, the eighth bit was added to double the number of available codes. In this new character set, called **extended ASCII** or **ASCII-8**, more specialized symbols, such as Greek letters and logical operators, could also be represented (Figure 2.2). **Unicode**, a later standard, uses 16-bit codes to effectively designate over 65,000 individual characters. This supports the digital encoding of many more written symbols and a wide range of languages.

Character	ASCII-8		
0	0011 0000		
1	0011 0001		
2	0011 0010		
3	0011 0011		
4	0011 0100		
5	0011 0101		
6	0011 0110		
7	0011 0111		
8	0011 1000		
9	0011 1001		
A	0100 0001	a	0110 0001
B	0100 0010	b	0110 0010
C	0100 0011	c	0110 0011
D	0100 0100	d	0110 0100
E	0100 0101	e	0110 0101
F	0100 0110	f	0110 0110
G	0100 0111	g	0110 0111
H	0100 1000	h	0110 1000
I	0100 1001	i	0110 1001
J	0100 1010	j	0110 1010
K	0100 1011	k	0110 1011
L	0100 1100	l	0110 1100
M	0100 1101	m	0110 1101
N	0100 1110	n	0110 1110
O	0100 1111	o	0110 1111
P	0101 0000	p	0111 0000
Q	0101 0001	q	0111 0001
R	0101 0010	r	0111 0010
S	0101 0011	s	0111 0011
T	0101 0100	t	0111 0100
U	0101 0101	u	0111 0101
V	0101 0110	v	0111 0110
W	0101 0111	w	0111 0111
X	0101 1000	x	0111 1000
Y	0101 1001	y	0111 1001
Z	0101 1010	z	0111 1010

Figure 2.2 ASCII codes.

2.3 Digital Files

A computer **file** is a container for binary code, which is the universal language of a computer. Everything a computer does, from startup to shutdown, must ultimately be represented as 0s and 1s. This includes the instructions, or programs, a computer follows to carry out its operations as well as the data it processes. A **file format** is the convention that specifies how instructions and data are encoded in a computer file. Without a specific file format, a binary code has no meaning.

File Sizes

The size of a file is usually measured in numbers of bytes. The term *kilo* designates one thousand in the metric system. Because computers use a binary system, storage capacities are given as powers of two. In computer parlance, a kilo represents 2^{10} or 1024—in other words, *approximately* 1000. A **kilobyte** (KB) is thus 1024 bytes. Similarly *mega* designates one million. When applied to computer codes, *mega* stands for 2^{20} or 1,048,576. A **megabyte** (MB) is 1,048,576 bytes or *approximately* a million bytes. Similarly a **gigabyte** (GB) is approximately one billion bytes and a **terabyte** (TB) is approximately one trillion bytes.

> **Bytes and Bits**
> KB and Kb are not the same. KB is the abbreviation for kilo**bytes. Kb** stands for **kilobits.** Similarly, Mb, Gb, and Tb are references to bits, not bytes. These bit measures are often used to describe electronic transfer rates, e.g. a 56Kbs (kilobits per second) modem or an 800Mbs (megabits per second) FireWire interface.

File Extensions

A **file extension** is a series of letters that designate a file type. File extensions follow a dot at the end of a file name and are usually limited to two to four letters. For instance, a file with the extension *.ai* is an Adobe Illustrator file, *.exe* is a Windows program file, *.doc* is a Microsoft Word document, and *.html* is a Web document. There are hundreds of extensions. Some of the more important ones for multimedia developers are listed in the text box on this page and discussed in later chapters.

> **Common Multimedia File Extensions:**
> .ai – Adobe Illustrator graphic
> .avi – Windows video
> .bmp – BMP graphic
> .doc – Word document
> .gif – GIF graphic
> .htm or .html – Hypertext Markup Language
> .jpg – JPEG graphic
> .mov – Quicktime video
> .pct – PCT graphic
> .pdf – Portable Document Format
> .png – PNG graphic
> .psd – Photoshop image
> .txt – ASCII text
> .wav – Windows audio

Extensions are important for multimedia developers for two main reasons. First, they immediately identify a file type and, often, even the program that created the file. This greatly simplifies the challenge of keeping track of the many media files and programs that make up a multimedia application. Second, file extensions are often used by a computer's operating system to identify and launch an appropriate program to open the file. A developer can simply double-click a file's icon and begin working on it. Removing the extension may require the user to identify a compatible application before the file can be opened. Given these advantages, it is good practice to maintain the extension when naming or renaming files.

File Compatibility

Although nearly all digital computers use binary codes, they do not necessarily use the same codes. Different computer systems, or **platforms**, use different hardware and software (see Chapters 3 and 4). As a result, a file that can be read and processed on one computer platform, such as a Windows PC, often cannot be used on another, such as a Macintosh. In addition, there are many variations in data file formats both within and between platforms. One of the most important concerns for multimedia developers is **file compatibility**, assuring that a computer can process the instructions or data that are encoded in a particular file format.

Program files give the computer its instructions. They include operating systems (Windows, OS X), programming languages (Java, C++), and applications (Word, Excel, Photoshop). Programs are developed for specific computer platforms and are generally not compatible with other platforms. Multimedia developers often use more than one computer platform (generally PCs or Macs). The first compatibility issue is whether or not the program they would like to use is compatible with the intended platform. Widely used applications such as Word or Photoshop are usually available for PCs or Macs but the developer will have to own separate copies for each platform.

Multimedia **data files**—text, images, sounds, video, and animations—pose two principal compatibility challenges. The first is whether or not the file format is *cross-platform compatible*. A format that is not cross-platform compatible cannot be used on other platforms. For instance, Microsoft developed the BMP image format and Apple developed PICT. These two formats are not cross-platform compatible and a developer would not use PICT images in an application destined for a Windows PC. Instead, either the PICT image would be converted to a Windows format or to a format that can be used by both platforms, such as TIFF.

The second compatibility issue for multimedia data is whether or not different application programs *on a given platform* can process the format. Multimedia developers create or edit the various elements of their applications in *media-specific software*, such as word processors, graphics programs, or video editing applications. In some cases, developers will work with different programs to create a particular media component. For instance, they may work with an image in a photo editing application and then add special effects using another program. The various media elements a developer creates or imports are then combined using *authoring software* (see Chapter 10). Throughout the process it is important to ensure that the files to be used are compatible with the media-specific and authoring applications that will be used. For example, some image formats, such as TIFF, can be used by most image editing applications and are also widely compatible with authoring software. Newer formats and those intended for specialized purposes may not be widely supported—it took time, for instance, for PNG, a rival to the GIF image format, to be supported by most image editing programs.

Native file formats are an important example of specialized files. These are coding conventions used by specific computer applications, such as Adobe Photoshop or Corel Painter. Native formats contain information specific to the application that created them. For instance, a file in Photoshop's native format (PSD) may contain information about filters and other effects applied to the image during editing. In general, native file formats are not compatible with other applications.

File Format Checklist for Multimedia Development

Is the format compatible with:
   the operating system of the development platform?
   the operating system of the delivery platform?
   the developer's media-specific software?
   the developer's authoring software?

Is a file conversion utility available to produce a compatible file?
Have copies of original files of all media elements been saved?

File Conversion

Problems with file compatibility can often be resolved through **file conversion**, the process of transforming one file type to another.

File conversion can be carried out by specialized applications, such as Equilibrium's DeBabelizer. It is also often possible to perform conversions using the "Save As" function in popular media-specific software. For example, a TIFF image captured by a scanner can be opened in Photoshop and readily saved as a JPEG image for use on the Web.

File Maintenance

The variety of formats that may be required to develop and deliver a multimedia application also makes it important to carefully preserve both original and derivative files. Good file maintenance can save time when applications need to be revised or updated. In addition, information is often lost or modified in file conversion. Preserving the original may be critical if the application needs revision or if high quality copies are required for future projects.

Effective file maintenance involves three major steps: *identification, categorization,* and *preservation*. Files should be clearly *identified* in terms of their specific contents, their general type, and/or their originating program. Contents should be identified by file names that clearly differentiate each item: *LargeLogo, OctSalePrices, MouseClickSound*. Much uncertainty and frustration in developing and revising applications can be avoided by creating meaningful file names. Standard extensions, as discussed above, identify file types or originating programs and should always be retained in file names: *LargeLogo.gif, OctSalePrices.doc, MouseClickSound.aif*.

Categorization is the process of meaningfully grouping related files. Electronic folders serve the same general functions as their paper counterparts. Files are more readily located when grouped as images, text documents, video clips, and so on. More specific categorization is often essential in multimedia development and may have the further benefit of indicating an application's overall structure: *JuneSalesImages, LessonOneAnswers, CellDivisionAnimations*. And of course we shouldn't omit another important category: *PhotoOriginals, SoundOriginals, SourceVideo*.

Finally, file *preservation* includes the preparation and storage of back-up copies as well as their distribution to individuals or departments that may need them for future work. Key considerations include the durability and the accessibility of the storage medium and ensuring that important files have been stored in more than one location.

2.4 Digitization

Multimedia developers work with a wide range of media, each of which is usually best handled in a digital format. Letters and numbers are discrete units. As such, they are readily represented in digital codes: a convention simply identifies particular letters or numbers with particular codes. These codes fully represent the letter or number. For example, the ASCII code 01001110 01001111 represents the letters *N* and *O* with complete accuracy.

Other data—still or moving images, and sounds—are often presented as continuous, or analog, phenomena. To take full advantage of the power of the computer, analog data must be transformed. **Digitization** is the process of converting analog data to a digital format. Digitization begins with sampling.

Sampling

Sampling is the process of analyzing a small element of an image or sound and representing that element in a digital code. Thousands of individual samples are usually collected. They are then combined to re-create the original analog data in a digital format.

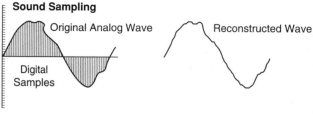

Figure 2.3 Sampling produces a digital version of an analog sound.

To digitize analog sound, thousands of samples of the varying amplitudes of the sound are collected each second. Each sample is assigned a binary code indicating its amplitude at that instant. The computer processes these values to re-create the sound from the individual samples (Figure 2.3). Analog images, such as photographs, are digitized by sampling their color at many different points. The re-created image is a grid of picture elements, or *pixels*, each having a particular color. If the grid is fine enough, the pixels blend together, producing the appearance of continuous areas of color (Figure 2.4).

Figure 2.4 Image sampling produces a grid of pixels. This section of the deer's eye is enlarged 1200%. See Color Plate 1.

Sampling can produce excellent digital reproductions of analog sources but it also often produces very large files. Multimedia developers must constantly balance media quality with the demands of effective and efficient delivery of their products. The two most important factors governing the quality of sampled media are *sample resolution* and *sample rate*. Sample resolution is directly related to another important issue in digital media production, *quantization*.

Sample Resolution and Quantization

Sample resolution is the number of bits used to represent a digital sample. **Quantization** is the process of rounding off the value of a sample to the closest available value in the digital code being used.

All sampling involves some degree of quantization. This is because analog phenomena are continuous and sampling always produces a series of discrete values. Since time and space are infinitely divisible, no finite recording of samples can capture all the information in an analog source: all samples are, in effect, "rounded off." On the other hand, high quality digital sampling can create virtually indistinguishable digital versions of analog media. Quantization only becomes a problem when sample resolution is too low. For example, photographs often contain thousands of shades of color. As sample resolution is reduced, fewer bits are available for coding and fewer colors can be represented. Some color samples must then be quantized—matched to the closest available substitute. If too few colors are available, much of the original image data may be lost. For example, a light pink and a burgundy might both be represented as the closest available match, a bright red. Figure 2.5 is an extreme example of quantization. Reducing the sample resolution from 24-bits to 2-bits reduces the range of individual colors from millions to just

Figure 2.5 Quantization. 24-bit v. 2-bit sample resolution. See Color Plate 2.

four. Browns and greens must be quantized to grey or black. Gone, too, are the various shades of blue in the sky.

Using codes with more bits, that is increasing the sample resolution, counters the effects of quantization. The 16.7 million distinct encodings of 24-bit sample resolution make it possible to assign a different code to every shade of color humans can distinguish. This produces images that rival the quality of 35mm analog photos.

Sample Rate

The second major factor determining the quality of digital images and sounds is sample rate. **Sample rate** is the number of samples taken in a given unit of time (sounds) or space (images). In the case of sound, the rate is given in kilohertz, thousands of samples per second. Sample rates for images are defined spatially and are referred to as **spatial resolution**. Spatial resolution typically varies from seventy-two to several thousand pixels per inch.

Low sample rates reduce the quality of digital images and sounds because they omit original analog information. For example, the frequency of a sound is determined by the rate at which its waveform repeats its highest and lowest amplitudes. If too few amplitude samples are taken, high frequency information will be omitted, producing a "flattened," lower-pitch version of the original. For images, a lower number of samples will miss details such as fine gradations of lines, often producing an incomplete, "fuzzy" reproduction (see Figure 2.6).

Figure 2.6 Spatial resolution. 300ppi (left) v. 50ppi (right). See Color Plate 3.

2.5 Digital Encoding of Media

All digital media, whether converted from analog formats or originally produced in digital form, must be represented in a binary code. There are two major approaches to digitally encoding media: **description-based** and **command-based**. In the descriptive approach, a digital media file contains a detailed representation of the many discrete elements that comprise the image or sound. An image is described by recording the colors of each of its many individual pixels thus creating a grid or "map" of their locations. This type of digital encoding is therefore often called a **bitmapped image**. Sound is described through thousands of individual amplitude samples and is known as **sampled sound**.

Descriptive digital encoding takes advantage of the computer's ability to store and process very large numbers of discrete media elements. Although descriptive encoding usually results in larger file sizes, it is often the preferred method for representing natural scenes and sounds. It also supports very detailed editing. Bitmapped images and sampled sound are the most common examples of descriptive encoding.

The second approach to encoding digital media takes advantage of another property of computers—their ability to execute commands. Rather than storing a detailed listing of constituent elements, the command approach stores a set of instructions that the computer then follows to produce digital images and sounds. These instructions, like all aspects of digital computing, are encoded as bits and bytes.

Sounds can be encoded as commands by specifying musical actions, such as striking a particular organ key with a certain force and duration. This is the approach used in the popular MIDI format (Musical Instrument Digital Interface; see Chapter 7). A MIDI file stores the commands used to produce sounds, rather than the sounds themselves. As the computer executes the commands, specialized software and hardware (*sequencers* and *synthesizers*) produce the corresponding sounds. Command-based sound is usually described as *synthesized sound*, sound "put together" by the computer. Similarly, digital images can be encoded as drawing commands. For example, commands might specify that a hexagon be drawn at a particular screen location, using one color for a border and another for its fill (see Chapter 6). *Draw programs*, such as Adobe Illustrator, produce images using the command-based approach.

Command-based media have important advantages over their descriptive counterparts. File sizes are usually much smaller, making them particularly useful in applications with limited bandwidth, as is often the case on the Web. They can also be scaled without introducing distortion, unlike most descriptive media. For

> Macromedia Flash, a popular authoring application for the Web, uses command-based graphics to lower file sizes and speed the delivery of animations.

instance, the size of an image can be increased without introducing "jaggies," the "stairstep" effect especially evident on diagonal lines when bitmapped images are enlarged. Similarly, the length of a synthesized sound can be changed without affecting pitch. On the other hand, it is usually more difficult to produce complex, natural media using the command approach. Photographs, or the human voice, for example, are usually more effectively encoded descriptively.

The distinctions between descriptions and commands for encoding digital media will recur throughout our consideration of the various media included in modern multimedia applications.

2.6 File Compression

A digital file can easily become very large. This is particularly true when the file involves description-based graphics, sound, and video. An 800 x 600 computer monitor displays 480,000 picture

> StuffIt, WinZip, PKzip are common compression utilities.

elements. At photo-quality resolution, each of these is represented with twenty-four bits. This requires the computer to store, read, and process over eleven million bits, or approximately 1.4 megabytes, of information. A video presents thirty of these images every second and adds sound as well. At well over 30 megabytes per second, this stream of digital data would quickly overwhelm the memory and processing capabilities of most personal computers.

Fortunately, the size of digital files can be significantly reduced by file compression. **Compression** is the process of re-encoding digital data to reduce file size. A specialized program called a **codec**, for COmpressor/DECompressor, changes the original file to the smaller version and then decompresses it to again present the data in a usable form. A basic understanding of compression is particularly important in multimedia development for two reasons. First, compression is one of the major strategies developers use reduce file sizes. Reducing file size leads to more efficient multimedia applications and is often essential for effective delivery on the Web. Second, the choice of a particular form of compression can dramatically affect media quality, and the range of compression choices is large and constantly evolving. Developers need to understand the fundamentals of compression to select the most appropriate option.

There are two major types of compression: *lossy* and *lossless*. In **lossy compression**, the number of bits in the original file is reduced and some data is lost. Lossy compression is not an option for files consisting of text and numbers, so-called *alphanumeric* information. Losing a single letter or number could easily alter the meaning of the data. However, it is often possible to maintain high quality images or sounds with less data than was originally present. **Lossless compression** substitutes a more efficient encoding to reduce the file size while preserving all of the original data. When the file is decompressed it will be identical to the original. Two examples can help to clarify the nature of compression generally and, especially, the differences between lossy and lossless techniques.

Lossy Compression—MP3

MP3 and Portable Music

MP3 also helped revolutionize portable music players. One megabyte can hold approximately one minute of MP3 sound. This allows iPods and other MP3 players to store hundreds of songs.

MP3 is a sound file format that incorporates lossy compression. It is part of a much broader set of compression standards established by the Motion Picture Experts Group (MPEG). MP3 (for "MPEG1, audio level 3") achieved its initial popularity because it made it possible to transmit near-CD-quality sound files over the Web. Without compression, the transmission of an original CD file is not practical for most web users. The CD audio standard uses 16-bit samples of the original music taken 44,100 times per second for each of two stereo channels. This results in files that contain 1,411,200 bits of information for each second of sound (44,100 samples $\times$ 16 bits per sample $\times$ 2 channels). A 56Kb modem would take approximately 25 seconds to receive this single second of sound (1,411,200 bits / 56,000 bits/second). At this data transfer rate, a three-minute song takes more than an hour to download. MP3 files compress this information, producing a file that is approximately 12 times smaller than the original. A modem can download the compressed file in a few minutes, and increasingly common broadband connections can reduce the time to seconds.

MP3 analyzes the sound file and discards data that is not critical for high-quality playback. For example, it removes frequencies above the range of human hearing. It may also evaluate two sounds playing at the same time and eliminate the softer sound. These types of data can be eliminated without significant impact on quality. The result is a lossy compression, because some information is discarded, but one that maintains near CD-quality performance.

Lossless Compression—Run Length Encoding

One of the simpler strategies to achieve lossless compression is run length encoding (**RLE**). Run length encoding is sometimes used to compress bitmapped image files, such as the Windows PCX format. As noted previously, bitmapped images can easily become very large since each pixel is represented with a series of bits that provide information about its color. Run length encoding generates a code to "flag" the beginning of a line of pixels of the same color. That color information is then recorded just once for each pixel. In effect, RLE tells the computer to repeat a color for a given number of adjacent pixels rather than repeating the same information for each pixel over and over. The RLE compressed file will be smaller, but it will retain all the original image data—it is "lossless."

2.7 Error Detection and Correction

Digital data consists of long strings of 0s and 1s. Changing or eliminating even a few of these bits can produce serious distortions. There are a number of ways in which these distortions can occur. For example, the pits and lands of a CD can be altered by a scratch or dust, or the magnetized surface of a floppy disk can be affected by stray magnetism or by heat. Data may also be lost or altered in electronic transmission. For digital data to be reliable, some means of detecting and correcting errors must be found.

There are many strategies for error detection and correction and, like compression, the multimedia developer seldom has occasion to enter very deeply into this specialized area. On the other hand, the storage requirements for data in various formats (such as CD and DVD) are significantly affected by the need to add code for detecting and correcting errors, and it is useful to understand the basics of its operation.

The first challenge in ensuring reliable digital information is to find a means of detecting an error. A simple strategy for doing this is the "parity bit." A **parity bit** is an extra bit added to a data code to maintain either an even or an odd number of 1s in the code. In this approach, the number of 1 bits in each block of data is counted. An extra bit is then added to make the total number 1 bits either odd, or even. The added bit is called a parity bit. If the number of 1 bits is intended to be odd the coding scheme is called "odd parity"; even numbers of 1s are "even parity." For example, the ASCII code for the letter A is 01000001. This code has an even number of 1 bits (two). In an even parity system, the parity bit added would be a 0 and the code for the letter would become 010000010. A letter such as C, with an ASCII code of 01000011, has an odd number of 1 bits (three). In even parity, a 1 would be added, producing a parity bit encoding of 01000111.

On receipt of the data block, the bits are again counted. If the number of bits is not the expected odd or even value (depending on the parity being used), an error must have occurred. This simple system can detect many errors, but it does have serious limitations. More advanced approaches are often used to detect errors. Once the error is detected, the second challenge is to correct it with accurate data bits.

For some applications, such as data transmission, knowing an error occurred may be enough. The data error will generate a request from the receiver to retransmit the flawed data item. The process continues until an error-free message is received. This strategy will not work for all types of digital media, however. For example, accurate playback of audio CDs requires *immediate* detection and correction of data errors. To accomplish this, error correction code is added to reconstruct the original bit sequence. This requires

B	E
0	0
1	1
0	0
0	0
0	0
0	1
1	0
0	1
0	1

Parity Bits

Even parity means that the number of 1 bits must be an even number. If it is, a 0 is added. If it isn't, a 1 bit is supplementary.

redundant data in the bit stream, which increases data storage requirements. It also dramatically improves reliability. CD audio discs devote approximately one third of their storage to error detection and correction.

2.8 Advantages of Digital Information

A computer is a revolutionary form of machine because in principle it is universal—it can become virtually any kind of information processing device. By changing the computer's instructions, or program, we can instantly change it from a word processor to a photo editor, to a graphing calculator, to a game station, and so on, indefinitely.

Computers can also control the delivery of analog information. For instance, computers have been used to control tape decks or laserdisc players displaying analog images. But the computer cannot edit those images while in their analog form. The chief advantage of digital information is that it can be directly manipulated and transformed by a computer. This has produced significant improvements in the reproduction, editing, integration, and distribution of a wide range of media.

Reproduction

Digital information can be repeatedly copied with no loss of quality. All of the information in the original file can be preserved in the copy, as well as in copies of the copy, and so on. This is not true for analog formats such as videotapes. A video copy does not preserve all the information of the master, and copies of copies soon produce significant distortions, a process known as **generation decay**. Digital information supports full-fidelity copies with no generation decay.

Editing

One of the earliest examples of the editing advantages of digital information was "word processing." Once words are represented in a digital code, a computer program such as Word can readily apply changes of font and formatting as well as operations such as search, replace, and spellchecking. These advantages soon drove typewriters from the forefront of text preparation.

Similar advantages apply to other media. Analog editing of photos tends to be slow and expensive, requiring specialized equipment and techniques. Once a photo is in digital form, programs such as Adobe Photoshop or Corel Paint Shop Pro can be used to instantly change its size, crop it, change its brightness or contrast, add special effects such as 3-D embossing, and so on. Digital information is readily and inexpensively edited.

Integration

By definition, multimedia is focused on the integration of different media. This may be as simple as tying the sound of a babbling brook to the image of a pristine mountain stream, or as complex as relating a control input to changes in the instruments and cockpit view of a flight simulator. This process is greatly simplified when all media are in a common digital format and can be stored and accessed by a single device, a digital computer. It is sometimes suggested that the computer has transformed multi-media into a sort of "uni-media" with digital code as its common language. A sound in this new scheme is still different from a photo, but common tools and techniques based on digital manipulations can be applied to both. Cut, copy, and paste, for instance, were once restricted to text. With the development of modern multimedia, these are common operations that are conducted in much the same way for all media.

Distribution

Distribution is one of the principal challenges in the evolution of modern multimedia. In the past, analog media such as radio, TV, and print enjoyed considerable advantages over digital multimedia. Their well-developed infrastructures and large customer bases allowed for rapid and widespread distribution of information. With the development and partial standardization of CD-ROMs, distribution of large multimedia files became more practical. The development of the Internet, particularly the World Wide Web, dramatically improved the distribution of digital information.

By the beginning of the twenty-first century it was evident that the future of all media was digital, and steps were underway to guide massive analog information systems, such as television, into the digital age. The existence of widely accessible digital networks, reaching into virtually every corner of the globe, has produced an information distribution system of unparalleled reach and scope. Not only can nearly everyone be reached, but nearly everyone can be reached by anyone else. The language of this revolutionary medium is digital.

2.9 Digital Challenges

Given these advantages, digital information will continue to displace analog formats. Digitization does involve significant challenges, however. Among these are file sizes, processing demands, standardization, bandwidth, and preservation. Each challenge will almost certainly be overcome with the further development of digital technology. But each is also a significant concern for today's multimedia developers.

File Sizes

Digitization often produces very large files. This is particularly true of dynamic media, that is media that changes over time, such as sound or video. A minute of CD-quality sound produces a file of over 10MB. A minute of uncompressed full-screen, full-fidelity (24-bit) video takes up approximately 1.7GB. At these sizes, digitized dynamic media soon tax the limits of available storage and processing in most personal computers.

Solutions to the challenge of large file sizes involve improvements in hardware and software. Many of these focus on compressing the original files. MPEG2, for instance, uses compression software in conjunction with specialized hardware to reduce the size of video files. It compresses video at about a 150:1 ratio and still retains excellent quality. Other solutions include hard drives with storage capacities in the hundreds of gigabytes and optical technologies such as DVD. DVD (Digital Versatile Disc) uses an optical disc the same size as a CD-ROM but increases the storage capacity from the CD's 650MB to a potential 17GB (see Chapter 3).

Processor Demand

Large digital files also burden a computer's processor (see Chapter 3). Some forms of digitization are particularly processing-intensive. In the final stages of producing a 3-D animation, computers must make many calculations. This process, called "rendering," may take many hours, or in the case of lengthy and complex presentations, days and weeks, to complete (see Chapter 9). In the case of the animated feature film, "Final Fantasy," 934,162 days of render time would be needed if only one processor was used. In fact, 1,200 processors were linked together to complete the project over two years.

Standardization

The development of multimedia technology is a competitive process in which different organizations pursue a variety of strategies to develop new software and hardware. As a result, a number of different conventions for encoding and manipulating digital data are created. These are often **incompatible**: data formats that work with one type of hardware or software do not work with others.

The absence of a common standard fragments the multimedia market and discourages the development of new applications. Over time, a combination of market forces and the work of standards committees generally produce a dominant standard. This, in turn, spurs the development of multimedia products and services. In the early stages of CD technology, different computer manufactures used different standards for encoding data. The development of a common standard (ISO 9660) made it possible for most computers to access the information on any CD, thus encouraging the development of many more multimedia applications.

Bandwidth

Computer networks, and especially the World Wide Web, greatly facilitate the distribution of digital multimedia. A basic challenge for network users is bandwidth. **Bandwidth** is the amount of digital data that can be transmitted over a communications medium, or band. In a standard 56Kb modem connection, the medium is the twisted pair copper wire of a telephone line. 56Kb (lowercase *b*) is 56 Kilo*bits* or 7 bytes of digital data transmitted each second. For large multimedia applications, this is a very small amount of data. Users of telephone modems are very aware of the limits of their bandwidth as they download data from websites with extensive graphics, sound, or animation.

Improvements in bandwidth include cable modems, DSL (Digital Subscriber Line, 1.5Mbps), digital lines such as T1 (1.54Mbps), and satellite communications (2Mbps).

Preservation

As digital media continue to displace their analog counterparts there is growing concern about the longevity and future accessibility of digital data in all its many forms. While digital encoding supports much more economical and accessible modes of archiving, serious challenges remain in two key areas: the durability and reliability of long-term storage media such as digital tape, CDs, and DVDs; and the availability of the hardware and software required to read the archived files. These are serious concerns for individuals and organizations alike. Individual family members may have much less access to the digital photos of earlier generations than their ancestors had to the analog prints preserved in albums in drawers, closets, and attics. Governments, courts, hospitals, law firms, and businesses of all kinds also clearly have a substantial stake in the preservation of digital data.

The challenges of preserving this data are already clear. Digital tapes must be periodically refreshed and the long-term durability of optical formats, especially the "recordable" and "rewritable" variants, is not completely known. Other widely used technologies, such as flash drives, are even more susceptible to degradation with repeated use. This is a widely recognized problem and a subject of active research that is likely to produce a better understanding of the prospects for media longevity. On the other hand, each new technology will continue to raise these questions and concerns about media preservation are likely to continue.

The second major challenge is to also preserve access to, and operability on, archived digital data. For this, appropriate hardware and software is essential. The rapid obsolescence of storage devices, processors, and software, including both applications and operating systems, means that perfectly well preserved files may no longer be readable. While it may sometimes be possible to preserve older software and hardware in operating condition, far more promising solutions are *migration* and *emulation*. Migration is the process of updating digital data to a form that can be read and manipulated by current hardware and software. In the context of preservation, emulation is the use of a new technology to reproduce the operability of an older one. In effect, new hardware and software mimics the capabilities of its predecessors. Both migration and emulation pose demanding challenges with respect to issues such as file compatibility and maintaining full interoperability, including the original functionality of advanced products such as interactive multimedia applications.

2.10 Summary

Data, or the observations, facts, and beliefs of experience, take two principal forms—analog and digital. Analog data is continuous and, in principle, infinitely divisible. Digital data is discrete—it is made up of indivisible units. Both analog and digital data are comprised of symbols, representations whose meanings are determined by conventions.

The symbols used in modern digital data are the binary digits (or bits), *0* and *1*. Eight-bit encodings called bytes, are fundamental to computing. The meanings of the strings of bits, or codes, used by computers are determined by conventions such as file formats. Codes are designed to be both effective and efficient. Effective codes successfully represent the desired range of data, while efficient codes conserve valuable computing resources. Effectiveness and efficiency are closely tied to sample resolution, the number of bits used to represent a data item. Every additional bit doubles the number of distinct data items that can be encoded, but it also increases demands on computer processing, storage, and transmission.

Good file maintenance is important in multimedia development. This involves identification, categorization, and preservation. Preserving original files from the specialized applications used to produce them is especially important for future revisions and/or the creation of new products.

A computer can only process digital data. Analog data must be converted to a digital format before computers can make use of it. Many of the most important concepts in multimedia development are concerned with this conversion process, called digitization. Digitization is based on sampling, a process in which many separate measurements are made of the continuously varying properties of analog media. Quantization, the rounding of the value of a sample to the closest available value of the digital code, may produce distortions in digital versions of analog phenomena. Ensuring that the samples are represented with adequate bit depth (also known as sample resolution) can lessen these effects. Sample rate, or the frequency with which samples are taken, also affects the quality of digitized media.

Media can also be directly created by the computer and digitally encoded. There are two major types of original digital media—description-based and command-based. Description-based media are encodings of large numbers of media elements—pixels for images and amplitude samples for sound. Description-based media are especially appropriate for the accurate representation of natural images and sounds such as photographs and human speech. Command-based media are encoded as commands that the computer follows to generate the image or sound. Files for command-based media are much smaller, offering significant advantages for delivery over the Web. They also have other advantages, including distortion-free scalability.

High quality digital media, especially dynamic media such as sound and video, can produce very large files. These often require compression before they can be practically incorporated in multimedia applications. Codecs compress digital data files to reduce their size and then decompress them for display or playback. Some codecs are lossless—they encode data more efficiently while preserving all of the original content. Others sacrifice data judged not to be essential and are described as lossy.

Because the meaning of digital data can be dramatically changed with the loss of just a few bits, error detection and correction routines often play an important role in the transmission and playback of digital data. *EDC/ECC* (Error Detection Code/Error Correction Code) can greatly improve the reliability of digital data.

Digital data has significant advantages related to reproduction, editing, integration, and distribution. It also poses challenges such as file size, processor demand, standardization, bandwidth, and preservation.

Key Terms

Analog data
ASCII
ASCII-8
Bandwidth
Bit
Bitmapped image
Byte
Codec
Command-based
Compression

Convention
Data
Description-based
Digital data
Digital encoding
Digitization
Effective code
Efficient code
Extended ASCII
File

File compatibility	Parity bit
File conversion	Platform
File extension	Program file
File format	Quantization
Generation decay	RLE
Gigabyte	Sample rate
Incompatible	Sample resolution
Information	Sampled sound
Kilobyte	Sampling
Lossless compression	Spatial resolution
Lossy compression	Symbol
Megabyte	Terabyte
MP3	Unicode
Native file format	

Review Questions

1. What is a symbol? Why is a bit considered a symbol?
2. What is the difference between data and information?
3. Why is an 8 bit code to designate the characters in English language effective? Is it efficient?
4. Why is file compatibility important for multimedia development?
5. What is a native file format? Give an example of such a format.
6. Why shouldn't you change a file named *zipIt.exe* to *zipIt.jpg*?
7. What are the three main considerations for file maintenance?
8. What is sampling?
9. What is sample resolution?
10. What is quantization?
11. What is sample rate?
12. Why is sample rate often referred to as spatial resolution?
13. Why is RLE compression lossless?
14. Why do CD audio discs contain redundant data on the disc?
15. What is a codec?

Discussion Questions

1. What is an efficient code? Why would a multimedia developer be concerned about using efficient codes?
2. Why are multimedia developers concerned about sample resolution and quantization when they scan a full color photograph?
3. Explain the distinction between "description-based" and "command-based" forms of encoding digital media. Give an advantage and disadvantage of each form of encoding.

4. What are the two major types of compression? Identify and explain which type is best for compressing an encyclopedia. Identify and explain which type is best for compressing a digital photo of the ocean.
5. How does MP3 maintain audio quality while also significantly reducing file sizes? Explain two specific strategies.
6. Identify and briefly describe two advantages and two challenges in the use of digital information.

■■■■ **Chapter 3**

Computer Hardware

Topics you will explore include:

Computer technology has transformed our lives for over 50 years. First introduced to alleviate the tedious work of calculating long data tables for the military, we now find computers recording and processing every aspect of our daily activity. The modern computer is no longer just a numeric calculator; it is a multimedia device that displays images, sound, and video through operating systems and applications that give the user unprecedented control over information. Visionaries such as Alan Turing and Vannevar Bush articulated the direction for such computers, but it was the development of micro-electronics that brought multimedia to our desktops. Powerful computing devices make multimedia applications possible. They capture and convert input from various analog sources; process and store the digital data; and output in ways that empower users to create, distribute, search, and share information as never before. Hardware powers the development and delivery of multimedia.

In this chapter you will explore the basic components of a computer system including the peripheral devices used for developing multimedia applications. Developers are concerned about the performance features of not only the processor, but also all input, storage, and output devices. After completing this chapter you should understand:

- Components of a computer system
- Types of computer systems
- Functions and components of the CPU
- Functions of the system board and hardware interface
- Peripheral devices and performance criteria for:
  - Secondary storage
  - Input
  - Output
- Network fundamentals

3.1 Computer Systems

A **computer system** is an integrated set of hardware and software designed to process data and produce a meaningful result. Every computer performs the basic functions of *input*, *processing*, *storage*, *output*, and *transmission of data*. Instructions and data are entered, processed into results that are stored for later use, and output in a useful format. Computers are connected to a larger network system for transmission of data and information.

Computer hardware is organized according to these basic functions. The *system unit* focuses on processing, while a variety of *peripheral devices* facilitate input, output, storage, and communication.

Types of Computer Systems

Computers are often identified by their size and power. Common categories of computer systems include *supercomputers*, *mainframes*, and *microcomputers*. Size traditionally refers to the computer's physical mass, while power refers to the computer's speed and the complexity of calculations it can carry out. Originally, mainframe computers were physically much larger than desktop microcomputers. Size is now less significant since microelectronics can package very powerful systems in very small spaces.

Supercomputers are the most advanced, powerful, and expensive computers of the day. They are characterized as having the fastest processing speeds and performing the most complex calculations. Today, those speeds can be trillions of instructions per second; tomorrow they will be even faster. Supercomputers are unlocking many mysteries of our universe. They are widely used in scientific research, artificial intelligence, defense systems, and industrial design. More recently, they have been applied to multimedia development. For instance, in the film industry supercomputers are used to carry out the rendering operations that transform digital animations into magical three-dimensional worlds.

> Supercomputing performance standards can also be achieved by combining individual computers. Virginia Tech combined 1,100 Mac G5 Xserve servers to achieve the third most powerful supercomputer, running at a sustained speed of 12.25 trillion operations per second.
>
> *(Mac Observer, 2003)*

A **mainframe computer** is an advanced multi-user machine typically used to manage the databases, financial transactions, and communications of large organizations such as banks, hospitals, retail stores, insurance companies, and government offices. While these applications don't require the computational complexity of super-computers, mainframes are still very powerful: they can process billions of instructions per second, support hundreds of users, and store terabytes (trillions of bytes) of data. Supercomputers and mainframes are very expensive and require a support staff to maintain daily operations. These computer systems are vital to the performance of many daily tasks but it was the personal computer that transformed the way most of us think and work.

A **personal computer** is a system that uses a microprocessor to provide computing to a single user. Personal computers have many different names and configurations including "**microcomputer**," "laptop," "desktop," and "tablet" (Figure 3.1). The first personal computers were developed in 1975 by computing enthusiasts who wanted their own computer rather than share a large centralized mainframe. Their efforts were energized in 1971 when Intel introduced the microprocessor. A **microprocessor** is a single silicon

Figure 3.1 Common microcomputer systems.

chip that contains all the elements of a central processing unit (CPU). This miniature CPU was not as powerful as a mainframe, but it was much smaller and cheaper. It was perfect for a single user who wanted computing capability on the desktop.

Altair, the first microcomputer, appeared in 1975 and launched the microcomputer revolution. Commodore Pet and Apple II soon followed in 1977. The IBM PC appeared in 1981. IBM used the Intel microprocessor to build office computers for word processing, spreadsheets, and databases. These applications focused on text-based data to improve business productivity.

On January 24, 1984, Apple introduced a different type of microcomputer that relied on images and sound to interact with the user. Steve Jobs and Stephen Wozniak captured the visions of Bush, Engelbart, and Kay when they delivered the first commercial multimedia computer. The Macintosh used an operating system with a graphical interface that resembled a standard desktop complete with folders and a trashcan. It relied on a mouse to manipulate data and programs. It included sound capabilities and dramatically introduced itself at the January 1984 debut. From that day on, advances in hardware technology supported the development of multimedia computing. Today's microcomputer is in every way a multimedia machine.

3.2 Computer Platforms

Computers have fundamental differences based on the hardware components, such as processors, and the operating systems that they use. An operating system is the software that manages the computer's resources and executes application programs. The combination of hardware and operating system is often called the **computer platform**. The two most common microcomputer platforms are Macintosh and Windows-based PCs.

The Macintosh platform utilizes hardware developed by Apple. Apple defines the hardware specifications and develops the operating system to control the hardware. Apple currently manufacturers multimedia computers in several configurations: iBook (end user laptop), iMac (end user desktop), and Power Mac (developer system).

The most popular personal computer today is a Windows/PC platform. These microcomputers utilize the Windows operating system developed by Microsoft. Many companies, such as Dell, Gateway, HP, and Sony, build Windows/PC computers. You might even build one yourself, since the hardware components are readily available from a variety of manufacturers.

Understanding the distinctions between computer platforms is important for multimedia development. Developers who plan to reach a wide market are concerned about **cross-platform compatibility**, the ability of an application to run on different hardware and operating systems. For example, images that are saved in a color palette and file format optimized for the Windows/PC platform may appear distorted on a Macintosh computer. Font technologies and typeface families also vary between the two platforms. Advances are underway to standardize digital media formats so they can be utilized on both platforms. Adobe's Acrobat, now in widespread use, provides one successful cross-platform format for text and images. The World Wide Web is a major catalyst for defining data formats so that they can be viewed on any computer through network connections and a browser.

3.3 Computer Hardware Basics

Computer hardware is divided into two main categories: the system unit and peripherals. The **system unit** contains the electronic components used to process and store data (see Figure 3.2). These components include the central processing unit (CPU), primary memory, and the system board. **Peripheral devices** are hardware used for input, auxiliary storage, display, and communication. These are attached to the system unit through a hardware interface that carries digital data to and from main memory and processors.

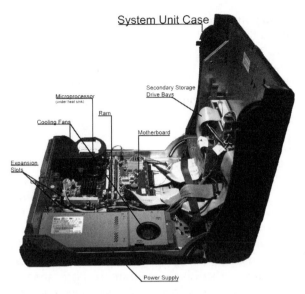

Figure 3.2 System unit.

System Unit

Central Processing Unit The most important component of any electronic computer is the central processing unit (CPU). A **CPU** is a complex integration of millions of transistors that execute program instructions and manipulate data. The Intel Pentium 4 CPU has 55 million transistors within a tiny two-inch chip. This ability to store a CPU on a single silicon chip ushered in the age of personal computers.

The CPU has three essential sets of transistors that work together in processing digital data: a control unit, an arithmetic logic unit, and registers. The **control unit** directs the flow of data and instructions within the processor and electronic memory. The **arithmetic logic unit (ALU)** contains programmed transistors that perform mathematical and logical calculations on the data. The **registers** are special transistors that store data and instructions as they are being manipulated by the control unit and ALU. New microprocessors also have additional high-speed memory on the chip called **cache** to store frequently used data and instructions.

Processing data and instructions are managed in a machine cycle. The **machine cycle** includes four steps that a processor carries out for each instruction: fetch, decode, execute, and store (see Figure 3.3). The control unit *fetches* data and instructions from a part of the computer's memory called RAM (Random Access Memory). It transports the digital bits through an electronic bus, stores the instruction in registers, and *decodes* the instruction for the arithmetic logic unit. The ALU *executes* the instruction and returns the result

> **The System Unit and the Box**
>
> Many refer to the rectangular box of the computer as the system unit. In fact, that "box" can contain several peripheral devices such as hard drives, optical drives, and even the monitor. As computer sizes shrink, manufacturers combine peripherals with the system unit in a single container. Apple's iMac is one computer with both the system unit and several peripherals combined in the display device.

to an accumulator register and storage register. When one machine level instruction is completed, a second one is sent through the cycle. Eventually there is an instruction to *store* the results and the control unit moves data from its temporary storage register to a specific address in RAM. Various performance features of the CPU determine the efficiency of this basic machine cycle. These include clock speed, word size, bus width, and techniques such as pipelining, RISC processing, multi-processing, and multi-core technology.

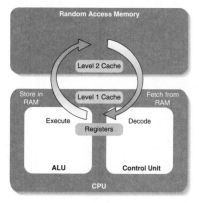

Figure 3.3 Sequential processing steps.

■ Clock Speed

An internal system clock synchronizes the machine cycle. On each clock tick, the CPU executes another instruction. **Clock speed** is the rate at which the CPU carries out its basic instructions. Computers execute instructions very rapidly, at speeds measured in hertz. One *hertz* is one cycle per second. Microcomputer clock speed is measured in *megahertz* (MHz, millions of cycles/second) or *gigahertz* (GHz, billions of cycles/second). Technological advances have dramatically increased clock speeds. Today's GHz microprocessors operate much faster than the original 4MHz Intel 8080 chip (see Table 3.1). Increasing internal clock speed is just one method of improving the performance of a CPU. Other performance features must also be optimized to take full advantage of the processor's power.

■ Word Size

One important factor that contributes to CPU power is the amount of data or instructions that are moved through a processor in one machine cycle. **Word size** refers to the group of bits that a processor can manipulate as a unit in one machine cycle. A 64-bit processor can manipulate 64 bits (or 8 bytes) of data at one time, clearly an advantage over a 32-bit (4 bytes) processor.

Table 3.1 Processor Ratings

Microprocessor	Transistors	Clock Speed	Word Size
Intel Pentium III	28 million	450–1200 MHz	32 bits
Intel Pentium IV	42 million	1.4–3.6 GHz +	32 bits
Intel Celeron	19 million	266 MHz +	32 bits
Itanium (Merced)	30–300 million	800 MHz	64 bits
Motorola PowerPC	3.6 million	133 MHz+	32 bits
Motorola G3	6.3 million	300 MHz	32 bits
Motorola G4	10.5 million	1–1.42 GHz	32 bits
Motorola G5	58 million	2 GHz	64 bits
AMD Athlon64	105.9 million	2.2 GHz	32 bits
AMD Opteron (dual core)	233 million	2.2 GHz	64 bits
Intel Pentium D (dual core)	230 million	3.2 GHz	64 bits

■ Bus Width

Another performance factor is the width of the system bus between the processor and memory. A **bus** is an electronic path for the flow of data. The **system bus** is an electronic pathway between the CPU, memory, and other system components. The processor has two bus connections to memory: the data bus and the address bus. The **data bus** is the set of pathways that carries the actual data between memory and the CPU. A 64-bit data bus can move 8 bytes of data to the processor in the same machine cycle. The data bus width should be matched to the word size of the CPU for optimum performance.

The **address bus** is the electronic pathway that carries information about the memory locations of data. The width of the address bus determines how much potential memory a processor can recognize. Larger address buses mean the processor can address more memory. Many microcomputers use a 32-bit address bus. This gives the processor access to a potential of 4GB of memory (2^{32}). The processor's ability to access a large address space is important for multimedia applications. Digital video, sound, and images produce large data files. Larger address buses support faster multimedia processing by allowing these files to be moved from hard drives, CD-ROMs, and other peripheral storage devices to the computer's electronic memory where they can be processed and displayed faster.

■ Pipelining

Microprocessor manufacturers such as Intel, Motorola, and IBM utilize additional techniques to maximize the CPU's speed. **Pipelining** increases CPU efficiency by reading an instruction, starting processing, and reading another instruction before finishing the previous one. Using pipelining, different steps of the machine cycle can be carried out on several instructions simultaneously (see Figure 3.4). This reduces CPU idle time and

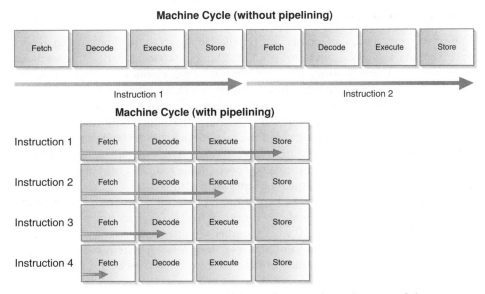

Figure 3.4 Modern processors support pipelining to increase the performance of the processor. In pipelining, instructions are sent to the processor in stages.

increases the speed at which instructions can be executed. Both Pentium and PowerPC chips take advantage of this technique.

■ RISC Processing

RISC (Reduced Instruction Set Computer) chips also increase overall speed of the CPU. **RISC** chips eliminate complex embedded microcode instructions and replace them with a simpler set of instructions for executing the most common commands used by the processor. These common commands are combined to carry out the less frequent, more complex processing tasks. This results in faster overall processing of routine operations. RISC technology is found in many microprocessors. The PowerPC G5 chip, developed by Motorola and IBM, was the first 64-bit RISC processor for desktop computers.

■ Multi-processing

> **Microcode** is a programming technique for implementing the instruction set of a processor. An **instruction set** is the set of instructions that a processor can carry out.

Multi-processing can also improve system performance. **Multi-processing** is a combination of multiple processors on the system board that execute instructions simultaneously. There are several approaches to multi-processing. Computers may have a CPU and math-coprocessor or graphics-coprocessor working together to increase the overall performance of a system. Apple's G5 computer has dual processors that speed CPU operations using 64-bit chips, reaching processing power comparable to a supercomputer. Multimedia development may also employ **parallel processing**, a technique of linking hundreds or thousands of processors to operate at the same time on a single task. Parallel processing is often used to speed the final stage of 3-D animation, known as rendering. Dreamworks employed a "render farm" of over 1,000 HP ProLiant DL145 servers to render the daily versions of its animated films, *Shrek 2* and *Madagascar*.

■ Multi-core Technology

Multi-core processors are an increasingly popular approach to multi-processing in personal computers. A processor "core" is a CPU's "computational engine," that is, those components that directly execute instructions. Older processors were single core. The CPU was built around a single computational engine that fetched and executed each command in the pipeline as fast as it could. To improve processing capacity, engineers increased clock speeds and made other improvements that added transistors to the CPU. However, the extra electronics increased the heat on the chip and did not achieve the performance gains necessary for current computing demands. Manufacturers looked for a different strategy to increase processing speeds while reducing heat and improving energy efficiency. The result was the multi-core architecture.

Multi-core technology combines two or more processor cores and cache memory on a single integrated circuit. A dual-core processor has two execution cores and two L2 memory caches. These two "cores" work together simultaneously to carry out different tasks. To achieve real computing gains however, the operating system and applications must be adjusted to take advantage of the dual core using a technique called multi-threading, or passing tasks simultaneously to different cores to execute.

Multi-core processors can significantly improve performance in multitasking work environments where one processor core can address one task while a second task is completed by the second core. For example, one core might be directed to writing a DVD and another one to editing images in Photoshop. A dual core processor would execute both tasks faster because each core could address a separate task. This can speed the process of multimedia development. The technology also has benefits for multimedia playback, particularly for graphics intensive applications. Multi-core processors are used in many video gaming consoles where they speed real-time rendering of complex graphics and player interactions.

The fetch/execute cycle of the CPU is optimized by a variety of techniques to increase speed and deal with more complex data types. By increasing clock speed, word size, and system bus, the control unit and ALU can process data faster. New developments in pipelining, multi-processing, and multi-core chips are producing faster processors that can handle increasingly complex commands for manipulating multimedia data.

Research continues to improve the speed and performance of the CPU. Moore's Law suggests that manufacturers can double the speed of a processor every 18 months. Future computers may use nanotechnology to achieve smaller and faster processors. Reliance on electronics may be replaced with optical circuitry to increase the speed of processing to "light speeds." Whatever the technique, we can expect new computer processors to continue to show improvements in performance.

> **Nanotechnology:** manufactured objects are designed and built by the specification and placement of individual atoms or molecules.

Primary Memory   Modern computers operate with electricity. The CPU processes electrically and uses basic instructions wired in the ALU's electronics. Therefore, data and instructions directly manipulated by the CPU must also be stored electronically. **Primary memory** is electronic storage that is directly addressed by the CPU.

There are several forms of primary memory on a computer system. **Random access memory (RAM)** consists of addressable storage areas for data and instructions in electronic format. This storage is volatile. Once electricity is powered off, the contents are lost. While not suitable for long-term storage, RAM provides the fast, electronic access to data and instructions required for processing by the CPU.

The amount of RAM storage is an important performance feature of computer systems. RAM is measured in units of Megabytes (MB) or Gigabytes (GB). Personal computers used to develop and play complex multimedia should have as much installed RAM as possible. Large RAM capacities are necessary to store the operating system, application software, and data for multimedia processing. Modern multimedia operating systems use large amounts of electronic storage. OS X and Windows XP require 128MB while Windows Vista recommends 1 GB of RAM. The application software to develop media also has large memory requirements. Developers like to keep more than one program open in memory. This practice of **multitasking** (running more than one program simultaneously) consumes large amounts of RAM. In addition, multimedia data files are often very large. Sound and video files, for example, can easily require 500MB or more of electronic storage. Larger capacities of RAM storage mean more data and applications can be open and readily accessed by the CPU. This translates to greater efficiency in the development and delivery of multimedia applications.

A second form of primary memory is **read-only memory (ROM)**. ROM is a special form of non-volatile electronic storage that contains frequently used instructions for the CPU. These commands are hardwired or embedded in the chip by the manufacturer; they can be *read*, but not changed. The instructions perform essential system checks and load the operating system from disk storage into RAM. ROM is activated when the power is on. The embedded instructions do not disappear when the power is off, unlike RAM storage.

A third form of electronic memory is called **cache** storage. This high speed electronic storage optimizes microprocessor speed by storing frequently used data and instructions close to the processor. This reduces the time it takes to locate and transport data from RAM. Primary cache (Level 1) is on the actual CPU chip. Level 2 cache is positioned between the CPU and RAM. It has higher capacity than primary cache on the CPU, but less capacity than RAM. Neither Level 1 nor Level 2 cache storage adds to the overall total of available RAM. However, cache is an important feature that improves processor performance.

System Board   The **system board** (also called the *motherboard*) is the main circuit board or the electrical foundation of the computer. In addition to CPU, RAM, and ROM chips, the system board contains:

- integrated circuits that convert analog signals to digital format
- expansion slots to add memory and hardware devices
- special purpose chips such as a digital signal processor
- video card to control the display monitor
- power supply
- I/O interface ports to capture and send data to peripheral devices

Multimedia computers are equipped with many built-in devices, but often a developer may want additional hard drives, a DVD burner, or a second video board, for example. Many computers have expansion slots to add these hardware components; others have limited or no expansion capability at all. An alternative to adding devices directly on the system board is to plug external devices into an interface port.

Hardware Interface   A **hardware interface** is a point of union between the system unit and a peripheral device. Data flows through the interface between the system board and peripheral devices in a serial or parallel path. **Serial data transmission** is a single stream of bits. One wire sends the bits and another wire returns the bits. This method is generally used for devices that don't transfer large volumes of data, such as a keyboard, mouse, or modem. **Parallel data transmission** is a series of bits transferred simultaneously. Each bit has its own wire in a parallel path. Parallel connections may move 8 or more bits of data at once, thus increasing the amount of data transferred in a given amount of time. One common parallel connection is a printer port where more data to the printer results in faster printouts.

Interface ports are connections to add peripheral devices to the system board (see Figure 3.5). They are generally located behind the system unit cabinet. PCs have RS-232C and LPT ports as common interface ports for modems, printers, or scanners.

Cable Lock   Phone   Ethernet   Firewire   USB Ports   VGA   Headphone
   Slot   Modem   Port   display

Figure 3.5 Interface ports for iMac.

Older Macintosh computers use a serial interface called the Apple Desktop Bus (ADB) to make connections to the printer, keyboard, and mouse and a faster, parallel interface known as SCSI (Small Computer System Interface) for devices such as scanners, Zip drives, and external hard disks. Current microcomputers are equipped with USB (Universal Serial Bus), FireWire (IEEE 1394), audio, video, and Ethernet ports.

Universal Serial Bus (USB) is an input/output bus to transfer data at higher speeds than older serial and parallel interfaces. USB has several advantages over previous bus systems. First, it is a widely supported standard. This simplifies purchasing external devices. A USB device can plug into any USB port, whether on an Apple or PC. Second, a USB cabling system creates its own independent bus where up to 127 devices can be daisy chained together and share a single port on the microcomputer. Third, USB devices are "hot swappable." A USB device can be disconnected and another device swapped (plugged) into the system without restarting the computer. Fourth, USB devices can be powered through the interface port rather than a separate power supply. This greatly reduces the number of power adapters (or "wall-warts" as they've been called) that clog up power strips. Finally, USB has faster data transfer. USB transmits data at speeds of 12Mbs compared to the RS-232C speeds of 115.2Kbs. USB devices such as printers, scanners, Zip drives, and keyboards benefit from faster transmission rates. The USB2 standard introduced even faster transmission rates (480Mbs) for devices that require higher rates of transmission such as MP3 players, removable hard drives, and DVDs.

IEEE 1394 (named **FireWire** by Apple) is a high-speed serial interface standard with data transfer rates of 400Mbs over cables up to 4.5 meters in length. It has its own bus system that can daisy chain up to 63 devices. Like USB, FireWire devices are hot swappable and power for these devices is drawn from the FireWire port. These ports are most often found on digital video cameras or large capacity external hard drives. A further development of the standard, FireWire 800, has twice the transfer speed and can maintain it across 100-meter cables. This opens efficient cabling possibilities to capture digital video and/or audio from cameras placed significant distances from the computer (Figure 3.6).

As the processing speed of CPUs increases, computer manufacturers continue to seek ways to increase the interface speeds between the user and the system board. Table 3.2 summarizes transmission rates for various standards. Note the advantages of improved technologies such as USB2 and FireWire 800 for connecting peripheral devices to the system board.

Figure 3.6 USB and FireWire cables.

Table 3.2 **Transmission Rates for Common Interface Standards**

Serial Port	115Kbs
Standard Parallel Port	115KBs
USB	12Mbs
SCSI-1	5MBs
SCSI-2	10MBs to 20MBs
Ultra SCSI	20MBs to 40MBs
Wide Ultra3 SCSI	160MBs
USB2	480Mbs
IEEE 1394 or FireWire	100–400Mbs
FireWire 800	800Mbs

Peripheral Devices

Peripheral devices are the hardware components that input, output, and permanently store data and applications for computer processing. Although often located close to the system unit, they are outside the main processing circuitry and thus are considered peripheral (Figure 3.7). The functions and performance characteristics of peripherals are important considerations for both multimedia users who may want the best display device for a video game, and for developers who seek high performance data capture and access.

Secondary Storage Devices   Computer systems are not complete without a means of storing data and instructions for future use. Random access memory is essential for the CPU to process data and instructions electronically; but RAM is volatile. Once the power is off, memory is cleared, and data is lost. **Secondary storage** is the media that holds data and instructions outside the system unit for long periods of time. It is also called *external storage* or *auxiliary storage* to distinguish it from primary electronic storage inside the system unit. Early forms of secondary storage were paper tape, punched cards, and magnetic tape. Secondary storage now includes hard disks with gigabyte capacities, optical discs that deliver high fidelity multimedia, and a wide array of portable storage ranging from zip disks to flash drives, and even portable music players (Figure 3.8).

Secondary storage has several advantages over primary electronic storage. In addition to being non-volatile, secondary storage is easily expandable and portable. If one disk fills with data, another disk is readily available. Data and applications are easily distributed and shared through secondary storage media such as CDs, DVDs, flash drives, or zip disks. Each of these addresses one or more of the five main uses of secondary storage: *saving*, *backup*, *distribution*, *transport*, and *archiving*.

Figure 3.7 With the miniaturization of today's mobile computing systems, the peripherals may not seem so distant. A PDA (Portable Digital Assistant, such as a Palm Pilot or Blackberry) embeds both the display device and keyboard on the system unit.

The most obvious use of secondary storage is to *save* the data that is in electronic memory for further processing. Multimedia developers frequently save data files to hard drives or other devices as they work. They know that RAM is volatile and that hours of effort can be lost in an instant with a system crash or power failure. Important performance criteria for saving include capacity, access time, and transfer rate. **Storage capacity** is the amount of digital data, measured in bytes, that a device can record. Multimedia developers require high storage capacities for large media files such as digital video. **Access time** is the time needed to locate data on the storage device. **Transfer rate** measures the speed at which data moves between secondary storage and RAM. Faster access times and transfer rates mean less time waiting for data and applications to load into RAM. This speed is especially important if developers are working with large sound or video files where fast access to data editing and playback is essential. See Table 3.3 for sample performance measures of magnetic storage.

Another use of secondary storage is to *backup* entire hard drives or important volumes on the hard drive. Data is a major asset for most organizations. It must be preserved in the event of damaged drives, theft, system crashes, viruses, or natural disasters. Backup systems should have large storage capacities and be able to transfer data quickly. Frequently, a hard drive is backed up to another hard drive since both have large capacities and fast transfer rates. Users should also consider backing up important data files to other devices, such as a zip disk, flash drive, or DVD, on a routine schedule. To further protect the data, the backup should be stored in another location, preferably off site.

Figure 3.8 The iPod is also a popular storage device. In addition to holding hours of music and video, the iPod can plug into a USB port to record data for transport.

A third use of secondary storage is *distribution* of data and applications. Networks improve data-sharing over communication lines, but data portability cannot be restricted to network connections. Data and applications can also be distributed by "snail mail" or as retail products such as "shrink-wrap" software. CDs, for example, are cheap to produce, have long storage life, and are lightweight. Most computers can read the disc, which makes them a good choice to distribute applications and data. Performance features to consider in distributing secondary media include cost, weight, data integrity, and adherence to standards for playback.

In addition to distributing data and applications, secondary storage media *transport* digital content. Commonly called "sneaker-net," users can carry their digital files on portable media such as floppy disks or flash drives. Adequate capacity, and the ability to

Table 3.3 Magnetic Storage Performance Measures

Device	Access Time	Transfer Rate	Capacity
Floppy drive	84ms	250–500KB/s	1.44MB
Zip drive	29ms	1.2 MB/s (USB 250)	100, 250, 750MB
Hard Drive	< 9ms	15MB/s–160MB/s	Variations of GBs & TBs

withstand temperature extremes, magnetic fields, and the wear and tear of a duffle bag are important criteria for digital data on the move.

Finally, a fifth use of secondary storage is to *archive* digital information for long-term preservation. Digital files abound in all the transactions of daily life and schools, hospitals, governments, businesses, and other organizations must preserve them for legal and historical purposes. In the past, this meant large vaults of file folders. Later, these files were transferred to tape and stored in special tape libraries. Archived data requires storage media with massive and expandable capacity, media longevity, and security. These include RAID (Redundant Array of Independent Disks) drives, WORM (Write Once Read Many) optical disk library systems, and digital tape.

The devices used for secondary storage fall into three broad categories based on the underlying technology used to represent digital data: magnetic, optical, or solid-state.

■ Magnetic Storage

Magnetic storage devices record and/or read digital content in magnetic form. These devices include floppy, hard, and cartridge drives. The drives record bits on a disk platter or card as positive or negative magnetic fields. A drive motor rotates the disk on a spindle, an access arm reaches across the disk surface, and a read/write head at the end of the arm transfers data to or from the surface of the disk and RAM. Fixed disk drives are mounted inside the computer enclosure and connected to the system board. Portable drives are plugged into USB or FireWire ports.

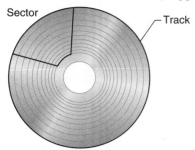

Magnetic disks are either floppy or hard platters. Data is stored on these platters in addressable tracks and sectors defined by the operating system. A **track** is a circular path along which data is stored. **Sectors** are pie-shaped logical divisions of a track (see Figure 3.9). Each sector holds a designated amount of data. The PC standard defines sector capacity at 512 bytes of data. The number of tracks and sectors determine storage potential.

The **floppy disk** is a thin plastic film coated with an iron-oxide substance that holds magnetism. Floppies were the earliest form of portable magnetic disk storage, but newer forms of storage are replacing them. Floppy disks are an inexpensive way to transport small amounts of digital content, but they have several limitations.

Figure 3.9 Track/sector addressing scheme for magnetic storage.

First, floppy drives are slow: they have high access times and low transfer rates. Secondly, the limited storage capacity of 1.4MB is not sufficient for most multimedia data files. Finally, data on floppy disks is vulnerable to destruction by heat, scratches on the disk surface, and the wear and tear of normal usage. Because of these limitations, floppy drives are disappearing from computer systems and diskettes are being replaced by other portable storage that is more reliable and has higher storage capacity.

Hard drives are composed of rigid platters mounted on a spindle in an enclosed drive container. The container regulates air pressure and filters the air that enters the drive to protect it from dust and other contaminants. A drive motor rotates disks at speeds of 7,200 rpm or more. Access arms with read/write heads move between platters to read tracks on both top and bottom surfaces (see Figure 3.10). These platters are formatted with higher track density and more sectors than a floppy disk, thus increasing storage capacity. Hard disks can have 10,000 or more tracks and 50 or more sectors per track. Hard disk units built inside the computer system can have storage capacities in the hun-

dreds of gigabytes, but even these disks quickly fill with large multimedia data files, applications, and modern graphics-based operating systems.

Portable hard drives and disk cartridges drives offer expansion alternatives for magnetic storage. Zip drives are external drives that are usually connected to USB ports. **Zip disk** cartridges are an affordable, portable alternative to the floppy disk. Zip drives support cartridges of 100, 250, and 750MB capacities. Cartridges are used to back up or transport files (Figure 3.11).

External hard drives supplement the fixed hard drive capacity while providing data portability and security. These drives often use FireWire for high-speed data transfer to the system unit. They are commonly used to back up and secure data, or store and edit large projects such as digital video. In addition to their large gigabyte capacities, external hard drives have faster access times and transfer rates than Zip drives (Figure 3.12).

Figure 3.10 Disk platters are rotated on a spindle. The access arms move to a track location and the read/write head transfers data to and from RAM. © vadim kozlovsly/ShutterStock, Inc.

Magnetic media can provide large capacity storage and rapid data access and transfer. Magnetic storage is also economical. Prices are currently in the range of a dollar per gigabyte and they continue to drop. But magnetic storage also has several disadvantages, not the least of which is its limited durability. Magnetism is easily destroyed or weakened over time, resulting in damaged or lost data unless backups are done frequently. Portable magnetic storage also has limited capacity. Floppy disks hold a mere 1.4MB and current zip cartridges are limited to 750MB.

Figure 3.11 Zip cartridges.

Figure 3.12 External hard drive.

▪ Optical Storage

Optical storage uses laser technology to read and write data on specially coated reflective discs. The origins of optical storage can be traced to the early 1980s.

In 1982, the CD (compact disc) revolutionized the music indus-try and spurred the development of multimedia applications. Philips and Sony first developed CDs to replace vinyl records with a medium that could deliver high quality sound on a small, lightweight platter. LP (Long Playing) records were limited to 45 minutes of analog music. Sound quality was governed by the

> **Disc and Disk**
>
> *Disc* refers to optical storage media as opposed to *disk*, which is used for magnetic media.

condition of the record and needle, and records themselves were bulky and difficult to manage. Portable music was restricted to tapes, also easily susceptible to damage. Compact disc storage and digital music provided a medium for permanent, high fidelity recordings. CDs were designed to hold a full 74 minutes of digital audio recording, sig-nificantly increasing music storage over the long-playing vinyl record.

The advent of optical storage also offered new potential for multimedia. A new CD standard, called CD-ROM, was developed especially for computer data. Now applications that required large storage could easily be distributed on a small 4.72″ disc. The first gen-eral interest CD-ROM was *Grolier's Electronic Encyclopedia*. Released in 1985, its 9 million words only used 12% of the CD-ROM's capacity. Optical storage technology developed rapidly. From music CDs of the 80s, technology expanded to DVD videos in the 90s.

Compact Disc Technology   CD storage uses a laser beam to read and write data to disc. **Lasers** are amplified light energy focused into a very precise beam. The basic process is simple: focus a laser beam on a reflective surface and measure the amount of light reflected back on a photo detector. By altering surface texture, light will either be reflected or deflected. The disc acts as a reflective mirror with pits and lands that encode digital content. **Pits** are indentations on the surface and **lands** are the flat area. Pits scatter light and lands reflect light (see Figure 3.13). Binary data once encoded as positive/negative magne-tism is now read as variations in light reflection.

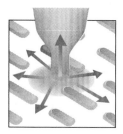 

Figure 3.13 Pits scatter light and lands reflect light.

CD-Audio and CD-ROM discs are manufactured by pressing pits into a plastic base. This process is called *stamping*. A reflective layer of aluminum is then added and finally a lacquer coating is applied to protect the surface. The laser beam scans the bottom of the disc surface where pits appear as bumps to scatter light. Lands reflect the full intensity of the light beam. Once the CD is stamped, data is permanent.

Optical storage has several advantages. The first is high capacity storage. Laser beams are extremely precise and pits and lands are extremely small, so data is densely recorded on a disc. Pits are approximately .83 microns long by .5 microns wide (about 30 times narrower than a human hair). Data is recorded in one continuous spiral from the center to the outside edge of the disc. There are about 20,000 windings of this single spiral on a CD, resulting in a total track length of 5000 meters or about 3 miles. This produces a storage capacity of 680MB.

Another benefit of optical storage is stability. CD data is more durable than data stored magnetically. Pits are pressed into the disc. This process makes it unlikely that normal handling and exposure to the environment will destroy the data. CD data is also encoded with special error detection and correction code (EDC/ECC) to further assure data integrity if the disc is damaged. Magnetic media, such as floppy disks, do not incorporate error detection and correction, with the result that damaged data is lost data. By contrast, the data on a scratched CD Audio disc can usually be repaired as it plays. CD technology is synonymous with high capacity, high quality, and durable storage.

> **Pits, Lands, and EFM**
>
> Pits and lands do not translate directly to bits. Instead, optical discs use an encoding system called "Eight to Fourteen Modulation" (EFM). Fourteen bits are used to encode the 8 bits of a data byte. The extra information is used to ensure the accuracy of the optical reading of each byte.

Optical Data Encoding   Optical data is organized in *tracks*, *frames*, and *sessions* on the disc. A track is the basic addressing scheme on a CD. A CD has a physical, continuous spiral from the center to the outside edge but it is further divided into logical units called tracks. A compact disc addresses one of up to 99 sequentially numbered tracks. Each track can handle only one data type so a CD with music and text would require at least two separate tracks (see Figure 3.14).

The basic unit of information stored on a CD is a **frame**. Frames define the physical format of data. Frames contain data code, error detection and correction code, synchronization code, and information about the track. Fifty-eight frames are grouped together to form the smallest addressable data unit called either *blocks* (CD Audio) or *sectors* (CD-ROM). Each CD audio block has 2352 bytes of user data, while CD-ROM sectors contain 2048 bytes of data code. There are fewer bytes of data code on the CD-ROM because

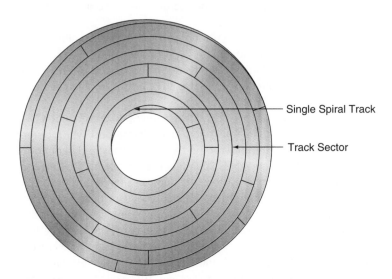

Single Spiral Track

Track Sector

Figure 3.14 CDs store data in a continuous spiral from the center to the outside of the disc. The single spiral is further divided into logical units called tracks. The smallest addressable data unit is called a block or sector.

these sectors contain more error detection and correction code that helps ensure the integrity of error-sensitive media such as text and numbers.

A **session** is a single recorded segment on the CD. Sessions may cover several tracks depending on the content of the application. For each session, a track table of contents is added to the disc. A *track table of contents* (TTOC) is an index of track contents. Early CDs supported only one session and one TTOC per disc. This is called a single-session CD. Newer CD formats support *multi-sessions*. Kodak used the first multi-session CD for their PhotoCD. Kodak initially records one set of photos on a CD, then adds another set of images with a separate track table of contents to the same CD at a later time. Today, multi-session storage is common on CD-R (CD-Recordable) discs.

Compact Disc Formats   One of the more important decisions made by optical disc manufacturers was to standardize the size of the disc. Disc size is fixed at 120mm with a 15mm center hole and 1.2mm thickness. As a result, all CDs will fit into any drive, making it possible to design newer drives with backward compatibility. *Backward compatibility* is the ability of more recent hardware or software to use data from an earlier product. The most important CD formats are CD-DA, CD-ROM, CD-R, and CD-RW.

> CD-ROM sectors have less data capacity than CD Audio blocks because they contain more error detection and correction code. This helps ensure the integrity of error-sensitive media such as text and numbers.

The **CD-DA** format was the first digital optical disc standard and it is still used in the production of music CDs. While these discs can typically be played on a computer CD drive, CD-DA cannot be used to record computer data. CD-DA specifies a high-quality audio file format that records 16-bit samples at a rate of 44.1KHz.

CD-ROM was developed to take advantage of CD technology for the storage of computer programs and data. CD-ROM discs are Read-Only Memory. They can be used to distribute pre-recorded data to various computers, but computers can only read them, they cannot change content by writing to the disc.

CD-R discs (CD-Recordable) use a different method of recording "pits" to allow computers to write, as well as read, a disc. Discs are coated with a photosensitive dye. This dye is translucent when the disc is blank. Light shines through and reflects off the metal surface. When data is applied, a laser beam heats the dye and alters its molecular structure to create opaque "pits" that will not reflect light.

Several dye materials are used to create these discs, each with a different color. CD-R discs are manufactured with predefined spiral tracks and sector formatting, which determines disc capacity. CD-R discs have different recording capacities measured in minutes of music and MB of data. One common capacity is 700MB and 80 minutes. CD-ROM and CD-R discs are similar in that once the data is written, it cannot be altered or removed.

CD-RW discs (CD-ReWritable) use a different material so the laser beam can read, erase, and write data. Discs have a special layer of "phase change" chemical compound. A laser beam heats the compound and changes it either to a liquid or crystalline structure. This compound in its liquid state becomes amorphous and absorbs light. The crystalline state allows light through to reflect off the aluminum surface. These crystalline and amorphous properties remain on the disc when it cools down. These discs require a special drive with a laser that alters the heat intensity as it adjusts to read, write, and erase operations. Most computers today are equipped with a rewritable optical drive. (See Appendix A for further detail on development of standards and formats for CD storage.)

Optical Drives   Optical drives are complex mechanical devices that move a laser light along a track on the disc. The laser reflects light back to a system of mirrors that direct reflections to a photo detector. A tracking mechanism controls the location of the laser beam on the disc (see Figure 3.15). Early optical drive motors varied rotational speed from 500 rpm, when the light was at the center of the disc, to 200 rpm when the light was at the outer edges. This allowed the drive to maintain a constant data transfer rate.

Transfer rate measures the speed at which data is moved to the computer or other device for playback. The CD-DA standard established a transfer rate of .15MB/s or 1X. This assured accurate playback of digital music. Altering this speed would distort the sound by speeding it up or slowing it down.

When CD technology was adapted for computers, higher transfer rates were needed to quickly move data from disc to RAM. One technique to produce higher transfer rates is increasing rotational speed. Current computer CD drives have transfer rates of 48X to 64X. If the drive is rated at 48X, the transfer rate is 48*.15MB or 7.2MB/s. Transfer rates are affected not only by rotational speeds, but also by the method used to store and access data on disc. There are two methods to locate and transfer data: CLV and CAV.

CD-audio drives read data from disc at a **constant linear velocity (CLV)**. A CLV disc stores pits and lands as closely together as possible in a uniform, continuous spiral from the center to the outside edge. This produces the highest possible storage capacity; but it also creates a problem. Because disc diameter is larger at the outside, a constant rate of spin will result in more data being read per second at the outer edge than at the inner edge. To keep the transfer rate constant, CLV drives spin the disc faster when data is

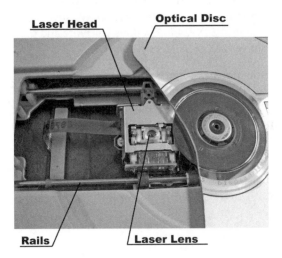

Figure 3.15 A beam of light produced by a laser is directed through a series of lenses until it is focused on the surface of the spinning disc. A drive motor moves the laser head along the rails to reposition the laser lens.

being read toward the center of the disc and slower as reading takes place toward the outside. This results in the same length of the data spiral being read each second, regardless of its location on the disc (hence, constant *linear* velocity). For audio data, varying disc spin rate is a reasonable mechanical adjustment since the rate of music playback is continuous and predictable from one song to the next.

Using CLV for computer data, however, poses a problem. An important performance feature of computers is random access. **Random access** is the ability to quickly read data from any location on the storage device. Random access is difficult to achieve with CLV because drives must constantly adjust spin rates depending on data location, speeding up if the data is located close to the center and slowing down if it is closer to the outside of the disc. When CD drives were first adapted for computer data, they maintained the CLV standard but increased the motor spin rates to improve transfer rates from 1X to 12X. However, it became apparent that CD drives needed to dramatically increase rotational speeds to keep up with faster processor demands. It was reasonable to alter spin rates from 200 rpm to 500 rpm, but much harder to go from 5,000 rpm to 12,000 rpm. A second method of storing and accessing data was needed.

Computer optical drives adopted the same technique used in hard drives, **constant angular velocity (CAV)**. These drives spin the disc at a constant high speed regardless of the location of the laser. Transfer rates vary from the inside to the outside track. While this would destroy playback of a symphony orchestra on a CD player, computers can compensate for the data flow variations by buffering data and storing it in RAM for later processing. Today, most CD drives that exceed 12X transfer rates are using CAV to control disc spin rate. Computer optical drives may also combine CLV and CAV techniques. CLV mode is used to write CD-Rs and CD-RWs, while CAV mode is used to read discs.

The transfer rates of current optical drives are still slower than a hard drive, but they are much faster than the original CD audio drives. CD-R and CD-RW drives have a range of transfer rates. CD-R has a write transfer rate and reading transfer rate. CD-RW drives have different rates for writing, erasing, and reading. A 52X–24X–52X drive will write and read at a 7.8MB/s transfer rate, but erase at a slower 24X or 3.6MB/s (Table 3.4).

DVD: Movies and More on Disc   The music industry sought ways to improve on vinyl records with the first CD. In similar fashion, the movie industry pushed development of DVDs to record full-length films on a higher quality medium than film or tape. CDs held promise for video, but their storage capacity was too low for a 133-minute movie, even with high levels of data compression.

Table 3.4 **CD Drive Rotational Speeds and Transfer Rates**

Drive Rating	Access Method	Avg Transfer Rate (MB/s)
1X	CLV	.15
8X	CLV	1.2
12X	CLV	1.8
12X–24X	CAV	2.7
12X–48X	CAV	4.5

DVD, or Digital Versatile Disc, first appeared in 1997. Originally, it was targeted as a storage format for movies and called the Digital *Video* Disc; but developers soon recognized its potential to store all forms of digital data and changed the name to "versatile." The versatility of DVD is reflected in its various designations: *DVD-Video* for motion pictures, *DVD-Audio* for high quality music, *DVD-ROM* for distribution of computer software. Competing standards and other uses of the technology have led to a proliferation of DVD specifications. See Table 3.5 for a listing of the most significant of these formats.

> 4.7GB of DVD storage can hold:
> - More than 400,000 text documents, the equivalent of eight 4-drawer filing cabinets stuffed with paper information.
> - 4,700 full-color digital photos @ 640X480 resolution.
> - 210 minutes, a full 3.5 hours of compressed MPEG-2 satellite quality video.
> - 120 minutes of compressed MPEG-2 theater-quality video
> - 14+ hours of MP3 compressed audio
>
> *Verbatim Corp.*

The main advantage of DVDs over CDs is storage capacity. The capacity of a CD is approximately 650MB. A DVD can hold up to 17GB. The higher capacity of DVDs is based on four major developments: a more precise laser light, multi-layer storage, new video compression algorithms, and improved error detection and correction code.

DVDs and CDs are the same physical size and share the same basic optical storage technology. But new lasers with a wavelength of 635 to 650 nanometers and powerful laser lens systems can focus on smaller pits to significantly increase storage capacity. DVD pits have a minimum length of .40 microns, compared to the CDs .83 microns (see Figure 3.16). Data is recorded on a spiral track that measures 7.5 miles, as compared with the CDs 3 miles. Each layer stores 4.7GB of data, two layers on the same side offers 8.5GB of storage. When all four layers are used, a total of 17GB is available, enough storage for 8 hours of movies.

The second factor contributing to increased capacity is multi-layer storage. Each side of a DVD can be divided into two layers. A DVD disc is a lacquer-coated sandwich of polycarbonate plastic, aluminum, and semi-reflective gold. The plastic is impressed with pits arranged in a continuous spiral of data. A coating of aluminum is added to the inner layer and a layer of semi-reflective gold is used for the outer layers. This provides two reflective surfaces. The laser first focuses on the outer layer of semi-reflective gold, then the lens mechanism focuses through the semi-reflective layer to the second layer of aluminum.

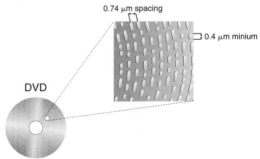

DVD players first appeared for commercial use as stand-alone systems to play DVD-videos. Each disc

Figure 3.16 Pits are closer together on a DVD disc.

could hold 133 minutes of video and an assortment of video add-ons such as trailers and outtakes. DVD drives with the capability of also handling CD and CD-RW formats were soon developed for use in computers. The drive is similar to a CLV CD. The motor rotates the disc from 200 rpm to 500 rpm to maintain a constant data transfer rate. A tracking mechanism moves the laser along a spiral track. It starts at the center and moves to the outside edge of the outer layer, then works from the outside back to the center on the inner layer to optimize the drive action.

DVD drives are rated according to rotational speeds (4X, 12X, etc.) just like CD drives, but the actual transfer rates are much higher for DVD drives. For example, a 1X DVD-ROM drive transfers 1.321 MB/s (as opposed to the .15MB of CDs). A 6X DVD drive transfers approximately 7.93 MB/s, equivalent to a 54X CD drive. There is no advantage to a 6X DVD player for playing movies. Speeds above 1X do not improve video quality, but they will impact the speed for reading computer data and playing games.

Table 3.5 **DVD Formats**

Format	Features	Players
DVD-ROM	Read only format Video or game content burned into the DVD First standard	Runs on any DVD-ROM equipped device
DVD-audio	Higher quality sound than CD 192kHz/24bit 74 min high quality sound 7 hrs CD-quality sound	Requires special player to read the higher quality sound files
DVD-RAM Supported by Panasonic, Toshiba, Apple, Hitachi, NEC, Pioneer, Samsung, Sharp	Writable DVD formats for use in computers Rewrite more than 100,000 times Life expectancy about 30 years	Removable storage for computers Not compatible with most players
DVD-R Supported by Panasonic, Toshiba, Apple, Hitachi, NEC, Pioneer, Samsung, Sharp	Writable DVD discs using organic dye technology 4.7GB	Compatible with most DVD drives and players
DVD-RW Supported by Panasonic, Toshiba, Apple, Hitachi, NEC, Pioneer, Samsung, Sharp	Phase-change erasable format 4.7GB Rewrite about 1,000 times Drives write DVD-R, DVD-RW, CD-R, CD-RW discs	Playable in many DVD drives and players
DVD+RW Supported by Philips, Sony, HP, Dell, Ricoh, Yamaha	Erasable format Holds 4.7GB/side Writes in a way compatible with many existing DVD readers Rewritten about 1,000 times	Readable in many DVD-Video players and DVD-ROM drives
DVD+R Supported by Philips, Sony, HP, Dell, Ricoh, Yamaha	Record only in CLV mode A write once variation of DVD+RW	Readable in many DVD-Video players and DVD-ROM drives

Data summarized from www.dvddemystified.com/dvdfaq.html#4.2

Despite a DVD's impressive 17GB capacity, a single disc still cannot accommodate the 110GB required for an uncompressed full-length movie. The third improvement, video compression, delivered movies on a DVD. Video compression reduces file size without compromising the quality of video content. The Motion Picture Experts Group (MPEG) developed a 40:1 compression ratio for MPEG2. This compression format combined with the storage capacity of the DVD now makes it possible to have movies and much more on a single disc.

Finally, DVDs also benefited from improved error detection and correction code. On a CD, ECC/EDC may take up as much as a third of the available storage space. DVDs reduce this to approximately 13%, making more disc space available for data.

DVDs have such extensive storage that manufacturers often package additional content with their films. Dolby digital surround sound, soundtracks presented in up to 8 languages, subtitles in up to 32 languages, as well as related content such as actor profiles and alternative endings can be easily accommodated by DVD storage. Some production companies' even plant "Easter eggs." These are hidden movie clips that are not on the index. You can explore the world of DVD Easter eggs at http://www.dvdeastereggs.com.

The Digital Versatile Disc gained acceptance as a medium to distribute movies, but a wide array of applications soon followed for this high capacity disc. Basic DVD formats were applied to the music industry (DVD-audio), and read/write computer drives. DVD formats include DVD+RW, DVD+RAM, DVD-R, and DVD-RW, but not all of these formats are compatible. Successful playback of a DVD recording will depend on the type of disc, recording drive, and the playback device.

The DVD standard introduced massive storage capability using a laser beam that was more precise than that used to create CDs. Full featured digital video was now possible on these discs but manufacturers were not satisfied with a mere 17GB of storage. HDTV programming and video games could benefit from even higher capacities and a new form of laser is making that possible. Blu-ray Disc (BD) developed at Sony holds 25GB on a single side and HD DVD by Toshiba stores 15GB per side. These storage densities are possible because a blue-violet laser has a shorter wavelength than the red laser used to record DVD discs. The result: as much as 50GB on dual layer discs or about 9 hours of high-definition video and 23 hours of standard defini-tion video on Blu-ray discs. HD DVD supports 30GB with 5 hours of high-definition video and 13 hours of standard playback.

■ Solid-State Storage

A **solid-state storage** device is a form of computer memory that contains no moving parts. Solid-state secondary storage is non-volatile memory that can be both read and written to. The use of solid-state devices for secondary storage has grown dramatically as their capacity has increased and their cost has fallen. Common examples include USB **flash drives**, **memory cards**, and the built-in memory used in MP3 players, digital cameras, and mobile phones. The technology used in all these devices is called **flash memory** (Figure 3.17).

Figure 3.17 Solid state storage devices have a variety of names. Memory stick, thumb drive, and travel disk are commonly used. The standard name is USB Flash Drive or "UFD."

Flash memory is made up of a grid of cells, each of which contains two transistors. A very thin layer of insulating oxide separates the transistors. One serves as a *control gate*. The other is a *floating gate*. The insulating oxide layer traps any electrons present on the floating gate, preserving the electronic information with no need for external power. The charge of the floating gate, in turn, modifies the electric field of the control gate. The voltage of this field is then read to determine the bit value (0 or 1) of the cell.

Solid-state memory has a number of advantages. The absence of delicate mechanical parts makes solid-state storage more durable. They are smaller and weigh much less than their mechanical counterparts. Finally, solid-state devices use less power.

These benefits will lead to increasing use of flash technology for secondary storage. Mechanical storage is not likely to be completely replaced, however. Flash storage is more expensive than magnetic and optical storage, and the capacities of most flash devices are significantly smaller. But perhaps the biggest concern is that flash memory has a limited life expectancy. In general, a flash device wears out with approximately 10,000 erase operations. As a result, magnetic, and especially optical, devices are currently the preferred media for long-term storage.

Input Devices for Multimedia Computers

Multimedia requires a variety of input devices to transmit data and instructions to a system unit for processing and storage. Keyboards and pointing devices, such as trackballs, touch pads, and touch screens, are central to interacting with GUI applications and operating system software. Other devices are necessary to input sound, video, and a wide array of images for multimedia applications. Some of these, such as microphones, are built into the system. Others, such as scanners, cameras, sound recorders, and graphics tablets, are plugged into USB or FireWire interface ports.

Scanners capture text or images using a light-sensing device. Popular types of scanners include flatbed, sheet-fed, and hand-held, all of which operate in a similar fashion: a light passes over the text or image, and the light reflects back to a **CCD** (Charge-Coupled Device). A CCD is an electronic device that captures images as a set of analog voltages. The analog readings are then converted to a digital code by another device called an **ADC** (Analog-to-Digital Converter) and transferred through the interface connection (usually USB) to RAM.

The quality of a scan depends on two main performance factors. The first is **spatial resolution**. This measures the number of dots per inch (dpi) captured by the CCD. Consumer scanners have spatial resolutions ranging from 1,200 dpi to 4,800 dpi. High-end production scanners can capture as much as 12,500 dpi. Once the dots of the original image have been converted and saved to digital form, they are known as pixels. A **pixel** is a digital picture element.

Need a larger image? Scale when you scan. Scaling during scanning captures more information from the original image. Scaling later, using an image-editing program, forces the computer to interpolate image information, producing a lower-quality enlargement.

The second performance factor is **color resolution**, or the amount of color information about each captured pixel. Color resolution is determined by **bit depth**, the number of bits used to record the color of a pixel. A 1-bit scanner only records values of 0 or 1 for each "dot" captured. This limits scans to just two colors, usually black and white. Today's scanners capture 30 to 48 bits for each pixel. This delivers a wide range of color possibilities for each pixel, making it possible to produce high-quality digital versions of photographs, paintings, and other color images.

Scanners work with specific software and drivers that manage scanner settings. Spatial resolutions and bit depth can be altered for each scan. These settings should reflect the purpose of an image. For example, if an image is a black and white photo for a website, the scanning software can be adjusted to capture grayscale color depth (8-bit) at 72 dpi. This produces an image suitable for most computer monitors that display either 72 or 96 pixels per inch. Scanner software also has settings to scale an image and perform basic adjustments for tonal quality (amount of brightness and contrast).

Optical character recognition (OCR) is the process of converting printed text to a digital file that can be edited in a word processor. The same scanners that capture images are used to perform OCR. However, a special software application is necessary to convert a picture of the character into an ASCII-based letter.

> **ASCII** is American Standard Code for Information Interchange, the basic digital code for alpha-numeric symbols.

This OCR software recognizes the picture of the letter C, for example, and stores it on the computer using its ASCII code (01000011). These characters are then edited and reformatted in a word processing application. Many image scanners today are shipped with OCR software that can recognize basic text formations. Specialized applications, such as *OmniPage* or *Readiris Pro*, are optimized to deliver high-speed, accurate OCR results. The final success of any OCR conversion depends on the quality of the source material and the particular fonts used on the page. Small print on wrinkled, thin paper will not deliver good OCR results.

OCR scanning is one method of capturing text documents. Scanners are also used to create a PDF (Portable Document Format) file. The scanner captures a specialized image of the page and saves it as a .pdf file. *Adobe Acrobat Reader* is necessary to view the contents of a .pdf file. This file format is cross-platform compatible, so it is particularly suitable for distributing highly formatted documents over a network. OCR scanning creates a file that can be edited in any word processing application. PDF scanning, on the other hand, creates a specialized file format that can only be managed by Adobe's Acrobat software.

Flatbed scanners are configured to meet a variety of uses. The scanner bed varies to handle standard letter to legal size image sources. Multi-format holders are available for 35mm filmstrips and slides (Figure 3.18). Some scanners have an optional sheet feed device. For small production, these adapters to a flatbed scanner may suffice. For larger projects, more specialized scanners should be considered. Slide and film scanners are specifically calibrated to capture high spatial resolution, some at 4,000 dpi. Sheet fed scanners are built to automatically capture large print jobs and process 15 or more pages per minute. In selecting a scanner for multimedia development there are many considerations. Image or text source, quality of scan capture, ease of use, and cost all factor into choosing the right scanner.

Digital cameras are a popular input source for multimedia developers (Figure 3.19). These cameras eliminate the need to

Figure 3.18 Slide and flatbed scanner.

Figure 3.19 Digital cameras have a variety of features including size, storage capacity, mega-pixel, and optical zoom ratings.

develop or scan a photo or slide. Camera images are immediately available to review and re-shoot if necessary, and the quality of the digital image is as good as a scanned image. Digital capture is similar to the scanning process. When the camera shutter is opened to capture an image, light passes through the camera lens. The image is focused onto a CCD (Charge-Coupled Device), which generates an analog signal. This analog signal is converted to digital form by an Analog to Digital Converter (ADC) and then sent to a Digital Signal Processor (DSP) chip that adjusts the quality of the image and stores it in the camera's built-in memory or on a memory card (Figure 3.20). The memory card or stick has limited storage capacity. Images can be previewed on the card, and if not appropriate, deleted to make space for additional images.

Digital camera image quality, like scanning, is based on spatial resolution and color resolution. Most consumer-grade digital cameras use 24-bit color resolution. This is quite adequate for most multimedia development. Professional digital cameras often use 42- or 48-bit color resolution, allowing them to capture a wider range of data for manipulation by image editing programs.

A digital camera's spatial resolution is measured in the number of pixels captured by the CCD. Early digital cameras were 1-megapixel. This means the maximum image resolution is 1,200 horizontal by 800 vertical ppi (1,200 × 800 = 960,000 or close to 1 million pixels). The physical size of the image depends on where it is viewed. If this image is viewed on a monitor at 72 ppi, the image will appear quite large: 16″ by 11″. If printed at 300 dpi, the image will be 4″ wide by 2.6″ high (Table 3.6). These camera images

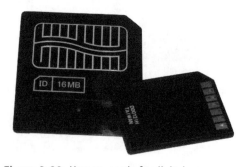

Figure 3.20 Memory cards for digital cameras.

are fine for web pages or sending email attachments, but they do not capture sufficient data to produce high quality "photo-like" printouts.

Newer digital cameras capture resolutions of 5- to 8-megapixels. Higher pixel ratings mean more realistic printed photographs. They also mean larger file sizes. If the camera is set to capture the highest quality image, the total number of stored images is reduced. Most cameras have adjustments to lower the resolution and capture more images on the memory card or stick.

> **Dots vs. Pixels**
> Spatial resolutions are measured in *dpi* for print material and *ppi* for electronic display.

Images are transferred to a computer from the memory card either through a USB adapter or a "memory card reader" that resembles a miniature floppy drive. Image catalog programs such as iPhoto help to manage digital images on secondary storage. These files can then be edited using programs such as Photoshop or Paint Shop Pro to enhance quality, adjust size, or add special effects. The digital camera has brought great efficiency to multimedia development. The costs of film, development, and time are reduced by digital source capture. It has also introduced a new level of creativity to the photo-editing process as developers take advantage of editing software to enhance and combine the digital photos.

Digital video (DV) cameras are another important input device for developers (Figure 3.21). Before DV cameras became effective and affordable, a developer captured video in analog format. Analog video was played through a VCR to a video capture board where the analog signal would be converted to digital format and stored on the hard drive. DV cameras eliminate that conversion process. Full motion capture is stored on a built-in hard drive, a mini-digital tape, or DVD. DV cameras have a FireWire interface to transfer a digital movie to other devices. Using applications such as Apple's Final Cut Pro or Adobe Premiere, a developer can edit and enhance the video in a wide variety of ways.

The performance of a DV camera is determined by several factors. The first is the method used to capture video data. Professional quality video requires a 3-chip camera. These cameras have a separate CCD for each

Figure 3.21 Digital video camera.

Table 3.6 **Comparison of Selected Megapixel Ratings and Image Sizes**

1 Megapixel	2 Megapixel	4 Megapixel
1200 h × 800 w = 960,000 total pixels	1600h × 1200 w = 1,920,000 total pixels	2700 h × 1704 w = 4,600,800 total pixels
Viewed @72ppi = 16″ × 11″ image size	Viewed @72ppi = 22″ × 16″ image size	Viewed @72ppi = 37.5″ × 23.6″ image size
Printed @300ppi = 4″ × 2.6″ image size	Printed @300ppi = 5.3″ X 4″ image size	Printed @300ppi = 9″ X 5.6″ image size

channel of RGB color. One chip captures the full range of reds, another greens, and the third blues. These three separate channels yield high quality color. Standard consumer DV cameras use a single CCD and rely on sharpening algorithms to reproduce three channels of color. This tends to over-sharpen the image and add artifacts to the moving images. While consumer DV cameras are an affordable means of capturing video footage and may suffice for some multimedia applications, a professional project will require the more expensive 3-chip cameras.

Lens and zoom quality are also important for high quality capture. An inferior lens affects the camera's ability to reproduce color and capture sharp images. DV and still-image cameras feature **digital zoom**. This simulates the effect of a stronger telephoto lens by digitally enlarging and cropping an image. Digital zoom inserts additional pixels based on an analysis of the original image, in effect creating a "best guess" enlargement. Digital zoom is not a good substitute for high quality optical zoom lenses that faithfully capture the details of the original image.

Most standard consumer DV cameras also have built-in automatic-exposure features, image stabilization (to compensate for the shaky hand), and preprogrammed modes that adjust video for backlit scenes, sports photography, snow, or spotlight scenes. A retractable LCD screen displays the video and can be an alternative to using the eyepiece to frame a shot. Many consumer DV cameras also have a still-capture media card and can be used to take photographs, though usually at lower resolutions than a digital still camera.

Sound capture devices transform analog waveforms into digital files. Microphones are built into many computers and are useful for capturing voice commands and recording directly into applications such as PowerPoint. Built-in microphones, however, can introduce interference and are not suitable for high-quality capture. Developers often connect high quality microphones directly to the computer's audio capture port for better results. CD and tape players can also be plugged into a sound capture board through the audio port. An ADC (Analog to Digital Converter) translates the analog sound wave into a digital file. Sound editing software, such as Sound Forge or Audacity, can then be used to remove unnecessary segments, enhance sound quality, or add special effects.

Graphics tablets have a flat drawing surface for freehand image creation (Figure 3.22). The artist uses a stylus to draw on a pressure sensitive surface. Software interprets the stroke pressure to control density and color, reproducing the artist's drawing as a digital image. Tablets are also useful for tracing existing art. Many developers work with graphics tablets because of the intuitive drawing control they provide. The digital artwork they produce can then be directly manipulated with popular image editing programs such as Photoshop or Corel Draw.

Figure 3.22 Artists and designers use graphics tablets and a stylus pen to input drawings for further editing.

Multimedia Output Devices

Computer output devices present processed data in a useful form. Output devices include screen displays, audio speakers or headsets, and hard copy. The quality of output for display, sound, and print is dependent on the performance features of these devices.

Display devices share their heritage with either Cathode Ray Tube (CRT) technology used in analog televisions or LCD (Liquid Crystal Displays) first used in calculators and watches. Both CRT and LCD technologies produce an image on a screen through a series of individual picture elements (pixels). As in scanners and digital cameras, the quality of a display image is largely determined by spatial resolution (the number of pixels) and color resolution (the bit depth of each pixel).

CRT monitors use **raster scanning** to generate a display. In this process an electronic signal from the video card controls an electron gun that scans the back of a screen with an electronic beam. The monitor's back surface is coated with a phosphor material that illuminates as electronic beams make contact. The electronic signal scans horizontal rows from the top to the bottom of the screen. The number of available pixels that can be illuminated determines the spatial resolution of the monitor (see Figure 3.23).

A spatial resolution of 640 by 480 produces a grid of 640 horizontal pixels and 480 vertical pixels, for a total 480,000 potential pixels the electron gun can address on the screen's surface. A resolution of 800 by 600 increases the screen's addressable pixels. This produces crisper images and text because the pixels are closer together. It also makes it possible to display more data on the monitor surface. As resolutions increase to 1024 by 768 or 2048 by 1536, the number of available pixels dramatically increases. These high resolutions are effective on large monitors where there is more area to illuminate. On small monitors of 14" or 15," text and images would be too small for most viewers.

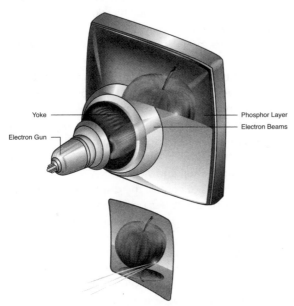

Yoke
Electron Gun
Phosphor Layer
Electron Beams

Figure 3.23 Raster scan CRT creates images through electron beams that illuminate a phosphor coating on the back of the monitor screen. RGB color monitors have three beams to illuminate red, green, and blue phosphors. See Color Plate 4.

Developers favor large monitors (17″ or 21″) with high resolution so they can organize more content on the screen at one time.

> **24- and 32-bit Color**
>
> 24-bit color assigns 8 bits to each of three color channels – red, green, and blue. This produces 256 variations for each channel and 16.7 million colors for their combination (256 * 256 * 256). The extra 8 bits in 32-bit color does not produce more color options. Instead, this is an "alpha channel," used to specify the transparency of each pixel.

Color resolution, or bit depth, is the second factor to influence display device performance. The number of bits per pixel determines the range of possible colors that are displayed. The video card controls bit depth. Video cards convert computer data to an electronic signal that illuminates the pixels. An 8-bit color monitor has a range of 256 color possibilities (2^8). This is sufficient for text and simple graphics, but a wider range of colors is needed for more sophisticated graphics and video. Current video cards generate 24- to 32-bit color, supporting 16.7 million colors.

CRT output is becoming less popular on many desktop systems because of its size, weight, and energy consumption. However, CRTs remain an inexpensive display device and continue to have sufficient advantages to keep them on the market. These monitors provide sharp text, crisp, color-rich graphics, and fluid video. Images are easily scaled up or down in different resolutions without a blurring effect. The viewing area of a CRT is also more durable than the LCD screen.

LCD displays use a different technique to create pixels. An **LCD** screen is a sandwich of two plastic sheets with a liquid crystal material in the middle. Tiny transistors control rod-shaped molecules of liquid crystal. When voltage is applied to the transistor, the molecule is repositioned to let light shine through. Pixels display light as long as the voltage is applied. Laptops borrowed this technology and improved its resolution, color capability, and brightness to make LCDs suitable for computer display (Figure 3.24).

Laptops use two forms of LCD technology. **Active matrix** screens use Thin Film Transistors (TFTs) and assign a single transistor to each liquid crystal cell to control the color and light that composes each pixel. Each pixel on the LCD is a bundle of subpixels (red, green, and blue) that are combined to generate the array of colors. These displays are brighter and have better color control. Motion images require fast response from each pixel. This is achieved when more transistors control the crystal's molecules. Active matrix is best for animation and video.

Figure 3.24 LCD screen on a laptop.

The **passive matrix** screen has fewer transistors to control the display; this results in less color and darker displays. Passive matrix displays use less power and are less expensive than active matrix. These screens may be fine for word processing applications, but active matrix is necessary for good multimedia display.

Resolution and brightness impact the quality of LCD output. LCD screens have specific resolutions controlled by the size of the screen and the manufacturer. This fixed pixel format is referred to as the "native resolution" of the LCD screen. A 15″ LCD screen has a native resolution of 1024 by 768 pixels: there are exactly 1024 pixels in each horizontal line and 768 pixels in each vertical line for a total of 786,432 pixels. Altering the resolution to lower settings, 800 by 600 for example, reduces the output quality. Most

LCDs use an expansion technique to fill the screen with the image at a lower resolution. Pixels are either doubled, producing a chunky effect or added using interpolated
colors, resulting in a blurred effect. Either way, the quality of the image is compromised.
LCD screens should remain in their native resolution for best results. The brightness of
light that shines through the screen is also significant in overall output quality. Brighter
screens display richer graphics.

LCDs became popular with laptop computers and are now standard in most system
configurations. Users prefer the smaller footprint of the LCD monitor and its light weight.
The display has no glare, is flicker free, offers sharp colorful images in its native resolution, uses less energy and generates less heat. As prices continue to drop, the LCD monitor has become commonplace on the desktop.

Speaker systems are essential components of modern computers. Most early microcomputers restricted sound output to warning sounds such as a loud beep when there
was an error message. Macintosh computers raised the bar on sound output when the
first Mac introduced itself to the world in 1984. A computer that could speak changed
the prevailing belief that all computer information needed to be in visual form. Sound
capability soon became a requirement for a multimedia computer.

Sound output devices are speakers or headsets. They are plugged into the soundboard where digital data is converted to analog sound waves. Soundboards can be a
part of the system board or added to a computer's expansion slots. Soundboard circuitry
performs four basic processes: it *converts* digital sound data into analog form using
a Digital to Analog Converter, or **DAC**, *records* sound in digital form using an analog-
digital converter (ADC), *amplifies* the signal for delivery through speakers, and *creates*
digital sounds using a synthesizer. A **synthesizer** is an output device that creates sounds
electronically. Synthesizers may be built into the computer's soundboard or added later,
usually as a card mounted in one of the system's expansion slots. The most common
standard for creating digital music using a synthesizer is MIDI (Musical Instrument Digital
Interface). MIDI specifies the format for musical commands, such as striking a piano key.
The computer sends these commands to the synthesizer, which then creates the appropriate sound.

Sound quality depends on the range of digital signals the soundboard can process.
These signals are measured as sample size and rate. *Sample size* is the resolution of the
sound measured in bits per sample. Most soundboards support 16-bit sound, the current
CD-quality resolution. *Sample rate* measures the frequency at which bits are recorded in
digitizing a sound. Modern boards accommodate the 48KHz sample rate found in professional audio and DVD systems. Soundboards control both sound input and output
functions. Input functions are especially important for developers because they need to
capture and create high quality sounds. End users are concerned with output; they want
high-quality sound for games, movies, and digital music.

Printers remain an important multimedia peripheral device, despite the fact that
multimedia applications are primarily designed for display. Storyboards, system plans,
schematics, budgets, contracts, and proposals are just a few common documents that are
frequently printed during multimedia production. End users print images and web pages,
as well as the standard text documents associated with most computer applications.

There are two basic printing technologies: impact and non-impact. *Impact printers* form images and text by striking paper. **Dot-matrix** printers use a series of pins that strike the paper through an inked ribbon. These printers are used for applications that require multiform output or high-speed printing. They are easy to maintain and relatively inexpensive to operate. However, limited color and graphics capability, combined with high noise levels, make impact printers undesirable for most printing needs.

Non-impact printers form printed output without physically contacting the page. These devices include inkjet, photo, and laser printers.

Inkjet printers are used in many homes and businesses. They are affordable, quiet, and versatile: inkjets can print everything from labels and envelopes to photo-quality color images.

An **inkjet printer** is a line printer. The print head moves across the page, one line at a time, spraying drops of ink. Different techniques are used to produce the ink spray, but the most common is the "bubble" jet method first implemented in 1977 by Cannon and later adopted by Hewlett Packard. As the ink cartridge moves across the paper, heat is applied to tiny resistors on the metal face of the print head. The surface of the ink boils, producing a vapor bubble. This bubble forces ink through a nozzle and onto the paper (see Figure 3.25).

Inkjet output quality is determined by printer resolution and type of paper. Printer resolution is measured in dots per inch (dpi). The drop of ink is a dot. An image printed at 200 dots per inch will have more ink applied than one printed at 100 dots per inch. Inkjet printers can support optimized resolutions of 4800dpi. Because the inks tend to blend together on the paper before they dry, inkjet printers can achieve higher quality

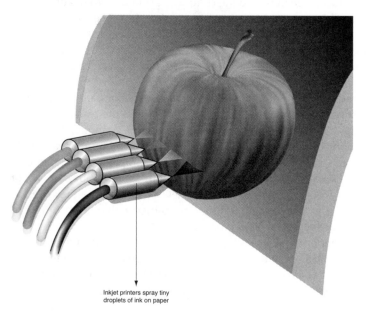

Inkjet printers spray tiny
droplets of ink on paper

Figure 3.25 Inkjet printers spray dots of colored ink to form an image. See Color Plate 5.

output with fewer dpi. Setting the print resolution to 200 dpi will deliver a reasonably good photograph and also reduce ink consumption.

Inkjet papers vary in surface texture. Glossy photo paper is used to transform digital images into printed photos, while matte finish paper can produce colorful reports. Papers with linen or cotton fibers and textured papers will bleed where ink is applied. For best results, use paper specifically designed for inkjet printers.

Printer speed is measured in pages per minute (ppm). Inkjet printers average 20ppm. Color printing is much slower than black and white output. A typical black and white speed is 18ppm while color output slows to 12ppm.

While most inkjet printers are very affordable, the cost of consumables can be high. Print cartridges are expensive to replace (Figure 3.26). Expect to replace color cartridges frequently if the output is full-size color photos. Specialty papers for high gloss photos are also expensive. Paper and ink costs should be factored into the decision to use inkjet printing for multimedia production.

Figure 3.26 Inkjet cartridges.

A **photo printer** is a color printer specifically designed to produce photos (Figure 3.27). The best photo printers can deliver photo-lab-quality output. Many consumer photo printers are based on inkjet technology. These printers use a media card from a digital camera and have a push-button panel to set the size, quality, and number of copies. Images do not have to be transferred to a computer before they are printed. This increases the ease and speed of sharing digital pictures. Some inkjet printers are configured as both a standard and photo printer by adding a media card slot and panel controls to manage the photo printing. More expensive photo printers use dye sublimation technology for output. **Dye sublimation** uses heat to transfer colored dye to specially coated papers. These printers are found in professional settings such as photography studios and digital imaging labs.

Laser printers use a copier-like technology to fuse text and image to the paper. They are called *page printers* because the entire page is transferred to the printer's electronic storage before it is formed on paper.

Laser printing begins with document transfer to the printer's electronic storage. A laser beam then scans an **optical photoconductor (OPC)** drum placing a negative electrical charge where text and images should appear. Toner, a form of powdered ink, is attracted to these charged areas. When paper moves through the printer, it passes under the OPC drum, which deposits the toner. Other rollers add heat and pressure to fuse print material on the page. Because lasers print an entire page at once, they are faster than inkjet printers.

Figure 3.27 Photo printers can crop, enlarge, and enhance the image before printing on special photo paper.

Laser printers have resolutions of 600 to 2400 dpi. Common print speeds range from 20 to 45 ppm. Laser printers are very popular in offices with large black and white print jobs where quality and speed are imperative. For years, inkjet printers held the advantage of color over a standard laser printer. Color laser technology is now delivering high quality color output at reasonable costs.

Color laser printers add cyan, magenta, and yellow toners to traditional black. Applying additional toners slows printing speeds. The laser scans each color separately to the OPC drum making a separate pass of the drum to collect each color for the entire page. Early printers moved the paper past the drum each time to collect a particular color, but the constant movement of paper back and forth through the printer rollers often misaligned the color output. Now "one-pass" color lasers simply move the drum four times around to collect toner for each color and then pass the paper once to transfer the final colored image. Color laser printers are significantly slower than standard black and white lasers because there is extra processing for each color.

Color laser printers require large electronic storage capacity. A full page, 600 dpi color image may require over 16MB of printer storage. If the printer cannot form the entire page in memory, it will only print the portion it can store. In some cases, insufficient memory produces an error message and the page is not printed at all. Color laser printers should have from 128MB to 512MB of primary storage.

Considerations for Selecting a Printer

- Resolution (measured in dpi)
- Speeds (measured in pages per minute)
- Cost of the printer
- Cost of consumables (paper, inks, toner)
- Paper handling features (duplexers, envelopes, labels, legal, continuous paper forms)
- Built-in memory capacity (more is always better)
- Computer and network interface (USB, parallel, Ethernet capable)
- Maintenance requirements (service contracts, cleaning requirements, operating environment)

Laser printers are desirable output devices because they have high quality and high-speed output. However, these printers are expensive to operate. Operational expenses include toner cartridges, service contracts, and paper. Laser printers also require special environmental conditions. Excessively dry or damp atmospheres will affect printer operation. Many multimedia development offices share laser printers through network connections, reducing the cost to individual users. Most laser printers have built-in network cards for Ethernet LANs (Local Area Networks).

In addition to standard printers, there are other print devices for specialized applications. Plotters, portable printers, and label printers are just a few. One hybrid device that combines printer, scanning, fax, and copier technology in one unit is called a **multifunction printer**. This single unit saves desk space and eliminates the need for purchasing separate output devices. All printing devices utilize either the basic impact or non-impact methods. When selecting printers for multimedia development, consider the purpose of the output and the media to print. If documents are text-based reports for staff members, high quality, expensive printers may not be necessary. If the media is detailed images for production design, then a printer with high color resolution is important.

3.4 Networks

Multimedia projects may require input from many individuals working independently on their personal computers. The integration of this work requires a network of computers. A **network** is a collection of computers connected through a communication link to share hardware, data, and applications. Networks also allow individual processors in each computer to work simultaneously on a single task. Complex rendering projects for animation sequences are frequently done with an array of networked computer processors called a "render farm." Networks are the backbone that ties together the work of individual developers and the resources of their personal computers.

Computer networks are categorized as *WAN* (Wide Area Network) or *LAN* (Local Area Network). The **WAN** connects computers over a wide geographic region using the communication lines of an outside service provider such as a telephone or cable company. A developer can transfer digital files via email attachments or use *file transfer protocols* (FTP) to add digital files to a remote network server. In both cases, the computer connects to other systems through external communication links.

The **Internet** is a special form of Wide Area Network. It is a network of networks that uses Transmission Control Protocol and Internet Protocol (**TCP/IP**) to send data from one host computer to another. **Protocols**, or rules for transmitting data, control the transfer and addressing of data between each host computer. The Internet started in 1969 as a government research project with four computer systems interconnected to share system resources. Twenty years later, the Internet exploded with possibilities when Tim Berners-Lee developed the HTTP (hypertext transfer protocol) protocols for the World Wide Web **(WWW)**.

The Web introduced interactive multimedia to the Internet. Web pages, written in *HTML* (Hypertext Markup Language), display multimedia through a browser such as Internet Explorer or Safari. **Hyperlinks** connect resources from one web page to another location. Hyperlinks are defined with a **uniform resource locator (URL)** that identifies the path to an Internet resource such as an image, web page, or video file.

The efficiencies of the Web are in its *client/server* model for distributing data. **Server** computers store and send data to a client computer. **Client** computers have software to open and process data files. Once data is downloaded from the server, applications on the client computer, such as browsers and plug-ins, display or play data content. Client computers process data locally, which is more efficient than processing it on a server computer shared by thousands of users.

> http://computerscience.jbpub.com/graphics/index.htm
> This URL identifies the http protocol, the host computer (computerscience.jbpub), the domain (.com), and the path to a specific page resource on that host (/graphics/index.htm).

Special data file formats are necessary to insure data is compatible on any client system. For example, image files include .jpg, .gif, or .png format and text files use .html or .pdf format. Incompatibilities between computer platforms and data file formats are slowly disappearing through the network connections and protocols of the World Wide Web.

A **Local Area Network (LAN)** is a series of computers connected within an organization. Many homes now have a LAN to share printers and access to the Internet. Multimedia developers connect computers to distribute files, access applications from a local server, or share hardware devices. Computers on a LAN can be connected using twisted pair cable that resembles a phone line, though wireless connectivity is increasingly common.

Ethernet is a common set of protocols to control the flow of data on a LAN. Ethernet defines how files are transferred, the speed of transfer, and the cables used to connect the computers. Many LANs are using wireless connections as computers become more mobile and users desire flexible network access. A wireless network requires an **access point** (AP) that broadcasts a radio signal within a cell area. The AP often contains a firewall to prevent unauthorized wireless network access. The AP is connected to a larger network system through a cable modem or **router** (a switch to control data flow on a network). Computers need a wireless card or built-in wireless capability to send and receive data via radio waves.

Wi-Fi and Bluetooth are two popular wireless standards. The **Wi-Fi** (WirelessFidelity), or 802.11b standard, transmits on 2.4GHz radio frequencies. Transmission rate is 11Mbs (Megabits/second) up to 300 feet away from the AP. Distance, interference, and number of users can adversely affect the transmission rate. The **Bluetooth** protocol was developed in 1994 to communicate between devices within 30 feet at 1Mbs speeds. Bluetooth is designed to transfer data between nearby computers and PDAs, or to communicate with a nearby printer or other peripheral device.

Networks have increased the power of individual computers and expanded the efficiency of computer users. Networks are also instrumental in fulfilling the visions of Bush and Nelson to build "trails" from one information point to another.

3.5 Summary

Computers are manufactured in many sizes and platforms. *Mainframe* and *supercomputers* are used in organizations with high volumes of data and complex processing requirements. *Personal computers* use *microprocessors* to bring computing power to the desktop of both multimedia developers and end users. Personal computers are defined by their *platform*, the combination of *hardware* and *operating system* they use. Multimedia developers must consider the *development platform* that meets their project requirements, as well as the *delivery platform*, the computer system available to potential users.

All computer hardware systems share the basic functions of *input*, *processing*, *storage*, *output*, and *transmission of data*. The *system unit*, consisting of the *CPU*, *primary memory*, *expansion ports*, and the circuitry that connects them, provides the foundation for processing digital instructions and data. *Peripheral devices* support processing through input and output interfaces on the system board. *Hard drives*, *CD* and *DVD* drives, and *solid state media* are common peripheral devices that support the main processing activity by storing software and data for later processing. Large capacities of permanent, portable storage are necessary to deliver the applications expected of today's multimedia computers. *Networks* unite computer hardware making it possible to share and distribute media within local organizations or over wide geographic areas.

The evolution of multimedia hardware is far from complete. New devices appear daily. The marvel of the digital computer is its scalability and adaptability. Computer microelectronics move ever-larger volumes of data at ever-increasing speeds. Processors transform those bits into wondrous images and sounds. But even the most advanced hardware is simply a collection of components awaiting instructions and data from a user. Software, the subject of the next chapter, transforms electronic computers into useful tools to create and manage an increasingly interconnected world of digital multimedia.

Key Terms

Access point	Interface ports
Access time	Internet
Active matrix	LAN
ADC	Land
Address bus	Laser
Arithmetic logic unit (ALU)	Laser printer
ASCII	LCD
Bit depth	Machine cycle
Bluetooth	Magnetic storage
Bus	Mainframe computer
Cache	Memory card
CAV	Microcode
CCD	Microcomputer
CD-DA	Microprocessor
CD-R	Multi-core
CD-ROM	Multifunction printer
CD-RW	Multi-processing
Client	Multitasking
Clock speed	Nanotechnology
CLV	Network
Color resolution	Optical Character Recognition (OCR)
Computer platform	Optical Photoconductor (OPC)
Computer system	Optical storage
Control unit	Parallel data transmission
CPU	Parallel processing
Cross-platform compatibility	Passive matrix
CRT	Peripheral devices
DAC	Personal computer
Data bus	Photo printer
Digital zoom	Pipelining
Dot matrix printer	Pit
DVD	Pixel
Dye sublimation	Primary memory
Ethernet	Protocols
FireWire	RAM
Flash drive	Random access
Flash memory	Raster scan
Floppy disk	Registers
Frame	RISC
Hard drive	ROM
Hardware interface	Router
Hyperlinks	Scanner
Inkjet printer	Secondary storage
Instruction set	Sector

Serial data transmission	TCP/IP
Server	Track
Session	Transfer rate
Solid-state storage	URL
Spatial resolution	USB
Storage capacity	WAN
Supercomputer	Wi-Fi
Synthesizer	Word size
System board	WWW
System bus	Zip disk
System unit	

References

Chaffin, Brian. "Virginia Tech's G5 Supercomputer Could Rank #2 In The World." *The MacObserver*, October 13, 2003. http://www.macobserver.com/article/2003/10/13.2.shtml.

Taylor, Jim. "DVD Frequently Asked Questions (and Answers)" *DVD Demystified*. January 10, 2005. 1 Aug. 2005 http://dvddemystified.com/.

Review Questions

1. What are the differences between a supercomputer, mainframe, and microcomputer?
2. What are the two main components of a computer system?
3. Why should a multimedia developer be concerned about cross-platform compatibility?
4. What are the two main categories of computer hardware? Explain the function of each.
5. Why is the system board an essential component of the system unit?
6. What are the three main sets of transistors on a microprocessor chip? Identify the main purpose of each set.
7. How do clock speed and word size determine the performance of a CPU?
8. What is the advantage of a 32-bit address bus over a 16-bit bus?
9. What are the differences and uses of RAM and ROM?
10. How does cache memory improve the overall performance of a processor?
11. What are the similarities and differences between USB and IEEE 1394 interfaces?
12. Why is the transfer speed of the hardware interface important to a multimedia user and developer?
13. What are the magnetic storage options for portable media?
14. How do pits and lands on an optical disc store digital data?
15. What is one advantage and one disadvantage of the CLV method of data storage?
16. Why does the *V* in DVD currently stand for "versatile"?
17. Why can DVDs store more data than CDs?
18. What are three input devices that would be useful for a graphics artist?

19. What are the two main options for computer display? Which option is increasing in popularity? Why?
20. What is an advantage and disadvantage of the following printer categories: inkjet printer, laser printer, photo printer, and color laser printer?
21. What is the distinction between a WAN and a LAN?
22. What features did the WWW introduce to the Internet?
23. What are the essential similarities and differences between Wi-Fi and Bluetooth?
24. Why is the Internet a special form of WAN?
25. Why is the "client/server" arrangement an efficient use of the server's processor and the network's bandwidth capacity?

Discussion Questions

1. Recommend four essential system unit performance features a video developer should consider when purchasing a computer to import, edit, and store digital video.
2. Identify the five main uses of secondary storage and recommend a storage medium for each one to manage 900MB of digital sound.
3. What are the three major categories of secondary storage devices? List the main advantages and disadvantages of each.
4. Do you think CD-RW/DVD drives will soon replace magnetic external storage devices? Explain your position.
5. As a video editor on a multimedia production team, what type of secondary storage would you use for composing and editing the digital video? Explain your choice.
6. Many organizations are storing all their vital data on secondary storage media to save paper and economize on space. Do you think this is a good idea or not? What are the most important issues to consider? Support your answer with Web research on these issues.
7. Locate a recent ad for a flatbed scanner and describe the performance features of that scanner.
8. Locate a recent ad for a digital camera and describe the performance features of that camera.
9. Do you think LCD technology will replace CRTs? Explain your position by referencing the performance features of each.
10. Research how "render farms" are used to develop digital animation sequences and report your findings.
11. Review the vision of Vannevar Bush and Ted Nelson and determine if today's networks and search engines are fulfilling their vision. Explain why they are or are not.

Chapter 4

Computer Software

Topics you will explore include:

A computer is a blend of physical components, or *hardware*, and sets of instructions, or *software*. This chapter presents the essentials of the different types of software that make multimedia development and delivery possible. After completing this chapter you should understand:

- The three main categories of software
- The functions of operating systems
- The main types and uses of programming languages
- The different types of software used to develop multimedia products

4.1 Categories of Software

Software is the collection of computer programs that govern the operation of a computer system. A **program** is a list of instructions that can be carried out by a computer. Without software, a computer can do nothing. With the appropriate software, computers can perform virtually any information-processing task. There are three main categories of software. *Operating systems* are software that control hardware devices and basic system operations. Programs that perform specific tasks are *applications*. *Programming language* software is used to create other software programs. Each of these three types of software has important uses in multimedia computing.

4.2 Operating Systems

Operating systems are taken for granted by most users. We power on the computer and quickly launch into a favorite application. Yet without the operating system there would be no access to hardware, applications, or data. The **operating system** is a collection of programs that provide a user interface, manage the computer's resources, and execute application programs. The user interface facilitates interaction with the computer system. Computer resources such as memory, CPU, printers, and disk drives are hardware components managed by the operating system. The operating system also manages and executes application software such as Photoshop or Excel. Operating systems are vital to making the computer a useful tool.

Operating systems vary from one computer platform to another because different platforms use different hardware. Versions of Windows (XP, Vista) manage hardware specific to the PC. OS X is an operating system designed for the hardware used in the Macintosh computer platform. Other operating systems such as Unix and Linux are multi-platform systems because they are easily adapted to control hardware from different manufacturers. While there are many operating systems on the market, all perform the same basic functions. Multimedia developers rely on the operating system to provide an intuitive, easily navigated user interface; to manage a wide range of hardware devices; and to control the operation of many different application programs.

User Interface

The **user interface** provides a means to communicate with the programs and hardware of a computer system. The user interface may consist of commands typed into the operating system directly, or it may be a series of icons and menu bars. Early computers used commands to manage computer operations. This *command-line interface* required knowledge of a specific command language and precise attention to syntax: misplace a comma or make a spelling error and the command would not execute. The command language interface discouraged widespread use of computers because it was neither intuitive nor forgiving.

Visionaries such as Douglas Engelbart and Alan Kay recognized the limitations of this interface. Their ideas helped to shape the first graphically controlled computer, the Alto, developed in 1973. Alto presented computer functions in windows where an operator could manipulate a mouse to visually control objects like papers on a desk. This early research into graphical computing paved the way for Steve Jobs to develop the first GUI (Graphical User Interface) for the Lisa computer. This operating system was revised in 1984 for the Macintosh, which used a desktop metaphor complete with folders, clipboard, and trashcan to control complex hardware functions. The operating system was slowly adapting to the way people work and freeing the user from learning arcane computer commands.

The Graphical User Interface is standard in most operating systems today. A **GUI** (or "gooey") presents the functions of the operating system as a series of icons, pull down menus, and dialog boxes. "Point and Click" and "Drag and Drop" now provide users with easily learned, intuitive procedures to control complex computer systems.

Managing Computer Resources

Operating systems control a variety of computer resources including processors, memory, peripheral devices, and networks. In many cases, the operating system (OS) performs its tasks behind the scenes with little or no user interaction. In other cases, the operating system may provide special programs, called *utilities*, to assist users in more directly controlling operating system functions (Figure 4.1).

The OS and the Processor

Operating systems control how programs are executed in the processor. Some processors are so powerful they can support many users simultaneously. Multi-user operating systems control the amount of processor time each user's pro-

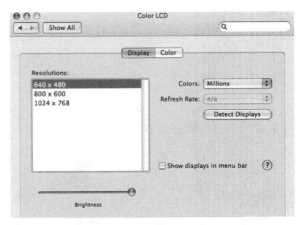

Figure 4.1 The Macintosh option to select monitor properties built into the operating system.

gram will have. This process is also called **timesharing** because the operating system allocates "slices" of processor time to multiple simultaneous users. First one user, then another, will be given a few microseconds of the processor's time.

Multi-user systems are also multitasking. **Multitasking** is the ability of the operating system to manage more than one application

A *microsecond* is one millionth of a second.

concurrently. Each user can be executing different programs to complete different tasks and all will appear to be running at the same time.

Multi-user systems are found on mid-range, mainframe, and supercomputers. These systems can support hundreds or thousands of users at one time. However, if a sudden increase in users occurs, everyone will notice a slowdown in computer performance because each user is competing for a "slice" of the processor's activity. Unix and Linux are common multi-user operating systems.

Operating systems for microcomputers such as the Macintosh and the PC are designed to support a single user. Microcomputer operating systems also support multitasking. Multitasking is particularly important for multimedia developers because they often work with several programs at once. Earlier microcomputers frequently crashed because the operating system lacked control over application execution. Multitasking often caused systems to "freeze" because one application monopolized computer resources and failed to release control to other applications. *Preemptive multitasking* gives the operating system additional control over system resources. The operating system can interrupt an application process and pass control to another program. The operating system can also regain control if one of the running applications suddenly stops. This results in more stable performance when multiple applications are open. Windows Vista and OS X are operating systems that employ preemptive multitasking.

The OS and Memory Management

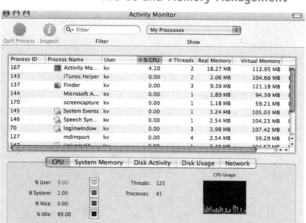

Memory management is another important function of every operating system. The operating system controls how much memory is accessed and used by application programs (Figure 4.2). Operating systems monitor use of memory and release memory when the processor no longer needs it. With today's multitasking environments, it is important to have the operating system allocate memory effectively between multiple programs. There is a finite amount of installed RAM and it is easy to fill it up with several open applications and large data files.

Virtual memory is a method to expand the amount of memory available for processing tasks. The operating system identifies a

Figure 4.2 Activity Monitor in OS X displays CPU and memory usage.

portion of the hard disk to simulate RAM. The operating system then swaps program segments between RAM and the hard drive through a process called "paging." While this swapping process may slow down processing time, it does make it possible to run large applications on a limited amount of RAM storage.

Virtual memory is sometimes helpful in multimedia development because it may make it possible to run several programs concurrently on a computer with insufficient RAM. However, virtual memory complicates and slows processing and is no substitute for RAM. The preferred solution to main memory shortages is always more installed RAM.

The OS and Peripheral Devices

Operating systems also include a number of programs to control peripheral devices such as monitors, printers, keyboards, mice, and storage devices. These programs are shipped with the computer system or later added as device drivers. **Device drivers** are programs that tell the operating system how to communicate with a peripheral device. When a new device such as a scanner is added, the operating system must be able to recognize and manage that device. Many of these peripheral devices are easily installed with advances in *"Plug and Play."* The operating system senses that a new device is plugged into an interface and automatically configures the system to support it.

In cases where the operating system does not automatically recognize the device, it may be necessary to install a device driver. For example, some operating systems do not recognize certain printers as "plug and play" until the correct driver is added to the operating system.

Managing Network Resources

The widespread use of microcomputers on networks requires operating systems to manage the access and security of networked computers. The operating system provides options to share files with other users on the network as well as connect to network servers and printers. Operating systems include commands to connect to wide area networks (WANs) as well as local area networks (LANs) (Figure 4.3). They also manage access to wireless networking. The Mac OS includes wireless network computing using Bluetooth and Airport (802.11b) capability. Windows Vista and XP on laptop computers are also configured for automatic access to wireless networks.

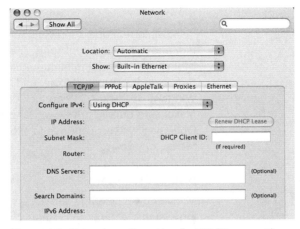

Figure 4.3 Network configuration for TCP/IP connection.

Networks are particularly important for advanced multimedia development in which teams of specialists need rapid access to planning documents and media files prepared by their colleagues.

OS Utility Programs

In addition to managing hardware devices to carry out basic system operations, operating systems also include various utility programs (Figure 4.4). **OS utility programs** provide tools to optimize operating system functions. Disk management tools are a common utility set. These programs include disk repair, disk defragmentation, disk partitioning, and backup routines. Other common utilities are programs to write CDs and DVDs, view graphics files, uninstall programs, and set up screensavers. The file manager is also an important utility that provides a graphic interface to managing data on secondary storage.

Name	▲	Date Modified	Date Created
▦ Activity Monitor		Sep 16, 2007, 4:01 PM	May 17, 2
🐾 Adobe Updater		Nov 10, 2006, 8:13 PM	Mar 16, 2
▸ ◻ Adobe Utilities		Nov 10, 2006, 8:12 PM	Apr 13, 2(
◎ AirPort Admin Utility		Jun 24, 2005, 1:31 AM	Jun 24, 2(
▨ AirPort Setup Assistant		Jul 10, 2005, 3:17 AM	Jul 10, 20
▪ Audio MIDI Setup		May 17, 2005, 1:33 AM	May 17, 2
◆ Bluetooth File Exchange		Nov 21, 2007, 10:01 AM	Jul 10, 20
✕ ColorSync Utility		Sep 16, 2007, 4:01 PM	May 17, 2
▦ Console		Apr 19, 2005, 2:56 PM	Apr 19, 2(
◉ DigitalColor Meter		May 17, 2005, 1:59 AM	May 17, 2
▨ Directory Access		May 27, 2005, 12:31 PM	May 27, 2
◪ Disk Utility		Sep 16, 2007, 4:01 PM	Jun 20, 2(
▨ Grab		May 17, 2005, 1:32 AM	May 17, 2
◉ Grapher		Apr 29, 2005, 7:35 PM	Apr 29, 2(
▪ Installer		Nov 21, 2007, 10:01 AM	Jul 10, 20
▸ ◻ iPod Software Updater		Jul 14, 2006, 12:38 PM	Jun 17, 2(
▸ ◻ Java		Sep 16, 2007, 4:01 PM	May 27, 2 ▲
◈ Keychain Access		Sep 16, 2007, 4:01 PM	May 31, 2 ▼

Figure 4.4 Utility programs provide tools to optimize the functions of the operating system.

Most current operating systems bundle multimedia utilities such as basic image editing, photo management tools, speech recognition, and sound controls. The Mac OS is thoroughly integrating multimedia data in its operating system with a series of utilities that includes iTunes, iMovie, and iPhoto, as well as the popular QuickTime program. Windows operating systems include Media Player for Internet radio and MP3 files, Movie Maker, and built-in drivers to transfer images directly from a digital camera or scanner. Operating systems continue to expand their multimedia functionality as new computer technology emerges.

Disk Management

Managing disk storage and access to data files is another important feature of operating systems. Operating systems prepare a disk for storage by **formatting** the storage medium. Formatting prepares a disk in three essential ways. First, it defines track and sector addressing on the disk platter. These physical addresses are used by the operating system to locate and retrieve data from a disk. Second, formatting defines a logical storage unit called a cluster. A **cluster** is the smallest unit of disk space that contains data. A single cluster can hold data from only one file. Depending on the operating system, the cluster may span one or several sectors on a single track of the disk platter. Finally, formatting defines the **file system** for the disk. This is a type of index to each file name and cluster location on the disk. When a file is retrieved, the operating system locates the cluster address based on the file system. When a file is saved, the operating system records cluster addressing with the filename properties. Different operating systems use different file systems. A com-

> **Disk Fragmentation**
>
> Disk fragmentation results when segments of a file (called *data blocks*) are scattered to non-contiguous locations on the disk. This slows access to the file and can decrease system performance. Defragmentation reorganizes file contents and saves them in contiguous locations. Some operating systems, including OS X, automatically defragment disks.

mon file system for the Windows OS is FAT (File Allocation Table) while Apple's OS X uses HFS+ (Hierarchical File System).

Disk management also involves deleting files and reuse of disk space. When the user deletes a file, it is marked for removal in the file system. Windows and Mac operating systems have a "restore" command that will undelete files. This restores the address to the file. But once the user empties the "recycle bin" or "trash can," it is more difficult to recover the deleted files because the file system frees up cluster addresses for other data or program files. Only special utility programs can recover the lost data.

File Management

Files are containers for data and programs. They have unique names and properties that are recognized by the operating system. Understanding how to manage files is also important for the user. If a file is not carefully named and saved in appropriate folders, it can easily be lost in the myriad of files stored on disk.

As we noted in Chapter 2, many filenames have two components separated by a dot: a prefix name and the **file extension**. The user defines a data file prefix. The prefix name should clearly indicate the contents of the file, for instance *RedRose*. The file extension can define two properties of a file: its source application or a file data type. *RedRose.psd* indicates that the file is a Photoshop document; *RedRose.gif* identifies the file type (Graphic Image Format).

Files are initially named when they are saved from RAM to secondary storage. The user must be aware of the filename conventions of the operating system. For instance, Unix filenames are case sensitive while Windows and Mac OS filenames are not. The allowable length and the characters that can be included are also important considerations for filenames. For years, DOS users struggled with very restrictive filename conventions. Filenames could only be 8 characters with no spaces or special symbols. Mac users could use 32 characters to define a file name that included spaces and no extension. Both Windows and Mac operating systems now allow more than 250 characters for prefix names, enough to meaningfully name just about any file.

In addition to filename rules, the user must be aware of the importance of the extension. Some extensions are unique to programs and must not be changed. For example, *Photoshop.exe* designates a Windows application file. If the extension is deleted or changed, the Windows operating system will not recognize the program. Application prefix names should not be changed either, since there are many supporting programs that locate the application based on its name.

> **Opening Files with Missing Extensions**
> In cases where an extension is missing, a data file can be opened within the application. Launch the application first, then use the File/Open command to locate the file in the directory of filenames.

Other extensions identify the program that created the data file. A Word file has a *.doc* extension, Photoshop uses *.psd*, and Adobe Acrobat has the extension *.pdf*. These extensions associate the data with the application. Macintosh operating systems use either an extension with the file prefix or an icon to associate the data file with the application.

File extensions are also useful for end users. If the extension is correct, the user can "double click" on a data filename and launch the application to view data immediately.

However, if the extension is deleted or changed, the operating system may not associate a source application with the data. In both Windows and OS X, a dialog box often appears to select an application from a long list of installed programs that could have created the data.

Extensions can also define a specific data format. These data files are not associated with any particular application; instead, they indicate the type of data stored in a file. For example, *book.txt* is an ASCII text file that can be opened with any text editor or word processing application. Extensions such as *.jpg*, *.gif*, and *.bmp* are graphics images that are opened in a variety of image editing applications. Like other extensions, those that designate data formats should not be changed. An *.aiff* extension indicates a sound file. If the extension is changed to *.txt*, this will not only confuse a user trying to locate a sound file, but also the operating system as it tries to relate it to an application.

Directories

In addition to observing file-naming conventions, effective file management also requires an understanding of directories. A **directory** provides a common storage label for collections of data files and program files. Directories are similar to folders in a file cabinet. Windows and Macintosh operating systems display filename information in directory windows (Figure 4.5 and Figure 4.6).

Directories are usually organized in a hierarchical pattern in which folders are placed within folders to create related subdirectories. The logical structure of directories and subdirectories can be defined either through *pathnames* or graphically through folders that can be opened to reveal other folders. Pathnames identify the main directory first

Name	Date Modified	Size	Kind
▶ Sound Effects	3/4/06, 10:26 PM	246.7 MB	Folder
placeCard.psd	3/5/06, 8:08 PM	2.7 MB	Adobe Phot... Element
▶ Flashold DataFiles	3/12/06, 9:08 PM	7.8 MB	Folder
LC Banner.fla	4/11/06, 10:51 PM	432 KB	Macromedia Flash Mov
LC Banner 2.fla	4/12/06, 11:22 AM	484 KB	Macromedia Flash Mov
LC Banner 2.swf	4/12/06, 11:22 AM	108 KB	Shockwave Flash Movi
▶ FlashLab2	4/12/06, 4:39 PM	2.2 MB	Folder
▶ Flash8 Data Files	7/21/06, 9:01 AM	20.6 MB	Folder
Pixar Ren...r Farm.doc	10/27/0...2:14 PM	56 KB	Microsoft Word docum
▶ noise_data	3/16/07, 4:09 PM	3.3 MB	Folder
▶ AudacityDemo	3/20/07, 7:42 PM	236 KB	Folder
▶ Sound Project06	4/9/07, 10:48 AM	50.8 MB	Folder
▶ FilePractice	8/20/07, 9:46 PM	68 KB	Folder
▶ PShopEle...s Data Files	9/26/07, 11:31 AM	285.8 MB	Folder
Dice8.fla	10/21/07, 8:14 PM	28 KB	Macromedia Flash Mov
▶ FlashTutorials Done	11/26/07, 2:14 PM	12.6 MB	Folder

Figure 4.5 Macintosh OS Finder: Files and Folders.

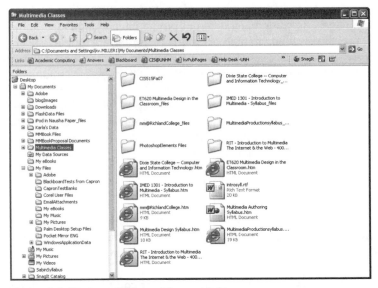

Figure 4.6 Windows Explorer: Files and Folders.

and then indicate sub-directories: "C: \Projects\AjaxCo\Website\Bid.doc" provides the path to a Word document, *Bid*, stored on the computer's hard drive (C).

Like file prefix names, directory names should also clearly identify file contents. For instance, a popular directory in the Windows operating system is "My Documents." This name clearly identifies the files as those created by the user.

Directories are also an important means of grouping related files for ease of access. For example, directories labeled "JonesProject" or "SmithProject" might store all the files associated with a specific multimedia project. These could be added as sub-directories within "My Documents." Such hierarchies of directories provide an efficient index to locate specific files.

Another important function of operating systems is to provide tools to create and manage directories. Windows has a file management utility named Windows Explorer that displays the contents of a disk directory. Users can move, copy, rename, and delete files as well as set up directories within the GUI window area. Windows Explorer is an important utility to control the contents of a disk. The Mac OS also provides a window to the contents of a storage device. Within each window of a directory the user can move, copy, rename, and delete files. New folders are easily created in each window to further organize files on the disk. Using meaningful file names and appropriate directories makes it much easier to locate specific files among the hundreds that are often created in the course of a multimedia project.

4.3 Programming Languages

The second major category of software is programming languages. A **programming language** is a defined system of syntax (or "grammar") and semantics (or "vocabulary") to write computer programs. All operating systems and software applications are written in a programming language. There are many different programming languages. Some languages, like *BASIC*, provide the fundamentals of programming and are simple to learn; others, like *C*, are difficult to master but very powerful. Some languages are better suited for scientific programs, others for business applications, and still others for multimedia programs.

Programming languages are divided between *low-level* and *high-level* languages. Low-level languages relate directly to specific processors, requiring programmers to understand technical details of the computer's hardware. High-level languages are not tied to specific hardware. They are more flexible and easier for programmers to understand.

Low-Level Languages

In the early 1950s, when computer hardware systems were limited, programs were developed for each specific computer using a set of commands that were recognized directly by the computer's processor. These machine-dependent languages are known as **low-level languages**.

Machine Code
0011110 0101101
1001100 0111001
0100110 0111001

The most basic low-level programming language is **machine code**, in which program commands are directly coded in binary digits to control specific computer systems. These commands are immediately recognized and executed by the processor. In fact, machine code is the only language the computer can directly execute. Ultimately every other language must be translated into machine code before it can be processed. But machine-code programming is very tedious. Programmers quickly tired of writing commands in strings of binary digits and turned to a series of abbreviations that were less error prone and easier to use. This form of low-level programming is known as *assembly language*.

Assembly Code*
A = add
C = compare
MP = multiply
STP = store
*Assembly languages have different sets of abbreviated codes.

Assembly language uses easily remembered combinations of letters as abbreviations for the 0s and 1s of machine coded programs. This greatly improves the efficiency of programming, but the assembly language abbreviations still have to be translated into machine code before the computer processor can execute the program. A translator program called an **assembler** converts abbreviated code into a binary program. Assembly code is also machine dependent, so a program written for a specific computer model could not run on a different computer system. Programmers still use assembly language to create fast and efficient programs because the commands are designed to correspond directly to machine-code instructions in a particular computer's CPU.

High-Level Languages

Computers and software proliferated in the 1960s. High-level languages emerged that were more English-like, less error prone, and not dependent on specific computer systems. **High-level languages** are those that abstract from specific hardware components, allowing programmers to concentrate on the program itself rather than the way it is implemented in the computer. Using high-level programming languages, programmers could ignore the operation of specific computers and write programs that could be run on a wide range of computer systems. Useful applications soon multiplied. Languages such as BASIC, COBOL, Pascal, and Fortran were widely used to develop software applications. While these languages are easier for programmers to use, they, too, must be converted to machine language before they can be executed. This process of converting "source code" written by the programmer to "machine code" for a specific computer system requires either an interpreter or a compiler.

Interpreters and compilers are programs written to read source commands and translate them to a string of 0s and 1s that the specific computer can process. **Interpreters** translate one line of the program into machine code, execute that line of code, and proceed to the next line in the program. Every time the program is executed it must be "interpreted" to binary code, one line at a time. This is a time consuming process, especially for software applications with millions of lines of code. The main advantage of interpreters is that programmers can more easily correct errors in a program that is translated line by line.

A **compiler** converts the entire source code program into machine code. This produces an executable file that runs on a specific computer. The compiled file is much faster to execute because the entire program is saved in its machine code format. Software applications such as Corel Draw or Paint Shop Pro are compiled programs that run on a specific computer platform. The compiler for Windows-based computers is very different from the compiler for Macintosh systems because the two platforms use different hardware. This is why software purchased for Windows cannot be run on the Mac OS.

New Programming Languages

Programming languages have evolved rapidly with advances in computer technology and demands for more powerful software applications. Two new categories, *object-oriented languages* and *visual programming* are making programming easier and faster.

Object-oriented languages use self-contained programmed objects that are repeatedly referenced in an application. These objects hold all the data and instructions for a particular task (Figure 4.7). This programming environment is much different than previous high-level languages where program code is processed as a list of instructions. By contrast, the object-oriented programming environment is modular. Independent objects with their own characteristics interact with each other based on a series of messages from other objects. The programmer structures the exchange of messages between objects to build up complex operations. Object-oriented programming allows developers to quickly test routines and easily incorporate routines from other projects. C++ and Java are common object-oriented languages.

Visual programming uses a graphical interface to expedite writing source code. Command segments are created using "drag and drop" procedures. Once a segment is developed it is compiled to machine language and can be used without having the entire application completed. Visual programming is often used for Rapid Application Development (RAD) because it offers an effective means of generating an application with various stages of

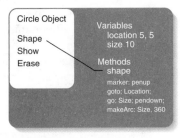

Figure 4.7 An object to manage a "circle" has three methods defined to shape, show, and erase a circle. The instructions to make the shape, as well as the data for the location and size of the circle, are contained in the object.

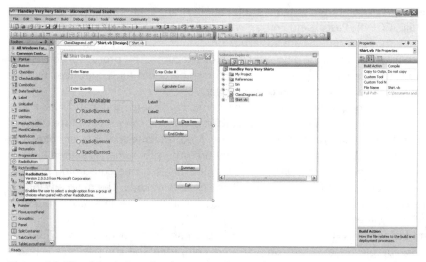

Figure 4.8 Visual Basic is a visual programming environment that allows programmers to build object-based programs. The programmer uses buttons and text boxes to assign properties and write code for each object. The segments can be individually tested as each set of properties and code is developed.

testing and usability. Visual Basic .NET is an example of an object-oriented language that includes visual programming (Figure 4.8).

Programmers often use object-oriented languages and visual programming to create customized routines for multimedia applications. Special features such as database interactions or user control of players, vehicles, and other objects in video games may be created using a language like Java or C++. These programs can then be compiled for use in the application.

Programming languages are essential for all software development. Every application and operating system is generated from these languages. While machine code remains the "lingua franca" of computer hardware, modern languages are making it easier to craft applications that address a wide range of computing needs. The computer is a word processor, 3-D game, or window to the Internet using the applications that are developed with programming languages.

4.4 Application Software

An **application** is software that performs a specific task. These programs combine with the operating system to make computers productive tools. Early software for microcomputers included word processing and spreadsheet applications. Today's business productivity tools also include database, presentation, project management, desktop publishing, and time management applications. These programs are often bundled together with a common interface and integrated set of commands. iWork, Microsoft Office Suite, and Open Office.org are examples of these program suites.

There are two major types of software for multimedia development. **Media-specific applications** are used to create and edit the individual media elements (text, graphics, sound, video, animation) that make up a multimedia product. **Authoring applications** contain software tools to integrate media components and provide a user interface. This chapter provides a brief overview of media-specific and authoring applications. More details about each of these topics will be found in Chapters 5 through 10.

Text

Multimedia developers use several types of application software to create and edit text. The most common are *word processors* such as Corel WordPerfect or Microsoft Word. These programs make it possible to readily create text in different fonts and styles, check spelling, search and replace words and phrases, and import and export text in a variety of file formats. These functions are just as important in multimedia development as they are in other forms of communication.

Text editor software, such as Notepad, generates ASCII text files. Unlike a word processor file, an ASCII file is compatible with any platform or application. The disadvantage of an ASCII file is that it does not include the advanced formatting and style options available in word processors. Text editors are very useful, however, for tasks that require only simple formatting, such as writing source code for computer programs. Notepad, for example, is commonly used to write XHTML code for web pages.

The development of the World Wide Web also introduced specialized programs designed to preserve the formatting of text documents and to support a variety of interactive features such as hyperlinking, text searching, and speech synthesis. Multimedia developers use Adobe Acrobat to produce PDF files that incorporate these features. Acrobat text files are cross-platform compatible, making them ideal to distribute highly formatted text over the Internet. PDFs are readily viewed using a free Acrobat Reader.

Multimedia text is further explored in Chapter 5.

Graphics

Graphics applications generate 2-D or 3-D paint and draw images. Developers may use several graphics applications, each specialized for the type of image they seek to create. **Paint programs** contain tool sets to create graphics objects as well as editing tools for digital photos or scanned images (Figure 4.9A). They offer a wide array of features such as filters (blur, emboss, pixelate), image adjustment settings (scale, brightness, rotate), and special effects (drop shadow, gradient overlay). Special control over individual image elements is possible using layers and mask options. Text tools are used to generate graphics text with distinctive patterns, shapes, and 3-D effects.

Draw programs contain a distinctive set of tools for creating basic shapes such as ovals, rectangles, Bezier curves, and polygons generated from mathematical formulas (Figure 4.9B). These shapes are grouped, filled, and scaled to produce complex drawn images. These programs create unique logos, designs, and graphics objects that can easily be resized for specific multimedia projects.

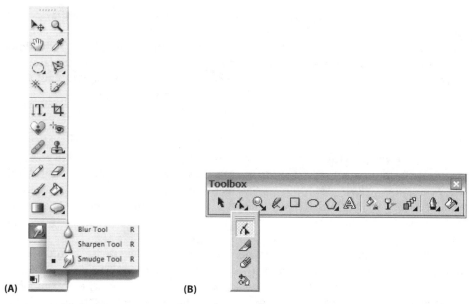

(A)   **(B)**

Figure 4.9 Photoshop paint tools palette and Corel Draw tool palette.

Many projects, especially animation sequences and gaming applications, require 3-D images. **3-D imaging programs** are used to model 3-D objects, define surfaces, compose scenes, and render a completed image (Figure 4.10). In *modeling*, the graphic artist

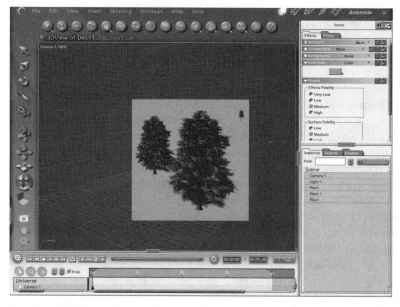

Figure 4.10 3-D graphics application (Carrara) to model, define surface, compose scene, and render objects.

Table 4.1 **Sample Graphics Applications**

Paint	Draw	3-D Graphics
Adobe—Photoshop	Adobe—Illustrator	Carrara—Eovia
JASC—Paint Shop Pro	Corel—Draw	Corel—Bryce 3-D
Corel—Painter	Macromedia—FreeHand	MetaCreation—Infini-D

creates the shape of an object; in *surface definition*, color and texture are applied; in *scene composition*, objects are arranged, lighting is specified, and backgrounds and special effects are added. Because the creation of the objects and scenes of 3-D graphics can be very time consuming, many 3-D applications provide libraries of clip objects that can be adjusted for individual projects. The final stage of 3-D graphics is rendering. *Rendering* creates a 3-D image from the specified scene. Rendering is both processor intensive and time consuming because the software must calculate how the image should appear based on the object's position, surface materials, lighting, and specific render options.

Image editing and creation is an important part of multimedia development. Graphic artists select the application they will use—paint, draw, or 3-D graphics program—based on the specific needs of the project (Table 4.1). *Graphics suites* bundle several applications that share a common command set and interface. Adobe and Corel each offer a graphics suite with paint and draw applications.

The different types and uses of graphics are further discussed in Chapter 6.

Sound

There are two major types of sound applications for multimedia development: *sampled* and *synthesized* (Table 4.2). **Sampled sounds** are captured from a microphone, CD, DVD, or any analog sound source. Software settings control the sound format of the sound recording. Sampled sounds can be edited in a wide variety of ways such as trimming to delete

Table 4.2 **Sound Applications**

Sampled Sound	Synthesized Sound
Sonic Foundry—Sound Forge	Steinberg—Cubase SX3
Bias—Deck 3.5	Cakewalk
Apple—SoundTrack Pro	Apple—Garage band

dead space, splicing to combine sound segments, setting fade-in and fade-out (enveloping), adjusting volume, and adding special effects such as echoes or sound reversals (Figure 4.11).

Synthesized sound applications use digital commands to generate sounds. These commands can be captured from a MIDI instrument such as an electronic keyboard or created with a "sequencer" program. Using sequencer programs such as Cakewalk or GarageBand, developers can enter music notations, determine instruments to play, layer instrument tracks to achieve a full-orchestra effect, and synchronize sound tracks to play a rich musical score. The musical file is then saved and played back on a computer's *synthesizer*, an electronic device to generate sound. MIDI applications are a good source of original music for multimedia applications. However the developer does need to know music notation and have musical talent to generate high quality sound files. Digital sound is further explored in Chapter 7.

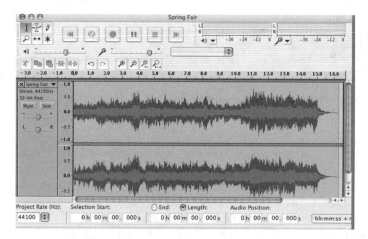

Figure 4.11 Audacity Edit window where analog sound is recorded to a digital file and edited. Special effects can be applied and additional tracks can be added and mixed to create a sound file for a multimedia project.

Video

Video applications provide an environment to combine source material called "clips," synchronize clips to a sound track, add special effects, and save the work as a digital video. High-quality digital video production once required specialized, expensive hardware and software only available to large multimedia development firms. The widespread use of digital video cameras, the development of more powerful microcomputers, and improvements to the Web made digital video production practical for most developers.

A video "project" starts by assembling film clips in a project window (Figure 4.12). The clips can be still images, animations, sounds, or digital video files. Video applications

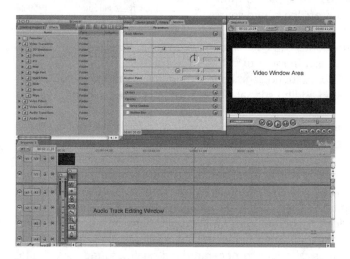

Figure 4.12 Video editing process with Final Cut. Clips are imported into the project window, arranged on a timeline, and previewed. Special effects and transitions are added before exporting the final video project.

provide tools to move and insert clips on a time line, set in and out points, trim the clip, and define transitions between tracks. Sound tracks, title fields, and special effects such as superimposing, transparency, and lens flare add to the video composition. Video editing applications also define playback size and frame rate. When the video project is complete, the application provides settings to save it in specific file formats and compression schemes. Video formats include .MOV for QuickTime, .AVI for Microsoft Windows, .RM for RealNetworks streaming video, as well as .MPEG for DVDs.

Table 4.3 **Digital Video Applications**

Home User	Developer
Apple–iMovie	Adobe–Premiere
Apple–Final Cut Express	Apple–Final Cut Pro
Eskape–My Video	IMSI–Lumiere
	Avid–Xpress DV

Basic software applications such as Apple's iMovie make editing and saving digital home movies easy and affordable. Developers rely on more robust applications such as Final Cut Pro or Adobe Premiere to create professional quality digital video (Table 4.3). Additional detail on digital video will be discussed in Chapter 8.

Animation

Animation software is used to create and edit animated sequences. **Animation** is the technique of using a series of rapidly displayed still

Table 4.4 **Animation Applications**

Informatix–Piranesi	Macromedia Director MX	Macromedia Flash MX

images to produce the appearance of motion. Animation software has greatly simplified the traditional work of animators (Table 4.4). Objects are drawn or imported into the software where they are manipulated in a series of still frames. Frames are played back in sequence to create an illusion of motion (Figure 4.13). Each frame represents a single instance of the animated sequence. Typical animation tools control the path of an object, object shape, and color changes over the frame sequence. Objects are placed

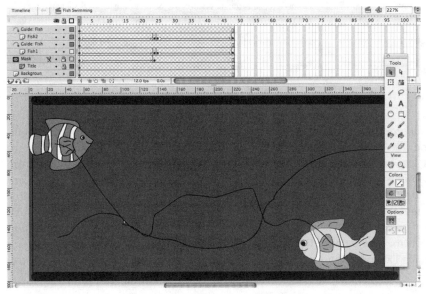

Figure 4.13 Animation sequence in Flash. There are 48 still frames in the sequence. The playback of these 48 frames gives the appearance of swimming fish.

on a timeline where effects can be applied to fade in, morph, rotate, spin, flip, or change pace. Multiple objects can be layered to interact with each other to create more complex animations.

Multimedia projects include a wide variety of animations ranging from simple animated logos to full-length feature films such as *Toy Story* or *Madagascar*. Additional details on animation are presented in Chapter 9.

Media Utilities

Developers use a wide array of media utilities in addition to media-specific applications (Table 4.5). **Media utility** programs add functionality to media-specific applications. Some utilities provide productivity features such as image or font cataloging; others perform specific tasks such as color matching or compression. These "enhancement" programs include:

- clip libraries of images, sounds, and animations
- color utilities to match Pantone color ink formulas for printers
- image cataloging programs to manage image files
- font utilities to manage, create, and convert type formats
- video production utilities to encode and publish streaming video and audio to an array of streaming formats and codecs
- compression applications to reduce file sizes of specific media and application projects

Table 4.5 Sample Utility Programs for Multimedia Development

Eye Candy (special effects)	MonocoEZColor (color management)	FontReserve (font utility)
PhotoObjects (royalty-free clip images)	Cleaner 6 (publish/compress video and audio)	SonicFire Pro (manage soundtracks for video projects)
Sorenson Squeeze.3 (compression suite)	Extensis Portfolio (image cataloging)	StuffIt (compress files)

Authoring Software

Authoring applications are programs specifically designed to facilitate the creation of multimedia products. They are used to assemble media elements, synchronize content, design the user interface, and provide user interactivity (Figure 4.14). Authoring programs fall into one of three main categories based on the metaphor they use to organize media elements. Programs such as Toolbook, PowerPoint, and SuperCard use a *card-based metaphor* in which elements are arranged much as they might be on index cards or the pages of a book. These applications are easy to use and are ideal for products such as information kiosks, lectures, and tutorials that do not require precise synchronization of individual media elements. Others, such as Director or Flash, use a *timeline* of separate frames much like a motion picture film. These applications provide the precise control

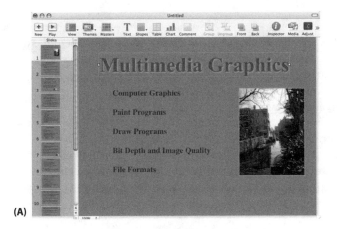

(A)

(B)

Figure 4.14 Two common authoring applications are Keynote (A) and Flash (B).

needed for advanced animations. Other authoring programs, such as IconAuthor or Authorware, use *icons* arranged on flow lines to quickly develop a wide range of multimedia products including advanced tutorials, product demonstrations, and simulations. Icons can represent both content (images, text, animations, video) and a wide range of interactions (play, stop, go to, calculate, etc.).

Authoring software and the authoring process are discussed further in Chapter 10.

4.5 Summary

Software is the collection of programs that make a computer a useful tool. *Operating systems* provide the "hidden programs" to control hardware devices, application execution, and access to data. *Programming software* provides the language to create operating systems and computer applications. *Application software* makes it possible for users to carry out an ever-expanding array of tasks with their computers.

Multimedia development requires a wide selection of applications to capture and prepare various media components. Media specialists such as graphic artists, sound specialists, and video editors use increasingly powerful *media-specific* application programs to prepare digital content for multimedia projects. Once the media components are completed, they are assembled using an *authoring application*. Authoring software integrates the media, provides interactivity, and produces the final multimedia project.

Key Terms

3-D imaging program	Low-level language
Animation	Machine code
Application	Media utilities
Assembler	Media-specific application
Assembly language	Multitasking
Authoring application	Object-oriented language
Cluster	Operating system
Compiler	OS utility program
Device drivers	Paint program
Directory	Program
Draw program	Programming language
File	Sampled sound
File extension	Software
File system	Synthesized sound
Formatting	Timesharing
GUI	User interface
High-level language	Virtual memory
Interpreter	Visual programming

Review Questions

1. What are the three main categories of software?
2. What is the main function of each category of software?
3. Why is the operating system critical to a computer system?
4. What are the two types of user interface presented by an operating system?
5. How does the operating system control access to the processor by multiple users?
6. Why is multitasking important for multimedia developers?
7. What is virtual memory and when is it helpful to a developer?
8. What are the three ways formatting prepares a storage disk for data?

9. What are two important considerations when naming a data file?
10. What are directories and how can they be used to manage media files effectively?
11. Why are programming languages an important type of software?
12. What is the essential distinction between low-level and high-level programs?
13. Why must all programs be translated to machine code?
14. What is the difference between an interpreter and compiler?
15. What are the advantages of using object-oriented languages?
16. What is the difference between a text editor and a word processing application?
17. What is the difference between a paint and draw application?
18. What is the difference between sampled and synthesized sound applications?
19. Why might a developer rely on media utility applications?
20. What is the purpose of authoring software?

Discussion Questions

1. Open the system preferences on OS X or the Control Panel on the Windows XP operating system. Explain how you can control five different hardware devices through the operating system.
2. Locate the operating system utility programs in OS X or Windows and list three OS utility programs.
3. Locate the yahoo.com directory of programming languages (Directory > Computers and Internet > Programming and Development > **Languages**). How many languages are listed there? Why do you think there are so many programming languages? Choose one language and report how it is used.
4. Point your browser to www.tucows.com. Search for popular media utilities for editing images or sound. Select one image editing and one sound editing utility and describe the main features of each.
5. Identify and describe the three main approaches to organizing media elements in an authoring application. Give an example of each.
6. Research the media you can add to a Word document. Do you think Word is an authoring application? Why or why not?

Chapter 5

Text

Topics you will explore include:

In 1518, Michelangelo sketched a series of simple images on the back of an envelope. This scrap of paper, today preserved at the Casa Buonarroti in Florence, is perhaps the most valuable shopping list of all time. Known simply as "Three Lists of Food," the sketch includes the artist's menu for a meal for two, including six rolls, two soups, and a fish. Apparently the person who was to fetch the ingredients was illiterate and so had to be told what to get in pictures. Michelangelo knew how to draw; but how much easier it would have been, even for him, if his assistants knew how to read. And if he had wanted a *thousand* fish, that one word would have been worth a thousand pictures. Writing, now as then, is sometimes the most efficient mode of communication.

The power and usefulness of text derives in part from its universality. Literacy is a requirement of modern social life. In much of the world it is a formal condition for citizenship. A few people can paint; nearly all can read and write. Multimedia developers often take advantage of the universality of reading. It is common to label new icons to make their meaning clear. When the new icon is widely recognized and has itself become a symbol, the label is often dropped. Developers also list contents, write out instructions for Help screens, and add their names to credits (as well as invoices). Text speaks to nearly everyone.

Text also has unique powers of expression. $E=mc^2$. Five symbols capture a set of concepts—energy, equivalence, mass, the speed of light, squaring—that are invisible to sense but made evident to the mind in text. No picture can replace this simple formula, though one might help to explain it. Multimedia developers, like other writers, continue to use text to express abstract concepts.

Text can also be powerfully suggestive, engaging a reader's imagination, creating its own images, or prompting a string of unexpected reflections. Byron writes of a looming battle and our minds fill in the images:

> *The Assyrian came down like the wolf*
> *   on the fold,*
> *And his cohorts were gleaming in pur-*
> *   ple and gold;*
> *And the sheen of their spears was like*
> *   stars on the sea,*
> *When the blue wave rolls nightly on*
> *   Deep Galilee.*
> *(Hebrew Melodies, "The Destruction*
> *   of Sennacherib")*

He speaks of his life and we reflect on our own, and on life itself:

> *My days are in the yellow leaf;*
> *The flowers and fruits of love are gone;*
> *The worm, the canker, and the grief*
> *   Are mine alone!*
> *("On This Day I Complete My Thirty-Sixth Year")*

Byron, as the poem's title suggests, was thirty-six, and this was the last year of his life.

The suggestive, engaging power of text does not belong to poets alone. Politicians use it: "Ask not what your country can do for you; ask what you can do for your country" (John F. Kennedy). And so do advertisers: "99 and $^{44/100}$ pure" (Ivory soap); and song writers: "I tried to forget you but you tied bells to your name. They jingled every time I thought of you, without shame" (Jewel). Multimedia developers also craft their words to capture the attention and to engage the imaginations of their readers.

Like all writers, multimedia developers value text for its universality, its clarity and efficiency, and its powers of abstraction, engagement, and suggestion. But unlike traditional writers, the multimedia developer has a wide choice of media, and this adds another step to the "writing" process. Developers must decide where and how to use text most efficiently and effectively. They generally avoid lengthy text presentations since reading is more difficult on-screen. They often provide instructions in text rather than sound because listening is more tiring than reading. Multimedia developers also make use of new tools for creating engagement with text. Words can be animated to attract attention. They can be linked to other words, sounds, or images to entertain or to inform.

Much of the creative challenge of multimedia development lies in effectively exploiting the potential of a new technology, of finding new uses for text and other media. Text also has a long history and a set of traditional conventions that remain important for multimedia development. These are the foundation on which developers build new forms of multimedia writing.

After completing this chapter you should understand:

- Key elements of traditional text, including typeface, font, style, case, weight, kerning, tracking, leading, and justification
- Fundamentals of computer text including codes, font technologies, anti-aliasing, and the problem of installed fonts
- Defining features and uses of multimedia text: editable vs. graphics text, text and sound (speech recognition and speech synthesis), hypertext and hypermedia, and multimedia text formats
- Major options for adding text to a multimedia application
- Basic guidelines for the use of text

5.1 The Text Tradition

Text was dramatically transformed by the invention of the printing press in the fifteenth century. In addition to greatly increasing the volume of written communication, the printing press also standardized many elements of text presentation. A number of the print-based text properties remain important to multimedia developers today.

Typeface

Characters are grouped into families that share a common design. These designs are traditionally called **typefaces**. Examples of typefaces include New York, Times, Helvetica, and Courier. Typefaces are carefully designed for specific purposes, and thousands have been created. Bell Centennial was created for telephone books and Spartan Classified was specially designed to improve the legibility of small classified ads in newspapers.

Serif ⟹
(Times @ 72 points)

Figure 5.1 Serif text.

Times: A serif typeface

Arial: A sans serif typeface

Edwardian: A serif typeface

Symbols: ∝│ℜ ♣ ♦ ⊗ ∅ ⊕ ℘ ≡ δ

Figure 5.2 Categories of typefaces.

Typefaces are commonly divided into two major categories: *serif* and *sans serif*. A **serif** is a fine line added to finish a letter stroke (Figure 5.1). Serifs tend to make letters flow into one another. This makes it easier for the eye to move from one word to the next in long segments of text. As a result, serif text is often used for the longer selections of text known as *body text*. **Sans serif** text is text without a serif (*sans* is *without* in French). This text typically has a clean, bold look. Sans serif text is traditionally used for headings. Other categories of typefaces include *script*, type that is designed to look like handwriting, and *symbols* (Figure 5.2).

Style

Typefaces generally contain several *styles* of letters. **Styles** are readily recognized variations in the appearance of characters that allow writers to adapt the typeface to specific purposes. Roman or plain text is usually used for body text while **bold**, *italic*, and underlined styles are often used for titles or for emphasis.

Point

A **point** is a measure of the size of type. The individual letters, numbers, and other characters that were mounted in printing presses were measured in points. A point is approximately 1/72 of an inch. Another traditional measure based on the point is the *pica*. A pica is twelve points; six picas is approximately one inch.

A typeface may be printed in many different sizes. The point size of a typeface measures the space within which each of its characters is designed. This is approximately the distance from the bottom of the *descender*, the portion of the letter normally written below a line (as in the dropped vertical line of a "p") to the top of an *ascender* (as in the rising vertical line of a "d").

The print industry also works with a variety of other measurements, including the height of capital letters (*cap height*) and the height of the small letter x (*x height*) (Figure 5.3).

Figure 5.3 Point size, cap height, and x-height.

Font

A complete set of characters of a particular typeface, style, and size is traditionally known as a **font**. *New York, italic, 12 point* is an example of a font. A typeface has many different fonts.

Some fonts are monospaced while others are proportional. **Monospaced fonts** assign the same width to each character, regardless of its shape. In monospaced fonts, narrower letters such as an "i" occupy the same space as wider letters such as an "m." Monospaced fonts have the somewhat choppy appearance of typewriter text. **Proportional fonts** adjust the width of a letter or other character based on its shape. Narrow letters are assigned less space than wider letters. Proportional fonts are usually easier to read and more elegant because they distribute characters more evenly (Figure 5.4).

Courier is a monospaced font.
Palatino is a proportional font.

Figure 5.4 Monospaced and proportional fonts.

Case

Small letters are traditionally labeled *lowercase*. Capitals are called *uppercase*. These designations refer to the containers or **cases** used to store the two different types of metal castings for use in printing presses. Capitals were stored in cases placed above the cases holding small letters.

Weight

Some typefaces are designed in multiple versions with lines of different thicknesses. **Weight** is the line thickness of a typeface. Thin lines are designated as *lighter* weight with thicker variations being *heavier* weights. A version of a typeface with particularly heavy weight is sometimes designated as "black." Arial, for instance, is light and **Arial Black** is heavy.

Kerning

The different shapes of letters sometimes result in distracting variations in letter spacing. At standard spacing, uppercase "A" and "W" appear to be further apart than uppercase "H" and "N" (compare AW & HN). This effect can be corrected by moving the pairs of letters either closer together or further apart. This process of adjusting the spacing between pairs of letters is **kerning** (Figure 5.5).

Before kerning: AW
After kerning: AW

Figure 5.5 Kerning.

Tracking

It is also often desirable to change the spacing of all characters, or **tracking**. More space between letters results in a looser track, less space produces a tighter track. A tighter track can usually be used on shorter lines of text; longer text lines typically require a looser track. Tracking adjustments are also often used to adjust the length of individual lines to avoid hyphenation (Figure 5.6).

This is a tighter track.
This is a looser track.

Figure 5.6 Tracking.

Condensed/Extended Text

Changing the proportions of the characters themselves can also alter the length of a text line. Instead of inserting more space between characters, as in tracking, the width of a character can be narrowed or widened. Narrowing the width of characters results in **condensed text**, widening results in **extended text** (Figure 5.7).

This is Futura.
This is Futura Condensed.
This is Futura Extended.

Figure 5.7 Condensed and extended text.

Condensed and extended text are usually used for space adjustments to an individual line of text or for artistic effect. Since fonts are carefully designed for specific purposes, condensing or extending the font in large blocks of text should usually be avoided.

Leading

The spacing between lines of text can also be adjusted. This is referred to as **leading** (pronounced "ledding"). The term is derived from the use of thin strips of lead to separate lines of text in printing presses. In general, as the number of words in a line of text increases, leading also needs to increase. Leading and tracking are also interrelated: a looser track typically requires greater leading and a tighter track less leading. This is because the distance between lines of text needs to be greater than the distance between words. If lines are spaced more closely than words the eye will tend to jump to the next line rather than moving to the next word on the same line (Figure 5.8).

A Looser Track with More Leading

Modern scholars have interpreted the various symbols in Lippi's works differently and perhaps Lippi's contemporaries did as well. We simply do not know exactly what the fifteenth century viewer would have seen in Lippi's art; but we do know that they would have approached his paintings with symbolic references in mind.

A Tighter Track with Less Leading

Modern scholars have interpreted the various symbols in Lippi's works differently and perhaps Lippi's contemporaries did as well. We simply do not know exactly what the fifteenth century viewer would have seen in Lippi's art; but we do know that they would have approached his paintings with symbolic references in mind.

Figure 5.8 Track and leading.

Alignment and Justification

Alignment and justification are also characteristics of print-based text that continue to be relevant in multimedia development. **Alignment** is the position of text relative to a document's margins. Text *aligned to the left* margin has a ragged (uneven) edge to the right. *Centered* text has ragged edges on both sides. Text *aligned to the right* margin has a ragged edge to the left. **Justification** is the process of adjusting line lengths to produce straight edges on both the left and right margins. This requires adjustments in the spacing of characters to make each line of text the same length. Traditionally, justified text has been used for more formal presentations and for the columns of text in magazines and newspapers. Left-alignment produces a more casual feel. Centered text and right-alignment are usually used for aesthetic effect (Figure 5.9).

Left Aligned	Centered	Right Aligned	Justified
....	....	....	....
....	....	....	....
....	....	....	....
....	....	....	....
....	....	....	....

Figure 5.9 Alignment and justification.

5.2 Computer Text

Text as it is treated by the computer shares many features with traditional text. Word processing programs allow their users to easily change the appearance of text and its

size by changing typeface, style, and points, for example. In almost all programs, however, typefaces are listed, somewhat inaccurately, as "fonts" (Figure 5.10). Strictly speaking, a font is not the whole collection of characters with a single design—this is a *typeface*. Instead, a font is a set of characters within the typeface of a particular size and style. Palatino, bold, 18 point is a *font*; Palatino is a *typeface*. The substitution of "font" for "typeface" is now well established in the computer industry, however, with nearly all references to computer font actually referring to type-

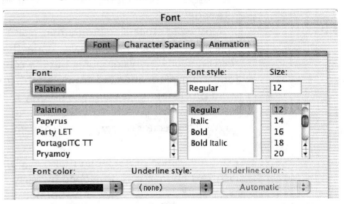

Figure 5.10 Word processors use "font" for "typeface."

face. In the sections below, the current convention of using "font" for what traditionally would be called a "typeface" will be followed.

Word processing programs also allow users to manipulate many other elements of traditional printing operations. Users can generally adjust kerning (the spacing between pairs of letters) as well as tracking (the spacing between all letters) and leading (the spacing between lines). Condensed (narrowed) and extended (widened) fonts are also often available.

Codes for Computer Text

All the data in a computer must be represented by a binary code, a combination of 1s and 0s. Developing such a code for text is relatively simple: each character (letter, number, symbol, punctuation mark, etc.) is assigned a unique combination of bits. Several different coding schemes have been developed for computer text. Two of the most important are ASCII and Unicode.

ASCII   **ASCII** stands for *American Standard Code for Information Interchange*. Virtually all computers can readily process ASCII files. The original version of ASCII was a seven-bit code. An expanded version of the code, known as "extended ASCII," uses an eight-bit code, thus doubling the number of characters that can be represented.

ASCII coding produces a very basic text file in which only letters, numbers, common symbols (for example "+" or "©"), punctuation marks, and a limited set of control functions (for example delete or carriage return) are represented. Notepad on the PC is an example of a basic ASCII text program.

> **Designing a Text Code**
>
> Binary codes are carefully chosen to facilitate specific tasks. For instance, the ASCII code was designed so that lowercase and uppercase versions of the same letter differ only by the value of one bit. Changing that single bit changes lowercase letters to uppercase and vice versa.

More advanced word processing programs, such as Microsoft Word, use proprietary coding schemes that support many more characteristics of text, such as styles (<u>underline</u>, *italic*), tabs, and so on. Computers that do not have these word processors or compatible programs installed will not be able to read these more elaborate codes.

Most word processing programs can also produce ASCII versions of files. Users simply save the file as ASCII or "text only," under the *Save As* or *Export* options. ASCII files can be read on nearly every computer, but the conversion process will strip away much of the formatting information (for example, tabs, text alignment, and text styles) in the original word processor file, leaving behind only those elements supported by ASCII code. The text itself will be preserved, however. If the objective is simply to create basic messages, an ASCII text editor is very effective and efficient.

RTF   A variation of ASCII that is also available in many word processors is RTF. **RTF**, or Rich Text Format, was developed by Microsoft to facilitate cross-application and cross-platform use of text files produced by different word processors. RTF is based on the ASCII code but it also includes special commands to reproduce the formatting of the original file. In this way, text files created using one word processor and operating system can be opened and edited using another word processor or operating system without loss of the original formatting. Like plain ASCII, RTF is often available as a file option under *Save As* (Figure 5.11).

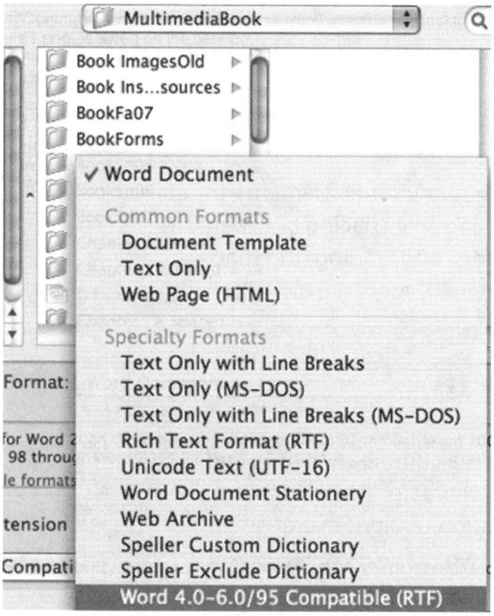

Unicode   Extended ASCII added, among other characters, a selection of Greek letters to the Latin letters and Arabic numerals available in original ASCII. However, many languages, such as Japanese and Chinese, do not use either Latin or Greek script. In an effort to more effectively present these languages, a new coding scheme was devised in 1988. Known as **Unicode**, the new standard is based on a 16-bit code that permits approximately 65,000 characters to be represented. The Unicode standard also specifies code subsets (called "surrogates" in the Unicode standard)

Figure 5.11 The RFT option in Word.

that permit a total of as many as one million additional characters. Unicode is continually evolving. Unicode 3.0 included 49,194 characters, covering virtually all languages in modern use and many historical languages as well. Unicode 5.0 specified over 100,000 characters. Unicode fully incorporates ASCII encoding as well as several other national and international standards.

The goal of the Unicode project is to define "a consistent way of encoding multilingual text that enables the exchange of text data internationally and creates the foundation for global software" (Unicode, 2001, 1). Unicode has been widely adopted for text representation. It is included in all modern computer operating systems and in HTML, XML, and Java.

> For current developments in the Unicode project, see http://www.unicode.org

5.3 Font Technologies

Standards such as ASCII, RTF, and Unicode specify the codes to be assigned to particular text characters. The codes 1010100 1100101 1111000 1110100 specify the word "Text" in ASCII, for instance.

Assigning a code is only the first step in the process of generating computer text. Text also must be displayed through monitors or printers. The techniques for displaying text are referred to as **font technologies**. There are two basic approaches to generating text display. The first makes use of *bitmapped fonts*; the second is based on *outline fonts*.

Bitmapped Fonts

A computer monitor displays a grid of pixels, or "picture elements." A monitor set to a resolution of 800 $\times$ 600 displays 800 vertical lines and 600 horizontal lines for a total of 480,000 individual pixels. Each of these pixels can be described with one or more bits. If a single bit is used, two color values, usually black or white, can be assigned to each pixel. Two bits can designate any one of four colors; three will allow eight colors and so on. The number of possible colors doubles with each additional bit used.

In a **bitmapped font**, each pixel of the letter to be displayed is described by a binary code. The listing of these codes constitutes a "mapping" of the text character as it will be displayed, hence a "bitmap." Because information must be saved about each pixel, bitmapped fonts require relatively large amounts of memory. This is particularly true if a wide range of colors must be available, since this requires more bits to be used for each pixel. A range of 256 colors, for instance, would require 8 bits to represent each pixel of the text character.

Bitmapped fonts have the advantage of giving font designers precise control over the appearance of text characters. Fonts can be edited down to the level of the individual pixel, ensuring that characters will appear exactly as intended. This degree of control can be particularly important in the use of smaller fonts since characters often become less precise and less readable as font size is reduced.

In general, different bitmaps must be designed for each size of text to be used. Bitmapped fonts do not scale well. Attempting to enlarge a 12-point bitmap to 28 points, for example, generally produces distortions in the text characters. This is because the computer must interpolate the additional pixels in the new, larger character rather than having the font designer directly select them. Effective use of bitmapped fonts requires separate bitmaps for each typeface, style, and point size to be used. This significantly increases memory requirements. It also limits flexibility in the use of computer text since the required font may not be available when needed.

Outline Fonts

Outline fonts represent a solution to the problems of memory and flexibility associated with bitmapped fonts. The basic strategy in **outline fonts** is to store a set of instructions to draw the character rather than a mapping of each of the character's pixels.

One common outline font technology is Adobe's PostScript. *PostScript* specifies a series of commands and parameters to produce text characters. The computer then draws the character to be displayed on screen or causes a printer to produce the character on paper. To produce a different font size, PostScript simply specifies a different drawing command. Outline fonts therefore scale much more effectively than bitmaps. Moreover, it is not necessary to store detailed descriptions of each character to be used, as is the case with bitmaps. All that needs to be stored are the drawing commands. As a result, files for outline fonts are much smaller than those for bitmapped fonts. PostScript commands can also be used to describe other elements of page layout, including illustrations.

Other outline fonts were developed following the success of PostScript. Apple and Microsoft, for instance, collaborated to produce *TrueType* for use on their computers. This allowed both companies to use an efficient, scalable outline font without paying royalties for the use of PostScript. TrueType is now very common on both Macintosh and Windows platforms. PostScript remains the standard of choice in professional publishing, however. Multimedia projects that include high-quality print materials often require the use of PostScript fonts.

Text Display and Anti-Aliasing

Both bitmapped and outline fonts are displayed on monitors as patterns of pixels. Many printers also use separate dots of color to compose text characters. Pixels are usually displayed as very small squares. Smooth lines can be created with a series of these small squares if the lines are vertical or horizontal. Curves and angled lines, however, will display with a stair-step effect that produces jagged lines (often called **jaggies**). This deviation from the text character's true form is called an *alias*. **Anti-aliasing** combats this effect by blending the color of the text with the color of the background on which it appears. The pixels adjacent to black text on a white background would be shaded gray; red text on white might use shades of pink. This shading blends the text to the background, minimizing the appearance of jagged outlines (Figure 5.12).

Figure 5.12 Anti-aliasing smoothes "jaggies."

Anti-aliased text is an option in image editing programs such as Photoshop and is often automatically applied in multimedia presentation programs such as PowerPoint. Producing clean, professional type usually requires the use of anti-aliasing.

The Problem of "Installed Fonts"

The coding schemes used for text, such as ASCII or Unicode, are so widely supported that multimedia developers seldom need to be concerned about their availability to users.

This is not true of fonts. Particular fonts (Palatino, Times, Chicago, etc.) must be installed in the user's operating system for text to be displayed as the developer intended. If the specific font is not available, the computer operating system will generally substitute another. The results may not be pretty. Text alignment may be lost and the psychology of the text display, its mood or feel, may be altered.

Developers employ two basic strategies to deal with the challenge of installed fonts. The first is to use only fonts that are widely available. Arial, Bookman, Courier, Times, and Lucida are available on nearly all Windows computers. Commonly installed fonts for the Mac include Chicago, Courier, Geneva, New York, and Times. Restricting a design to one of these fonts generally assures that users will view text as the developer planned.

The second strategy is to make the required font available to the user. This is done by including the font, with instructions for installation, among the application files. The user then installs the required font or fonts prior to using the multimedia application. As with all software, the developer must determine the conditions of licensing associated with the font prior to distribution. Some fonts may not be available for distribution at all while others may require payment of fees.

Cross-platform compatibility is another aspect of the problem of installed fonts. Fonts that share the same name may not appear the same on different computer platforms. The Windows Times font, for instance, will not produce the same text display as Times on the Macintosh. Developers who target their applications to both platforms need to test their products on each.

5.4 Multimedia Text

Computer text added powerful new tools to those traditionally available to the printing industry. Typesetting tasks could be carried out much more efficiently using specialized computers. Individuals using personal computers could create their own sophisticated designs and layouts with "desktop publishing" programs such as InDesign or QuarkXPress.

Multimedia further expands the possibilities of text by transforming it from a static to a dynamic medium. Text becomes dynamic as it is linked to other media and takes on new forms of interactivity. Text can change color with user interactions; it can be animated, spinning and rotating its way onto a screen; and it can be linked to charts, tables, photos, sounds, and video.

Text and Picture

The multimedia developer treats text in one of two main forms, either as the editable computer text discussed above or as graphics text. **Editable text** is the text produced by basic text editors and word processors. Editable text can be easily revised, searched, spell-checked, and reformatted. Multimedia developers take advantage of these capabilities for much of the text content of their applications.

Graphics text, on the other hand, is essentially a picture. Like other pictures, text in the form of a graphic can be manipulated to produce a wide range of artistic effects. Letters can be rotated, reshaped, variously colored, or animated. Such capabilities are often used in the creation of original logos or attention-grabbing headings. The words that make up graphics text are coded only as a pattern of shapes and not as the identifiable letters represented by ASCII or Unicode. In effect, the computer cannot "read" or process these images as words. For this reason, operations such as spell checking or search and replace are not applied to graphics text.

Graphics text allows developers to apply their artistic talents to words. The result is often an original, engaging word-picture. There is also another important use of graphics text. As noted previously, one of the challenges of computer text is ensuring that users have the appropriate fonts installed on their computers. If text is presented as a graphic, this problem disappears. Because graphics text is simply a picture, virtually any computer will be able to display it, and it will appear exactly as the designer intended it. For this reason, developers sometimes convert the editable text in their applications to a graphics text format.

Text and Sound

Just as the flexibility of text has been enhanced by its associations with graphics, so, too, has the use of text benefited by its newly developed connections to sound. The interconnection of text and sound takes two principal forms: speech recognition and speech synthesis.

In **speech recognition**, specialized software analyzes the sound patterns of human speech to identify individual words. These can then be converted into the corresponding text and displayed on screen as if the user had typed the words. Programs such as Dragon's NaturallySpeaking allow users to speak the text they would like to write into a microphone connected to the computer. The success of such programs depends upon techniques developed in another area of computer science, artificial intelligence. Speech recognition continues to improve, but because of the variations between speakers' voices, speech recognition programs sometimes require adjustments such as carefully separating words with pauses or "training" the system to respond correctly by speaking particular words or phrases to it.

In **speech synthesis**, text is given voice. Specialized software is used to analyze text for the distinctive elements of speech sounds that comprise spoken language. Speech synthesis has been extensively developed. Printed texts are "read" to the blind. Directory assistance is automated, as are a wide range of telephone ordering and marketing systems. Text to Speech (TTS) capabilities provided in OS X and Windows can synthesize speech from any selected text as well as read system alerts. Users can select a variety of voices and speech rates. Both Windows and OS X also support speech recognition. Users can directly control certain computer operations by voice commands such as "Switch to Microsoft Word" or "Get my mail."

Text and Interactivity: Hypertext and Hypermedia

The terms "hypertext" and "hypermedia" were first proposed by Ted Nelson in 1963 to describe new ways of representing and accessing information. Nelson's vision was powerfully extended and given practical implementation in the 1980s with Tim Berners-Lee's development of the elements of the World Wide Web.

Hypertext is linked text, text that leads to other text. The linkages may be very simple and direct, as in words linked to definitions—clicking on "mitosis" leads a user to a definition of that term, for example. Linkages may also be more sophisticated and complex. The Help functions in many applications provide hyperlinks based on different criteria such as content lists or an index. Searching for a particular topic may return a list of links ranked according to relevance.

The content items joined through hypertext are referred to as **nodes**. The point of departure in a hypertext link is called a **link anchor**. Clicking on the anchor leads to the related information, or node. **Link markers** indicate links. Underlined blue text is a common link marker on the Web, although linking has become so common that virtually any distinguishing text feature can now be used as a marker.

The development of the multimedia computer transformed hypertext into hypermedia. **Hypermedia** is an information structure in which a variety of media are used as nodes or link markers. Words, for instance, might be linked to illustrative graphics or to a sound file providing a pronunciation. Similarly a picture might be linked to a text description.

Hypermedia fulfills many of the dreams of Vannevar Bush and other early multimedia theorists. It provides readily accessible, powerful tools for storing, organizing, and accessing information. It dissolves disciplinary boundaries, promotes multi-sensory understanding, and engages its audience in ways never before possible.

Like any new mode of communication, hypermedia has been applied to the wide range of human needs and interests. Tim Berners-Lee's vision of improving scientific research through a web of readily exchanged multimedia resources is one use. Lecture presentations, tutorials, interactive texts, and simulations are among the educational applications of hypermedia. Advertising, shopping, political campaigning, and the many facets of entertainment (from video games to books, film, radio, and television) have all been affected by hypermedia.

HTML and XHTML

HTML, or Hypertext Mark-up Language, is a standard for the display of text and other media through browser software. A **browser** (such as Safari, FireFox, or Microsoft Internet Explorer) is a program running on the *client* (user's) computer that displays information received via a network from another computer that acts as a *server*. As its name suggests, HTML also provides for hyperlinking.

HTML encloses the information to be displayed between "tags" that specify the structure of the document and the formatting of text or other media elements. For instance, the following HTML coding causes the browser to display "This Month's Specials" as a large red heading: <h3><font color="#ff0000"> This Month's Specials </font></h3>. HTML provides only limited control of the appearance of text. While developers can specify a desired font in HTML, if the font is not available on the client machine, a substitution will be made. In addition, the formatting of text (that is, line lengths and spacing) is difficult to preserve in HTML. This means that text may not be displayed on a user's machine in exactly the way a developer intended.

Cascading Style Sheets (CSS) are an addition to HTML that makes it easier for developers to preserve consistency in the appearance of text. Like HTML, style sheets are text files that provide instructions to a browser as to how to draw a page. When used in conjunction with HTML, the style sheet specifies the *appearance* of the web page, while HTML specifies page *structure*. Instead of including coding for font color directly using HTML, the developer specifies this property for a category of text (such as a main heading) in the style sheet. HTML is used to specify paragraphs, tables, images, and other structural elements of the page. Changing the font, size or style of text on the site can then be easily accomplished by simply changing the style sheet, rather than editing each of the many tags that would otherwise appear in the HTML code. Style sheets also make it simpler for organizations to maintain a consistent appearance across a wide range of web pages.

Style sheets are an integral component of the successor to HTML, XHTML. **XHTML**, eXtensible Hypertext Markup Language, is a blending of HTML with XML (eXtensible Markup Language). **XML** is a *metalanguage*, a set of specifications or rules for creating other languages. The metalanguage allows developers to create more specialized languages for the specific needs of their field or project. Such languages can then be used in browsers that support the XML specifications. XML supports powerful data manipulation options that are useful for searching, sorting, and delivering data from various sources such as spreadsheets, databases, or content delivered from other websites. XHTML has the advantage of supporting user-defined tags that can improve page displays on computers or adapt to new mobile devices for Web access such as PDAs and cell phones. XHTML has replaced HTML as websites incorporate more sophisticated uses of data and as greater numbers of users access the Internet with small, portable devices.

PDF

It is often important to maintain the original formatting of documents delivered via networks. Business and government forms, for example, are difficult to use if the browser alters the original typefaces, spacing, and placement of graphics. Other text documents may be carefully designed to convey a particular mood or style, features that may not survive HTML display.

PDF, or Portable Document Format, was developed by Adobe Systems to preserve the original formatting of text documents. PDF documents are both platform and application-independent. They will maintain the same appearance whether they are displayed on a Macintosh, Windows, or Unix computer regardless of the program used to create the original files.

PDF supports multiple media and a range of user interactions. These include:

- Sound
- Animation
- Video
- Hyperlinks
- Speakable files for the visually impaired
- Copy/paste prohibitions

With its wide range of features, PDF quickly became a standard for electronic document exchange.

Two different forms of software are required for the creation and use of PDF documents. The *Acrobat* program, offered for sale by Adobe, is used to translate documents to the PDF format, add hypermedia features such as sound and interactivity, and implement options such as password protection and digital signatures. The translation process produces a file that can contain text in editable format, fonts from the original document, vector graphics, and bitmapped graphics. The locations of these elements on a page are encoded and compression is applied to graphics. The result is a file that preserves the original formatting of all page elements and also supports text searches and editing. PDF converters can also be found within popular word processors and as shareware utility programs.

A second program, *Acrobat Reader*, makes it possible to open and use any PDF document. Acrobat Reader is available for different operating systems including Macintosh, DOS, Windows, and Unix, and is distributed free of charge by Adobe.

5.5 Adding Text to a Multimedia Application

An *authoring program* is the software used to integrate individual media (text, sound, graphics, video, animation) and build the user interface (menus, hyperlinks, video controllers, etc.). Authoring applications such as Director, Authorware, or PowerPoint provide several ways for developers to incorporate text. These include direct entry, copy and paste, and file importing.

Direct Entry of Text

In direct entry, the developer simply types the desired text in the authoring program. Editable text is generally typed into an area defined for this purpose, a *text box* or *text field*. Text boxes or fields may have different properties depending upon the authoring program and the purpose of the application being developed. Some may be intended simply to display text information to the user. Others provide areas for users to enter information of their own such as responses to questions or search queries. Graphics text is often simply typed onto any area of the screen and then positioned or further manipulated by rotating, stretching, filling with color and so on, like any other graphic.

Copy and Paste

Copy and paste allows developers to select text from another source, copy it to the computer's "clipboard," and paste it directly into their project. Copy and paste is an essential, time-saving tool for the multimedia developer that is used not only for text, but also for all media.

File Import

Finally, text can be entered by file import. In this case the text to be incorporated already exists as a file, having been previously typed, scanned, or converted from speech. The authoring application will typically provide a dialogue box in which the developer selects the file to be imported. File import is particularly useful for larger amounts of text since it is much faster than re-entering text and more direct than copy and paste.

Scanning and OCR

Developers often need to incorporate text that exists only in its traditional format, the printed page. Scanning and optical character recognition (OCR) produce a computer text file from printed sources.

Scanning text for use in multimedia applications is a three-stage process. First, the text is scanned using one of several different types of devices (hand scanner, flatbed scanner, etc.). In this process light and photoreceptors are used to produce, in effect, a picture of the page. Like the graphics text described above, the scan only records the shapes that make up the text and not the identity of the individual characters.

In the second stage, specialized software is used to identify the characters represented by the scanned shapes. This is called **optical character recognition**, or **OCR**. The accuracy of OCR varies because, with so many different typefaces available, significantly different shapes may represent a particular letter, number, or symbol. In addition, imperfections on the printed page complicate accurate character recognition. OCR programs have continually improved and the best among them correctly identify a high percentage of characters. Some mistakes are nearly inevitable, however. This leads to the final stage of the process, proofing the text file produced by OCR.

Proofing is usually expedited by first using a spell-checker on the text file. Characters that have been misidentified (a "t" for an "i," for instance) will often show up as spelling errors. Spell-checkers will not catch all errors, however. Scanned files should always be carefully proofread.

5.6 Guidelines for the Use of Text

The effective use of text in multimedia applications is governed by the principles of good writing in general. Readers appreciate carefully crafted words whether they find them on screen or on paper. Conversely, poor word choices, spelling mistakes, and grammar errors rapidly undermine user confidence in the content of a multimedia application.

Multimedia also raises writing challenges and opportunities of its own. Some of the more important of these are addressed in the following guidelines.

1. **Be selective.** Use text where it conveys information more effectively than other media:
   - To present facts and abstract concepts
   - To label unfamiliar icons
   - To solicit or respond to user input
2. **Be brief.** Reading large amounts of text on a computer screen soon tires the user.
   - Eliminate unnecessary words.
   - Choose words carefully. Strive for precision and economy.
   - Break text into short, logical segments.
   - Use bullets.
3. **Make text readable.**
   - Preserve open space. Don't crowd the screen with too much text.

- Test fonts for legibility.
- Use anti-aliased text for a cleaner, more professional appearance.
- Match fonts to backgrounds:
  - Choose font/background colors carefully—for instance, red on black is much harder to read than yellow on black.
  - Avoid small fonts on textured backgrounds—the texture will obscure letter shapes.
- Adjust tracking and leading when changing line length.
- Limit the number of fonts. Too many fonts ("ransom note typography") will distract the user.

4. **Be consistent.**
   - Maintain a tone to match the purpose of the application: professional, formal, casual, or humorous.
   - Use the same fonts for each of the major categories of text: page headings, menus, body-text, buttons, etc. Font consistency helps to orient users.
   - Vary font size to reflect the relative importance of information.
   - Use a grid to consistently locate different types of text (headings, body text, navigation aids, text entry boxes).

5. **Be careful.**
   - Proofread. Spelling and grammatical errors quickly undermine your credibility.
   - Avoid plagiarism. Identify and credit your text sources.
   - Check for font availability on playback systems.
   - Check for font compatibility on cross-platform applications.

6. **Be respectful.**
   - Avoid stereotypes and disparaging usages (that is, racist or sexist language).
   - Use humor with care. What is funny to one person may be offensive to another.
   - Limit the use of animated text and "word art." These can easily become distractions, shifting the user's focus away from the meaning or message of the text.

7. **Combine text with other media.** Use sound, graphics, video, or animation to reinforce, explain, or extend the text message. For instance:
   - Spoken word pronunciation
   - Animation of a physical process (cell-division, nuclear fission)

8. **Make text interactive.** Much of the power of multimedia derives from interactivity. Try to engage users with text.
   - Solicit user input.
   - Use hyperlinks to tie words to related information.
   - Use mouse-overs:
     - to display definitions of unfamiliar terms
     - to pose a question
     - to make a comment

5.7 Summary

Often considered the least glamorous of the various media, text is nonetheless an important element in many multimedia applications. Text is often the most efficient communication medium and it is essential for the presentation of abstract ideas and theories. Well-crafted words can also be powerfully engaging and provocative.

Multimedia text is built on a long-standing text tradition and on the powerful editing tools of computer-generated text, but it has also made its own contributions to the expanding uses of the written word. These include many dynamic elements. Multimedia text can be animated, morphed, linked to any other medium, and automatically generated from speech. Like all written communication, multimedia text should be clear, grammatically correct, and delivered in a style appropriate to its audience.

Text is effectively combined with other media through a variety of resources including HTML and XHTML for web pages, PDF files for consistent delivery of highly formatted multimedia documents, and a wide range of authoring programs. Scanning and file import complement direct entry techniques to expedite the inclusion of text in multimedia applications.

Key Terms

Alignment
Anti-aliasing
ASCII
Bitmapped fonts
Browser
Case
Condensed text
Editable text
Extended text
Font
Font technologies
Graphics text
HTML
Hypermedia
Hypertext
Jaggies
Justification
Kerning
Leading
Link anchor

Link markers
Monospaced font
Nodes
OCR
Outline fonts
PDF
Point
Proportional font
RTF
Sans serif
Serif
Speech recognition
Speech synthesis
Style
Tracking
Typeface
Unicode
Weight
XHTML
XML

References

Unicode. Unicode 3.0. http://www.unicode.org/book/uc20ch1.html. (accessed March 10, 2006).

Review Questions

1. What are the main text properties derived from the print industry?
2. What are the two main font technologies?
3. Identify an advantage and disadvantage for each of the two main font technologies.
4. What is the process of "anti-aliasing"?
5. What is a benefit of graphics text?
6. What is one limitation of graphics text?
7. What is the main distinction between ASCII and RTF text files?
8. When should a person save a file created in Word as an RTF file?
9. What is hypertext?
10. What is one benefit and one limitation of OCR text input?
11. What are two advantages of PDF files?
12. What is the problem of "installed fonts"? How can multimedia developers resolve this problem?
13. What are two advantages of XHTML?
14. Identify and define the two principal uses of combining text and speech.
15. What are four methods to add text into a multimedia authoring application?

Discussion Questions

1. The characteristics of typography have their origins in the manual print industry. Identify and explain three features of typography that began in the print trade.
2. When should you consider using graphics text in a multimedia application? Why?
3. Locate and print the first page of your campus website. Circle two examples of graphics text and highlight two examples of editable text. Explain why these specific text elements were presented as graphics or editable text.
4. As the text editor of a multimedia tutorial, explain why you will only accept file formats that are .rtf.
5. As the text editor of a multimedia book, why will you convert your final chapters to a .pdf format?
6. Provide three guidelines you would follow to create the text-based content in a PowerPoint multimedia kiosk to announce your campus events.

Color Plate 1 Image sampling produces a grid of pixels. This section of the deer's eye is enlarged 1200%.

Color Plate 2 Quantization. 24-bit v. 2-bit sample resolution.

Color Plate 3 Spatial resolution. 300ppi (left) v. 50ppi (right).

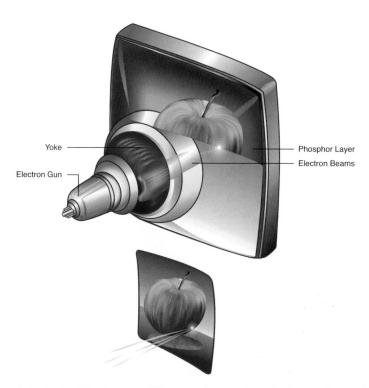

Yoke

Electron Gun

Phosphor Layer

Electron Beams

Color Plate 4 Raster scan CRT creates images through electron beams that illuminate a phosphor coating on the back of the monitor screen. RGB color monitors have three beams to illuminate red, green, and blue phosphors.

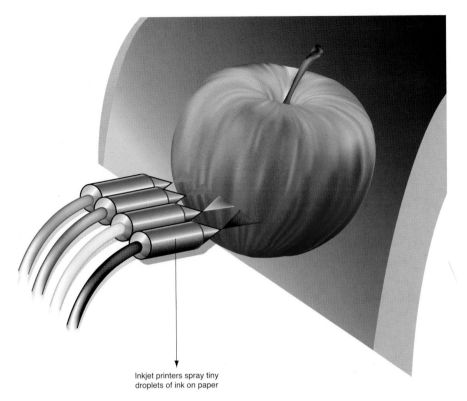

Inkjet printers spray tiny
droplets of ink on paper

Color Plate 5 Inkjet printers spray dots of colored ink to form an image.

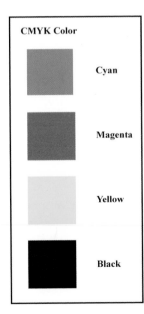

CMYK Color

Cyan

Magenta

Yellow

Black

Color Plate 6 CMYK color.

Color Plate 7 Ancient mosaic (Ephesus).

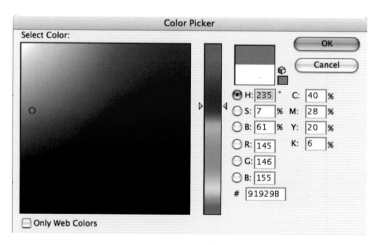

Color Plate 8 Color picker with HSB, RGB, and CMYK color models (Photoshop).

Color Plate 9 An image at 200 ppi.

Color Plate 10 The same image at 50 ppi.

Color Plate 11 Stretching the bounding box of a bitmapped graphic degrades the image quality.

Color Plate 12 Quantization may produce color banding.

Color Plate 13 Venice canal—24 bit.

Color Plate 14 Venice canal—3 bit.

Color Plate 15 Autotracing a bitmapped image (top) can reduce the file size and create interesting artistic effects (bottom).

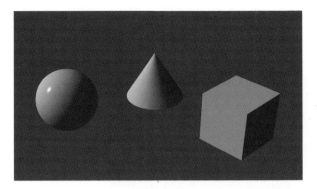

Color Plate 16 Primitives.

Color Plate 17 Boolean CSG: Union (top), Difference (center), Intersection (bottom).

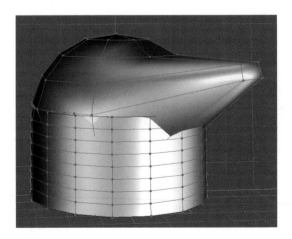

Color Plate 18 Polygon object.

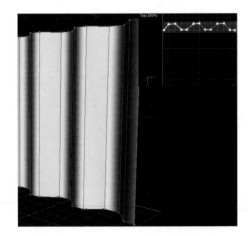

Color Plate 19 Extrusion. A line (top right) extruded lengthwise to produce a curtain.

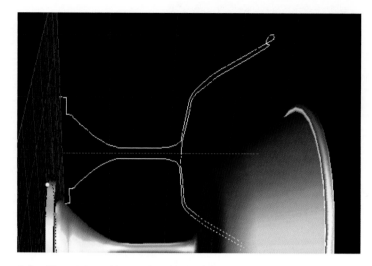

Color Plate 20 Lathing. A bowl lathed from a 2-D line.

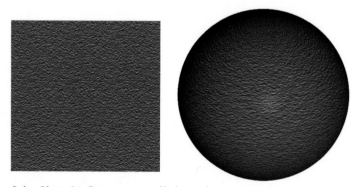

Color Plate 21 Bump map applied to sphere.

Color Plate 22 Rendering options: wire frame (top), smooth shading (middle) and ray tracing (bottom).

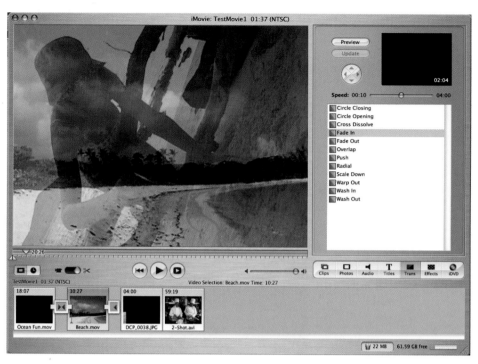

Color Plate 23 A dissolve in i-Movie. The beach scene in the background is gradually replaced by the close up of the girl.

Color Plate 24 A radial wipe in i-Movie. As the line sweeps the image, the wide shot of the beach replaces the close up of the crab.

Color Plate 25 The fog effect in i-Movie.

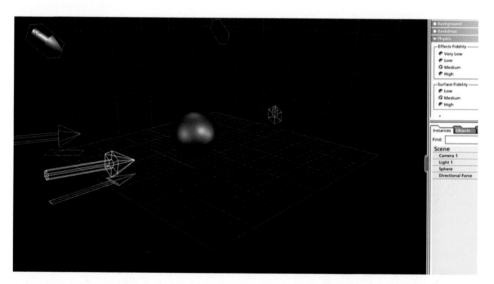

Color Plate 26 Applying a force in Carrara. The arrow indicates the direction of the force. The object automatically follows a trajectory based on its properties and the force.

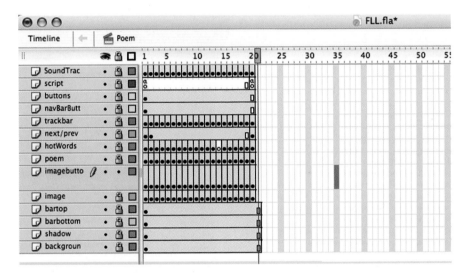

Color Plate 27 This timeline from Flash shows media organized in frames. Frame 1 is one instance of the display sequence. Each frame has 14 layers. Two layers have a special purpose: one layer contains program code to control the playback sequence and the top layer contains sound tracks synchronized to each frame. The playhead, the rectangle at the top, is currently on frame 21.

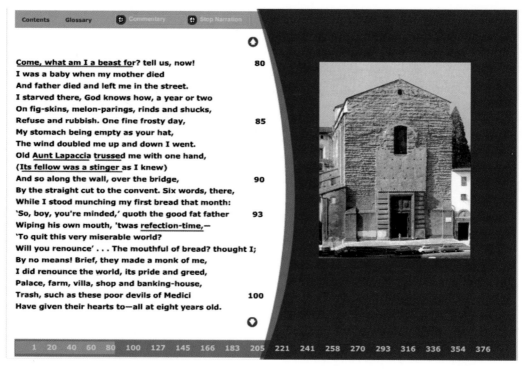

Come, what am I a beast for? tell us, now!   80
I was a baby when my mother died
And father died and left me in the street.
I starved there, God knows how, a year or two
On fig-skins, melon-parings, rinds and shucks,
Refuse and rubbish. One fine frosty day,   85
My stomach being empty as your hat,
The wind doubled me up and down I went.
Old Aunt Lapaccia trussed me with one hand,
(Its fellow was a stinger as I knew)
And so along the wall, over the bridge,   90
By the straight cut to the convent. Six words, there,
While I stood munching my first bread that month:
'So, boy, you're minded,' quoth the good fat father   93
Wiping his own mouth, 'twas refection-time,—
'To quit this very miserable world?
Will you renounce' . . . The mouthful of bread? thought I;
By no means! Brief, they made a monk of me,
I did renounce the world, its pride and greed,
Palace, farm, villa, shop and banking-house,
Trash, such as these poor devils of Medici   100
Have given their hearts to—all at eight years old.

1 20 40 60 80 100 127 145 166 183 205 221 241 258 270 293 316 336 354 376

Color Plate 28 A production screen—All media and functions complete (Exploring *Fra Lippo Lippi*).

Chapter 6

Graphics

Topics you will explore include:

- Traditional Graphics
  - Contone and Line Art
  - Image Reproduction
  - CMYK Color
- Computer Graphics
  - Bitmapped Graphics
    - Spatial Resolution
    - Color Resolution
    - Types of Bitmapped Graphics
    - Sources of Bitmapped Graphics
  - Vector-Drawn Images
    - Draw Shapes and Layers
    - AutoTracing
  - Comparing Bitmapped and Vector Graphics
- 3-D Graphics
  - Modeling
  - Surface Definition
  - Scene Composition
  - Rendering
- Guidelines for Using Graphics

In multimedia development, the term *graphics* covers a wide range of pictorial representations from simple line drawings to blueprints, charts, graphs, logos, paintings, photos, and the individual frames of animations and movies. Graphics were the first of the nontext media to be effectively processed by computers. The GUI or "graphical user interface" and early paint and draw programs transformed computers into multimedia machines.

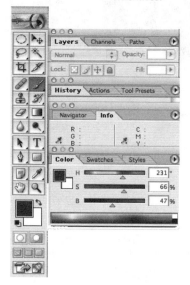

Figure 6.1 Photoshop tools.

Once images were represented digitally, computers were able to carry out many of the traditional tasks of artists and graphic designers. Graphics could be created using digital versions of tools such as paintbrushes, spray guns, image masks, and Bezier curves. They could be copied, cropped, rotated, skewed, and otherwise modified. More complex modifications such as blurring and sharpening images, applying gradient fills or embossing, could be carried out much more rapidly with computers than with traditional technology (Figure 6.1).

The arrival of multimedia authoring applications provided new uses for graphics. An image could now be a button and buttons could be linked to text, other images, sounds, or video. Animated graphics could attract attention. Pie charts, diagrams, maps, and other images could be linked to text for ready illustration of facts and ideas. Graphics facilitate navigation, stimulate interest, and convey information. They are an essential component of nearly every multimedia application.

The use of computer images also poses a number of challenges. Digital image files are often very large, slowing downloads and processing. Sometimes they are noticeably inferior to their traditional counterparts. The variety of file formats in use leads to compatibility problems. Images display differently on different monitors and printed versions often vary even more, sometimes emerging in different colors and sizes.

Multimedia developers routinely navigate between the worlds of traditional graphics and the newer digital formats. They scan images from photos or printed media and they sometimes also need to convert their digital images to formats suitable for printing. Performing these tasks efficiently and effectively requires an understanding of basic features of traditional graphics as well as mastery of current digital techniques.

In this chapter we briefly review some key features of traditional graphics and discuss the major varieties of digital images. After completing this chapter you should understand:

- Key elements of traditional print graphics such as contones, line art, linescreen, and CMYK color
- Features, uses, and development considerations for bitmapped graphics including spatial resolution, color resolution, device dependence, indexing, dithering, and file formats
- Features, uses, and development considerations for vector-drawn graphics including vectors, layers, grouping, device independence, and autotracing
- Essentials of 3-D graphics such as modeling, surface definition, scene composition, and rendering
- Basic guidelines for the use of graphics in multimedia applications

6.1 Traditional Graphics

There are several traditional graphics concepts that are important for multimedia developers. These include image types (contones, line art) and basic aspects of the process of reproducing images (linescreen, halftones, CMYK color).

Contones and Line Art

A **contone** is an image that is composed of continuously varying shades of color. A traditional black and white photo, for instance, is a contone image made up of continuously varying shades from white, to grays, to black (Figure 6.2). In computer graphics, these are called **grayscale** images.

Another technique for producing images is line art. In **line art**, combinations of lines are used to create images. Since each line is distinct, line art is not continuous tone. Line art uses only two colors. These are usually black and white, though other combinations may be used (for example blue on yellow). The terms *one-bit* and *bitmap* are often used for line art in computer graphics (Figure 6.3).

Figure 6.2 A contone image.

Image Reproduction

There are several traditional techniques for reproducing images. Sometimes copies are made using the same technology that produced the original: a painter copies an original masterpiece; another photographic print is made from an original negative. These methods can produce high-quality reproductions but they are not suitable for making copies for mass distribution. To reproduce paintings, photos, drawings, and other graphic works in books, magazines, and newspapers, another strategy is needed.

Making a negative image of the drawing, as in a woodcut, is one way of reproducing line art. The wood block is then inked and pressed to a paper surface. Creating the block is time consuming and a new woodcut is needed for each new image. A more flexible approach uses lines of very small dots to reproduce the image. These are then rearranged to reproduce other line art images. This is the technique used by printing presses—images are made up of dots of ink. Large dots produce a coarser copy with less detail; small dots preserve more of the original image.

Figure 6.3 Line art.

The size of the dots making up an image is indicated by the *linescreen* or lines per inch (lpi) used in the printing press. Newspaper presses use larger dots, for instance 85 per inch (an 85 line screen, or 85 lpi). Higher quality magazines use smaller dots, resulting in linescreens of 150 lpi or more.

Contone images can also be reproduced with dots of ink. The various shades of gray in a printed black and white photo use dots of black on a white background.

Figure 6.4 Halftone image. Grays are made from dots of black and white.

Concentrating the dots produces darker grays, wider spacing results in lighter tones. These images are called **halftones** because only half of the original tone is used to print the image—black/white, no grays (Figure 6.4).

The black dots making up these images are not necessarily the same size. Larger dots may be used for darker areas. The shape and pattern of dots is also often varied—dots may be round or elliptical and may be arranged as lines or crosses, for instance. The particular pattern used is called the *halftone screen* (Figure 6.5).

The various sizes and patterns of the dots used in printing can be seen using a magnifying glass and may be apparent to the naked eye in lower linescreens such as news-

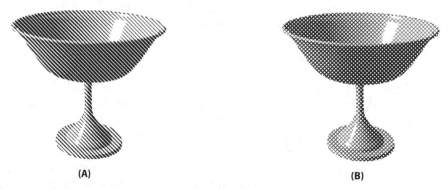

        (A)   **(B)**

Figure 6.5 (A) Halftone—Line shape (35 lpi); (B) Halftone—Cross shape (35 lpi).

papers. One reason that a basic knowledge of linescreens is important to multimedia developers is that scanners can also detect these patterns. This sometimes results in distortions in scans made of printed images.

CMYK Color

Color contone images are also printed with dots of ink, but in this case more than two colors are used. In the common "four-color" printing process dots of four different transparent inks are combined to reproduce the various colors of the original. The colors used are cyan, magenta, yellow, and a key color, which is usually black. This is so-called **CMYK** color (Figure 6.6). Very small dots of the correct combinations of these few pigments can reproduce many different colors. (Equal amounts of cyan and magenta, for instance, will produce a blue.)

Color is created on printed surfaces through a **subtractive** process—light from an independent source (the sun, incandescent or fluorescent light, etc.) is reflected from the surface. The pigments used to form the image absorb (or *subtract*) some of the colors from the white light. The remaining colors reach the eyes to produce the image.

The color on computer monitors, by contrast, is **additive**—color is produced by adding together varying amounts of red, green, and blue light. Developers of computer graphics often have to convert from the RGB (Red, Green, Blue) format used on monitors to CMYK when their images need to be professionally printed. Many graphics programs can convert between the two color models but the match may not be exact. One reason for this is that the two approaches use fundamentally different forms of color production. Computer monitor color is additive; printed color is subtractive.

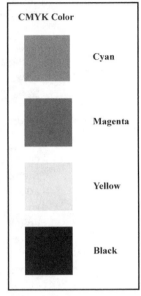

Figure 6.6 CMYK color. See Color Plate 6.

6.2 2-D Computer Graphics

Computers create either 2-D (width and height) or 3-D images (width, height, and depth). There are two main types of 2-D computer graphics: *bitmapped* and *vector-drawn*.

The bitmapped approach is particularly well suited for images with fine detail, such as paintings or photographs. Vector drawing is used for graphic designs ranging from simple drawings and logos to sophisticated artistic creations (Figure 6.7).

Bitmapped Graphics

A bitmapped graphic is very similar to a traditional mosaic. A *mosaic* is an image made up of many small, colored elements such as pieces of stone, tile, or glass (Figure 6.8). The overall image is a blend of each colored element.

Bitmapped images are also created as a pattern of discrete elements. The elements in this case are called **pixels** or "picture elements." Pixels are usually defined as small squares. Each pixel is assigned a code that designates its

Figure 6.7 Vector graphic (Adobe Illustrator sample file).

Figure 6.8 Ancient mosaic (Ephesus). See Color Plate 7.

color. The number of bits used in the code determines the number of different colors that can appear in the image. One bit allows any two colors to be represented. Each additional bit doubles the number of colors: two bits broaden the color range to 4, and so on. The location and color of each pixel is recorded in a rectangular grid of rows and columns called a *matrix* or *array*. The array is a mapping of the locations and colors of the pixels that comprise the image, or a **bitmapping**.

Types of Bitmapped Images

There are three major types of bitmapped images: line art, grayscale, and color.

> The term "bitmap" is misleading since one-bit images are only one kind of bit-mapped graphics—but the term is also well entrenched in the computer industry.

Line Art   As in traditional printing, computer-generated line art is produced using just two colors, usually black and white. For each pixel of the image only a single bit is required—for instance, 0 for black or 1 for white. Since only one bit is used, line art images are also often called **bitmaps**.

Line art provides crisp, clear images and is useful whenever the sharp division between black and white is appropriate. Diagrams, charts, handwritten signatures, and pen and ink illustrations are often represented in bitmap mode. Images that use color or shades of gray can also be converted to bitmaps when a reproduction that reduces the image to simple lines is desired. In these cases darker colors or shades of gray are represented as black with lighter shades all converted to white. Graphics programs allow users to specify the threshold at which a shade will be converted to black or white. Another important advantage of line art is its relatively small file size.

Figure 6.9 A grayscale image.

Grayscale Images   Grayscale images are composed of black, white, and different shades of gray (Figure 6.9). These are the so-called "black and white" images of traditional graphics. Computer grayscales are generally 8-bit images. This makes possible 256 gradations of shading, enough for excellent digital versions of black and white photos. Grayscale is also effective in representing the variations of shading in many drawn and printed non-color images.

Grayscale versions of pure black and white line drawings, on the other hand, are often less clear than line art would be. The incorporation of slight shifts away from pure black or white tends to make the edges of the lines somewhat blurry in grayscale images.

Color Bitmapped Images Bitmapped color images consist of patterns of colored pixels. The number of colors that can be used depends on the bit depth of the graphic. As previously noted, a one-bit image can produce black and white line art images. One bit may also be used to designate two other colors—red and blue, for instance. The most common bit depths for color images are 8-bit (256 colors) and 24-bit (16.7 million colors). If the range of color in an image is limited, 8-bit images are often adequate. For photo-realistic results, however, 24-bit color is usually required.

A **color palette** is a set of specific colors available to the computer at any given time. Just as painters can choose to place different colors on their palettes for different paintings, so too can computer artists designate different palettes for their digital images. Specifying a palette (sometimes also called a *CLUT*, or Color Look-Up Table) of 256 (2^8) selected colors produces eight-bit color. Macintosh and PC computers use different 8-bit palettes. As a result, images displayed on monitors using 8-bit color may differ on the two types of machines. The "web-safe" palette is made up of a selection of colors that are common to these two types of computers. Images that are created using this specialized palette will appear more or less the same on both platforms. This is a significant advantage for developers of web-based applications.

Twenty-four bit color images are defined by a different technique. Computers display color by combining different amounts of red, green, or blue light. Most 24-bit color encodings assign eight bits to each of the three color channels, telling the computer how much of each type of light to blend together to produce a particular color. A value of 0 for each channel produces black. The maximum value (255) for each channel produces an intense white (equal amounts at lower values produce various shades of gray). Other values produce all the colors in-between. For instance, values of 255 for red and green and 0 for blue, produces a bright yellow. The result is 16.7 million possible colors (256 × 256 × 256). Higher bit depths are also used. Thirty-two bit color makes another 8-bit channel available for additional image properties such as transparency or special effects. Forty-eight bit color assigns 16 bits to each of the three channels. This produces a possible range of over 281 trillion different colors, permitting more accurate sampling and color reproduction by scanners and cameras.

HSB Color

Color can also be defined by hue, saturation, and brightness. This is the HSB color model.

Hue is spectral color. Hue is specified by degrees beginning with reds (0 degrees) and ranging through yellows, greens, blues, and violets back to reds (359 degrees).

Saturation is the strength or purity of a color. Saturation is determined by the amount of gray added to a hue. The purest color is fully saturated—it contains no gray.

Brightness is the lightness or darkness of the color. Brightness is determined by the amount of white added to a hue. More white creates a brighter color.

The HSB model allows developers to specify colors using sliders for hue, saturation, and brightness. The HSB sliders above are from Flash MX. A medium green has been specified with a hue of 124 degrees, saturation at 91% and brightness of 69%.

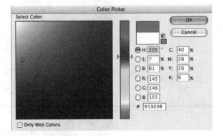

Figure 6.10 Color picker with HSB, RGB, and CMYK color models (Photoshop). See Color Plate 8.

Bitmapped graphics programs generally allow developers to choose colors by specifying values for each of the three color channels. They also often support other popular color models such as CMYK and HSB (see Figure 6.10 and "HSB Color").

Bitmapped Image Quality and File Sizes

Because bitmapped graphics files contain information about each individual pixel in the image, they are often very large. A full-screen black and white picture on an 800 × 600 resolution monitor requires 480,000 bits (800 × 600) or nearly 60 KB of information. Full fidelity color (24 bits per pixel) increases the file to 1.4 MB. The size of a multimedia application can swell rapidly as high quality graphics are added. To conserve storage and processing resources, developers often must make compromises in the quality of bitmapped graphics. Making the right choices requires an understanding of the factors that determine image quality.

The Quality of Bitmapped Images: Spatial and Color Resolution

The quality of a bitmapped image is determined by two factors: the density of the pixels, or **spatial resolution**, and the number of different colors each pixel can display, or **color resolution**.

Spatial Resolution The spatial resolution of images displayed on monitors is measured in **ppi** or pixels per inch. When the image is printed, spatial resolution is given as **dpi** or dots per inch. Scanners, digital cameras, and software for creating bitmapped images typically allow for different spatial resolution settings.

In general, higher spatial resolution captures more detail and produces sharper, more accurate images. This is because high-resolution images are made up of many very small, closely packed pixels. Lower spatial resolution uses fewer pixels, each of which must be larger than those of a high-resolution image. Since pixels can have only one color, an image with a low spatial resolution has larger areas of any given color and will capture less detail. Low spatial resolution produces images that appear fuzzy, or blurred, compared with their higher resolution counterparts (compare Figures 6.11 and 6.12).

Figure 6.11 An image at 200 ppi. See Color Plate 9.

Figure 6.12 The same image at 50 ppi. See Color Plate 10.

Although higher spatial resolution produces more detailed images, it is not always desirable to create or capture a bitmapped graphic at the highest possible ppi. One reason for this is that file sizes are larger for high-resolution images. If a lower resolution produces an acceptable image, it should generally be used to reduce the overall file size of the application. A second important consideration is that bitmapped graphics are *device-dependent*.

Spatial Resolution and Device Dependence In discussions of spatial resolution, **device-dependent** means that the dimensions at which an image is displayed depend on the spatial resolution of the output device. Computer monitors, for instance, are designed for relatively low spatial resolution, generally in the range of 72 ppi (Macintosh) to 96 ppi (PC). Printers, on the other hand, often produce output with much higher spatial resolution. A bitmapped image with a spatial resolution of 300 ppi will print in its original dimensions (for instance, 3″ × 4″) on a 300 dpi (dots per inch) printer. On a computer monitor, however, the image will be greatly enlarged. The 300 pixels in one inch of the image are spread over more than four inches of a Macintosh screen (see Figure 6.13). To display the image at its intended size we must reduce the spatial resolution to match the monitor's capabilities. In the case of a Macintosh monitor, this would mean resampling the image to a resolution of 72 ppi. The practical consequence of device-dependence is that different files are needed to produce the same size output on devices with different resolutions. Multimedia developers therefore often produce bitmapped images in several spatial resolutions to match their intended use (monitor, projector, low- or high-resolution printing, etc.).

Figure 6.13 The same image on a Macintosh screen at 72 ppi (top) and at 300 ppi (bottom).

Resampling a Bitmapped Graphic The need to produce bitmapped graphics files at different spatial resolutions often leads to **resampling**, the process of increasing or decreasing the number of samples described in the file. Popular image editing programs such as Photoshop allow users to select or deselect resampling when they alter image dimensions (see Figure 6.14). Adding samples to increase the spatial resolution of a file is known as **upsampling**. Reducing the number of samples in an image is called **downsampling**. Since each sample represents a pixel, upsampling increases the number of pixels described in the file while downsampling reduces the number of pixels.

Figure 6.14 Photoshop dialog box to select or deselect the resampling option.

Upsampling is used to enlarge the physical dimensions of an image on a given device. Figure 6.15 shows a dialog box from Photoshop in which image dimensions were increased from 2″ × 2″ to 3″ × 3″ using resampling. Since the image was enlarged, upsampling was required to produce the additional pixels. The "pixel dimensions," or number of pixels described in the file, increased from 300 to 450 while the file size increased from 88K to 198K. Upsampling is also used to maintain the original physical dimensions of an image when it is produced on another, higher resolution device. For example, an image that is displayed on a computer monitor at 2″ × 3″ will require additional pixels to be produced at the same physical dimensions on a 300 dpi printer.

Figure 6.15 Image dimension is increased from 2″ to 3″. Note the change in pixel dimension and file size.

Unfortunately, upsampling usually degrades the appearance of a graphic. In effect, the computer has to guess the color values for the additional pixels. While there are a variety of sophisticated algorithms for upsampling, the process usually produces an image that is noticeably inferior to one originally captured by a scanner or camera at the higher resolution. This is the reason that multimedia developers pay close attention to the intended use of bitmapped graphics: images that may need to be enlarged on screen or printed at high quality should always be captured or created at high spatial resolutions.

Downsampling, on the other hand, generally results in smaller images of very good quality. In this case, the computer is dropping information that is contained in the file, rather than adding new information. An image captured at a high resolution can be readily reduced to display with excellent quality at the lower resolution of a computer monitor. For instance, a developer may have a high-resolution source image from a digital camera to add to a website. Reducing spatial resolution to 72ppi with downsampling will create a new, smaller file that displays a high quality screen image at the intended dimensions. Given the advantages of downsampling over upsampling, a general rule of thumb is to capture at the highest possible spatial resolutions whenever possible.

The effects of upsampling and downsampling can also be observed on-screen when bitmapped graphics are re-sized in image editing programs. Stretching the bounding box of a bitmapped graphic forces the computer to generate more pixels to fill the larger area, degrading image quality. Reducing a bounding box dimension produces a smaller image that usually retains the quality of the original (see Figure 6.16).

Figure 6.16 Stretching the bounding box of a bitmapped graphic degrades the image quality. See Color Plate 11.

Resizing Bitmapped Graphics without Resampling   A bitmapped graphic can also be resized without resampling, that is, without changing the total number of pixels described in the file. This is usually done to change the size of a printed image without introducing the distorting effects of upsampling. The printer produces the larger image at a lower, but acceptable, resolution. There are limits to enlargement without resampling. The lower resolution printout contains the same number of pixels, which must now be physically larger to fill the expanded area of the new image. Excessive enlargement distorts images by producing a blocky, mottled surface appearance and accentuating the stair-stepped, jaggy appearance of diagonal lines (see Figure 6.17). Photoshop warns users when resizing without resampling would reduce the resolution of printed output to unacceptable levels (for instance, to less than 150 dpi). Reducing the size of a bitmapped image without resampling, on the other hand, generally produces very acceptable results. Pixels are packed more closely together, producing a high quality printout.

Resizing without resampling has no effect on an image displayed on a monitor. With no change in numbers of pixels, a computer monitor will display the image just as it did before, at exactly the same physical dimensions on screen.

Figure 6.17 Excessive enlargement distorts images by accentuating the stair-stepped appearance of diagonal lines (chair spindles).

Color Resolution   The second factor determining the quality of a bitmapped image, color resolution, is a measure of the number of different colors that can be represented by an individual pixel. As noted above, the number of bits assigned to each pixel, or **bit depth**, determines color resolution.

Simple images with a limited range of colors do not require high color resolution. A drawing using sixteen distinct colors, for example, would only require four bits per pixel. Using a code with greater bit depth produces a larger file with no increase in quality.

Other types of images, such as photographs, often contain a very wide range of distinguishable colors and do require greater color resolution. In fact, producing "photo-realistic" digital images typically requires millions of possible variations of color for each pixel.

The Effects of Low Color Resolution   Low color resolution means that fewer colors will be available. If the image being displayed contains a small number of colors, low color resolution is not a problem. Black and white line art images, for instance, can be precisely duplicated on a computer using a one-bit palette containing the colors black and white.

In many cases, however, images will contain colors not found in a lower resolution palette. Missing colors will have to be matched to the closest color available in the palette. This is called quantization.

Quantization is the process of rounding off a sample to the closest available value in the digital code being used. A grayscale image, for instance, contains shades of gray as well as black and white. If a grayscale is displayed on a computer using the lowest color resolution of one-bit, darker shades of gray will be quantized as black with lighter shades

Figure 6.18 Grayscale image (8 bit).

Figure 6.19 Image converted to a bitmap (1 bit).

becoming white. Significant image detail may be lost in the process (compare Figures 6.18 and 6.19).

Figure 6.20 Quantization may produce color banding. See Color Plate 12.

The effects of quantization in color images will vary greatly depending on the range of colors in the image and the specific color palette being used. In general, quantization leads to noticeable breaks in shades of continuous color since it is the subtle variations that are lost when values are rounded. This is known as **color banding**. In Figure 6.20, the bit depth of the lower image was reduced, resulting in bands of separate colors rather than the smooth transitions of the upper image.

In photographs, quantization often produces larger areas of a single color. This may create a "mottled" or "blotchy" effect. Figure 6.21 is a 24-bit image. With millions of possible colors to choose from, the photo captures the different shades of brick and nicely reproduces the surfaces of the plants and water. Figure 6.22 shows the effects of quanti-

Figure 6.21 Venice canal—24 bit. See Color Plate 13.

Figure 6.22 Venice canal—3 bit. See Color Plate 14.

zation. This 3-bit indexed version of the original presents the image using only 8 colors. Large areas now share a common color producing a less detailed, coarser image.

Color Resolution: Indexing and Dithering   The effects of low color resolution can often be mitigated by color indexing or by another process known as dithering.

In **color indexing** a specific palette of colors is chosen to optimize the appearance of the lower resolution image. The choice of colors for this special palette is made in several different ways. In **adaptive indexing** colors are selected based on an analysis of the dominant colors in the original. If the image contains many shades of green the indexed palette will use more greens. In another approach, **perceptual indexing**, the selection is based on the colors to which the eye is most sensitive. Another form of indexed color is the **web-safe color palette**. This palette specifies 216 colors that will be displayed more or less the same by different Web browsers and operating systems (notably Macintosh and the PC) on computers that are limited to 8-bit color. Image editing programs allow users to select different indexing options, including the number of colors in the indexed palette.

Indexing significantly improves the quality of images with lower color resolution but it can have a price. If a series of images with different optimal color palettes is displayed to a monitor, a flash of unusual colors may occur as the display shifts to the new palette. This is known as **palette flashing**. Using the same indexed palette for all images eliminates palette flashing, but some images may have less than optimum appearance.

Dithering is the process of combining pixels of different colors to produce another color that is not available. Dithering is based on the fact that the eye will perceive a grouping of small areas of different colors as a blend of those colors. For example, different shades of gray can be produced from different patterns of closely spaced black and white pixels. Combinations of red and yellow pixels can produce orange and so on. This technique is also often used in color printing. Dithering can significantly improve image quality without increasing bit depth. As in indexing, a variety of strategies for dithering are available. Dithering can be applied in regular patterns or diffused to random patterns. Developers can also control the amount of dithering applied to optimize the appearance of their images.

Color indexing and dithering are still important considerations for developers who need to reduce image file sizes to optimize the performance of their applications, particularly on the Web. Much of the original impetus for these strategies, however, was based on the limitation of earlier multimedia computers to 8-bit color. As the availability of 24-bit "true color" computers expands, concern about issues such as web-safe palettes and palette flashing will continue to diminish.

Sources of Bitmapped Images

Multimedia developers have five main sources for bitmapped images: paint programs, digital cameras, scans, clip art, and screen grabs.

Paint Programs   A **paint program** is specialized software for creating and editing bitmapped graphics. Paint applications such as Corel Painter or Adobe Photoshop include many tools built on a painting metaphor—brushes of various sizes and shapes, color palettes, paint buckets, airbrushes, and so on. Paint programs allow developers to create original art and edit existing images. In addition to tools for creating shapes, typical editing options include paint opacity (the degree of transparency), color adjustments (brightness, contrast, saturation), fill patterns (such as checkerboard, bubbles, wrinkles, etc.), gradient fills (fills with different colors blending from one to another), and special effects such as sharpen, smear, or emboss. Paint programs provide exceptional editing control by allowing users to manipulate each pixel of an image.

Since digital photographs are also bitmapped images, photo editing is a popular application of paint programs. Rotating, cropping, adjusting brightness and contrast, applying specialized effects (sharpen, blur, fill flash), and a host of other transformations can be easily previewed and carried out. The same procedures can be applied to other types of bitmapped images such as scanned objects and original digital artwork. Paint programs allow users to save bitmapped files in a variety of formats to match the intended use of the image (see the upcoming section on Bitmapped File Formats).

Digital Cameras   Digital cameras create bitmapped images by capturing information about the color and brightness of many very small samples of an image. The size of the individual picture elements, or pixels, sampled by the camera determines the camera's spatial resolution. This is usually measured in **megapixels** or millions of pixels. A 2-megapixel camera is capable of capturing an image at a spatial resolution of 1600 $\times$ 1200 pixels (1600 $\times$ 1200 = 1.92 million). Pixels are usually sampled by charge-coupled devices or "CCDs." A CCD measures the light from a segment of the image and records it as an electrical signal. This information is then digitally encoded and stored as one of the samples making up the image (see Chapter 3).

Still cameras with much higher spatial resolution are available. High-end digital studio cameras are intended for highly detailed professional work. These models support resolutions of 6000 $\times$ 7500 (45-megapixels) or more. Consumer-grade cameras in the 5- and 6-megapixel range have hastened the shift from traditional to digital photography.

As with all bitmapped images, higher spatial resolution translates to larger files. Different quality settings allow digital cameras to produce lower resolution images with smaller file sizes. This allows more images to be stored in a camera's memory. Since bitmapped files are device-dependent, the choice of the camera quality setting will be determined by the intended use of the image. Images that will be printed at high resolution or larger sizes will require higher spatial resolution than those intended for display on monitors. For instance, a 3" $\times$ 5" print at 300 dpi requires an initial spatial resolution of 900 ppi $\times$ 1500 ppi; the same size image on a Macintosh monitor requires a resolution of only 216 ppi $\times$ 360 ppi.

Cameras may include built-in memory and generally also support removable memory cards. Cards are manufactured in several different standards (Compactflash, Smartmedia, etc.) and in different capacities ranging from 32MB to 1GB or more. The images stored in a camera's built-in or removable media can be uploaded to a computer directly using interfaces such as USB or FireWire.

For a description of scanning technology and different types of scanners, see Chapter 3, Computer Hardware
For a description of the scanning process see Appendix B.

Scanning   Scanning is an important source of graphics in multimedia applications. In addition to photographs and printed images, scanners can also be used to produce digital versions of original works such as crayon sketches or paintings. Unusual designs can also be created from scans of three-dimensional objects such as coins or flowers.

Clip Art **Clip art** is "canned" artwork available on disk, online, or as part of paint or draw programs. Clip art has many advantages. It is ready to use, easily obtained, and available in many file formats. It offers a wide choice of subjects and styles and can often be distributed as part of a multimedia application at low cost. In fact, some clip art is royalty-free. Licensing agreements for clip art do vary widely, however, and developers need to review the terms of use carefully.

The principal drawback to clip art is that others have access to it as well. Extensive use of clip art makes it difficult to maintain the unique or distinctive appearance of a multimedia production.

Screen Grabs The images displayed on a computer monitor are bitmapped graphics. Both Macintosh and Windows computers can capture these screen images and save them as files that can then be used in multimedia applications.

Almost anything displayed on screen can be captured. **Screen grabs** or "screen dumps" are often used to illustrate steps or procedures in manuals or tutorials (Figure 6.23). Using paint programs, any part of the screen image can be selected and edited. The principal disadvantage of screen grabs is that they are relatively low-resolution images that do not enlarge well and are often not suitable for printing.

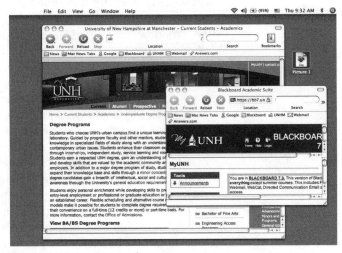

Figure 6.23 A screen grab.

Using the Mac OS:
- Press "Command-Shift-3" to capture the entire contents of the desktop. File "Picture1.png" is saved on the desktop.
- Select Finder/Services/Grab to select a portion of the screen to save as "Picture.png."

Using Windows OS:
- Press "printscreen" command to save the contents of the desktop to the clipboard.
- Open Word or image editor, paste the image to a new file. Edit and save.

Bitmapped File Formats Bitmapped file formats fall into three broad categories: native formats used by image editing programs, general-purpose bitmapped-only formats, and metafiles. *Native formats* (such as Photoshop's .psd) contain information essential to specific editing software. Generally, files in a native format cannot be used by other applications unless they are converted to a general-purpose format. *General-purpose formats* support widespread distribution either within or across platforms. Many different types of programs will be able to use these files. *Metafiles* are formats that can contain both bitmapped and vector images.

One of the most important characteristics of bitmapped graphics is relatively large file size. Many multimedia applications, particularly those intended for delivery on the Web, require significant image compression for efficient delivery. Several compressed file formats have been developed for bitmapped graphics. Some are lossy while others are lossless. **Lossy** formats discard some of the information in the original image. **Lossless** formats re-encode image information in a new, compressed form but recover all the original information on decompression.

Commonly used bitmapped and metafile formats include: PICT, BMP, TIFF, JPEG, GIF, and PNG. Developers choose among these formats based on application requirements, file compatibility with editing and authoring software, and compatibility with delivery platforms (Windows, Macintosh, etc.).

PICT—Macintosh PICTure format. PICT is a relatively old format that is widely supported by Macintosh applications. It supports different compression levels and 24-bit color depth. PICT is a metafile format: files can be either bitmapped or vector-drawn images. PICT is a flexible format, appropriate for most applications on the Macintosh platform.

BMP—Windows BitMaPped file. BMPs support 24-bit color. Compression is optional. Windows uses BMP for its screen grabs and screen background images ("wallpaper"). BMP is widely supported in Windows applications.

TIFF—Tagged Image File Format. TIFF is a very versatile cross-platform format that supports all major color modes (bitmap, grayscale, all color depths, and both RGB and CMYK). TIFF was originally designed for use with scanners. It is the format multimedia developers usually use both for scanned images and for files to be used in authoring applications. TIFFs can be compressed using a lossless compression called LZW (for the names of the developers, Lempel, Ziv, and Welch). The TIFF format is also suitable for professional printing, unlike PICT or BMP. TIFF is a good choice for the vast majority of non-web images.

JPEG—Joint Photographic Experts Group. JPEG is a cross-platform format designed to efficiently compress bitmapped images such as photographs that contain a wide range of colors. It is widely used in digital cameras and is the format of choice for photo-quality images on the Web. JPEG supports 24-bit color and interlacing. **Interlacing**, as applied to network transmission of images, is the process of progressively displaying an image: incomplete, low resolution, versions can be seen before the complete file is downloaded. This avoids having a blank screen while the download process is underway.

JPEG compression is lossy—some information is discarded and cannot be recovered. Developers can control the amount of information lost. A JPEG image can be saved without compression or with one of several different levels of compression. Saving without compression preserves all the information from the original. This is usually not advisable, however, because minimal compression produces a much smaller file with little loss of quality.

Repeatedly saving a JPEG image with compression progressively degrades the image. For this reason, developers should edit images in another file format, such as the native format of the editing software or TIFF. Only when the editing process is complete should the image be saved as a JPEG.

GIF—Graphics Interchange File. (Pronounced either "jif" or "gif" with a hard "g" as in "gift".) GIF is a cross-platform format with lossless compression. CompuServe originally created it for images transmitted over relatively slow Internet connections. The maximum color resolution for a GIF is 8-bits (256 colors). Lower bit depths can be used, further reducing file size. GIF supports interlacing, transparency, and a simple form of animation. GIF animation uses a "page-flipping" approach, rapidly displaying a series of different still images to suggest motion. GIF animations are very popular on the Web because of their low file size. GIF is a good choice for line art, grayscale, and color images with a small number of solid colors. It is not appropriate for most color photos because of its limited color resolution.

PNG—Portable Network Graphic (Pronounced "ping.") PNG is a cross-platform, lossless compression format that was created as a free replacement for GIF, which required commercial developers to pay licensing fees. PNG supports indexed color, grayscale, and true color images with resolutions up to 48-bits. PNG also supports transparency and interlacing. It does not directly support animation. PNG is a much more versatile format than GIF because of its support of high-resolution color images. Although intended primarily for web applications, PNG rivals the flexibility of TIFF and is likely to become increasingly popular with multimedia developers.

> **The RAW File Format**
>
> RAW is a bitmapped graphic format that is becoming more familiar in multimedia development. Actually, RAW is a family of formats, rather than a single standard. They are proprietary file formats used by camera manufacturers to save digital photos in a form that preserves more image information than is captured by JPEG. RAW image files are generally larger than those of other formats. They are intended for use in photo editing software where they support a wider range of editing options because they contain more information about brightness and other image properties. RAW images are converted to JPEG, TIFF, and other formats for use in multimedia applications.

6.3 Vector-Drawn Graphics

In bitmapped graphics, the computer is given a *detailed description* of an image that it then matches, pixel by pixel. In vector-drawn graphics, the computer is given a *set of commands* that it executes to draw the image.

Vectors, Shapes, and Drawn Images

A **vector** is a line with a particular length, curvature, and direction. **Vector graphics** are composed of lines that are mathematically defined to form shapes, such as rectangles, circles, and polygons. Vector-drawn images are made up of combinations of these shapes. **Draw programs** are the software used to create vector-drawn graphics. They can produce a wide range of images from simple line drawings to complex architectural renderings and original art works (Figure 6.24).

For relatively simple images, the list of drawing commands takes up much less file space than a bitmapped version of the same graphic. A draw program might use a command similar to "RECT 300, 300, RED" to create a red square with sides of 300 pixels. The file for this image contains 15 bytes that encode the alphanumeric informa-

Figure 6.24 Adobe Illustrator image with Tool and Layers palettes.

tion in the command. The same image could also be created with a paint program as a bitmapped graphic. Using 8-bit color resolution (one byte per pixel), this file would require 90,000 bytes (300 × 300). The much smaller files sizes of drawn images can be a significant advantage for multimedia developers.

Tools, Layers, and Grouping

Many of the tools used in draw programs resemble those of the traditional draftsman. These include pen tools; fixed shapes such as circles, ellipses, and rectangles; polygons; and Bezier curves. The shapes created in draw programs include anchor points called **handles**. Handles are "grabbed" and pulled to resize or reshape an object. "Hot spots," such as the corners of rectangles are used to rotate an object by clicking and dragging.

Objects are drawn on **layers**. Objects on higher layers overlap and usually cover those in lower layers. Layers make it possible to edit each object separately without affecting other components of the image. When all the objects are properly shaped, scaled, colored, and placed, they are grouped. *Grouping* objects freezes their properties by joining them together on a single, new conceptual layer. Grouped objects can then be moved or combined with other objects as a unit. *Ungrouping* returns the component objects of an image to their individual layers where each can once again be edited.

Device Independence

Draw images are **device-independent**—the same file can be used with different devices without altering the size of the image. Bitmapped images require different files for devices using different resolutions. For example, a 72 ppi file is appropriate for use on a monitor but a higher spatial resolution is preferred for printers. Draw files are commands for drawing. Different devices simply follow those commands at their own output resolutions. This preserves the original dimensions of the image.

Making Drawn Graphics from Bitmapped Images: Autotracing

Drawn graphics can also be produced from bitmapped images through autotracing. In **autotracing**, the original bitmapped image is analyzed for separate areas that can be treated as shapes. These shapes are then mathematically defined to convert the image to a vector graphic.

Autotracing is quite efficient with relatively simple bitmapped images. But if the image is complex, containing many constituent shapes and subtle shifts of color, the new vector file will not preserve the appearance of the original and may actually be larger. Judicious use of autotracing can significantly reduce file sizes and can also create interesting artistic effects (see Figure 6.25). Autotraced files are particularly useful in web-based applications where their smaller size reduces download times.

Making Bitmapped Graphics from Vector Graphics: Rasterizing

Vector graphics are readily converted to bitmapped images by a process called **rasterizing**. Rasterizing rapidly samples the vector image and saves it in bitmapped form. Vector-based editing programs such as Adobe Illustrator can perform the conversion. Vector graphics displayed on screen can also be captured as bitmaps through simple screen grabbing. Developers often create graphics in draw programs to take advantage

Figure 6.25 A & B Autotracing a bitmapped image (left) can reduce the file size and create interesting artistic effects (right). See Color Plate 15.

of strengths such as scalability and small file size and then convert them to the more widely used bitmapped format.

File Formats for Vector Graphics

Like bitmapped formats, vector graphics files fall into three categories. Native formats, such as Adobe Illustrator's .ai, support the needs of specific editing software while general-purpose formats are either vector-only or metafiles. General-purpose vector formats include: EPS, PDF, and SVG.

> **EPS**—Encapsulated Postscript. EPS is a variant of Postscript (PS) that supports page preview. EPS uses Postscript's page description language to draw vector graphics. It can also contain bitmapped information, though it is not itself a bitmapped format.
>
> **PDF**—Portable Document Format. PDF is a widely used, very versatile cross-platform file format for encoding full pages of text and graphics. PDFs can contain both bitmapped and vector images. Adobe Illustrator vector images can be saved in a form that preserves the editing capabilities of the native .ai format but, in general, PDF files support only limited editing. PDF files require Acrobat reader or a similar program to be viewed. Acrobat is free and widely distributed, making PDF a very practical distribution format.
>
> **SVG**—Scalable Vector Graphics. The newest of the general-purpose vector formats, SVG supports 2-D graphics on the Web. SVG is built on XML (eXtensible Markup Language) and supports still images, animations, and various forms of user interactivity.

6.4 Bitmapped and Vector Graphics Compared

The two major types of graphics are each optimized for particular uses. Multimedia developers choose between paint (bitmapped) or draw (vector) programs based on their knowledge of the strengths and weaknesses of each and the needs of the project. The relative advantages and disadvantages of the two approaches can be summarized as follows.

Paint Advantages:

- Accurate representation of complex contone images such as photographs
- Full-featured photo editing (sizing, cropping, tone and color adjustments, special effects, etc.)
- Wide range of artistic effects (gradient fills, smudges, blurs)
- Precision editing (can edit individual pixels)

Paint Disadvantages:

- Large file sizes
- Loss of precise shape when scaled or rotated
- Device-dependent image resolution

Draw Advantages:

- Smooth scaling and reshaping (no jaggies)
- Ease of editing objects
  - Layers
  - Grouping/ungrouping
- Low file sizes
- Device-independent image resolution

Draw Disadvantages:

- Less detailed representation of complex contone images
- No photo-editing capability
- Limited artistic control

Paint and draw programs continue to improve. In the process, software developers often find ways to incorporate the strengths of the alternative approach while limiting some of the inherent disadvantages of their own. For instance, the layers used in draw programs make editing an image much more efficient because one part can be changed without affecting others. Paint programs, such as Photoshop, have also adopted layers by including specialized information in their native file formats. Similarly, the subtle shifts of color in gradient fills were once the exclusive purview of paint programs. This capability has now been added to many draw programs.

Despite these improvements, fundamental differences remain. A multimedia developer would not use a draw program to adjust colorcast in a photograph. And a paint program is still a poor choice for a logo that will be resized for different uses on a website or for different types of printed output such as business cards, pamphlets, or posters.

6.5 3-D Computer Graphics

3-D graphics add realism and visual impact and they are an increasingly important area of multimedia development. They are also challenging. 3-D graphic artists must visualize scenes in which objects can move in any direction, floating in a potentially infinite space. They must select a point of view and arrange objects to match it. They must think about light sources—the type of light, its intensity, location, and strength. Surfaces and their interaction with light must be defined. And all these elements have to be combined to produce the illusion of depth on the flat surface of a monitor or printed page.

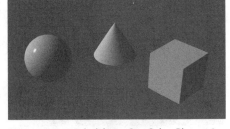

Figure 6.26 Primitives. See Color Plate 16.

3-D graphics applications are the sophisticated, powerful programs that make all this possible. In 2-D graphics, the computer is a helpful assistant. In 3-D graphics, it becomes a virtual partner in the creative process, using complex algorithms to create the finished images specified by the artist. There are four interconnected steps in the creation of 3-D images: modeling, surface definition, scene composition, and rendering.

Modeling

Modeling is the process of specifying the shape of a 3-D object. There are two major approaches to modeling. The first is to create a new object by combining simple cubes, cones, cylinders and other 3-D shapes that are supplied with the graphics program. These objects are called **primitives** (see Figure 6.26). *Parametric primitives* are objects that can be changed by specifying different parameters, such as the radius of a sphere. Parametric primitives can be scaled, rotated, moved, and combined to form a wide range of objects. In *constructive solid geometry (CSG)*, primitives are added to or subtracted from one another using Boolean operators (see Figure 6.27). Boolean *union* joins two or more objects; Boolean *difference* subtracts one from another, and Boolean *intersection* produces just the shape shared by the objects.

Figure 6.27 Boolean CSG: Union (top), Difference (center), Intersection (bottom). See Color Plate 17.

More complex forms of parametric primitives may also be provided. These include objects such as plants or trees that can be adjusted according to species, trunk angle, number and size of leaves, and so on. Environmental primitives such as clouds and fire can be similarly adjusted to produce a wide range of shapes, colors, and opacities.

The second approach to modeling is to create shapes directly using a **modeler**. Four popular 3-D modeler options are *polygons*, *splines*, *metaballs*, and *formulas*.

In **polygon modeling**, the object is defined as a pattern of straight-edged polygons, usually triangles or quadrilaterals (see Figure 6.28). To produce an image of the three-dimensional object, the computer first calculates which surfaces will be visible based on a viewing angle specified by the artist. Viewable surfaces are then divided into small polygons that define the shape of the object.

The polygon approach is similar to bitmapped two-dimensional graphics in that the object is defined by a fixed number of elements—polygons for 3-D graphics and pixels for 2-D bitmapped graphics. One advantage of polygon modeling is precise editing control: the individual lines and surfaces of polygons can be manipulated directly by

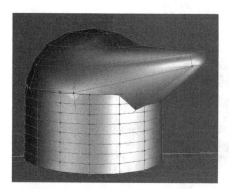

Figure 6.28 Polygon object. See Color Plate 18.

NURBs:

- Non-uniform—more easily bent in some areas than in others.
- Rational—based on mathematically defined ratios.
- B-splines—variants of Bezier curves.

the artist. The technique can also produce high-quality, realistic surfaces by increasing the number of polygons and manipulating their shapes and shading. The main disadvantages of polygon modeling are relatively large file sizes and scaling distortions. Increasing the number of polygons may produce files too large for some applications, such as 3-D game playing, in which images need to be generated in real time. And just as a bitmapped graphic deteriorates as it is enlarged, so too does a polygon model.

Spline modeling is curve-based and is similar to two-dimensional vector graphics. The term derives from *splines*, thin strips of wood or metal that can be readily bent to guide the drawing of curves. Different forms of spline modeling are available. One popular approach is the NURB. A **NURB** is a Non-Uniform Rational B-spline. Like a vector graphic, a NURB defines an image using mathematical formulas that can be adjusted to vary its size and shape. Spline modeling does not provide the precise editing control of polygons. On the other hand, this method produces smaller files and more flexible objects. A NURB-based object can be readily enlarged without the deterioration in quality associated with the polygon approach.

Metaball modeling creates objects as combinations of elements called *blobs*. Blobs are variously shaped (spheres, cubes, cylinders, etc.) and are either positive or negative. A positive blob adds its shape to the object, a negative blob subtracts its shape. Building an object with metaballs is similar to working with lumps of clay. The technique is useful for creating objects with soft edges, such as cushions and organic shapes like animal bodies (see Figure 6.29).

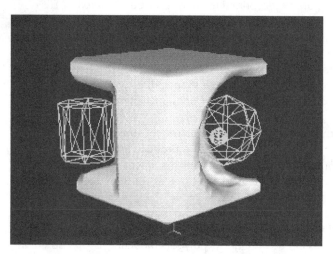

Figure 6.29 Negative metaball cylinder and sphere modifying a positive cube.

r1=8*p1;
r2=8*p2;
t=2*PI*u;
p=PI*(v-0.45);
x=r1*cos(t)*cos(p);
y=r1*sin(t)*cos(p);
z=r1*sin(p);
x=x+r2*cos(t);
y=y+r2*sin(t);

Figure 6.30 Formula model.

Formula modeling creates objects by specifying mathematical formulas that are subsequently drawn by the computer. This approach requires knowledge of programming and advanced mathematics. Formulas produce either simple or very complex objects that require very little file space and are drawn quickly by the computer (see Figure 6.30).

3-D graphics programs typically provide a choice of modelers. Developers choose a modeling method based on the type of object to be created and the way it will be used in the multimedia application. Many objects, such as buildings or furniture, are readily modeled as polygons. Others, like animal bodies or bushes, are better represented using spline curves or metaballs. Sometimes the type of application (interactive game vs. static image) or delivery considerations (web or DVD) favors one modeler over another. Spline and formula objects typically have smaller files and can be rapidly drawn. They are often used for games or web applications.

A modeler may also be chosen for its ability to extrude or lathe. **Extrusion** is the process of extending a 2-D shape through space to create a three-dimensional object. For a simple illustration of extrusion, think of a two-dimensional rectangle raised in a straight path from its surface to create a three-dimensional box. Similarly, a circle can be extruded to form a cylinder. Any two-dimensional line or object can be extruded. In addition, an extrusion can be oriented to a particular view. For example, a curved line can be viewed from the top and extruded lengthwise to produce a corrugated panel or a curtain (see Figure 6.31).

Lathing is the process of creating a three-dimensional object by rotating a two-dimensional line on an axis. For example, the profile of one-half of a bowl can be rotated 360° to trace the surface of the three-dimensional object (see Figure 6.32).

Figure 6.31 Extrusion. A line (top right) extruded lengthwise to produce a curtain. See Color Plate 19.

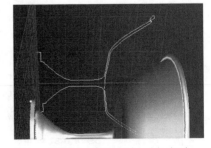

Figure 6.32 Lathing. A bowl lathed from a 2-D line. See Color Plate 20.

Surface Definition

Modeling defines the three-dimensional shape of an object but not its surface texture. In **surface definition**, developers specify textures that are then applied to the model's

surface. Surfaces can be defined according to a range of materials available as menu choices—fabric, wood, stone, glass, metal, and others. These different surfaces will vary in color, in transparency, and in the ways they reflect light. Metal surfaces, such as stainless steel, for example, may be highly reflective while glass may be only partially reflective. Graphic artists can vary the appearance of these surfaces by changing properties such as color, opacity, and reflectivity.

Custom surfaces can also be created as *image maps*: photos, drawings, or other images that are transferred or "mapped" to an object (Figure 6.33). Scanned photos, drawings produced with bitmapped or vector programs, and bump maps are some of the more popular sources for image maps. A *bump map* is a three-dimensional texture produced by varying shades of color. Lighter shades appear to be higher, while darker areas appear lower. Bump maps are readily created in image editing programs such as Photoshop. The "bumpy" surface of a basketball, for instance, can be simulated as an image map and then transferred to a sphere (Figure 6.34). Another common use of image maps is the creation

Figure 6.33 Image map (above) applied to a cup.

of labels, logos, and other designs that are then applied to the surfaces of objects such as bottles, cans, and boxes. Some programs also support the use of video as an image map, allowing animators to create realistic 3-D television or movie screens by mapping the video to previously created cabinets or walls.

Figure 6.34 Bump map applied to sphere. See Color Plate 21.

Scene Composition

In **scene composition**, objects are arranged, backgrounds are introduced, environmental effects are added, and lighting is established. Arranging objects includes situating them on the x, y, and z-axes as well as operations such as alignment, grouping, and linking that are familiar from 2-D drawing.

Much of the realism of a 3-D graphic is produced by accurately representing the interplay of light with the various objects that comprise a scene. This includes specifying the type of light, its direction, and its behavior as it interacts with the object. Types of lighting include: *omni lights* that spread light equally in all directions, like the light of the sun; *directional lights* that spread light in a specified direction; *spot lights* that focus a cone of light on a relatively small area; and *volumetric light* to represent the shafts of light from movie projectors, street lamps, and other sources. The various forms of light can usually be adjusted for properties such as brightness, color, and *attenuation*, the rate at which light intensity falls off with distance. Being able to control the color and intensity of light allows digital artists to simulate a variety of natural and artificial light sources. Lights can be located at virtually any angle and their effects—for instance, the types of shadows they cast or the way in which light is reflected or absorbed by surfaces—can also be controlled.

Rendering

Rendering is the process through which the computer creates the scenes specified by the artist. There are two main approaches to rendering: *pre-rendering* and *real-time rendering*. Pre-rendering is used for most still graphics and for animation and video with limited interactivity. Pre-rendering is discussed below. Real-time rendering is used for highly interactive 3-D applications such as video games. This is covered in Chapter 9, Animation.

Rendering is always the final step in creating a 3-D graphic but it is also a critical element in earlier stages. Artists need to be able to visualize their scenes as they place objects, plan their camera angles, add textures, and adjust lighting. They use various forms of rendering to create these test scenes (Figure 6.35).

Wire frame rendering is the simplest technique. A wire frame is a series of lines used to define the shape of an object without defining its surface. Wire frame rendering is a good choice for testing an object's basic geometry and placement because the computer can draw a wire frame model very quickly.

To test lighting effects, surfaces must be added. To create a surface, a model is usually *tessellated*, that is, broken into a pattern of polygons. Different shading algorithms, or **shaders**, may then be used to calculate the color values of the pixels making up these polygons. *Flat shaders* render an image relatively quickly but with imperfections such as jaggies. *Smooth shaders* produce a higher quality image but at the cost of slower rendering and larger file sizes. *Ray tracing* creates a more realistic surface by tracing each ray of light and calculating its path as it interacts with objects in the scene. *Radiosity* adds even more realism to a scene by recreating the changes resulting from the interaction of different wavelengths of light. When light is reflected from an object, both its path and its quality are changed. Light striking a blue object on a white surface, for example, creates a faint glow of blue in the immediate vicinity of the object. Radiosity applies mathematical formulas to calculate the effects of the thermal radiation responsible for these color transfers. Ray tracing and radiosity are computationally demanding forms of rendering. They are sometimes used to test particular scenes but are most often reserved for the final rendering process.

After scenes have been tested and refined, the final rendering process translates 3-D information to a 2-D image for use as a still graphic or as a frame in an animation or movie. 3-D graphics programs typically provide users with a variety of controls over the final rendering process. Many finished works are intended to be photorealistic but other forms of rendering that simulate painting or classic cartoons, for example, may also be available. These different rendering styles are described as *rendering engines*. Once an engine is selected, the user can control a series of rendering parameters. Important photorealistic parameters include raytracing, shadows, reflection and refraction, bumps, transparencies, and lighting effects such as indirect lighting and skylight. Users can choose to include or omit individual effects and

Figure 6.35 Rendering options: wire frame (top), smooth shading (middle) and ray tracing (bottom). See Color Plate 22.

they can specify quality settings for those that they do include. Each effect adds to the rendering process, which can easily stretch to hours for complex images. Compromises are often necessary, further reinforcing the need for test renderings of image samples.

3-D graphics is one of the most creative and challenging areas of multimedia development. In the hands of skilled artists, ever more powerful hardware and software can create convincing reproductions of the world around us. They can also produce an unending stream of engaging fantasy worlds. The uses of 3-D graphics, both as still images and as the frames of sophisticated animations, will continue to expand, making it increasingly important for developers to master the complexities of modeling, surface definition, scene composition, and rendering.

6.6 Guidelines for the Use of Graphics

Graphics are a critical element in nearly all multimedia applications. Both the development process and the final product can often be improved by observing basic graphics guidelines.

- Identify the purpose of the graphic.
  - To inform (maps, diagrams, pie charts)
  - To attract attention
  - To warn
  - To guide (navigation buttons, progress indicators, image maps)
- Choose the best format for each image.
  - Paint (bitmapped) for:
    - Complex contone images (photographs, paintings)
    - Scanned images
  - Draw (vector) for:
    - Images composed of regular shapes
    - Images to be scaled
- Match graphic design to purpose.
  - Avoid gratuitous decoration.
  - Match style to application content and audience:
    - Whimsical, artistic, sophisticated, primitive, professional
- Locate graphics. Establish a layout grid.
  - Use similar locations for graphics with similar purposes (navigation buttons, user alerts, explanatory drawings).
- Preserve image quality.
  - Store original photos, prints, and other scanned graphics carefully.
  - Avoid multiple saves in lossy compression formats (e.g., JPEG).
  - Retain copies of original, high resolution scans.
  - Keep copies of images in native file formats of editing applications (e.g., .psd).
- Economize. Use graphics efficiently.
  - Match resolution to output device.
  - Reduce sizes in image editing software, not by dragging a new size in authoring software.
- Organize graphics.
  - Maintain folders for original images, edits, and final production versions.

6.7 Summary

While most multimedia graphics are created for screen display, developers sometimes distribute images in printed form. They also often capture printed originals using scanners. For these reasons, key elements of traditional printing, such as *contones*, *line art*, *halftones*, and *CMYK color* remain important considerations for multimedia developers.

Digital graphics can be either two-dimensional or three-dimensional. There are two major types of 2-D computer graphics: *bitmapped* and *vector-drawn*. Bitmapped graphics are defined as patterns of *pixels*, or *picture elements*. They can include very fine detail and can be extensively edited. Developers pay close attention to *spatial resolution* and *color resolution* as they create bitmapped images using *paint programs*, or capture them using *scanners*, *screen grabs*, or *digital cameras*. The bitmapped approach is essential for highly detailed images such as photographs, but it also produces very large file sizes. These large files have given rise to a variety of *compression* strategies and *file formats* to match bitmapped graphics to their intended uses. Other challenges in the use of bitmapped graphics include *device-dependence* and *scaling* limitations.

Vector-drawn graphics are defined as a *set of commands* that the computer uses to produce an image for display or printing. Drawn graphics range from simple blueprints to sophisticated, naturalistic images produced by skilled illustrators. The advantages of vector-drawn images include much smaller file size, excellent scaling, and *device-independence*. Their principal disadvantage is that they do not support the detailed, pixel-level editing of bitmapped graphics and so are not suitable for photographic images.

3-D graphics take advantage of powerful computer processing to create a different type of digital image. In 2-D graphics, whether bitmapped or drawn, the artist uses digital versions of traditional tools to directly create a finished image. In 3-D graphics, the artist skillfully combines elements to specify an image that only the computer itself can produce in finished form. This new relationship between artist and computer is reflected in the multi-stage process of producing 3-D graphics: *modeling*, *surface definition*, *scene composition*, and *rendering*. 3-D graphics applications have steeper learning curves and require more powerful computers than their 2-D counterparts, but 3-D image making is advancing rapidly and is an increasingly important part of modern multimedia development.

Key Terms

Adaptive indexing	Color palette	Formula modeling
Additive color	Color resolution	GIF
Autotracing	Contone	Grayscale
Bit depth	Device-dependent	Halftone
Bitmap	Device-independent	Handles
Bitmapping	Dithering	Interlacing
BMP	Downsampling	JPEG
Clip art	Dpi	Lathing
CMYK	Draw program	Layers
Color banding	EPS	Line art
Color indexing	Extrusion	Lossless

Lossy	Pixel	Shader
Megapixel	PNG	Spatial resolution
Metaball modeling	Polygon modeling	Spline modeling
Modeler	Ppi	Subtractive color
Modeling	Primitives	Surface definition
NURB	Quantization	SVG
Paint program	Rasterize	TIFF
Palette flashing	Rendering	Upsampling
PDF	Resampling	Vector
Perceptual indexing	Scene composition	Vector graphics
PICT	Screen grab	Web-safe color palette

Review Questions

1. What is the difference between contone and line art images in traditional print graphics?
2. Why is CMYK called subtractive color?
3. Why is RGB called additive color?
4. Explain how bitmapped computer graphics are formed.
5. What are three forms of bitmapped graphics?
6. What is a color palette?
7. Why are color palettes significant considerations for developers?
8. What is spatial resolution?
9. How does spatial resolution affect the quality of a bitmapped image?
10. How does bit-depth determine color resolution?
11. How can quantization produce color banding?
12. What is color indexing? What is the benefit of using indexed colors?
13. What is dithering and how can it improve a color image?
14. Why might a developer use a series of screen grabs in an application?
15. What is the difference between lossy and lossless graphic file formats? Give an example of each.
16. How are vector graphics formed?
17. What are three major advantages of vector graphics?
18. What is autotracing? How is it related to vector images?
19. What is rasterizing? How is it related to vector images?
20. What are the benefits of a .pdf file format?
21. What is 3-D modeling?
22. How does an extrusion modeler create a shape? Give a specific example.
23. What is lathing?
24. Why is surface definition a key step in 3-D graphics?
25. What is rendering and why is it the final step in 3-D graphics?

Evaluate the following as True or False.
1. Contone images reproduced with dots of black ink are called halftones.
2. Color is created on a printed page using an additive process.
3. Vector drawing is typically used for illustrations and logos.

4. Monitor resolution of a bitmapped image is given in dots per inch.
5. Line art is produced using two or more colors.
6. A 4 bit color image can display 32 possible hues.
7. If each channel of RGB color is set to 255, the result is white.
8. Spatial resolution of bitmapped images determines the color quality of an image.
9. PPI means points per inch.
10. Higher spatial resolution results in sharper, more accurate images.
11. Quantization is likely to occur in images with high bit depth.
12. Dithering is used to produce web safe colors.
13. Paint programs provide editing control at the pixel level.
14. GIF files have greater color resolution than PNG files.
15. Draw programs produce device-independent images.
16. Polygon modeling produces large 3-D file sizes.
17. A circle can be extruded to form a sphere.
18. Custom surfaces on a 3-D object are made from NURBS.
19. Spline modeling is similar to vector graphics.
20. Real time rendering is used in highly interactive 3-D applications.

Discussion Questions

1. Identify three challenges of using images in multimedia documents and explain how each challenge is overcome.
2. Locate a copy of the Wall Street Journal in your library and magnify an image of one of their writers. Based on your understanding of contone image reproduction, explain how that image is constructed.
3. Identify and explain one advantage and one disadvantage of line art and color bitmapped graphics.
4. What does it mean to say that a bitmapped image is device-dependent? What is the connection between device-dependence and spatial resolution? Give an example from your experience with digital cameras, inkjet printers, or computer display devices.
5. Explain how color indexing and dithering can improve a bitmapped graphic with low color resolution.
6. What are the main sources of bitmapped images? Give a benefit or feature of each source.
7. Explain to a digital photographer why (s)he should not edit and resave multiple versions of a JPEG image file.
8. Do your think the PNG file format will replace JPEG and GIF formats for web graphics? Explain your position.
9. Why are 3-D graphics applications called a "virtual partner in the creative process"? Locate a 3-D graphic image and identify several features that were possible because of a 3-D application.
10. Identify and explain the two basic approaches to 3-D modeling.
11. In what ways is polygon modeling similar to 2-D bitmapped graphics?

12. In what ways is spline modeling similar to 2-D vector graphics?

13. Using 3-D graphic terminology, describe how you would create an image of a beach ball with your college logo on it resting on a sandy beach using a 3-D graphics application.

14. Why does 3-D rendering require powerful computers?

15. Identify three guidelines for using graphics that you think a graphic artist developing a college web site should follow. Specifically explain the importance of each guideline in relation to creating a college website.

Chapter 7

Sound

Topics you will explore include:

Digital technology dramatically changed the creation, distribution, and uses of sound. From the earliest CDs of the 1980s to digital phone services, Internet and satellite radio, and the MP3 players and podcasts of the early 21st century, digital sound transformed whole industries.

> *Podcasting* is a means of distributing audio content over the Internet. Podcast software (such as iPodder or iTunes) allows users to subscribe to regularly updated feeds of digital audio files (often MP3s) or to download selected episodes.
>
> Virtually any kind of audio—a child's first words, broadcast news reports, interviews, town meetings—can be quickly distributed worldwide through podcasting.

Early visionaries like Alan Kay understood the potential of the computer to capture, create, and distribute sound. Just as his Dynabook would allow people to express themselves in words and images, so, too, would it empower them to speak and to compose. But sound is a dynamic medium—it changes over time. Keeping up with the demands of real-time capture and delivery of sound required improvements in processors and memory. Making the computer speak was a surprise (and an effective marketing ploy) when Steve Jobs let the Macintosh introduce itself to the world in 1984.

Rapid progress in computer hardware was the key to expanding the sound capabilities of personal computers. Soon, "speaking" computers were commonplace, and it wasn't long before they were expected to listen as well. Built-in microphones allowed users to speak to their machines and ports were provided to connect musical keyboards. The microcomputer, with its processor devoted to a single user, now enabled one person with a single keyboard to create the sounds of an entire orchestra. For many observers, it was sound that transformed the computer from a "workstation" to a full-fledged communication device that could entertain, move, and persuade as well as calculate, sort, and inform.

The sophisticated sound production capabilities of modern computers allow multimedia developers to pursue a wide range of expressive possibilities. Sound can set a mood or a pace, as it routinely does in films. It can suggest a time (the crowing of a rooster) or a space (the canyon echo). It can reinforce simple interactions, as in the audible click of a button, or it can provide a fully developed alternative experience, as in programs for the visually impaired. Sound can engage and inspire all by itself, as the enthusiasm for digital sound libraries and MP3 players well attests. And it can be powerfully combined with other media to produce the compelling immersive experiences of video games and other interactive multimedia products.

In this chapter we consider the fundamental concepts, tools, and techniques of multimedia sound. After completing the reading you should understand:

- Key elements of sound such as frequency and pitch, amplitude and volume, and sine waves
- Defining features, uses, and limitations of sampled sound: sampling, sample resolution, quantization, clipping, sample rate, aliasing, and file formats
- Defining features, uses, and limitations of synthesized sound: MIDI, messages, synthesizer, sequencer, frequency modulation, and wavetable synthesis
- Sound on the Internet such as downloads and streaming audio
- Basic guidelines for the use of audio in multimedia applications

7.1 The Nature of Sound

Sound is a form of mechanical energy transmitted as vibrations in a medium. The medium is usually air, though sound can also be transmitted through solids and liquids. A clap of the hands produces sound by suddenly compressing and displacing air molecules. The disturbance is transmitted to adjacent molecules and propagated through space in the form of a wave. We hear the hand clap when these vibrations cause motions in the various parts of our ears.

Sound waves are often compared to the ripples produced when a stone is thrown into a pond. The stone displaces the water to produce high points, or wave peaks, and low points, or troughs. We see these alternating peaks and troughs as patterns of waves moving outward from the stone's point of impact. The clap of the hand also produces peaks and troughs as high air pressure is followed by a return to lower pressure. These changes in air pressure produce patterns of waves spreading in all directions from the sound's source.

The simplest sound wave patterns belong to so-called **pure tones**. A pure tone (such as the note produced by a tuning fork) can be represented as a simple wave that regularly repeats a smooth transition from high to low pressure. Such "periodic" waves are called *sinusoidal* or **sine waves**. A sine wave can be envisioned through a simple drawing in which the horizontal, or *x*-axis, represents the passage of time and the vertical, or *y*-axis, represents changes in air pressure (Figure 7.1).

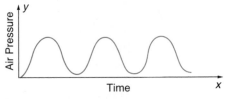

Figure 7.1 A sine wave.

A sine wave captures three essential features of sound: *amplitude*, *frequency*, and *duration*. **Amplitude** is a measure of sound pressure or the amount of energy associated with the sound. This is represented by the vertical, or *y*-axis, of the sine wave. Amplitude is perceived as the sound's **volume**, which is usually measured in **decibels** or *dB*. In general, sounds with higher amplitudes are experienced as *louder*. The range of human hearing is approximately 3 to 140 dB. Each 10 dB increase roughly doubles the perceived volume of a sound.

Frequency is the number of times a waveform repeats in a given interval of time. This is represented on the horizontal axis as the distance between two wave peaks or troughs. Frequency is measured in *hertz* or *Hz*. One **hertz** is one repetition of a waveform in one second of time. Frequency is perceived as **pitch**. High frequencies produce sounds of higher pitch and low frequencies produce low pitch. Pitch is the psychological perception of sound frequency. Humans can perceive a frequency range of 20 Hz to 20,000 Hz (or 20 *kHz*, *thousands* of hertz), though most adults cannot hear frequencies above 16 kHz.

The *duration* of the sound is the length of time it lasts. The total length of the horizontal axis represents duration (Figure 7.2).

Most sound waves are much more complex than the simple wave forms of pure tones. Different musical instruments playing the same note, for instance, produce different wave patterns (Figure 7.3). This is how we can tell the difference between a piano and

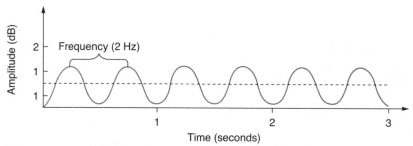

Figure 7.2 Amplitude, frequency, and duration.

trumpet. The sound of an entire symphony orchestra is an extremely complex blending of varied waveforms.

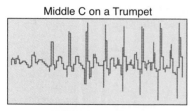

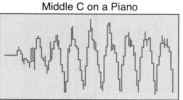

Figure 7.3 Comparison of the same note played on different instruments.

Sine waves, nonetheless, are central to acoustical theory and to the reproduction of sound. This is because *every* sound—a whisper, a lion's roar, a symphony, a crack of thunder—can be re-created as a combination of sine waves at particular frequencies.

7.2 Traditional Sound Reproduction

Sound waves are continuously varying, or analog, phenomena. Traditional approaches to capturing and reproducing sound were also analog. Sound waves vibrated the diaphragms of early microphones, which in turn caused a stylus to inscribe a continuous pattern on tinfoil or on a wax cylinder. To reproduce the sound, the process was reversed. The drum was rotated while in contact with a stylus. The movements of the stylus were electrically amplified to vibrate the drum of a speaker, which created the changes in air pressure that produce sound.

Over time, analog sound systems became very sophisticated. Technical improvements in sound capture and reproduction made possible very high quality or *high-fidelity* sound. Hi-Fi components such as amplifiers and speaker systems remain important in modern multimedia. These analog devices are still used in the final output of digital sound.

7.3 Digital Sound

Digital techniques represent sound as discrete (or discontinuous) elements of information. There are two major types of digital sound: *sampled* and *synthesized*.

Sampled sound is a digital recording of previously existing analog sound waves. A file for sampled sound contains many thousands of numerical values, each of which is a record of the amplitude of the sound wave at a particular instant, a *sampling* of the sound.

Synthesized sound is new sound generated (or synthesized, "put together") by the computer. A file for synthesized sound contains *instructions* that the computer uses to produce its own sound.

Multimedia developers usually use sampling to capture and edit naturally-occurring sounds such as human speech, musical and dramatic performances, bird calls, rocket launches, and so on. Synthesized sound is generally used to create original musical compositions or to produce novel sound effects.

Sampled Sound

In digital sampling, sound is captured by recording many separate measurements of the amplitude of a wave using an **ADC** or *Analog to Digital Converter*. An analog device, such as a microphone or the amplifier in a speaker system, generates a continuously varying voltage pattern to match the original sound wave. The ADC samples these voltages thousands of times each second. The samples are recorded as digital numbers. These digital values are then used to re-create the original sound by converting the digital information back to an analog form using a **DAC** or *Digital to Analog Converter*. The DAC uses the amplitude values to generate matching voltages that power speakers to reproduce the sound.

Digital sampling replaces the continuous wave form of the original sound with a new wave created from a fixed number of discrete samples (Figure 7.4). Some information is always lost in sampling since a continuous wave is infinitely divisible and sampling always yields a finite number of values. The quality of sampled sound is dependent on two factors directly connected to this sampling process: *sample resolution* and *sample rate*.

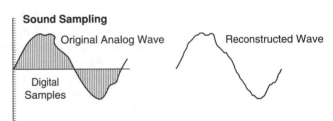

Figure 7.4 Sound sampling.

Sample Resolution   Each measurement of amplitude made by an ADC is recorded using a fixed number of bits. The number of bits used to encode amplitude is known as **sample resolution**. The two most common sample resolutions are 8-bit and 16-bit, though higher resolutions, such as the 24-bit DVD standard, are also used.

Eight bits can record 256 different amplitude levels. This is adequate to capture the variations in limited decibel ranges such as those between a human whisper and a shout. A higher sample resolution is needed to accurately reproduce sounds with a wider range of amplitudes, such as musical performances. CD-quality sound uses 16-bit sample resolution. This makes it possible to separately represent over 65,000 different amplitude levels. Inadequate sample resolution can distort sound in two different ways: *quantization* and *clipping*.

Quantization   Just as low color resolution can produce distortions in a bitmapped representation of a photograph, so can low sample resolution distort a sound recording. Each amplitude sample must be assigned one of the numbers available in the code being used. If the number of distinct values is too few, perceptually different amplitudes will be assigned the same number. Rounding a sample to the closest available value is known as **quantization**. In the case of sound, excessive quantization may produce a background hissing or a grainy sound. The solution is to record with a higher sample resolution (for instance, by using 16 rather than 8 bits).

Clipping   A different form of distortion related to wave amplitude is **clipping**. Sound sampling equipment is designed for a selected decibel range. If the source sound exceeds this range, (as, for instance, when someone yells into a microphone held close to their lips) higher amplitudes cannot be encoded, since no values are available to represent them. The waveform of a clipped sound shows square tops and bottoms marking the point at which the highest amplitudes could not be captured (Figure 7.5). Clipping can produce a harsh, distorted sound.

The solution to clipping is to lower the amplitude of the source sound to record within the limits of the ADC circuitry. Recording equipment usually includes some form of meter such as a swinging needle, colored bars, or lights to show input levels and alert users when the amplitude range has been exceeded. The familiar "Testing—one, two, three" is often used to establish the proper distance and speech level when recording with a microphone.

Clipping can also occur during the mixing of different audio tracks. **Mixing** is the process of combining two or more sound selections, or *tracks*, into a single track. For example, a background music track might be mixed with a voice track of a poetry reading. This combination of two or more tracks may produce an amplitude that exceeds the available range. Adjustments to the volume of each track can eliminate the problem. Another solution is to use higher sample resolutions (for instance, 24-bit) to provide a wider range of amplitude values.

Sample Rate   **Sample rate** is the number of samples taken in a fixed interval of time. As noted above, a rate of one sample per second is designated as a Hertz. Since sound samples are always taken thousands of times each second, sample rates are usually stated in thousands of Hertz, or *kilohertz* (kHz).

Sample rate affects sound quality by determining the range of frequencies that can be represented in a digital recording. At least two measurements are required to capture each cycle of a sound wave—one for each high value, or peak, and one for each low value, or trough. The highest frequency that can be captured is thus one-half of the sample rate. CD-quality sound captures 44,100 samples per second (44.1 kHz sample rate) and can represent frequencies as high as 22,050 Hz or 22.05 kHz. Since this is above

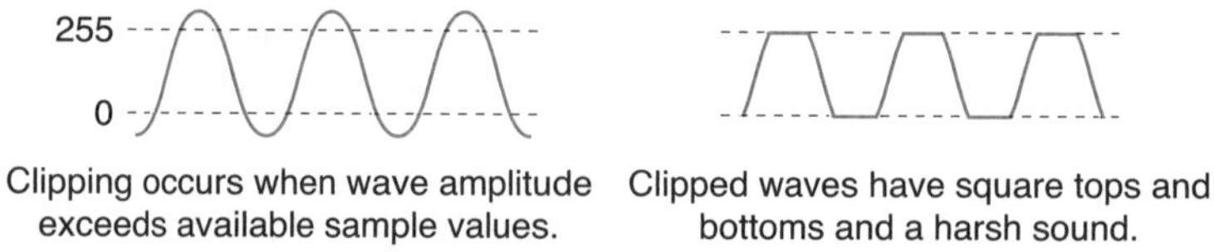

Clipping occurs when wave amplitude   Clipped waves have square tops and
    exceeds available sample values.   bottoms and a harsh sound.

Figure 7.5 Clipping.

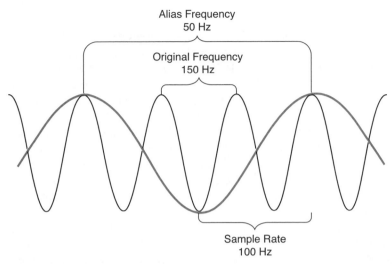

Figure 7.6 Aliasing—A higher frequency is falsely reproduced as a lower frequency. Original wave is in black. Reproduced wave is in blue.

the range of human hearing, CD sampling rates are generally considered adequate for full-fidelity sound recording.

Sounds that do not contain high frequencies can be more efficiently represented using lower sample rates since this will produce a smaller overall file size. One potential problem with lower sample rates, however, is aliasing.

Aliasing   **Aliasing**, as it applies to sampled sound, is the false representation of high frequencies as low frequencies. Aliasing occurs when the frequency being sampled is greater than one-half the sample rate being used. For instance, if a 150 Hz sound is sampled at a rate of 100 Hz, the resulting sound will be 50 Hz (see Figure 7.6).

Aliasing can be eliminated by applying electronic filters to the source sound to eliminate frequencies above one-half of the sample rate. Such filtering is often applied automatically by recording equipment.

Another approach to the problem of aliasing is to *oversample*. **Oversampling** uses a higher sample rate to accurately capture the frequencies above the desired range. For instance, the human voice has a limited range of frequencies. These can generally be captured with a sample rate of 11.025 kHz. But any background sounds with frequencies above approximately 5.5 kHz would be falsely included as lower frequencies. Using a higher rate such as 44.1 kHz will accurately capture these frequencies. The higher frequencies can then be eliminated with less expensive and more efficient digital filters. Once these frequencies are removed, the file is *downsampled*. **Downsampling** is the process of reducing the sample rate in an audio file. This reduces the size of the file to that required to capture the frequency range of the desired sound. In this case, the sample rate would be reduced from 44.1 kHz to 11.025 kHz.

Balancing File Size and Sound Quality

The most significant challenge in the use of sampled sound is large file size. One minute of a single channel of CD-quality sound (16-bit sample resolution and 44.1 kHz sample rate) produces a file of 42,336,000 bits (16 * 44,100 * 60) or approximately 5 MB. Stereo requires a second channel and doubles the size for a total of 10 MB per minute of sound. DVD Audio creates even larger files by using higher sample rates (96 kHz), a larger sample size (24 bits), and more channels to produce "surround sound."

Fortunately, it is not always necessary to use CD or DVD quality sound. Some sounds, such as normal speech, contain relatively low frequencies and a limited range of amplitudes. In these cases, higher sample rates and sample resolutions do not improve sound quality—they just create needlessly large files. Using a rate of 11.025 kHz for voice recording results in a file only one-quarter the size of CD-quality sound. In addition, 8-bit sample resolution and monaural sound are usually adequate for speech. This further reduces file size by a factor of four—one minute of monaural, 8-bit, 11.025 kHz sampled sound requires only 650 KB, one-sixteenth the size of a stereo CD recording.

These dramatic differences in file sizes make it important for multimedia developers to match sample resolutions and rates to the type of sound being recorded. This often requires testing a given sound at different resolutions and rates to determine a quality level appropriate to the application. One reason for including audio specialists on a multimedia development team is that they can draw on their experience to greatly expedite this process.

Determining the Size of Sampled Sound Files   Sound file sizes for monaural sound can be readily calculated by simply multiplying the time of the recording, the sample rate, and the size of each sample. The formula is:

*Monaural Sound File Size = Sample Rate * Sample Size (in bytes) * Sample Time (in seconds)*

For example, a sound sampled at 44.1 kHz, using a 16-bit (2 byte) sample size for 10 seconds produces a file size of 882,000 bytes (approximately 860 KB). To calculate stereo requirements, double the size of the monaural sound file. Comparisons of file sizes for one-minute of sound at different qualities are given in Table 7.1.

Sound Compression   Lowering the sample rate and reducing sample resolution are two ways to reduce the size of a sampled sound file. These methods work well for sounds at relatively low frequencies and narrow amplitude ranges. They are not effective for

Table 7.1 **Size and Quality Comparisons for Sampled Sound**

Resolution	Rate	Stereo/Mono	Size (1 Minute)	Quality
16	44.1 kHz	Stereo	10 MB	CD
16	22.05 kHz	Stereo	5 MB	FM radio
8	11.025 kHz	Mono	650 KB	AM radio
8	5.5 kHz	Mono	325 KB	Bad telephone

sounds that contain wider ranges of both frequency and amplitude, such as musical performances. In these cases another strategy can be used, *file compression*.

As we have seen in earlier chapters, file compression can be either *lossless* or *lossy*. Lossless compression uses more efficient coding to reduce the size of a file while preserving all the information of the original. Lossy compression discards some of the original information.

Lossless compression is essential for files containing computer programs and alphanumeric data since any change in this information could easily disable the program or distort the data. Images and sounds, however, often remain recognizable and usable when relatively large amounts of information are sacrificed. Since lossy strategies produce much smaller files, they are the preferred technique for sound compression.

Lossy sound compression **codecs** (coder/decoders) use various techniques to reduce file sizes. Some of these take advantage of *psychoacoustics*, the interplay between the psychological conditions of human perception and the properties of sound. For instance, while humans with optimal hearing can perceive frequencies as high as about 20 kHz, most people cannot distinguish frequencies above approximately 16 kHz. This means that higher-frequency information can be eliminated and most listeners will not miss it. Higher amplitude sounds in one stereo channel will also typically "drown out" softer sounds in the other channel. Again, this is information that usually will not be missed.

Lossy compression also uses other techniques such as variable bitrate encoding (**VBR**). In VBR, sounds are encoded using a different number of bits per second depending on the complexity of the sound. For simple passages of sound with limited frequencies, a smaller number of bits per second is used than for more complex passages, such as those with many different instruments and higher frequencies.

Lossy codecs such as the widely supported MP3 can reduce file sizes by as much as 80% while remaining virtually indistinguishable from the original CD-quality sound. Sound compression is a constantly evolving area of research and development. There are several competing formats and many different opinions about the relative merits of each.

Sampled Sound File Formats

A variety of file formats have been developed for sampled sound. Some are specific to particular computer platforms while others are intended for specialized audio capture and editing programs or for specific uses, such as Web broadcasting.

AIFF **AIFF** or Audio Interchange File Format is an Apple Computer format widely used on Macintosh computers. AIFF can support a wide range of sample resolutions, sample rates, and audio channels. Because AIFF files are not compressed, they tend to be relatively large. AIFF files use the extensions .aiff or .aif and can be played on Windows computers as well as Macs.

WAV **WAV** was developed by Microsoft and IBM and is the standard sampled sound format for the PC. Nearly all sound-capable Windows applications support WAV. WAV files can be monaural or stereo, and either 8 or 16-bit. This format also supports a variety of sample rates. Like AIFF, WAV files are uncompressed, high quality sound files that can be played on both Macintosh and Windows platforms. WAV files use the extension .wav.

AU   **AU** was developed by Sun Microsystems. This format is widely used on the Internet for transmission of relatively low-quality sound files. AU files use the extension .au.

RealAudio   Developed by Real Media, the **RealAudio** format supports streaming audio at low bandwidths. *Streaming audio*, discussed at the end of this chapter, is sound that can be played as audio files are being received by the computer. This allows users to begin playing sounds without the waiting required to download a complete file. It also supports real-time broadcasts of events such as concerts and the live reception of radio over the Internet. RealAudio files use the extension .rm.

MP3   **MP3** (MPEG-1, audio layer 3) is a popular audio format that supports significant compression while preserving excellent quality. It is widely supported across different computer platforms and is frequently used on the Internet. MP3s are often "ripped" from CDs. Ripping transfers the CD file to a user's computer and converts it to MP3 format. This creates small, high-quality versions of the original sounds for use on the Web or in portable MP3 players. MP3 files use the extensions .mp3 or .mpga.

Synthesized Sound

In sound synthesis, the computer sends commands to a specialized electronic device called a **synthesizer**, which then generates the corresponding sounds. The most common format for these commands is **MIDI** or Musical Instrument Digital Interface. As its name suggests, MIDI was developed to provide a standard method of connecting musical instruments, synthesizers, and other digital devices.

MIDI is an audio format for representing the elements of a musical composition in a digital code. Codes are provided for:

- Specific instruments
- Notes
- The force and duration of musical actions (pressing a key, striking a drum)
- Routing commands to different synthesizer channels to produce music with multiple simultaneous parts (such as a guitar and a bass drum)
- A variety of specialized control functions (enabling multi-channel play, etc.)

Prior to the development of MIDI in 1983, there was no guarantee that synthesized music played on two different systems would sound the same. One system might designate a guitar sound with a binary code that another system used for a flute. Developers could only be confident that their sounds would play properly when they controlled every aspect of the playback system. MIDI standardized synthesized sound.

MIDI Messages   MIDI commands are known as **messages**. Messages can be sent to the MIDI system as a whole or directed to any one of 16 individual channels. Different instruments, or *voices*, can be assigned to each of these channels and *program change* messages can be used to repeatedly change the instrument in any given channel. Most

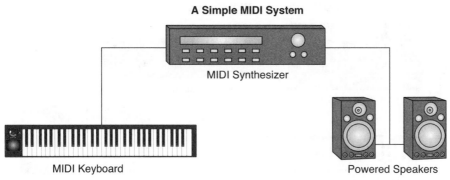

A Simple MIDI System

MIDI Synthesizer

MIDI Keyboard   Powered Speakers

Figure 7.7 Simple MIDI system.

MIDI systems are *multitimbral*—they can play multiple instruments at the same time by simultaneously processing the information in different channels.

Performance messages include note on, note off, the note played, and the velocity at which it was played. These messages cause synthesizers to play a particular note with a given amplitude, for a specified length of time. MIDI systems are generally *polyphonic*—they can play more than one note at once and so they can reproduce, for instance, the sound produced by striking five piano keys simultaneously.

Components of a MIDI Sound System   The simplest MIDI sound system has three major components: a digital musical instrument to generate MIDI messages based on the performer's actions, a sound synthesizer to interpret the messages and produce the corresponding analog wave forms, and an amplifier/speaker system to output the analog sound (see Figure 7.7). In this basic system, a keyboard might be set to play a piano on channel 5 through a synthesizer in real time. The sound would be produced as the performer played.

Since a MIDI performance produces a stream of digital messages, MIDI commands can be captured, edited, and reused. In fact, a single keyboard can be used to individually compose the parts of several instruments for a band or symphony performance. All that is needed is a device to regulate the flow of the MIDI commands to the appropriate channels of a multitimbral synthesizer. Such a device is called a **sequencer**. A sequencer controls the flow or sequencing of the MIDI data. The sequencer could send the piano part of the composition to channel 5, a harmonica part to channel 1, a drum part to channel 2, and so on (Figure 7.8). The result would be a synthesized band performance.

MIDI on a Multimedia Computer   Computers emulate MIDI systems through soundcards and sequencer software. Soundcards include synthesizers and interfaces to MIDI-supported input devices. A keyboard or other instrument can be connected to the computer through standard MIDI jacks on the soundcard. The computer can then be used to directly play any MIDI instrument.

The computer can also be used to create a composition without playing an instrument. Using sequencer software, an original composition is created by simply placing

Multi-Instrument MIDI System

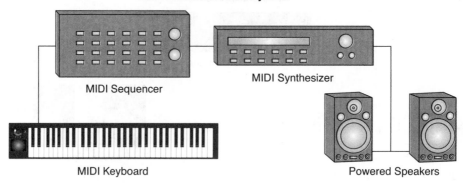

Figure 7.8 MIDI system with sequencer.

notes on a musical scale (Figure 7.9). Other compositions, including those produced by performers, are imported. Any part of the composition can then be edited in a wide variety of ways. Pitch, tempo, the duration and volume of notes, and the arrangement and timing of instruments are all readily altered with the sequencer.

MIDI dramatically changed music composition by placing control over a virtually unlimited range of instruments and musical scores in the hands of a single individual.

Figure 7.9 A sequencer. (GarageBand)

7.4 Sampled and Synthesized Sound Compared

Sampling and synthesis are very different techniques for incorporating sound in multimedia applications. Their relative strengths and weaknesses can be summarized as follows.

Advantages of Sampled Sound

Sampled sound can be played on virtually any modern computer at a consistently high quality. It is also easily created and edited.

- *High Quality:* The evolution of digital technology made it possible to capture many thousands of samples per second and to record these at bit depths that minimize the effects of quantization. In addition, the creation in the 1980s of CD-Audio, a nearly universal standard for high-fidelity music, promoted widespread acceptance and support of sampled sound. Other standards, such as DVD Audio, have expanded the capabilities of sampled sound. The result is high quality audio files and a wide range of supporting hardware and software.
- *Ease of Creation:* Sampled sound is a recording. A computer, equipped with a microphone and appropriate software, can readily capture any naturally occurring sound.

Sound capture software is easy to use and requires no specialized knowledge of the sound source. We can capture a symphony, for example, without knowing anything at all about musical composition.

- *Ease of Editing:* Once captured, sampled sound is readily edited. Sound editing software allows users to view sound in graphical form, select portions of sounds, and cut, copy, and paste in ways similar to familiar text and graphics operations (Figure 7.10). A wide range of adjustments and enhancements are possible, including filters to alter frequency ranges, mixing of sound tracks, and numerous sound effects (reverberation, echoes, etc.). Specialized knowledge of audio theory, while helpful, is not necessary to edit and test sampled sounds.

- *Consistent Playback Quality:* Every computer processes sampled sound in the same way. Provided that playback systems have comparable speaker capabilities, users will hear sounds just as the developer intended.

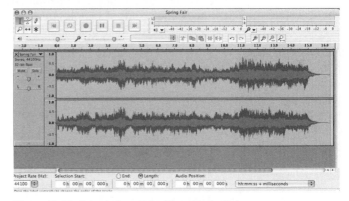

Figure 7.10 Sampled sound editor. (Audacity)

Challenges of Sampled Sound

Sampled sound, like bitmapped graphics, has certain disadvantages derived from the demands of the sampling process and the way samples are used to re-create the original sources. These include large file sizes and editing limitations.

- *Large Files:* The major disadvantage of sampled sound is large file size. Each second of sampled sound is re-created from thousands of samples, each of which must be separately recorded and processed. The demands that these files place on storage and processing often require that developers carefully compromise sound quality in the ways described previously.

- *Editing Limitations:* Sampled sound is easy to edit and computers make possible a wide range of editing options. However, once the various elements of a sound track have been mixed, it is not possible to extract and edit individual components. In addition, it is often desirable to alter the length of a sound source to coordinate its play to an animation or video. Sampled sounds can only be lengthened by small amounts before the process produces distortions, particularly in pitch.

Advantages of Synthesized Sound

The main advantages of synthesized sound are editing control and small file sizes.

- *Editing:* Synthesized digital sounds, such as MIDI performances, have the advantage of exceptional editing control—compositions can be edited at the level of the individual note. One significant advantage of this approach over sampled sound is that the duration of a MIDI sound can be readily altered without producing distortions. Another editing advantage of MIDI is that it allows a single skilled musician to create and play an original composition that otherwise would require the efforts of many skilled professional performers and technicians. This has provided multimedia developers with a source of significantly less expensive original music.

- *Small Files:* MIDI sounds on computers also have another striking advantage: small file size. A MIDI file is a listing of alphanumeric messages. These take up far less space than the many thousands of samples per second recorded for sampled sound. In fact, MIDI files may be up to 1000 times smaller than comparable sampled sound files.

Challenges of Synthesized Sound

The challenges for the use of MIDI in multimedia productions concern expertise, playback consistency, and reproduction of natural sounds.

- *Expertise:* Unlike the process of capturing an existing sound, the creation and editing of MIDI sound does require knowledge of musical theory. Sampled sound can be captured by virtually anyone and non-specialists can easily master many editing changes. MIDI sound, on the other hand, demands at least basic understanding of notes, scales, and other elements of music.
- *Playback Consistency:* The playback quality of synthesized sound is less consistent than it is for sampled sound. Every computer processes sampled sound in essentially the same way. Given comparable amplifiers and speakers, sampled audio will sound the same no matter where it is played. MIDI sound must be synthesized, that is, artificially created by the computer's soundcard. The synthesizers built into soundcards differ significantly in quality and may produce very different results. There are several reasons for the differences in sound synthesizer quality.
    - Some synthesizers use a process known as **frequency modulation**. FM synthesis produces the variety of sounds by using one signal to modulate the frequency of another signal. This can be very effective if the desired output is a novel electronic sound. If the goal is the natural sound of traditional instruments, however, a second approach is usually more effective.
    - The second major approach to synthesizing sound is called **wavetable synthesis**. This uses very short samples of naturally produced sounds to generate new, synthesized sound. Wavetable synthesizers differ in the number and quality of their sound samples as well as in the means they use to generate new sounds from their samples. The result is significant variation in output quality.
- *Natural Sound:* The third major challenge in the use of MIDI is that synthesized sound is generally not effective for the representation of non-musical natural sounds such as the human voice. If a multimedia project requires speech and other natural sounds, sampled sound is usually the better choice.

7.5 Combining Sampled and Synthesized Sound

The challenges in digital audio can sometimes be met by combining synthesized and sampled approaches.

Developers can take advantage of the editing control of MIDI and minimize its playback limitations by composing original MIDI scores and then converting these to sampled sound. This is accomplished by sampling the MIDI performance or by using a specialized program to convert MIDI data directly to waveforms. In either case, the result is a recording that will deliver reliable playback on any computer.

In another approach, developers can take advantage of the superiority of sampled audio for the reproduction of natural sounds while minimizing its storage costs. Much smaller MIDI files can be used for major sound components of the application and MIDI commands can be used to call and play sampled sounds as required. For instance, MIDI might be used for long-playing background music with sampled sounds for briefer spoken passages.

7.6 Advantages of Digital Sound

Digital sound, whether sampled or synthesized, has a number of advantages over traditional analog formats.

- *Noise Reduction/Recording Accuracy:* The circuits of analog audio devices typically generate unwanted noise, such as hums and crackling, which do not occur in digital circuitry. Digital audio can also capture a wider dynamic range (range of amplitudes). This makes digital recording particularly effective for representing symphony performances, for example.
- *Superior Copies:* Analog copying usually results in **generation decay**— sound quality is lost because a copy of a copy does not preserve all the information of the original. A copy of a copy of a cassette tape, for instance, will not be as good as the first copy. By contrast, digital copying normally results in no loss of information over successive generations of copying.
- *Durability:* Digital audio is also more durable than its analog counterpart. Repeated play of traditional analog media such as vinyl records or magnetic tape results in wear that lowers sound quality. Needles wear the grooves of records and the magnetic oxide of tapes gradually decays with use. Digital audio files are stored using optical and electronic devices that are unaffected by normal use.
- *Random Access:* Digital audio also permits direct, or *random access* to any point on the recording. Analog sources such as tapes are sequential and require the user to physically move through other sections of the recording to reach the desired portion. Random access greatly improves interactivity and is critical to the success of modern multimedia.
- *Editing/Distribution:* Finally, digital audio benefits from the typical editing and distribution advantages of digital media in general, as discussed in Chapter 2. Editing is easier and less expensive than analog techniques. Copies can also be distributed much more readily, particularly through computer networks.

7.7 Sound and the Internet

By the early 21st century, both sampled and synthesized sounds were readily shared over the Internet. The development and widespread distribution of software such as

QuickTime, Windows Media Player, and RealAudio Player simplified user access to all forms of audio. Improvements in bandwidth provided through DSL, cable, and satellite services also improved access to large digital sound files, as did advances in audio compression. Particularly significant was the MP3 format, which dramatically reduced the size of CD-quality audio and led to a revolution in the distribution of music.

There are two major strategies for delivering sound on the Internet: *downloading* and *streaming audio*. **Downloaded audio** transfers a complete audio file from one computer (the server) to another (the client) according to a set of file transfer protocols. Users await the complete delivery of the file and then use player software to open the file and listen to the audio. The file remains on the user's computer and can be edited and replayed at will. These are significant advantages, but downloading also has serious shortcomings. Downloads take time, they consume hard disk space, they are not easily updated, and they cannot be used to broadcast live events. One approach to shortening the delay between starting a download and hearing the audio is *progressive downloading*. As in normal downloading, progressive downloads save a file to the client computer's hard disk, but they also buffer content in main memory and begin to play the sound as it is being downloaded. Progressive downloads are relatively easy to deliver using common protocols such as HTTP and TCP/IP and they can deliver high quality audio files over a wide range of connection speeds. Their main disadvantages are that playback during the download process may be interrupted on computers using slower network connections and users will not be able to access later portions of a recording until the download is complete.

Streaming audio provides a solution to these limitations. **Streaming audio** is "real-time" sound that is heard as it is being delivered and is not saved to the client computer. Streaming audio uses special protocols such as RTSP (Real Time Streaming Protocol), special servers, and special media formats and players, such as RealMedia. The protocols used to deliver streaming media are optimized for efficient, real-time delivery over networks rather than delivery of error-free downloads. The special requirements for preparing and delivering streaming audio make it more difficult to implement than downloads. In particular, developers must choose between competing streaming formats as they prepare files and arrange for their distribution. On the other hand, streaming is the only way to provide audio of live events over networks. It provides more reliable playback than progressive downloads, does not consume hard disk space on the client machine, and can be readily updated.

7.8 Guidelines for the Use of Sound

Multimedia development typically demands careful planning and frequent revision. The challenges of digital audio can be more readily met by following a few basic guidelines.

- Identify the purpose of the sound. Sound can be memory and processor intensive—use it for good reasons.
  - To attract attention (chimes, bells)
  - To inform (oral histories, speeches)
  - To illustrate (word pronunciations, musical selections, animal sounds)
  - To establish a mood or setting

- ▪ To provide feedback (audible mouse clicks, spoken alert messages)
- ▪ As an alternative to text for the visually impaired
- ▪ Use high-quality sound. Poor audio gives an immediate negative impression.
- ▪ Conserve file space. Calculate sound file sizes. Choose the most efficient sound format.
  - ▪ Lower sample rates and sizes for speech.
  - ▪ Consider MIDI sources.
  - ▪ Consider compression options such as MP3.
- ▪ Consider the playback environment.
  - ▪ Public vs. private use
  - ▪ Quality of synthesizers for MIDI sound
  - ▪ Compatibility of sound formats with playback hardware and software
  - ▪ Give users control:
    - ▪ over volume
    - ▪ to stop or start play
- ▪ Avoid excessive use of sound—sound can be more tiring for users than images or text.
- ▪ Organize sound files. Preserve original sources.

7.9 Summary

There are two basic approaches to creating digital sound. The first is *sampled sound*, a recording made up of many thousands of samples of existing sounds. Sampled sound has several strengths including effective representation of natural sounds, ease of creation and editing, high quality, and reliable playback. The disadvantages of sampled sound include large file size and limited editing control.

The second form of digital audio is *synthesized sound*, sound created by the computer itself. *MIDI* is the most widely used form of synthesized sound. A MIDI file contains commands that the computer follows to artificially generate sound. These files are much smaller than sampled sound files. They also permit knowledgeable developers to edit music at the level of the individual note for any of the various instruments used in a composition. The length of synthesized sound tracks can be altered without affecting pitch. The disadvantages of synthesized sound include limitations in the production of natural sounds such as human voices, the need for knowledge of musical theory, and less consistent playback quality.

Sampled and synthesized sounds have a number of advantages over traditional analog formats. These include high quality copies, durability, random access, and ease of editing and distribution.

Sound has become an essential element in many multimedia applications and is widely distributed over the Internet either as *downloads* or *streaming audio*. The challenges of digital sound make it particularly important for developers to carefully consider the purposes sound serves in their applications and the techniques they use to optimize the quality and efficiency of multimedia sound.

Key Terms

ADC
AIFF
Aliasing
Amplitude
AU
Clipping
Codec
DAC
Decibel
Downloaded audio
Downsampling
Frequency
Frequency modulation
Generation decay
Hertz
Message
MIDI
Mixing

MP3
Oversampling
Pitch
Pure tones
Quantization
RealAudio
Sample rate
Sample resolution
Sampled sound
Sequencer
Sine waves
Streaming audio
Synthesized sound
Synthesizer
VBR
Volume
WAV
Wavetable synthesis

Review Questions

1. What is sound?
2. Identify and define the three essential features of sound that are captured by a sine wave.
3. What is pitch? How is it related to sound frequency?
4. What is sampled sound? What is synthesized sound?
5. What is sample resolution? How does it affect the quality of sampled sound?
6. What is quantization? How does it affect a sampled sound?
7. What is clipping? How does it affect a sampled sound?
8. In what way is quantization related to sample resolution?
9. What is sample rate? How does it affect the quality of a sampled sound?
10. What is aliasing? How does it affect the quality of a sampled sound?
11. What is downsampling? Why would a developer convert a 44.1 kHz file to 11.025 kHz?
12. What are two ways to reduce the file size of a sampled sound?
13. Why is lossy compression better for sound files than text files?
14. What are the similarities of .aiff and .wav files?
15. What is a synthesizer?
16. Identify and explain the three major components of a basic MIDI sound system.
17. How did MIDI change the nature of music composition?
18. What are the main advantages and disadvantages of sampled sound?
19. What are the main advantages and disadvantages of synthesized sound?
20. Identify and explain the two main strategies for delivering sound on the Internet.

Discussion Questions

1. Identify three expressive possibilities for using sound in multimedia applications. Locate one example of a multimedia animation on the Web and describe the uses and importance of sound in this application.
2. Determine the sound file size for a stereo music recording of 2.5 minutes, 8 bit, 11.05 kHz.
3. Explain why MP3 file compression became such a popular format for digital music.
4. If you are the audio specialist for a development team, should you save the original sound files as .aiff format or MP3 format? Explain your selection.
5. If you are the audio specialist for a web development team, should you create the background music for an animated cartoon in MIDI or sampled format? Explain your choice.
6. Describe a situation where an audio specialist may combine sampled and MIDI sound for an animated cartoon.
7. Describe how a computer application can create MIDI sounds.
8. What are the benefits of converting an audio tape library to CD format?
9. Identify and explain three relevant guidelines to incorporate the sound of cathedral bells in a public kiosk on the history of Chartres Cathedral.
10. Consider the distinction between bitmapped and vector graphics and explain how that distinction is similar to the difference between sampled and synthesized sound.

Chapter 8

Video

Topics you will explore include:

- Analog Video
  - Standards and Characteristics
  - Uses in Multimedia Development
- Digital Video
  - Video Quality
  - Codecs
  - File Formats
  - Shooting
  - Editing
  - Rendering
- Guidelines for Video

For most of the twentieth century, the creation of "motion pictures," whether film or video, was a restricted specialty demanding teams of skilled professionals and expensive equipment. Home movie cameras and camcorders gave amateurs little more than a tempting entrée to the world of video. To be sure, they could capture moving images; but raw video is exactly that—it is only with the revision and refinement of editing that a video "draft" becomes a memorable message. And analog editing was expensive and complex. Few non-professionals had the skills or the resources to create effective analog video.

As in all media, the computer transformed video and film, adding expressive possibilities that were impossible to produce using analog techniques. The result has been new forms of expression ranging from special effects to convincing digital simulations of human actors. Cutting-edge digital film and video still require expertise and computing resources beyond the budgets of most multimedia producers. But there has also been a revolution in desktop digital video. Improvements in microcomputers, digital cameras, and video editing software have made it possible for individuals and small production teams to effectively add video to a wide range of multimedia applications.

After completing this chapter, you should understand:

- Key elements of analog video: standards, aspect ratio, scan methods, color reproduction
- Uses of analog video in digital multimedia: as source footage, as a delivery mode
- Design and delivery considerations for multimedia uses of analog video: flicker, safe action and safe title areas, illegal colors
- Key elements of digital video: resolution, frame rate, compression strategies, codecs, file formats
- Main development considerations for each of the three stages of creating digital video: shooting, editing, and rendering
- Basic guidelines for the use of video in multimedia applications

8.1 Moving Pictures

To understand both the power and the continuing challenges of digital video, we must turn first to the elements of video and to its origins in the analog technologies of the last century.

Film and video are composed of a series of rapidly displayed still images. We perceive these stills as continuous motion for two reasons. First, each image captures an instant of motion, recording the changes in the positions of moving objects. One image shows the feet of a running horse in one position and the next captures their new position an instant later. The second factor is persistence of vision: images formed on the retina remain for a short time after an object is gone. If the still images are changed rapidly enough, persistence of vision fills the time between them resulting in the perception of a continuous flow of motion.

Traditional film and video are analog media. Film records individual images as continuous areas of color on a transparent medium that is then projected to a screen. Analog video records images as continuously varying electrical voltages. These voltages are then used to produce images on cathode ray tubes (CRTs) or projection screens. Sound tracks for both traditional film and video also use analog techniques.

Digital formats are rapidly displacing analog video, but many multimedia applications either make use of analog source material or use analog TVs for display of their products. For these reasons, a basic understanding of the older video standards continues to be relevant to multimedia development.

8.2 Analog Video Formats

Analog video was initially intended exclusively for broadcast television. This resulted in several compromises that produced images of relatively low resolution with limited color fidelity. Despite these limitations, the original television standard, called **NTSC** (National Television Standards Committee), dominated broadcast TV in the United States for more than fifty years.

The NTSC Standard

In 1952, the NTSC established the format for televised video in the United States. The NTSC standard included specifications for the aspect ratio, resolution, scan rate, scanning method, and broadcast techniques used to create images on American televisions.

Aspect ratio is the relationship between the width and height of the still images, or frames, that make up a film or video sequence. This also determines the shape of the screen used to view film and television. The NTSC aspect ratio for television is 4:3—for every four units of width there will be three units of height. A television screen that is 16 inches wide will be 12 inches high. Smaller and larger TVs will preserve the same ratio.

The **resolution** of NTSC video is the number of lines used to re-create images on screen. NTSC established a maximum resolution of 525 lines to reproduce each frame. The CRTs, or *cathode ray tubes*, used in most analog television sets create images by using an electron gun to sweep lines of differently colored phosphorus dots, causing them to glow in a particular pattern. The rate at which the screen is scanned was established by NTSC at 60 Hz, or sixty times per second. This took advantage of the cycle rate (60 cycles per second) of the alternating current used in the United States.

The scanning method used in NTSC video is known as *interlacing*. An **interlaced scan** is one in which alternating lines of the image are produced in each scanning pass. The electron gun first sweeps across the odd numbered lines and then returns to sweep the even numbered lines in a second pass. Each pass produces a partial image called a **field**. The two fields are produced very rapidly and blend together to present the completed image, called a **frame**. Scanning each of the two fields in one-sixtieth of a second produces a **frame rate** of thirty frames per second (30 fps).

The NTSC standard also provided for overscanning. **Overscanning** is the process of transmitting a larger image than will appear on the screen of the TV. This assures that the transmitted image will completely fill the television screen. As a result, the maximum visible resolution of an NTSC TV screen is reduced from 525 to 484 lines.

> The current frame rate for NTSC Video is actually 29.97 fps. This slight departure from 30 fps was made when color information was added to the original black and white signal.

To broadcast color television images, NTSC uses a composite signal. A **composite color** signal is a mixture of two other signals, one of which represents *luminance* and the other *chrominance*. **Luminance** is the amount of brightness, or white, in an image. **Chrominance** is color hue. Composite color is inexpensive to create and transmit. This technique also made it possible to continue using black and white TVs after color television was introduced. Older sets continued to use the luminance information while ignoring chrominance.

> The limited range and purity of NTSC color has led critics to quip that the acronym actually stands for Never The Same Color.

Although NTSC color TV is broadcast as a composite signal, it is displayed on a TV screen using a different color model. TV displays, like computer monitors, use the **RGB** (**R**ed, **G**reen, **B**lue) color model. Each pixel of the image is colored by blending different proportions of red, green, or blue light. RGB is **component color**: each color component is represented separately. RGB can produce a virtually unlimited range of very pure colors. In order to produce RGB color on a screen, a television must first translate the composite color information of the broadcast signal to component RGB mode. The composite signal cannot record color as precisely as component color, however. As a result, NTSC color displayed on TVs lacks the range and purity of full RGB color, as displayed on a computer monitor.

All analog video broadcasts in the U.S. use NTSC composite color. The original production of video, however, is done in other formats and most of these make use of component color. This allows producers to create and edit images with the superior color range and fidelity of the RGB format.

Other Analog Video Broadcast Standards

While NTSC is used in most of North America, other incompatible analog TV standards are in use elsewhere in the world. The two major competitors are **PAL** (Phase Alternate Line) and **SECAM** (*Sequential Couleur Avec Memoire*). PAL is used in England and much of Europe. SECAM is found in a number of countries including France and Russia. These standards are also interlaced but they use different scan rates (50 Hz), frame rates (25 fps), and screen resolutions (625 lines). Video produced for one format cannot be played on devices intended for another format. This means that NTSC videotapes cannot be played in Europe, and European video productions cannot be played in the U.S. without specialized VCRs.

VCRs, Camcorders, and Videotape Standards

The development of VCRs and video camcorders in the 1980s provided another mode of creating and distributing analog video. VCRs use a variety of tape formats, the most important of which are VHS, S-VHS, 8mm, and Hi8. There is limited compatibility between these formats: S-VHS decks can also play VHS tapes, and Hi8 decks can play 8mm tapes, but no other combinations are possible.

■ **VHS:** The first widely adopted format was VHS. The VHS format has a relatively low resolution of 240 lines. It can support hi-fi audio but it uses composite color. As a result, the overall quality of VHS video is slightly lower than analog TV broadcasts.

- **S-VHS:** Introduced in 1987 by JVC, S-VHS was an improvement on VHS. S-VHS increased resolution to 400 lines. It also improved color quality by maintaining separate luminance and chrominance signals, rather than mixing the two types of information as in composite color. This is a variant of component color known as **Y/C** (for luminance/chrominance). Y/C color is also called "pseudo-component" because it is not as precise as RGB color. It does represent a significant improvement over composite color, however. S-VHS is an improvement over NTSC broadcast video.
- **8mm:** The 8mm format was a smaller tape that made possible more compact, lightweight video cameras. It supported a screen resolution of 230 lines and provided near-CD-quality sound.
- **Hi8:** Hi8 improved the resolution and color of 8mm in ways similar to the improvements of S-VHS over VHS. Resolution increased to 400 lines and Y/C component color was added.

S-VHS and Hi8 offer significant advantages as source media for digital conversion because of their superior resolution and color quality. None of these formats compares very favorably, however, with the expensive broadcast quality video used for TV production. These provide full RGB component color and resolutions of approximately 1000 lines.

Analog Video and Digital Multimedia

Digital video will eventually replace analog video. This will greatly simplify the creation and distribution of multimedia applications of all kinds. In the meantime, however, the conversion of digital multimedia to analog video remains an important concern for developers since many projects are still destined for display on analog televisions. This includes the development of commercials and TV programs as well as videotapes and DVDs. There are several challenges in the conversion process. To understand these we need to turn first to the differences between the display devices used by computers and analog TVs.

Analog televisions and many computer monitors share the same 4:3 aspect ratio. For instance, many computers use 640×480, 800×600, or 1024×768 screen resolutions. In other ways, however, the two technologies differ significantly.

First, televisions use interlaced scanning to produce a single frame from two separate fields. Computer monitors use progressive scanning. **Progressive scanning** reproduces each line of the image in a single pass. Second, televisions overscan and computer monitors underscan. Overscanning, as we have seen, transmits a larger image to the screen than it can display. This clips off portions of the original image and assures that the entire screen will be filled. **Underscanning** sends a smaller image to the screen, assuring that the entire image will be viewable. Finally, televisions presenting NTSC broadcasts display colors derived from a *composite* signal, while computer monitors display *component* color. These three key differences lead to specific cautions that must be observed by multimedia developers delivering products through analog television. Developers need to be alert to *line widths*, *safe action* and *safe title areas*, and *NTSC safe colors*.

Line Width: Avoiding Flickers   A one-pixel line drawn on a computer screen occupies a single line of the display. Computer monitors scan progressively. These thin lines are refreshed on every pass of the scanning process and appear just as steady as wider lines. But when the image is converted to the interlaced NTSC format, each line will only be scanned on every other pass. A one-pixel line will be completely missing from one of the two fields making up the video frame. The result is that the line may appear to flicker as it is dropped and then picked up again in the scanning process. Widening the line will reduce this effect since part of the line will remain visible in each field. To deal with this problem, multimedia developers avoid thin lines and delicate fonts with thin serifs in applications intended for analog video output.

The Safe Action and Safe Title Areas   Televisions do not display the full image they receive; computer monitors do. For this reason, an image that appears close to the edge of a computer monitor may not be visible on a television. The **safe action area** of the computer monitor is the area that will be displayed on a television. This is approximately the inner 90% of the computer screen. If it is important not to cut off the ear of a person appearing at the edge of the screen, be sure to stay within the safe action area. The **safe title area** is the portion of the monitor in which effective display of text is assured on a television. Since text is not normally displayed at the very edge of the screen, the safe title area is placed inside the safe action area. The safe title area on a computer monitor is the inner 80% of the screen (Figure 8.1).

NTSC Safe Colors   The range of colors available in a video is called its **color gamut**. The gamut of NTSC video is smaller than the gamut of the RGB video used by computers. As a result, colors created on the computer may not be accurately displayed on a television. In the worst case, these color mismatches produce distortions such as shimmering that can dramatically degrade the television image. Computer-generated colors that can-not be reproduced in NTSC video are called **illegal colors**. Graphics and video editing applications often provide warnings that a particular color is "out of gamut" or "illegal"

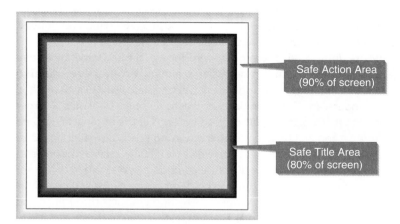

Figure 8.1 Safe action and safe title areas.

for NTSC use. Developers use this information, or predetermined NTSC color palettes, to select colors that will display properly on televisions.

8.3 Digital Television

Television, as its name suggests, began as a broadcast medium. The digital revolution in video will be complete when analog TV broadcasts are replaced with digital transmission. In the U.S., the federal government has mandated that television broadcasters switch to digital transmission, and many digital programs are already available. Digital transmission of converted analog broadcast material is even more common: the small-dish satellite receivers of services such as Direct TV transmit MPEG-2 encoded digital video. This is not yet digital television (**DTV**), however, because analog-to-digital conversion takes place both at the source and at the end-delivery point of the video. The video source is the analog signal of traditional television. This is converted to the digital MPEG-2 format for transmission via satellite. At the receiver, this digital signal is processed to return it to the standard NTSC analog format for display on an analog monitor.

By contrast, DTV is digital at each stage of video creation and delivery. The video is produced with digital cameras and transmitted as a digital signal to a digital television. The NTSC signal, with all its analog limitations, is completely eliminated. Crisper, clearer images are produced as a result of higher screen resolutions and richer colors. DTV also differs from NTSC analog video in two other ways: it changes the shape of the screen and it provides a choice of screen resolutions.

Aspect Ratio

DTV introduces a new aspect ratio for the television screen. Instead of the 4:3 format of analog television, DTV uses a wider, 16:9 aspect ratio. This is closer to the format used in film, thus promoting the merger of film, video, and computers. Under the NTSC standard, conversion of film to video required modifications that either filled the television screen but sacrificed part of the original film image ("full screen") or left horizontal bands above and below the film when shown on a TV ("letter box").

Screen Resolution: SDTV and HDTV

Broadcasters are allotted a transmission bandwidth for digital television of 19.39 Mbs. The codec used for transmission (MPEG) is scalable: different data rates can be selected for any given video. Some programs, such as talk shows, can be more efficiently compressed than others because they present less complex scenes and less motion. These programs will consume less bandwidth than, for instance, a major sporting event, which would probably be broadcast with less compression and at a higher screen resolution. Broadcasters can divide their assigned bandwidth into sub-channels to simultaneously distribute several programs or they can choose to devote their resources to a single high-quality transmission.

To support these options, DTV specifies Standard Definition (**SDTV**) and High Definition (**HDTV**) digital television standards. *SDTV* provides a screen resolution of 704 × 480 pixels and supports either interlacing (480i) or progressive scan (480p). *HDTV* increases the screen resolution to produce higher quality images. There are two major options within HDTV: 1280 $\times$ 720 pixels using progressive scan (720p), or 1920 $\times$ 1080 pixels either in interlaced (1080i) or progressive scan format (1080p).

8.4 Digital Video

The future is digital. And nowhere is this more evident than in film and video. But digital video poses very significant challenges for multimedia developers. The most important challenge is large file size. Like its analog cousin, digital video is composed of a series of rapidly displayed individual images. Each image is made up of very small picture elements or *pixels*. Each pixel is assigned a color. To reproduce a photo-realistic range of colors requires a 24-bit code for each pixel. The lowest resolution computer monitors display a grid 640 pixels wide and 480 pixels high. This translates to 307,200 pixels and nearly a megabyte of digital data for each screen. Full motion video requires display of thirty of these screens each second. A computer must store and process almost 30 MB of data for every *second* of uncompressed digital video. This was well beyond the processing and storage capabilities of earlier microcomputers. Dramatic improvements in hardware and compression techniques have largely overcome earlier limitations for desktop display of full-screen video. DVD players are common additions to personal computers and small, portable devices, such as PDAs and iPods, also effectively display digital video. Large video files are still a major challenge, however, particularly when an application is intended for distribution over the Web. Multimedia developers must often make compromises as they try to incorporate high quality digital video in their applications.

> Sound also adds to the size of video files. CD-quality stereo sound requires approximately 10 MB per minute.

Digital Video Quality

The quality of digital video depends on three main factors: *screen resolution*, *frame rate*, and *compression method*. **Screen resolution** is the number of horizontal and vertical pixels used to present the video image. Screen resolution determines how large the video will appear to the user, for instance, as a window 720 pixels wide and 480 pixels high. Frame rate is the number of individual video frames displayed per second. The compression method, or **codec**, is the particular algorithm or set of algorithms used to compress and then decompress the digital video. Large display sizes and higher frame rates require more processing and greater bandwidth. This in turn often demands greater compression.

Screen Resolution   The smaller the screen resolution of a digital video, the less processing, storage, and transmission it requires. Developers often reduce screen resolution to match the capabilities of the output medium. This is called the **output resolution** of the video. The output resolution of the relatively high quality DV (Digital Video) format is 720 $\times$ 480 pixels. This requires the computer to process and transmit information for nearly 350,000 pixels at rates of up to 30 times per second. Slower delivery options such as CD-ROM and Internet video streaming cannot transfer data at this rate. Reducing display size to 320 $\times$ 240 for CD-ROM cuts the number of pixels to less than 80,000; using 240 $\times$ 180 for Internet video reduces pixels to just over 43,000.

Frame Rate   The standard frame rate for video in the U.S. is 29.97 frames per second. Video intended for streaming over the Internet is often delivered at a rate of just 15 frames per second, effectively cutting the required data rate in half.

The perception of continuous motion in video is dependent on two factors. First, images must be displayed rapidly enough to allow persistence of vision to fill the interval between frames. Second, the changes in the location of objects from frame to frame must be relatively gradual. Lowering the frame rate both slows the delivery of individual images and drops out frames of video. If the rate is low enough, viewers will experience a string of still images with abrupt changes of content—in other words, a jerky video. In general, frame rates below 15 fps will not maintain the perception of smooth motion, although this is also affected by the complexity and amount of motion in the video itself. To assure acceptable results, developers often test various frame rates for a particular video.

Compression Strategies   Compression is the key to the successful delivery of digital video. All digital video delivery formats incorporate some form of compression, and advances in compression algorithms have made major contributions to expanding the use

> A codec provides instructions for a computer to compress a file and then decompress it to display a version of the original.

of high quality digital video. Multimedia developers seldom venture into the technicalities of video codecs. On the other hand, they routinely make choices based on their knowledge of the basic strategies supported by different compression options. These strategies include *intra-frame*, *inter-frame*, and *variable bit rate* encoding techniques.

Intra-frame Compression   **Intra-frame compression** re-encodes the information in a single frame of video (*intra* means *within*). Lossless strategies such as *RLE* (Run Length Encoding, see Chapter 2) can be used for intra-frame compression. The result is a smaller, more efficient file that reproduces all of the information of the original. Most intra-frame compression, however, is *lossy*, that is, some of the original information is lost when the file is decompressed. A popular lossy codec is JPEG. JPEG files are widely used on the Web to encode photorealistic still images at the smaller sizes required for network transmission. JPEG compression is **scalable**—compression can be accomplished at various levels from high to low quality. Low quality images will have very small file sizes and may be useful for links or buttons leading to a higher-quality, larger image. The video version of JPEG is called **M-JPEG** (Motion-JPEG). Individual images are compressed and linked together as motion sequences that can then be edited using digital video software.

Some video compression strategies, such as the popular DV format, use intra-frame compression alone. This is often the best choice for video intended for editing since it preserves each individual frame of the video. The video editor can then cut or modify the individual frames as needed.

Inter-frame Compression   **Inter-frame compression**, by contrast, eliminates some intervening frames, saving only the changes between frames (*inter* means *between*). **MPEG** (Motion Picture Experts Group) is a codec specifically designed for video that uses both intra-frame and inter-frame compression. Many video sequences can be dramatically compressed using inter-frame compression. For instance, a video of a newscaster reading a story contains a series of frames in which very little motion occurs. One frame may differ from another only in the position of the lips of the speaker, while others may shift only slightly more as she moves her head or shoulders. MPEG saves some frames as complete, compressed images. These are called *I-frames*, for "intra-frames," since they do not differ from the strategy used in intra-frame compression. Subsequent frames record only the parts of the image that have changed between I-frames and discard the rest of the image. These are designated either as *P-frames* (predictive frames) or *B-frames* (bidirectional frames). P-frames record more significant changes. B-frames are the frames between I and P frames; they record smaller changes. MPEG encoding produces much smaller files than can be created by intra-frame compression alone. When an MPEG file is decoded, the processor reassembles the dropped frames by using I-frames as references to re-create the intervening frames with the changes stored as predictive or bi-directional frames.

Interframe compression is an excellent choice for the *distribution* of digital video because it compresses the original video files so effectively. This technique is not the best choice for *recording* source video intended for editing, however. Dropped frames must be reconstituted in order to edit the sequence and less original information is preserved.

Variable Bit Rate Encoding   There are two major approaches to encoding digital video data. The first uses *constant bit rate encoding* or *CBR*. **CBR** assigns the same number of bits per second to all parts of the video, independent of content. Both simple and complex video sequences are encoded using the same number of bits per second. **VBR**, or *variable bit rate encoding*, analyzes the video content and assigns more bits to encode complex scenes and fewer bits for simpler scenes. In effect, this invests computing resources where they are most needed, allowing a higher quality reproduction of complex scenes. VBR is a common rendering option in video editing software.

Common Video Codecs   There are many different video codecs. Among the more widely used are MPEG, M-JPEG, and RealVideo. MPEG includes several different codecs, including MPEG-1, MPEG-2, and MPEG-4. MPEG-1 is a widely supported format that effectively delivers shorter amounts of video on Video CD, an optical disc format. MPEG-2 produces higher quality video for the larger capacity, faster, DVD format. MPEG-2 is also widely used in the transmission of digital video for television. MPEG-4 is optimized for the delivery of video over the Web where relatively low bandwidths require higher levels of compression. RealVideo uses proprietary codecs to encode streaming video for the Web and is widely available as a plug-in for browsers. Of course, not all video is intended for immediate distribution. Multimedia developers often need to render video in a form suitable for authoring or archiving. In these cases the format often chosen is **DV**. DV uses another codec, M-JPEG, to produce less-compressed higher quality files free from interframe compression.

Digital Video File Formats

The variations in digital video file formats reflect the different uses that can be made of the medium. Some formats support very high resolutions and use minimal compression. These are generally intended for high-quality video cameras and editing systems.

They are used in the production of broadcast quality video or film. Others are specialized for particular output options, such as CDs, DVDs, streaming websites, or digital television. Developers use these formats to render their final projects in a form suitable for delivery.

- **D1** is a high-resolution component color format used in expensive cameras and editing systems for the production of broadcast quality TV using 19mm tape.
- **D2** and **D3** are less expensive composite color formats used for TV production. They also use a 19mm tape.
- **DV** is a smaller tape format (6mm) widely used in both consumer and professional production and editing. DV uses component color and M-JPEG intraframe compression.
- **CD-video** is a widely supported format for the distribution of video on CDs that uses component color and MPEG-1 compression.
- **DVD video** is a component color format that uses MPEG-2 compression and provides a screen resolution of 720 $\times$ 480 pixels. This is the format used for the distribution of video on DVD optical discs.
- **QuickTime** is a cross-platform format for the distribution of video, animation, and sound files. QuickTime supports a variety of codecs and screen resolutions. QuickTime files use the .mov file extension.
- **Video for Windows** is a PC format for video distribution. Video for Windows uses the .avi file extension.
- **RealVideo** is a streaming format for delivery of video over the Web.
- **SDTV** and **HDTV** define a new aspect ratio and several screen resolution options.

8.5 Sources of Digital Video

Multimedia developers have two ways to acquire digital video: they can convert existing analog video to a digital format or they can purchase or create original digital footage.

Making Digital Video from Analog Video

Analog video is often a source for digital video. Analog tapes and laserdiscs can be sampled and converted to digital format for use in fully digital multimedia applications. Analog video is converted to a digital format by the sampling techniques familiar from graphics and sound. The output from a VCR or laserdisc player is connected to a digitizing board that samples the signals and records the value of each sample. Digitizing boards are often installed in computers as add-on cards. They may also be connected as an external device.

Digitizing boards contain **ADC**s, *Analog to Digital Converters*. These devices sample the electrical currents produced by playing the analog source and store the resulting voltage levels as digital values. In much the same manner, ADCs are also used to capture the audio content of analog video. Measurements of the voltages that produce sound are taken and stored as digital values. Many digital video cameras can also digitize analog video. A VCR or laserdisc player is connected to the camera's analog input port and played while the camera is in *record* mode. This samples the analog video and stores the resulting digital file on the camera's tape, disc, or drive.

The quality of digitized video depends on the format of the analog source video and the method used to connect the analog playback device to the digitizing device. Formats such as S-VHS and Hi8 support higher resolutions and Y/C color and can produce better digital video than their lower resolution composite counterparts. These advantages can be easily lost, however, if proper cabling is not used. S-VHS and Hi8 devices typically provide output options for both composite and Y/C color. Common composite connectors include coaxial cable and RCA jacks (Figure 8.2). The output from either of these mixes the Y/C signal into a composite signal, just as in NTSC broadcast or the lower quality VHS or 8mm formats. To maintain the advantage of Y/C color, a special **S-Video** cable that transmits luminance and chrominance information through separate wires must be used. S-Video connectors are provided on S-VHS and Hi8 devices and on most digitizing devices.

Figure 8.2 S-Video & RCA connectors.

Creating Original Digital Video

There are three main steps in creating an original digital video: *shooting*, *editing*, and *rendering*.

Step One: Shooting   Effective shooting of digital video requires planning. Developers review the intended uses of the video. They list the shots that will be required. They consider weather, lighting conditions, and the availability of personnel. They also consider the ways in which video will be integrated with other media in the completed project.

Stand-alone videos are sometimes shot with the intent of doing little more than recording a particular event and immediately sharing the result with others. **Shooting to record** attempts to capture the ultimate form of the video as the shooting is done. Lighting decisions may involve little more than keeping the sun to the shooter's back and the identification of essential shots may be a short list committed to memory. But video destined for a multimedia application is seldom shot in this way.

In a multimedia product, video works with text, graphics, and other elements to inform, entertain, or persuade a user. The effective integration of video with other media almost always demands careful editing of the original footage. **Shooting to edit** captures source footage with editing in mind. The videographer carefully plans the shoot, concentrating on acquiring a variety of individual video sequences, or clips, that will later be trimmed, re-ordered, and blended to effectively communicate a message.

Recording the Shots: The Digital Video Camera   The highest quality digital video requires expensive equipment and trained professionals. Such shoots are carefully budgeted and painstakingly planned. In recent years, the development of higher quality, affordable cameras and increasingly powerful desktop editing systems has put digital video within the reach of a wide range of multimedia developers. Like the video professional, these developers will generally "shoot to edit," trying to record a variety of video images as source material for the editing process.

Shooting to edit requires a camera designed to record high-quality source footage. The most important considerations include the number and quality of CCDs, lens quality, microphone location and quality, storage file format, and light sensitivity.

- *CCDs:* A **CCD**, or *Charged Coupled Device*, generates different levels of electrical voltage based on variations in the intensity of light striking its surface. These voltages are then converted to digital values to store data about each pixel of a digital image. The size of CCDs varies from approximately 1/16 to 1/2 inch or more. Larger CCDs are used in more expensive cameras. The number of CCDs is also important. To digitally record color, each sample must include information about the proportions of red, green, and blue light. Two approaches are taken to defining these RGB levels. In the first, a single CCD is used. The incoming light is passed through filters and the CCD records the level of each filtered color. In the second approach, the light is split into the three-color components by a prism and three separate CCDs are used to record red, green, and blue levels. Three-CCD cameras produce clearer, more accurate color. While these cameras remain more expensive than single CCD models, prices have fallen and good three-CCD options are increasingly available in the "prosumer" category.
  The resolution of the CCD is also important. Higher resolution CCDs sample smaller elements of the image and produce more accurate digital images. This is reflected in larger horizontal and vertical dimensions. Higher resolutions are particularly important when the camcorder will be used to capture still images. For motion capture, resolutions that are higher than the format used to store the video (for instance, 720×480 for DV) are not necessary.
  Whether the camera is used for still or for video capture, the resolution of the CCD itself is the most important measure of camera resolution. Camera resolutions are sometimes stated based on digital enlargement rather than CCD resolution. *Digital enlargement* uses software to interpolate new pixels to increase image size. The results never match the accuracy of a higher resolution CCD. Camera selection should always be based on the resolution of the CCD itself.
- *Lenses:* As in still cameras, the quality of an image is greatly affected by the quality of the lens. Higher quality cameras use lenses from better vendors and they also support higher zoom ratios through the use of camera optics, rather than software. In fact, digital video producers often suggest that software zoom capabilities be ignored in selecting a camera, since they produce inferior results to optical zoom. In addition, software zoom, if desired, can always be applied during the editing process on a computer.
- *Microphones:* Microphone placement, type, and quality are important for accurately capturing sound in a digital video. Microphones are designed differently to capture different types of sound. *Omni-directional* microphones are optimized to capture a broad range of background sound. *Unidirectional* microphones are intended to record sound from a narrowly defined location. *Zoom* microphones match their pickup patterns to the camera's zoom lens. At wide zoom, they act as omni-directional microphones, picking up ambient sound. At narrow zoom ratios, they act like unidirectional microphones, focusing on the sound directly in the camera's path. Some cameras include "shoes" to which a variety of types of microphones can be attached. Microphones on some cameras are built into the camera case. These are more likely to pick up camera noise. Others largely avoid this problem by mounting the microphone on a handle toward the front of the camera. The use of headphones during shooting is often recommended because they provide a direct indication of the effectiveness of the microphone while the shoot is in progress.

- *File Format:* The file format supported by a digital video camera is also important. Source footage should not be highly compressed and should be captured at the highest resolution available. Desktop video producers often chose the DV format because it limits compression to approximately 5:1, uses M-JPEG compression, and has relatively high resolution (720 × 480). As noted previously, M-JPEG has the advantage of using only intraframe compression, a significant advantage for source video destined for editing.

- *Light Sensitivity:* Cameras vary in their ability to effectively capture images in low light conditions. This is measured in units of lux. Lower lux ratings indicate that a camera can operate in lower light conditions. DV camcorders vary in their low-light capabilities from approximately 2 to 8 or more lux. A variety of auto exposure presets are also often available for different lighting conditions—for instance, sunlight, moonlight, spotlight, or dusk. Supplemental lighting can also often be attached directly to cameras or provided through stand-alone lights.

> A *lux* is the light given off by one candle over a one square meter surface.

Shooting Basics   Like still photography, effective videography requires an understanding of the capabilities of the camera and an awareness of basic "best practices." Developers prepare for shoots with extra batteries, tapes, external mikes, and headphones. They know the automated focusing and light modes the camera supports and also how to shift to manual control when necessary. They also note the advice of professionals for *framing shots*, *camera motion*, the use of *pans* and *zooms*, and taking care of *time code*.

> **White Balancing**
>
> *White balancing* is the process of adjusting a camera to correctly record white in different lighting conditions. Different types of light—the sun, incandescent bulbs, fluorescent tubes, and so on—produce different hues of white. A camera that is not white balanced may produce video with an inaccurate color tint. Most cameras can be automatically white balanced by briefly recording a white object. Videographers often carry a piece of white cloth for this purpose: they aim the camera at the cloth and record for a few seconds. White balancing is particularly important when changing from one artificial light source to another or between indoor and outdoor recording.

- *Framing a Shot: The Rule of Thirds*

The **rule of thirds** is perhaps the most widely embraced guideline for framing a video shot. To use the rule, mentally divide the camera image into thirds both vertically and horizontally by inserting two equally spaced lines in both directions. Subjects are then aligned on the intersection of these lines (see Figure 8.3). The choice of left or right vertical line or upper or lower horizontal line is based on the direction of the motion. In general, the subject should be moving toward the open area of the frame. A shot of a runner on a track moving to the left of the camera, for example, frames her body on the right vertical line, with her eyes on the intersection of that line and the uppermost horizontal line. Using the rule of thirds, rather than simply centering the image, preserves its interest and meaningfully relates it to the action that is taking place. It also helps to ensure adequate side and headroom, thus avoiding an unintentionally cramped or cropped image.

- *Minimizing Camera Motion: Shakes, Pans, and Zooms*

Excessive camera motion is a distraction. This is particularly true of the jumpy images produced by unsteady hands, but many professionals also caution against the intentional motions introduced by pans and zooms.

Figure 8.3 The rule of thirds.

Digital video cameras often include image stabilization technology to minimize shakes and jitters. While these may be helpful, they are no substitute for the use of tripods or basic techniques, such as using flat surfaces to support the shooter's hands and arms or holding the camera close to the body when no other source of support is available.

Pans (moving side to side) and zooms (enlarging camera images by lens changes) can serve useful functions. The slow pan of the vast, empty sea from the perspective of the life raft helps to tell a story. Zooms can readily vary the amount of detail conveyed in a scene and are also often useful. But both techniques are difficult to use effectively without specialized equipment to stabilize the camera. Professionals generally restrict their use by panning slowly in just one direction, rather than also panning back. Similarly, they zoom slowly to a fixed point rather than repeatedly zooming in and out. For most video shots, the best rule is to capture moving images with a *still* video camera.

■ *Taking Care of Time Code*

Digital video cameras write a **time code** as they are recording images and sound. The code is in the form hours: minutes: seconds: frames. A time code of 01:21:36:05 indicates a location at one hour, twenty-one minutes, thirty-six seconds, frame five. This code can be viewed on each frame of the video and it serves as the frame's address. Time code makes it possible to easily locate specific video segments. Editing software uses time code to carry out splits, trims, transitions, and other effects. Digital video cameras will record a single, continuous time code for the full length of a tape provided that they begin a new recording session at a previously recorded point. If the tape is advanced beyond an earlier recording point, however, the time code will be broken and a new code sequence will begin when the camera resumes recording. This may happen when the camera is shifted to VCR mode to view a previously recorded segment and then advanced beyond the last recorded frame before recording is resumed. Since there is no time code on the tape, the camera treats it as it would a new tape and starts the code over again. The result is that different frames will share the same time code or "address." In order to avoid this conflicting information and the complications it creates for cataloging and editing video, it is important not to break the time code. Cameras often provide an "End Search" control to automatically locate the end point of recording.

■ *Getting the Right Shots*

Video planning also includes the identification of particular types of shots needed. Video is used to convey a message. Just as a traditional author chooses words carefully, so, too, the videographer carefully selects images. One consideration is *coverage*—the source video needs to cover all the important elements of the subject being recorded. A documentary of a figure skating competitor might require source footage of her arrival at the arena, practice sessions, discussions with her coach, and the nervous anticipation of her parents, as well as the competition itself.

In addition to covering all aspects of the subject, videographers are careful to include a variety of different types of shots. Some shot variations reflect changes in the camera's *field of vision*.

■ *Close up* shots (CUs) fill the screen with the subject, focusing the viewer's attention on its details. Close ups are often used for dramatic effect—the tension in the face of the coach as the skater approaches a difficult jump. These are often among the most powerful video images.
■ A *medium* shot (MS) frames the whole subject. Medium shots are used to present the main action or tell the story. The camera frames the skater's whole body as she begins her routine. The greater part of most videos consists of medium shots.
■ A *wide shot* (WS) presents the subject as relatively far away and is often used to orient a viewer to the scene of the action. The camera moves out from the skater, showing the stands and the cheering spectators.

There are variations on these basic shot categories—a BCU (big close up), for example, is an extremely close shot of a subject, while an MCU is a medium close up. Other important basic shots include establishing shots, cutaways, point of view shots, reverse angles, and over-the-shoulder shots.

■ An *establishing shot* orients viewers by providing an image identifying the subject. This may be a wide shot, such as the skating arena framed against the city skyline. It could also be a medium shot of a banner presenting the name of the event or a close up of a ticket stub.
■ A *cutaway*, as its name implies, momentarily takes the viewer away from the main subject to a related image. As the skater completes the most difficult part of her routine, a cutaway displays the crowd reaction.
■ A *point of view* shot shows what the subject would see—a camera behind the skater captures the bouquets of flowers being thrown from the stands at the end of the performance.

- A *reverse angle* shot is sometimes called a shot/reverse shot. A shot of the subject is taken from one angle and another shot is taken from a different angle. This may be accomplished either by using two cameras or by moving the camera and re-staging the scene. This technique is often used in interviews. One image shows the skater as she responds to a reporter's animated questions after her victory. The reverse shot is taken behind the skater and includes the face of the reporter. This heightens the sense of interaction between the two individuals.
- *Over-the-shoulder* shots include the subject as well as others observing the subject. With the competition over, the skater tells her story to a gathering of friends. The video is shot from behind the crowd of friends, showing portions of them, while focusing on the skater. Over-the-shoulder shots can efficiently present the interaction of a main subject with other elements of the scene.

With source footage in hand, the digital videographer is ready to begin the editing process and transform a scattered collection of images into a coherent video presentation.

Step Two: Editing   Video editing software ranges from basic consumer packages (iMovie, Movie Maker) to increasingly powerful "prosumer" applications (Final Cut Pro, Premiere, Pinnacle Edition), to specialized, expensive software for professional video and film production. The prosumer category provides desktop multimedia producers, and even some professional videographers, with a powerful complement of video editing tools.

Digital video editing involves four major tasks:

- capturing video from an external source
- arranging separate video sequences or "clips"
- splitting and trimming clips and
- adding transitions and special effects.

Editing software provides the tools to perform these tasks. Editors include windows in which each of the activities takes place. The names and specific features of these windows vary from product to product but virtually all include variants of preview, library, and construction windows.

A *preview window* displays the source video prior to capture and also is used to preview the current project at any time during the editing process. VCR-like controls are provided to rewind, fast-forward, pause, and play. Clips that have been transferred to the computer are located in a *library window*. The library window may also display titles, transitions, and effects that can be applied to the video. Clips are edited and combined in a *construction window*. The construction window presents the assembled video clips either as a **storyboard** or as a **timeline**. The storyboard is a more general overview in which each clip is represented by a single video frame. The storyboard shows the order of clips and the transitions between them. This makes it easy for an editor to review the overall organization of project elements. The timeline is a more precise representation of the project. Timelines show the duration of the video and include multiple tracks. Tracks

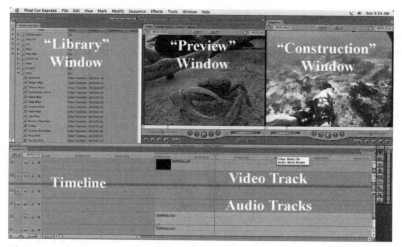

Figure 8.4 Windows, Timeline, and Tracks in a basic video editor (iMovie).

are used to store different video clips and audio recordings. Timelines can be zoomed out to display the entire project or zoomed in to show individual video frames.

Capturing/Importing Video   The first step in the editing process is getting the video from the camera to the computer. This is described as *video capture* or *video importing* depending on the program being used. Some digital video cameras record directly to DVD discs. In these cases the computer's DVD drive can be used to transfer the video. As noted previously, however, DVDs use MPEG2 compression, a format that is not as well suited to video editing as DV tapes. In addition, DVD recording does not produce the time code found on DV tape. For these reasons, many cameras continue to use tape to store digital video. Transfer to the computer is done through a FireWire connection. FireWire supports transfer rates as high as 800Mbps, making it very suitable for the transfer of large video files.

Scene detection is a technique that can improve the efficiency of video capture. In addition to the time code found on DV tape, digital video cameras also record several data items along with sound and images. These are typically the date and time of day. Editing software can use changes in this data to identify different recording sessions as separate scenes. These can then be captured individually. This makes it easier to select segments for editing since the source footage is broken into identifiable sections rather than appearing as one long video sequence. Scene detection can also be based on changes in video content. The editing software examines the incoming video for major image changes and establishes scene breaks as these changes occur. Content-based scene detection is less reliable than scene detection based on the data code, though the editing software may allow users to change the parameters being used to improve the accuracy of scene identification. Content-based techniques are particularly useful when data code is not available, as, for example, with video converted from an analog format.

Batch capture is the process of transferring only those portions of a source tape that have been specifically selected. The video editor scans the tape, selects "in points" to mark the start of a desired scene and "out points" to mark the end of the scene. Once all desired scenes have been identified, the capture process is started. The editing software rewinds the tape and starts transferring the desired video scenes to the computer. Captured video clips are then stored on the computer's hard drive. They are visible in a library window and ready for the next editing step, arrangement on the storyboard or timeline.

Basic Video Editing Operations   Captured clips represent **source video**, raw video that will be used to create a finished product. Source video is selected for editing by dragging the clip's image in the library window to the desired point in the construction window. Once placed in the construction window, the clip becomes part of the master video. **Master video** is the sequence of clips as they are being developed in the editing environment.

The storyboard view of the construction window provides an easily grasped overview of the general structure of the master video. The editor can readily identify which clips have been added, their order, and any transitions that have been applied. Clicking on a clip will display it in the preview window where it can be played. The timeline provides a more precise view. Video can be inserted in different tracks. Audio can also be included in separate tracks. The timing of video and audio sequences, as well as transitions and special effects, can also be set on the timeline.

Splitting is the process of dividing a clip into multiple parts. Shooting to edit involves capturing many different types of shots. A particular clip may contain a wide shot that is ideal for orienting a viewer early in the video and another that makes an effective closing shot. Splitting allows these segments to be used wherever they are most effective. Splitting can be done on the timeline and is sometimes supported in the library window as well.

Video editors are constantly searching for the most effective way to use their source material. This often involves deleting frames from clips. **Trimming** is removing unwanted frames from the beginning and/or end of a video clip. The editor identifies a new start point and a new end point. The software then deletes the frames that fall outside this range. Trimming can be carried out on the timeline. More advanced programs also provide a separate window or windows in which the clip is displayed together with the specific controls needed for trimming: frame-by-frame advance, preview controls (play, stop, rewind), and buttons or sliding calipers to mark start and end points.

Trimming eliminates frames and therefore shortens the overall video. In some cases, it is important to maintain a particular video length. For instance, a commercial may need to be exactly sixty seconds or an image sequence may be designed to complement the reading of a poem that takes two minutes and ten seconds. One approach is to manually extend another video clip in the project to compensate for the lost frames of the trimmed clip. Another is to use a two-sided trim, also called a rolling edit. In a *rolling edit* trimming one clip automatically produces a lengthening of the next clip. This preserves the original duration of the video.

Transitions are the effects used to move into or out of a clip. Transitions are usually applied between clips, but they may also be used at the beginning of the first clip of a video or at the end of the final clip. While there are hundreds of variations on transitions, the major categories are *cuts*, *fades*, *dissolves*, and *wipes*.

- The *cut* is the simplest of transitions because, in a sense, it is not a transition at all. In the cut, one clip ends and another begins with no intervening effect.
- *Fades* are transitions between an image and a black screen. The beginning of a video is sometimes introduced by fading from black to the first image of the clip. The final clip may fade from the last image to black. Fades are also used between clips, often to suggest a major shift of scene.
- In a *dissolve*, the last image of one clip blends into the first image of the second. Dissolves often provide a subtle shift between scenes and tend to be used to suggest continuity between related actions (Figure 8.5).
- A *wipe* replaces one image with another by moving each in a particular pattern. A radial wipe, for instance, rotates a line around the screen with one end fixed at the center. As the line sweeps the screen, the first image replaces the second (Figure 8.6).

Video editors also provide a variety of tools for the creation of titles, credits, and other text. In addition to the usual control over font, size, and color, many editors provide special text effects, such as titles that appear to be typed onto the screen or rolling credits. The flexibility of digital editing assures the ready availability of many other special effects that can be applied to any part of the video. Everything from fog and rain to earthquake effects and fairy dust can be readily applied to digital video (see Figure 8.7).

Step Three: Rendering   The editing process creates master video that can only be used within the editing application. In fact, the master is actually a series of pointers and instructions for performing operations on the original source footage. Editing does not alter the source footage and it does not create a new video. This strategy preserves the original video information and it saves a great deal of file space.

To be useful in other applications or as a stand-alone production, the master video must be converted into a new, independent, video file. This usually involves the creation

Figure 8.5 A dissolve in i-Movie. The beach scene in the background is gradually replaced by the close up of the girl. See Color Plate 23.

Figure 8.6 A radial wipe in i-Movie. As the line sweeps the image, the wide shot of the beach replaces the close up of the crab. See Color Plate 24.

Figure 8.7 The fog effect in i-Movie. See Color Plate 25.

of new digital content—for instance, dissolves require new frames that combine elements from two or more different images and special effects will require modifications to many frames. **Rendering** is the process of applying the editing operations specified by the master video to produce a new, independent video file. Given the wide range of editing options available, rendering can become a very time-consuming, processor-intensive operation.

During rendering, the developer also specifies output options based on the video's intended use. Video intended for DVD distribution is rendered differently than video for the Web. The rendering options provided by digital video software include the video compression method; the resolution, or screen size; the frame rate; the video data rate; and the audio format and audio data rate.

One of the most important decisions is the choice of a *codec*. All digital video intended for distribution must be compressed. The particular codec used will largely determine the quality of the resulting video as well as the ways in which it can be effectively delivered. Editing software generally provides a range of choices, often including the various versions of MPEG and streaming formats such as RealVideo.

Screen resolutions also vary depending on the mode of delivery. A resolution of 720 × 480 is generally used for DVDs while a lower resolution such as 320 × 240 is more appropriate for the lower-capacity, slower CD media. Again, the lower bandwidths of many Internet connections result in the use of a lower resolution such as 240 × 180 for streaming video and video e-mail attachments.

The frame rate is another important factor in the size of video files. Reducing frame rates can dramatically reduce the amount of video information the computer must process in a given time. Computer hardware and network bandwidths continue to improve, but frame rates for videos streamed via the Web often must be reduced to ensure that a wide range of users can effectively view them.

Having selected an appropriate codec, resolution, and frame rate, developers then specify the *video data rate*. Codecs typically can compress at different quality settings. Setting a relatively low data rate will require more compression and will usually produce lower quality video. This is often essential, however, to ensure effective delivery. Rates vary from as low as 20 to 30Kbps for low-quality streaming video to approximately 9Mbps for DVDs. In addition to selecting a data rate, developers often also have the option to select either *constant* or *variable bit rate* encoding. VBR is sometimes done using two passes, one to analyze the video data to determine which scenes to record at a higher or lower rate, and a second to do the actual encoding. This slows the rendering process but usually results in higher quality than CBR.

Finally, most video also includes sound. Sound is recorded on tracks separate from video and can also be encoded using different codecs and data rates. When file size and data rates are not as critical, sound is often recorded in the uncompressed, widely supported PCM (Pulse Code Modulation) format. Compression options include MP3 and the Dolby Digital AC-3 formats.

8.6 Guidelines for Video

The production of high quality video has traditionally required expensive equipment, highly trained professionals, and generous budgets. Today, the availability of affordable, powerful digital tools—cameras, editing software, and computers—has made video a practical addition to many multimedia projects. Video is also complex and demanding, however. The successful use of video requires attention to basic guidelines for shooting, editing, and rendering.

Shooting

- Choose a camera carefully. Consider:
  - CCDs
  - Optics

- Microphones
- File formats
- Lux rating
- Steady the camera—use a tripod or lean against a solid surface.
- White balance prior to shooting, especially when changing between different lighting conditions.
- Avoid shooting into light and backlit scenes.
- Limit pans and zooms.
- Frame the subject—use the Rule of Thirds.
- Make an inventory of required shots.
  - Different angles
  - Wide shots, medium shots, and close-ups
  - Establishing shots, reverse angles, over-the-shoulder, and point of view
- Use the highest resolution available.
- Add external microphones if required.
- Use headphones to monitor sound quality.
- Record background sounds for use in editing.
- Don't break the time code.

Editing

- Protect source video.
  - Keep copies of original sources at the highest resolution and lowest compression.
  - Lock and label source tapes.
  - Store tapes away from televisions, computers, and other sources of magnetism.
- Save a copy of the master video prior to rendering.

Rendering

- Match codec, resolution, frame rate, and data rate to intended use and delivery medium.
- Use variable bit rate encoding when available.

8.7 Summary

Powerful microcomputers and sophisticated editing software have made it possible for all multimedia developers to add high quality video to their productions. While multimedia developers prefer to acquire and distribute video in a digital format, there are still many important uses of analog video. Developers therefore need to be aware of *basic analog formats* and several *design issues* that affect conversions between the two formats.

Digital video is characterized by very *large file sizes* that place significant burdens on processors, storage devices, and, especially, computer networks. Multimedia video is tailored to specific uses by adjusting *screen resolutions* and *frame rates* and choosing appropriate *compression* options.

Digital video can be produced from analog sources by *digitizing*, a process in which the continuous data of the source footage is sampled and converted to digital values. More frequently, digital video is acquired using *digital cameras* or as downloads of previously created digital video files. Relatively inexpensive digital camcorders can produce high quality *DV format* video that can be effectively edited by multimedia developers. Most multimedia development will require a *shoot to edit* approach in which careful planning identifies the range of necessary video clips. Editing software can then be used to *capture* video, *arrange clips*, carry out *splitting* and *trimming*, add *transitions* and *effects*, and finally render the *master video* as a new video file suitable for distribution.

Key Terms

8mm	Output resolution
ADC	Overscanning
Aspect ratio	PAL
CBR	Progressive scan
CCD	QuickTime
CD-video	RealVideo
Chrominance	Rendering
Codec	Resolution
Color gamut	RGB
Component color	Rule of thirds
Composite color	S-VHS
D1	S-Video
D2	Safe action area
D3	Safe title area
DTV	Scalable compression
DV	Screen resolution
DVD video	SDTV
Field	SECAM
File format	Shooting to edit
Frame	Shooting to record
Frame rate	Source video
HDTV	Splitting
Hi8	Storyboard
Illegal colors	Time code
Inter-frame compression	Timeline
Interlaced scan	Transitions
Intra-frame compression	Trimming
Luminance	Underscan
Master video	VBR
M-JPEG	VHS
MPEG	Video for Windows
NTSC	Y/C

Review Questions

1. What is the distinction between film and video?
2. What are the three broadcast analog video standards? Which one is used in the U.S.?
3. Define aspect ratio. What does it describe on a TV monitor?
4. What are three significant distinctions between computer and analog TV display technologies?
5. What does the "resolution" of NTSC video describe?
6. What is the difference between component and composite color?
7. What is a color gamut?
8. Why are some colors "illegal" for NTSC display?
9. What is the difference between progressive and interlaced scanning? Which does TV utilize and which does a computer use?
10. What is screen resolution and what does it mean for digital video?
11. Why do developers often need to adjust the output resolution of digital video?
12. What is a codec?
13. Identify and define the three main strategies for compressing digital video.
14. Identify one advantage and one disadvantage of inter-frame compression.
15. What is the distinction between MPEG2 and MPEG4 video compression?
16. Why is the DV format often used to archive digital video?
17. What are the three steps in creating original digital video?
18. Identify and explain the two main approaches to shooting video.
19. Describe the "rule of thirds" and explain its importance in shooting video.
20. What is time code and why is it important in shooting video?

Discussion Questions

1. Identify and explain the three factors that influence the quality of digital video output.
2. Why would a producer of a TV mini-series use component color if the video broadcast standard is NTSC?
3. You plan to convert all the family videos from analog tapes to a DVD. The source tapes include VHS, Hi8 and S-VHS formats. Which sources will deliver the best digital conversion and why?
4. Based on the distinctions between analog and digital video displays, would you recommend viewing a movie on a TV monitor or a computer monitor? Explain.
5. Why does digital video produce large data files?
6. How do developers control these large data files?
7. You are sent to shoot the source footage for a video promoting your college. Identify and explain three important considerations for shooting this digital video.

8. Your college plans to have one version of the video promotion on the college website and a second version on a DVD to accompany the admission's catalog. Identify and explain the important considerations when you render the video project for each of these uses.

9. Describe the features of a digital camera that are important to consider if your multimedia project requires professional quality digital video.

10. Locate a 45–90 second video clip on youtube.com. Discuss the quality of the video, including shot selection, camera control, and editing. How could the clip be improved?

Chapter 9

Animation

Topics you will explore include:

9.1 The Brave New World of Digital Animation

Animation is the pinnacle of modern multimedia. It incorporates and draws inspiration from each of the other media. And more than any other medium, animation exploits the creative and transforming potential of the computer as a "universal machine."

Computers have dramatically lowered the costs and increased the ease of creating many different types of animation. *Motion graphics*, for example, is the art of making titles, credits, and other graphic objects move across movie and television screens. For many years only large studios could afford these services. Now individuals and small groups readily create a wide array of flashing text, spinning logos, and image morphs to complement websites and other multimedia productions. Virtually every form of traditional animation from the simplest "flipbook" to the extraordinary creations of the great Disney Studios has been transformed by digital technology.

The revolution in animation is not just about economy and efficiency. The computer also provides developers with entirely new capabilities that have resulted in animations that were inconceivable a generation ago. These new creative powers draw on three principal capabilities of computers.

First, the computer supports *interactivity*. Traditional animation is a passive medium, intended simply for viewing. By contrast, the computer supports user participation. We do not *watch* video games or flight simulators. We *play* and *fly* them.

Second, computers can convincingly *simulate three-dimensional sensory experience*. Traditional animations were largely two-dimensional fantasy worlds that playfully presented improbable behaviors such as singing mice and flying men. The computer now supports an entirely different form of fantasy by creating realistic 3-D characters and scenes that are often indistinguishable from those of video or film.

Third, computers can *embody and implement rules of behavior*. A traditionally animated character does what it is *drawn* to do. Computer-animated characters do what they are *told* to do. There are many different types of "rules of behavior." Some determine how the object is to appear. Computers create realistic 3-D images through algorithms that, in effect, tell the object how to respond to simulated light. The rules may also determine motion. *Inverse kinematics* provides rules of behavior for the various limbs of animated characters so that the hipbone really is connected to the thighbone—and both move as they should. The airplane in a flight simulator flies realistically because the computer is implementing a set of rules to reproduce the responses of simulated airfoils to different flight conditions. The behaviors may also be psychological, as with game characters that react to certain situations, such as the presence of weapons or food, in particular ways whenever they happen to encounter them.

The computer transformed the work of animators by providing powerful tools of creative expression and new ways to engage their audiences. The potential of these new forms of animation is already clear in video games that addictively immerse their players in alternate realities and in films that convincingly substitute fully digital actors for human performers. As the film producer Jeffrey Katzenberg once remarked, thanks to computer-generated animation, "If we can imagine it, we can make it." These new powers follow directly from the programmability of the computer, from the fact that it is a universal machine with, in a practical sense at least, unlimited potential. Digital animation is indeed a "brave new world," one that will almost certainly continue to generate enthusiasm, revenue, and debate. To understand both the practice and the potential of this powerful new medium, we must first consider the basic elements of animation and the ways in which it was traditionally created.

Once you have finished this chapter, you should understand:

- The basic elements of animation: persistence of vision, frames, frame rates, flip books
- Fundamental animation techniques: shooting on twos, cycles, holds, ease-in, ease-out, stretch, squash
- Cel animation: cels, key frames, tweens, storyboards, pencil tests, scratch tracks, Leica reels
- 2-D digital animation: animated GIFs, rotoscoping, tween animation, programmed animation
- 3-D animation: modeling, surface definition, scene composition, motion techniques, rendering
- Basic animation guidelines

9.2 Animation Basics

Over the course of the twentieth century, animation evolved from a simple recreational pastime to a major communications industry. It was the development of the camera and "motion pictures" that finally gave animators the practical tools they needed to display their creations to large audiences. The basics of animation were known long before, however, and they continue to be relevant today.

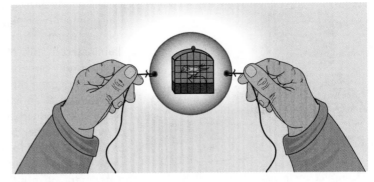

Figure 9.1 Thaumatrope.

All animations are a rapidly displayed sequence of individual, still images. The earliest animation devices worked with only a few images and offered little control over display rates. The *thaumatrope* was a simple disc, with strings attached, and just two images, one on each side. Operators held the disc between their hands and spun it by winding and then pulling on the strings. The spinning of the disc merged the two images. A picture of a man's head on one side and a hat on the other results in a combined image of a man wearing a hat. Figure 9.1 shows a bird in a cage. One side is a free bird and the other an empty cage. The thaumatrope illustrates the first basic feature of all animations: its dependence on a peculiarity of human vision. The images formed by the retina persist for a short time after the stimulus has disappeared. The persistence of the picture on one side of the thaumatrope causes it to blend into the other, producing a single, combined image. Animation, like film and video, makes use of this **persistence of vision** to produce the illusion of motion. Because one image fades into the next, a series of images, each differing slightly, can be used to produce the illusion of continuous motion.

The familiar **flipbook** can present dozens of images on a series of pages, each showing a different stage of a motion. As the pages are rapidly flipped beneath the thumb, the motion, such as a person walking, is displayed. The flipbook illustrates several additional elements of animation. First, the *quality* of the motion will depend on the rate of display—very slow flipping produces jerky, unnatural motion. Second, assuming an adequate rate of flipping, the *speed* of the motion will depend on the differences between the images—larger variations in the positions of arms and legs from one drawing to the next will produce the illusion of a faster walk. Third, each drawing must be a variation on its predecessor, usually with slight changes between the two. To produce a new image, it is important to be able to use the preceding one as a reference. This is accomplished by laying a new page over the drawing. If the paper is thin enough, the previous image will show through. Thicker papers will require a light table to illuminate the underlying image. This process of drawing with reference to preceding images is traditionally known as **onionskinning**. Finally, the flipbook also illustrates *registration*, another basic requirement of animation. Registration is a way of physically aligning the images with one another. The binding of a simple notepad accomplishes this. Drawing on a set of loose sheets requires pre-punched holes and peg systems or some other form of registration.

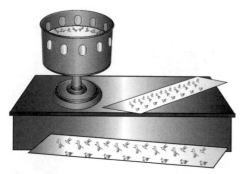

Figure 9.2 Zoetrope.

The nineteenth century saw the development of mechanical animation display devices. One, the *zoetrope*, was a rotating drum with slits on its side (see Figure 9.2). A light illuminated a strip of drawings fastened inside the drum. As the drum turned, the viewer caught a glimpse of each successive image through the passing slits. When the drum was rotated at an appropriate speed, persistence of vision blended the individual images and produced the perception of motion. Another device, called the *praxinoscope*, was used by Emile Reynaud to project short animations to audiences at his Théâtre Optique in Paris during the 1890s. This early experiment gave little more than a hint, however, of the enormous influence of fully developed animation.

9.3 Traditional Animation

Traditional animation is film-based. Individual images of the animation sequence are photographed and recorded as separate frames on a long strip of transparent film. The film is passed in front of the light of a projector and the animation appears on-screen. Later, video was used to encode the images and sounds of film on magnetic tape for television display. Movie theaters and televisions provided animators with the mass communication possibilities that drove the commercial development of traditional animation.

Film dramatically enhanced the expressive possibilities of animation. Multiple reels could hold any desired number of individual film images. This made it possible for animators to create longer animations with more subtle motions. Projectors reliably displayed images at frame rates that produced natural motion. And, finally, film allowed animators to add sound to their creations.

The Challenges of Traditional Animation

To bring their characters to life, animators must overcome a series of challenges. One major challenge is the sheer number of images to be created. Film is projected at 24 frames per second. Animators must somehow produce 1,440 individual images for every minute of animation. *Shooting on twos*, *cycles*, and *holds* are among the more popular strategies they use to manage this task.

Shooting on twos cuts the number of required images in half. Animators found that convincing motion can be achieved using pairs of identical images—each drawing, or set of objects, is usually photographed twice. In this way twelve images can do the work of twenty-four. Since each shot requires a separate scene setup, shooting on twos saves a great deal of production time.

A **cycle** is a series of images that can be re-used to extend repetitive actions. A common example is a set of drawings depicting a character walking. If the series is drawn so that the last step blends smoothly with the first, a long walk can be created by simply repeating the cycle as many times as desired (see Figure 9.3).

Holds are a sequence of identical drawings that express a particular state or action. For instance, a character's face and body may be drawn to express surprise. This drawing can then be repeated 24 times if the script calls for the character to express surprise for one second.

The animator also faces a series of artistic or creative challenges. Photographers and videographers capture the world before them. Animators must create their own worlds. We can catch a glimpse of this challenging creative process by briefly noting some of the common strategies animators use to bring their characters and scenes to life.

Effective portrayal of motion requires an awareness of how things actually move in the world. For instance, objects have mass and accelerate more or less gradually depending upon how heavy they are. The snowball starting its roll down the hill should move slowly at first and gradually gain speed. As it reaches level ground, it should gradually slow. Animators routinely use such gradual increases and decreases in rates of motion, called **ease-in** and **ease-out**, for many types of motion.

Objects often *overshoot* their resting-points. The snowball, slowed by a gradual piling up of snow in its path, makes a final forward lurch and settles back into its track as it comes to rest.

Figure 9.3 A cycle.

The different components of objects often move independently of one another. If the snowball strikes a tree at the bottom of the hill, the motion of the branches will, at first, lag behind the motion of the trunk. As the trunk comes to temporary rest at the extreme point of its motion, the branches will continue to move. Paying attention to such *overlapping motions* helps animators produce convincing, lively motions.

Close observation of the natural world is important for successful animation. But most animators are not trying to simply duplicate natural motion. Instead, animation usually derives its power from the skillful exaggeration of motion for dramatic effect. Often the exaggeration is simply in the rate of motion—the snowball eases into its downhill motion, but it gains speed with an unnatural rapidity and quickly grows to enormous proportions, scattering the terrified people in its path. Other forms of exaggeration focus on distortion. **Stretch** and **squash** are staples of the traditional animator's art (see Figure 9.4). The speeding snowball hits a bump and flies into the air. As it rises, it stretches to form a vertically elongated ellipse. It hits the ground and is squashed into a horizontal ellipse; it snaps back to a round shape and races on. Stretch and squash wildly exaggerate the effects of gravity to enliven the snowball's journey.

Normal   Squashed   Stretched

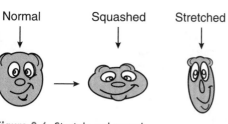

Figure 9.4 Stretch and squash.

These strategies have been applied to the wide range of animation subjects. In fact, anything that can be photographed is a candidate for animation. Paper cut-outs, clay figurines, puppets, and all sorts of natural objects have been posed, photographed, reposed, and photographed again to create the individual photo-frames of filmed animation. But the technique that most directly influenced the development of digital animation was cel animation.

Cel Animation

Cel animation was perfected and popularized by the Disney Studios of the early and mid-twentieth century. **Cel** originally referred to the drawings of individual animation frames made on sheets of celluloid, the same flexible, transparent material used for early films. These drawings were then photographed to produce the animated film. Today, acetate has replaced celluloid but the technique is still known by its traditional name.

The main advantage of cels is that they save enormous amounts of drawing time by allowing animators to break scenes into those parts that stay the same and those that must be changed from frame to frame. A single drawing can then be used over and over for the unchanging elements of the scene. For instance, if a character skips down a village path, the path, the village buildings, sky, clouds, trees, and so on are unchanging background items. These can be placed on one cel. Objects that change can be placed on another layer of cels. The skipping child will require a series of drawings, each depicting different positions of her arms, legs, head, and torso. Only the child will be drawn on this layer of cels. To create the individual frames of the animation, the two layers are stacked over a light source and the composite image—background village scene and one stage of the skipping child—is photographed. For the next frame, the top cel is removed and replaced with the cel image of the next stage of the skip. The background can be left in place—it needed to be drawn only once.

The cel animation technique saved time and also gave animators precise control over the elements of their creations. Individual cel layers could be used to reproduce interdependent, complex motions. For example, yet another layer of cels could be used for the drawings of lip positions to sync with a sound track of the girl singing as she skips down the path.

> At Disney it is estimated that each new animated film may entail the creation of a million drawings, sketches, and paintings.
>
> *Tim Campbell*

Cel animation also encouraged division of labor and promoted high artistic standards. One technique, keyframing, divided drawing tasks among various specialists. Master artists produced original sketches for major actions, the **key frames**. These are also often called *extremes* because they typically present just the extremes, or limits, of the action. The first key frame, or extreme, might show a cat as he begins his leap toward an unsuspecting mouse. The second key frame captures the collision with a wall as he misses his target. Assistants then painstakingly draw the sequences of step-by-step changes, called **tweens**, to produce the illusion of motion. Tween drawers take advantage of onionskinning to guide their work. The key frame drawing is placed on a light table and another sheet of paper is placed over it. The lower image shows through (as light shows through an onionskin) and is used to guide the drawing of the next stage of the action.

Key frame and tween drawings are then transferred from paper to celluloid by *inkers* who specialize in applying the lines to one side of the cel, while another set of specialists, *opaquers*, carefully apply colors to the other side. These artists must work with great precision and care. They wear cotton gloves to protect the soft acetate sheet and they work in dust-free environments to minimize the appearance of speckles in photographs of the cels. The results of their efforts are impressive. Individual cels are often works of art in their own right and many are highly valued collector's items.

Many additional specialists are required for the production of a traditional cel animation. These include producers, directors, script writers, audio specialists, camera operators, and even checkers, specialists in assuring that all the individual cels have been properly prepared, ordered, and aligned (or "registered").

Producing Cel Animation The cost and complexity of cel animation makes it important to carefully plan each step of production. *Storyboarding*, *pencil tests*, *scratch tracks*, and *Leica reels* are important planning and production guides. Many of these traditional practices have important counterparts in modern multimedia production.

A **storyboard** is a sequence of drawings that sketch out the content of major scenes in the animation. Storyboarding is a way for animators to develop and test their ideas and it is essential for successful animation. There are simply too many interdependent images and sounds in an animation to proceed without this critical guide. Major studios devote large, cork-covered walls in dedicated storyboarding rooms to the creation and display of these overviews of proposed animations.

A storyboard will sketch the action of the animation and note the dialogue or other sounds for each scene. The amount of detail presented varies with scenes. In some cases, it may be important to produce relatively complete, colored images to explore color schemes or lighting effects. In others, simple pencil sketches to explore proposed actions may be adequate. These sketches often become the basis for the **pencil test**, a series of simple sketches that are photographed and projected to test the design of animated sequences. This allows directors, artists, and others to check the movement of objects and characters and refine their ideas before committing the team to the development of fully drawn and colored cels.

The sound track is a critical element of most animations. Spoken dialogue, sound effects, and music create much of the dramatic effect of the production and they must be precisely synchronized to their corresponding images. A **scratch track** is a draft of the animation's audio track. Like the storyboard, the content of the scratch track varies with purpose and scene content. A completed musical score may appear relatively late in the development process, but dialogue will probably be an early addition to the scratch track because it is a critical guide to creating the motions of speaking characters. As production continues, animators test the interplay of sound and image by combining the scratch track with a projected version of the storyboard. Eventually, this testing may cover the full length of the animation, although many drawings and sounds will remain incomplete. This working draft of the complete animation is sometimes called a **Leica reel**, a reference to the relatively inexpensive Leica cameras originally used to photograph test cels.

The cel technique also requires specialized equipment and materials. Each layer of acetate filters out approximately five percent of the original light. This produces a noticeable difference in the perceived hue of the colors on lower layers. To compensate for this, specially prepared sets of paints in different hues are used. In this way, a red appearing on one layer will match the red of another. In addition to specialized cameras and lighting, cel animation also requires devices to:

- track changes in the paths of animated characters (animation stands, pantographs)
- precisely align stacks of cels for each of the thousands of individual camera shots (cel punches, peg plates), and
- synchronize and edit the final film (viewers, editing machines, splicers).

Cel animation, in short, is a complex, demanding, and expensive form of animation. It has also produced many of the finest examples of the animator's art.

By the 1960s, rising production costs curtailed most large-scale cel animations, and other forms of commercial animation were experiencing similar pressures. The computer dramatically improved the prospects for animation by placing new tools in the hands of an ever-wider audience of creative animators.

9.4 Digital Animation

Digital animation takes two different forms: 2-D and 3-D. Two-dimensional digital animation evolved from traditional techniques, particularly cel animation. Three-dimensional digital animation exploited capabilities unique to the computer to produce an entirely new form of animation.

2-D Animation

Developers can produce simple 2-D digital animations by mimicking basic traditional techniques such as the flipbook. *Animated GIFs* consist of a series of individual GIF images that are rapidly displayed in sequence. Simple software lets animators insert or delete images, vary the rate of display, stop or loop the animation, and so on.

Other forms of traditional animation also have digital counterparts. *Cutout animation* uses figures cut from paper or other flat material. These are often made up of separate parts, such as arms or legs that can be positioned differently to produce the various states of motion needed for the animation. Producing the figures, manipulating their parts, and photographing each set-up are time-consuming tasks. Digital paint and draw programs can be used to create and modify cutouts much more rapidly and with greater control of detail. Animation programs can then be used to quickly import these images, arrange them on a time line, set timing and transitions, and produce the final animation as a digital movie.

Rotoscoping was also transformed by digital techniques. **Rotoscoping** is the process of producing an animated sequence by tracing the individual frames of a film or video. This can be especially effective for animating complex motions, such as the twisting and turning of people dancing. Traditionally, the filmed dance would be projected one frame at a time to a surface on which an artist could trace the outlines of the dancers. The sequence of tracings captured the pattern of motion and the tracings themselves could then be developed by the artist to fit the subject and mood of the animation. Rotoscoping was labor-intensive and required specialized equipment usually available only at larger production studios. The computer makes rotoscoping a practical tool, available to virtually any animator. Film or video is simply converted to digital form or shot with digital cameras. Individual frames are then imported to image editing programs such as Photoshop that allow the artist to add a transparent layer and trace the desired parts of the scene. The original image layer is deleted leaving behind the traced layer. This can be further developed and saved as an animation frame. The individual frames are then imported to an animation or video program such as After Effects or Premiere where they are sequenced and edited.

More complex productions can be created using 2-D animation software that mirrors many of the elements of traditional cel animation. Animations are composed of a series of individual *frames* like the film frames used to present a cel animation, the frames are synchronized to one or more sound tracks, graphic elements can be placed on different layers corresponding to traditional cels, major changes in scenes are designated as *key frames*, and the illusion of motion is created by producing a series of tweens based on key frames.

Digital animation programs such as Flash or Director present frames as a horizontal row of small rectangles in a window called a **timeline**. Developers can easily move to different frames by clicking on a frame or by using simple controls similar to those on VCR or DVD players. The contents of the frame are displayed in another window where they can be edited. The timeline makes it possible to precisely control each frame of the animation.

A frame in a digital animation may be composed of multiple *layers*, just as a frame in a cel animation may be composed of several transparent sheets of "celluloid." As in cel animation, layers have a stacking order. The lowest layer is used for background elements, those images that remain the same as others are changed to produce the appearance of motion. Animators can easily change the order of layers. And unlike traditional animation, there is no need for precise registration devices to maintain alignment or different paints for different cel layers to compensate for the effects of opacity.

The *key frames* and *tweens* of traditional cel animation are also important components of digital animation. The creation of frames is facilitated by another digital variant of a traditional technique, *onionskinning*. Here the computer imitates the process of using one drawing as a reference for a new image by creating a faint image of the original on one layer and allowing the animator to draw on a second, higher layer. Animators can produce each successive frame manually. This is known as **frame-by-frame animation**, a technique that provides complete control over frame content, but is also very time-consuming.

Tween Animation   A powerful alternative to the frame-by-frame approach is tween animation. In **tween animation**, the animator creates the key frames and the computer automatically produces the tweens. There are several different types of tweens. A simple **motion tween** can be used to move an object from one position to another. The first key frame places the object in one position and the second places it in another. The program then fills in the intervening frames (see Figure 9.5). Tweening is also used to produce **path-based animation**: the animator draws a path from one key frame to another and the computer fills in the intervening images, spaced out along the path, to produce the desired motion (see Figure 9.6).

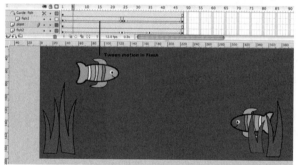

Figure 9.5 Motion tween defined in the timeline using Flash MX.

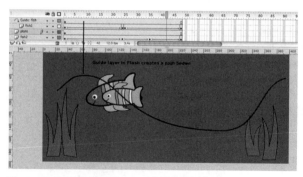

Figure 9.6 Path "motion guides" in Flash determine the location of each animated object.

Tweening is also used to animate other properties of objects. One common example is *morphing*, also known as *shape tweening*. In **morphing**, the shape of one image is gradually modified until it changes into another shape. The image of a child might be morphed to that of an adult or a drawing of a pen might be morphed to a rocket ship. The key frames in this case are the two images and, again, the animation program creates the tweens, the sequence of frames over which the program gradually alters the shape of the object, little by little, to complete a transition from one to the other (see Figure 9.7). Animators can control the way in which objects change by specifying the points of

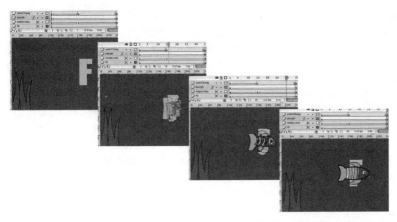

Figure 9.7 Shape tween or morphing in Flash MX. The letter F gradually changes into a fish.

the beginning and ending images that should correspond. These are called *hints*. Setting hints for eyes, ears, nose, and mouth, for example, creates a morph focused on those parts of a face.

Objects can also be readily enlarged or reduced on stage by **size-tweening**. Here the first key frame is the object at its initial size and the second is the final size. Color and transparency can be animated using key frames representing initial and final image properties using **alpha-tweening**. A flesh tone, for example, can gradually blend to a red to produce a blushing cartoon character. The opacity of two images can be adjusted to transition from one to another with the first fading as the second becomes more opaque (see Figure 9.8).

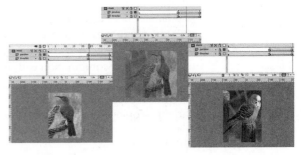

Figure 9.8 Alpha tween alters the opacity of two bitmap images over the timeline in Flash MX.

Other traditional animation tasks, such as the drawing and painting of images, are also completed more easily using the computer. Animation programs contain image-editing tools, usually organized in floating windows, or *palettes*. These allow animators to create new graphic objects or edit imported graphics.

Animation development is supported by a number of other tools: palettes for precisely placing and aligning objects on-screen; text tools to select fonts, styles, colors, kerning, and leading; basic sound control such as fades, enveloping, looping, and synchronization; and a number of tools and strategies to support interactivity.

Programmed Animation Applications such as Flash and Director are powerful digital versions of traditional tools and techniques. These allow animators to work with familiar metaphors such as key frames and tweens. Relatively little knowledge of computer languages or procedures is required to produce an animation using these techniques.

Programmed, or procedural, animation is a different approach. In **programmed animation**, animators write commands and the computer generates the animation. This requires knowledge of programming languages and the mathematical techniques required to specify patterns of movement as well as the other changes (size, shape, color, etc.) that occur in the animation.

> **Programmed Animation in Flash**
>
> The following script is a simple example of rotating an object through programming, rather than tweening:
>
> OnClipEvent (enterFrame) {_rotation += 9}

Programmed animation has several advantages. Files sizes are smaller because much of the animation consists of commands, rather than a series of images. This reduces storage, bandwidth, and processor requirements. As a result, programmed animations load and play more quickly, allowing them to be used on a wider range of computers and networks.

Another advantage is the relative ease with which different versions of an animation can be created. For instance, if an animation requires a large flock of birds, a single bird can be animated procedurally. The animator can then create different birds by simply altering the parameters governing direction, speed, wing motion, and so on.

Programmed animation also supports more complex forms of interactivity. In computer games, developers often provide users with a wide range of choices. Programmed animation allows the developer to specify the content of the animation that the computer will create based on the user's actions. The animation is then generated "on the fly."

Animation software may support both tweening and programmed animation. The scripting languages (Actionscript, Lingo) in Flash and Director, for instance, can be used to produce programmed animations. Once a programmed animation is created, it can be used alone or in combination with tweened animations.

The computer provides flexible, novel animation possibilities through programming and it transformed traditional 2-D animation techniques such as cel animation, cutouts, and rotoscoping. It had an even greater impact on 3-D animation.

3-D Animation

Traditional 3-D animations are created with sequences of photographs of three-dimensional objects such as clay figures, puppets, toys, models, and people. The animator sets up one scene, photographs it, makes changes to the figures to be animated, takes another photograph, and so on until the animated sequence has been completed. This is a time-consuming process requiring painstaking attention to the positions of the animated objects as well as careful control of camera angles and lighting.

The earliest applications of the computer to 3-D animation simply facilitated traditional approaches. For example, specially designed and programmed computers were used to precisely control the motion of cameras across a stage area. The computer allowed operators to shoot each frame, reposition objects, and shoot the next frame from a new position. When the frames were projected, the motion of the camera would appear perfectly smooth because of the precise positional control provided by the computer.

As the graphics rendering capabilities of computers improved, their role in 3-D animation changed. Now computers could be used to create convincing representations of three-dimensional objects themselves and then set them in motion. This eliminated the need for elaborately built stages and models and soon led to the creation of novel animations that could not be produced using traditional techniques. This new form of 3-D animation involves three major, interrelated tasks: *creating objects and scenes*; *defining motions*; and *rendering*.

Creating Objects and Scenes   Animators create their objects and scenes in much the same ways as 3-D graphics artists do—through *modeling*, *surface definition*, and *scene composition*. As discussed in Chapter 6, modeling defines the shapes of objects using techniques such as polygons, splines, and metaballs. Surfaces are defined by specifying materials (glass, metal, wood, etc.), applying image and bump maps, and establishing properties such as opacity and reflectivity. Animators compose scenes by placing objects and defining camera angles, lighting, and environmental effects.

Defining Motions   The second major task in 3-D animation is to define motions. The elements of a 3-D animation include the objects and sounds viewers will experience as well as the cameras and lights used by the animator to define the finished product. Virtually all of these elements can be set in motion. Cameras can move in and out of a scene as if they were on tracks or booms, lights can follow characters and, of course, the characters themselves can be transformed in all the ways established by the animation tradition. Stretch and squash, ease-in and ease-out, exaggeration and anticipation—all these traditional manipulations and more remain directly relevant to 3-D animation.

As in 2-D animation, 3-D developers use key frames to designate major changes in an animation with intervening frames produced by the computer. The movements captured in key frames can be created in several different ways. Models can be placed at different points in a scene to define a path that is then completed through computer tweening. Similarly, shapes, colors, transparency, and texture can be changed using key frames and tweens. The most complex motions typically involve models of humans and animals. Here it is necessary to manipulate individual body parts to achieve realistic motion. *Motion capture*, *forward kinematics*, and *inverse kinematics* are three of the major techniques used to animate animals and humans.

Motion capture, also known as *performance animation*, is the technique of recording the motions of actual objects, such as human or animal bodies, and mapping these motions to a computer-generated animated character. The "performers" are equipped with sensors to track the motion of various body parts as they create the actions to be animated. This information is transmitted to the computer and processed to produce the corresponding motion in the animated character on screen. In this way animation producers and performers can see the results of the performance and immediately make any necessary adjustments. Performance animation is often used to capture complex natural motions that would be difficult to create using other techniques. The technique has been used to reproduce the movements of highly realistic "virtual actors" and "virtual models" that are intended to be indistinguishable from real humans. In other cases, the results of performance animation are deliberately modified to be less realistic to fit the style of a specific production.

Kinematics is the study of the motion of bodies or systems of bodies. Animals are systems of body parts. The motion of one part, such as a knee, produces related motions in others—thigh, shin, and foot. In **forward kinematics**, objects are modeled as collections of separate elements that can be individually adjusted by the animator. To begin a walking motion the animator might slightly rotate the hips, move the thigh forward, rotate the knee, move the shin back, and slightly arch the foot. These adjustments can be made in different key frames with the smooth, finished walk produced by the computer through tweening. Forward kinematics is relatively simple to implement. The models are easily defined and computer processing is kept to a minimum. The quality of the finished product depends on the skill of the animator, however, and the process can be quite time consuming.

Inverse kinematics (IK) is the process whereby the motion of one body part produces related motions in other body parts. This allows the animator to move one object—a foot, for instance—and have the computer carry out the motions of related body elements—shin, knee, thigh, hips, and so on. The "legal" range of motion of each of these elements is pre-defined: a foot cannot revolve 360 degrees nor can a leg be bent forward past its straight position at the knee. Inverse kinematics greatly simplifies the work of animators and helps assure consistent, realistic motions.

IK presupposes basic anatomical knowledge and an elementary skeletal or bone system for the animated character. The trend in advanced 3-D productions is to extend the power of IK by incorporating more and more anatomical knowledge in the animation software. For example, DreamWorks created a program to simulate the interrelated motions of muscles. It was first used to create realistic facial expressions and was subsequently extended to the whole body for the major characters in the animated film, *Shrek*. The program, which they called a "shaper," simulated not only bones and joints but also underlying muscle and flesh. An arm movement shifts related bones and also produces the motions of the biceps and other muscles. These movements are then carried through to subtle motions of skin or clothing thus producing a very realistic animation.

Inverse kinematics requires careful planning and innovative programming. It also demands far more computer processing than forward kinematics. But IK has the potential to powerfully augment the work of animators by providing them with tools to quickly reproduce natural patterns of motion. Another technique to automate the animation of objects takes advantage of the computer's ability to model physical laws.

Animating with physics specifies motions based on the properties of objects and the laws of physics. Instead of the animator trying to envision the changes that gravity would produce on the path of a baseball, the animation program directly produces the ball's motion by calculating the forces acting on it. The animator simply specifies the direction and force of the hit (see Figure 9.9). Similarly, the animation program can calculate the bounce of different objects based on what they are made of (rubber, glass, lead, etc.), the forces acting on them, and the composition of the object they strike. Eventually, a 3-D animation program may automatically create virtually any form of interaction: a glass shattering against the floor, a basketball rebounding from a hoop, a fighter recoiling from a punch—all based on pre-programmed physical principles. These and other refinements, such

Figure 9.9 Applying a force in Carrara. The arrow indicates the direction of the force. The object automatically follows a trajectory based on its properties and the force. See Color Plate 26.

as IK, free animators from some of the more laborious aspects of 3-D animation, allowing them to concentrate on creating engaging characters and stories.

Rendering   As in static 3-D graphics, rendering is the final step used to produce the frames of a 3-D animation. **Rendering** creates the final animation frames by applying the modeling, surface definition, scene composition, and motion specifications created by the animator. An animation may be either *pre-rendered* or rendered *in real time*, "on the fly." The former approach is appropriate for applications with little or no interactivity, such as animated films. The latter is essential for highly interactive animations such as video games because the final form of the animation depends on the user's choices.

Pre-rendering of an animated feature film such as *Toy Story* or *The Polar Express* requires enormous processing resources. Each of the film's many thousands of individual frames is a high-resolution bitmapped image. The individual pixels that make up these images are defined by complex calculations carried out by the computer to implement the object properties, lighting, camera angles, and motions specified by animators. To render *Toy Story*, the first fully digital feature-length animated film, Pixar Animation used a "rendering farm," a network of 117 workstations, each with at least two processors. The task required 800,000 computer hours (a single computer would have taken 43 years to complete this task).

> **OpenGL and Direct 3-D**
>
> OpenGL and Direct 3-D are APIs, *Application Programming Interfaces*. OpenGL is a widely implemented cross-platform API while Direct 3-D is a Microsoft standard for Windows PCs.
>
> APIs specify standard definitions and functions that can be implemented by a range of software and hardware. For instance, OpenGL provides functions to draw 3-D objects from primitives, apply textures, set camera angles and lighting, and render scenes in real time. Programmers can use these functions with all OpenGL compliant hardware and software. This simplifies application development and also encourages rapid adoption of new devices such as improved video cards.

The luxuries of rendering farms and weeks of rendering time are not available for video games and other highly interactive 3-D animations. In these cases the computer must produce the animation immediately. More powerful computers and specialized *play stations* with powerful graphics processing capabilities are part of the solution to this challenge. Simplifying the animations themselves by creating objects with low polygon counts and minimizing the use of complex textures and shading is also important. The animated objects of a video game are usually created through programming languages such as C++ and then rendered in real time by rendering routines provided through Direct3-D or OpenGL.

9.5 Animation Tips and Guidelines

Animation covers an extremely wide range of productions from the very simple, such as spinning logos that can be produced quickly by individuals, to complex feature-length films that require years of coordinated effort by hundreds of artists and technicians. Nonetheless, many of the guidelines appropriate to larger productions are also useful for individuals and small teams. Animation typically requires greater computational resources than static media such as text, drawings, or photos and the process can easily become expensive and unwieldy without careful planning.

- Don't forget the learning curve! Animation programs are typically more difficult to master than other media-specific software.

- Design for delivery. Complex animations rapidly consume bandwidth and processing. Be sure your animation can reach its intended audience. To minimize animation file size:
  - Use simple backgrounds.
  - Simplify and limit the number of objects.
  - Limit the number of lights and the use of reflections and transparencies.
  - Experiment with different rendering options to pick the best combination of file size and quality.
  - Be sure to preserve an original uncompressed file.
- Consider clip animation. An appropriate animation may be available at little or no cost.
- Consult the tradition. The staples of the animator's art will often ease the development process and enliven a digital production. Consider:
  - Cycles
  - Holds
  - Shooting on twos
  - Tweening—motion, size, color, shape
  - Stretch & squash
  - Ease in & ease out
  - Overshoot & overlapping motion

9.6 Summary

The dramatic accomplishments of digital animation are based on a rich animation tradition, a powerful new set of digital tools, and, above all, the creativity of a new generation of writers, producers, animators, and programmers. The "universal machine" plays a two-fold role in their work.

On the one hand, computers serve as very efficient assistants in the animation process. In the hands of skilled developers, digital versions of traditional tools for creating, editing, and combining media save time and money. On the other, the computer has extended its role, becoming not simply a tool but also a virtual partner in the creative process. The key to this transformation lies in the computer's "universality"—its ability to embody any form of knowledge and intelligence that we can either define ourselves or find a means of empowering the machine to define for itself.

The practical effects of machine intelligence are already evident in 3-D animation techniques. We have seen them in advanced forms of rendering and in the variety of algorithms used to produce natural motions and behaviors. Here the computer creates scenes that animators simply could not know how to create on their own. New animation software will incorporate increasing amounts of knowledge and intelligence, allowing animators to express an unprecedented range of experience from the hyper-realistic world of virtual humans to otherworldly forms limited only by their imaginations. Together, advanced computers and talented animators will ensure that digital animation remains the cutting-edge frontier of modern multimedia for some time to come.

Key Terms

Alpha-tweening

Animating with physics

Cel

Cycle

Ease-in / Ease-out

Flipbook

Forward kinematics

Frame-by-frame animation

Holds

Inverse kinematics

Key frame

Kinematics

Leica reel

Morphing

Motion capture

Motion tween

Onionskinning

Path-based animation

Pencil test

Persistence of vision

Programmed animation

Rendering

Rotoscoping

Scratch track

Shooting on twos

Size-tweening

Storyboard

Stretch / Squash

Timeline

Tween animation

Tweens

Review Questions

1. What is persistence of vision? How is it related to animation?
2. What basic elements of animation are illustrated in a simple flipbook of images?
3. What were the advantages of film for traditional animation?
4. What is a keyframe? How did it improve the efficiency of developing traditional animation?
5. Why was celluloid significant in the development of traditional animations?
6. What is onionskinning?
7. What is a storyboard?
8. What is a pencil test?
9. What is a scratch track?
10. What are animated GIFs? In what way are they similar to a flipbook animation?
11. Describe the process of rotoscoping. How is it used in 2-D animation?
12. What are the features of 2-D animation software that mimic traditional animation?
13. What is the difference between frame-by-frame animation and tween animation sequences?
14. What is morphing?
15. How do program commands generate animation?
16. What are the advantages of programmed animations?
17. Describe the process of motion capture for creating 3-D animation.
18. When is performance animation frequently used for 3-D animation?
19. What is kinematics? What is the difference between forward and inverse kinematics?

20. Identify and explain which form of kinematics requires more computer-processing power.
21. What are the advantages of animating with physics?
22. What is pre-rendering and when is it used?
23. Why is real-time rendering often found in computer video games?
24. Identify and explain two guidelines that will be important to follow if you need to create an animated web logo for a client's website.
25. Identify and explain two guidelines that will be important to follow if you need to develop a computer-animated children's fable.

Discussion Questions

1. Identify the major challenge of traditional animation and explain three methods to overcome that challenge.
2. Identify the role of the *storyboard*, *pencil test*, and *scratch track* in developing a traditional animation.
3. Why is cel animation described as a "complex, demanding, and expensive form of animation"?
4. What specific efficiencies did animation software introduce to the 2-D traditional animation process?
5. Identify and explain four types of tweening found in typical 2-D animation software applications.
6. In what ways do the power of new computers alter the development of 3-D animation?
7. Research and explain how Claymation animation is produced. Is this an example of computerized animation or not? Explain.
8. If you train as a 3-D digital artist, would you have the necessary skills to become a 3-D digital animator? Explain your response.
9. List the steps for creating 3-D animation and identify the main purpose of each.
10. Would a 3-D animator prefer to use forward or inverse kinematics to develop an animated sequence of a school of dolphins? Explain your answer.
11. Identify a current animation sequence from a movie, TV, or website and analyze how you think the developer may have created it. Refer to specific techniques for computer animation.
12. Video games are a major product in the entertainment market. Based on your knowledge of animation, what techniques might an animator use to make sure the gaming animations remain current, flexible, and responsive to the player?
13. Why do the authors suggest that computer animation is the "pinnacle of modern multimedia"? Do you agree with this assessment or not? Explain.

Chapter 10

Authoring

Topics you will explore include:

In the last five chapters we've explored the tools and techniques for creating and editing text, graphics, sound, video, and animation. Powerful *media-specific software* allows developers to work with each of these media with ever-increasing ease and sophistication. In this chapter we consider the ways in which developers integrate different media elements to produce a completed multimedia application. There are two major approaches to this final stage of multimedia development: *programming* and *authoring*.

In **programming**, a developer uses a *programming language*, such as Visual Basic or C++, to directly specify the many ways in which media are presented and user interactions are carried out. Programming is extremely powerful because it provides the developer with precise control over every aspect of the application; but this power comes at a price. Programming requires a thorough command of the programming language and it is also time-consuming. This limits application development to a relatively small number of specialists. To make multimedia development a practical possibility for a wide range of people another approach was needed.

This alternative approach is called **authoring**. Authoring is the process of integrating and presenting media elements using software, called *authoring applications*, specially designed for this function. Authoring applications allow developers to concentrate on the appearance and functionality of their creations by automatically generating the specific instructions a computer executes to present a multimedia product. In effect, the computer becomes its own programmer by creating the code to implement the decisions of the developer. Authoring opened multimedia development to the vast majority of computer users, allowing virtually anyone to participate in this new communication medium. The result was a proliferation of multimedia products of all kinds from slide presentations to advertisements, games, films, encyclopedias, tutorials, interactive novels, simulations, and more. In this chapter we consider the tools and strategies of multimedia authoring. After completing this chapter, you should understand:

- The meaning and advantages of authoring
- The functions and major types of authoring applications
- The major tasks in the authoring process
- Basic criteria for selecting an authoring application

10.1 Authoring Applications

The tools of a traditional author include pens, typewriters, and word processors. The central tool of the multimedia author is called an **authoring application**. An authoring application is software specially designed for the creation of multimedia projects. Authoring applications are used to *assemble media elements*, *synchronize content*, *design the user interface*, and *provide user interactivity*. As noted above, each of these tasks can also be accomplished through programming languages, but programming requires mastery of the specific commands and syntax of the language and is often very time-consuming. Authoring software, by contrast, allows a developer to focus on the design, interactivity, and performance of the project rather than code syntax.

An example of the advantages of authoring over programming can be seen in the creation of multimedia web pages. Websites are developed by writing individual HTML programming codes for each element on the page. Text properties, image locations, and page properties are defined within the code. Web authoring tools such as FrontPage or Dreamweaver, on the other hand, automatically generate HTML code based on the choices made by developers as they type text, drag and drop images, and define interactions through simple menu choices. This allows developers to work more rapidly and to concentrate more directly on project design.

Authoring Metaphors

Authoring applications are grouped around three different metaphors: *card*, *icon*, and *timeline*. A **metaphor** is a comparison of one thing (usually familiar) to another (usually new or unfamiliar) to enhance understanding. Macs and PCs use the metaphors of desktops, folders, and trashcans to help users understand how to operate a computer. Authoring metaphors help orient developers to how the software organizes media elements, sequences events, and presents a final multimedia project.

Card Metaphor   Authoring tools based on the **card metaphor** are the most intuitive and simplest to use. Media content is organized in sequential order on a stack of cards, much like a Rolodex; as a collection of slides, like a slide show; or as a sequence of pages, as in a book. HyperCard, developed by Apple Computer in 1987, was the first authoring application to use the card metaphor (Figure 10.1). Current authoring applications such as Toolbook and SuperCard derive much of their operating environment from HyperCard. Presentation applications such as Microsoft's PowerPoint and Apple's Keynote organize media as sequences of individual screens called slides.

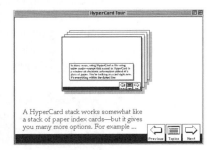

Figure 10.1 HyperCard—An early authoring program.

The card metaphor is most appropriate for projects using static media such as text or images, and for content that is normally experienced in sequence, one screen display at a time. Playback of these applications proceeds from one screen to the next, unless the developer includes navigation objects such as hyperlinks, menus, or buttons to change the order of presentation.

Cards have two *layers*. The **background layer** contains elements that are shared such as navigation buttons or background images. The **foreground layer** contains content specific to that card (Figure 10.2). There are three main advantages to dividing content

Figure 10.2 These slides from a PowerPoint presentation contain two layers. Text and images are placed on the foreground layer of each slide. The background layer design is repeated for all slides. Slides are viewed in linear sequence.

by layers. Development time is saved because the content for backgrounds is created once and repeated for multiple cards. A unified, consistent design is easier to achieve because the common background layer has the same appearance and organization each time it appears. Finally, file sizes are minimized by the use of common background layers because media elements do not need to be duplicated for each card.

Icon Metaphor   Authoring tools based on the **icon metaphor** organize media content and interactivity on a flowline. A **flowline** is a graphical representation of the relationships between the components of a multimedia application. In authoring, **icons** are graphic symbols that define media (a text box, an image, sound, video) as well as different forms of interactivity (menu choices, buttons, user responses). Each icon is dragged onto the flowline to create the structure of the application. The project can be segmented into separate flowlines and single icons or whole flowline segments can be rearranged using simple drag and drop procedures. Flowlines allow developers to quickly visualize and adjust the structure of an application, making them ideal for the organization of branching applications such as the lessons of multimedia tutorials.

Each icon has a dialog box with properties and parameters that the developer specifies. Sophisticated branching routines are easily defined with "Decision" and "Interaction" icons. Complex, sophisticated applications can be built using the visual programming techniques of icon-based applications, such as Authorware and Icon Author, without requiring the developer to master the complexities of specialized programming languages (Figure 10.3).

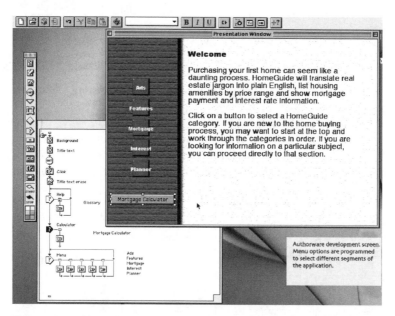

Figure 10.3 This Authorware flowline organizes the events in a logical sequence. It also groups other flowlines into maps. Menu options give the user access to different segments of the flowline.

Timeline Metaphor   The **timeline metaphor** organizes media content and interactivity as sequences of **frames** much like the frames of traditional films and animations. Media elements are first imported into a *library* or *cast* window. They can then be used repeatedly in many different frames without significantly increasing file size. Each frame can have multiple *layers*. Layers define the stacking order of the media. A graphic that is shared by several frames is placed on the bottom layer to create a background. Other media intended to appear in front of the background are placed in higher layers. Sounds play in a separate layer and extend over multiple frames. Transitions can be applied to a sequence of frames to fade items in or out of the viewing area. The timeline controls the presentation of events and interactivity. As the "play-head" moves across the timeline, individual frames appear on the screen. The rate of playback, in frames per second, can be regulated, and navigation menus or buttons can be placed in a frame to alter the flow of the playhead on the timeline (Figure 10.4).

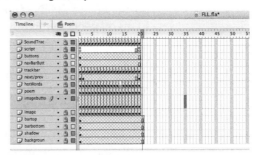

Figure 10.4 This timeline from Flash shows media organized in frames. Frame 1 is one instance of the display sequence. Each frame has 14 layers. Two layers have a special purpose: one layer contains program code to control the playback sequence and the top layer contains sound tracks synchronized to each frame. The playhead, the rectangle at the top, is currently on frame 21. See Color Plate 27.

The timeline metaphor is especially appropriate for dynamic media, such as video and sound, which change over time. Timeline applications, such as Director and Flash, are powerful authoring tools that allow developers to precisely synchronize the elements of animation sequences based on fractions of seconds. They are also more difficult to learn and are usually chosen only when animation or video is the dominant element in a multimedia project.

10.2 The Authoring Process

Multimedia authoring involves a series of interrelated tasks. Developers *design* the application. They *import* or *create*, and *edit* various media elements. They *integrate* and *synchronize* media. They *establish navigation structure* and they may *program* more sophisticated user interactions. They may also add *database support*. They *preview, test* and *debug* their applications. Finally, they prepare (or *publish*) their products for delivery. Just as authoring applications differ in terms of their basic metaphors, they also vary in their capabilities to perform these essential tasks.

Application Design

Authoring software may include a number of features to support the design process. Presentation programs, such as PowerPoint, usually provide an outline view in which authors can organize the basic structure of a presentation. More complex multimedia projects often make use of storyboards. A **storyboard** is a series of sketches of screens used to guide the development process. Storyboards include layouts of screen elements such as media and navigation controls as well as directions to guide the work of animators, programmers, and other members of the development team.

Authoring applications with good support for design can speed the development process since it is usually easier to build an application from a design created in the same program.

Importing Content

Multimedia content is frequently created in media-specific applications such as paint or draw programs that use their own ("proprietary") file formats. Media content can also be purchased in a variety of formats from clip library sources. To make use of these different forms of media, authoring applications can usually import several different file formats. Not all formats are supported by all authoring applications, however. For example, images in .psd (Photoshop) format or sounds saved as MIDI files may not be directly supported by the authoring application. Such files can usually be converted to supported formats such as TIFF for .psd files or QuickTime for MIDI, but this adds another step to the development process.

Creating and Editing Content

Media-specific applications have powerful tools optimized for the tasks each performs. The development process would be very inefficient, however, if every element of a multimedia application had to be created and edited in different, specialized applications. For this reason, all authoring applications include some media creation and editing capability. For example, all applications have tools to enter text either as a graphic or in editable text form. Text content is often easier to create and edit within the authoring application when the supporting media are visible on screen. Adjustments to font size, color, and style are also easier to make within the authoring environment.

Many authoring programs also include basic image and sound editing capabilities. This makes it possible to quickly create graphics for buttons, make simple adjustments to imported images, or shorten sounds. The power and flexibility of these tools varies widely from product to product. PowerPoint includes a basic draw program while the capability of Flash draw tools is more advanced. Similarly the paint capabilities of Authorware or SuperCard are less powerful than those of Director.

Media Integration, Synchronization, and Playback

Once the content is developed, authoring software is used to integrate and synchronize various media elements and determine the order in which they are played for a user. Techniques for media integration vary with authoring metaphor. Media may be placed on a card surface, represented as an icon and dragged to a flowline, or selected from a library or "cast window" and placed on a timeline. The position and order of objects may be determined by placement in layers.

Synchronization is critical for dynamic media. Sounds, animations, and transitions must be timed to present a coordinated and unified flow of information. Authoring tools approach synchronization in various ways. Objects can be held on screen for specific times (20 seconds) or paused on screen until another event occurs such as the end of a sound segment. In these cases, timing properties are assigned to the objects themselves. More complex synchronization is done on timelines. Media objects are placed on the timeline to play for a specified number of frames. In similar fashion, an animation can be synchronized to a sound track by placing each on a different layer of a common sequence of frames.

Variations in computer processor speeds, access times for storage devices such as hard drives or optical discs, and network transmission rates make synchronization particularly important for multimedia developers. Dynamic data such as video places high demands on computer systems. Less powerful, slower systems often cannot process the information rapidly enough to maintain smooth motion and consistent sound. An animation with a high frame rate created on a fast processor may slow to a crawl on less capable systems or not play at all. To assure adequate performance on different systems, authoring applications optimized for dynamic media often have options to synchronize media automatically. Timing controls can be applied to various media components or the final project may be defined with parameters to drop out images to keep up with sound playback.

Establishing Navigation Structure

Authoring tools are also used to determine the order in which content is presented to the user, which is known as playback. Playback is determined by navigation structure. There are four basic navigation structures: *linear*, *hierarchical*, *networked*, and *conditional*.

The simplest form of navigation is **linear** or *sequential*. Screens are viewed one after the other, much like the pages of a book. Linear navigation is appropriate whenever information is best presented as an unvarying sequence, such as a recipe for baking a cake. Some authoring applications, such as PowerPoint, are particularly well suited to linear navigation. While other navigational structures can be created in PowerPoint, the normal flow of information is from one slide to the next as a user clicks a mouse.

A second navigation structure is **hierarchical**. Navigation starts at the top with the most general topic and filters down to more specific options. Authoring software is used to structure menu options or create other forms of hierarchical navigation such as *image maps*. An **image map** is a graphic with "hot spots" where a user can click to navigate to a particular topic. For example, a state tourist map might include the counties as hotspots. Clicking on a particular county leads to a description of tourist attractions in that region.

Networked is the third common navigational structure. A networked structure allows users to explore more freely by replacing sequences or hierarchies with a variety of user options. One common form of a networked structure is the hyperlink. **Hyperlinks** are connections between two data items, for instance between the title of a painting and a photo of the painting. A single website may be organized in a hierarchical structure of web pages by the author, but the hyperlinks within each page can send the user on a "web" of exploration with no prescribed path (Figure 10.5).

Finally, navigation structures may be **conditional**. Access to information is contingent on the user's responses or progress in the application. A specific project may require that certain conditions be met before the user proceeds to the next step. A multimedia tutorial on video editing, for example, may prevent users from jumping to the last chapter if they haven't completed the previous sections. In these cases, programming code specifies conditional navigation.

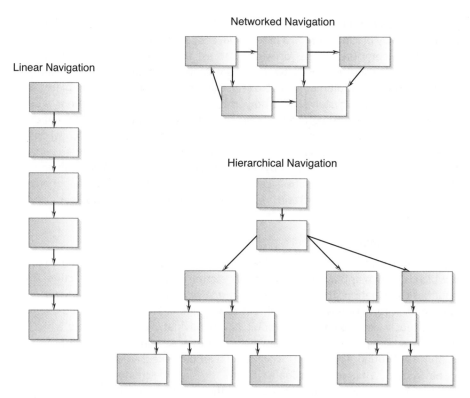

Figure 10.5 Navigation structures.

Navigation control is an important consideration for developers. It governs how the content is structured and controls the playback sequence. Multimedia developers plan navigation structures as part of the design process and they choose authoring applications based in part on how well they support navigation.

Programming

All authoring applications can create basic navigation structures as well as other simple interactions such as playing a sound or video. Applications such as PowerPoint use a series of dialog boxes to specify the actions of screen buttons, add hyperlinked terms, and create simple forms of animation.

These simple interactions are adequate for basic multimedia presentations but more complex projects require more flexibility and control. Projects with extensive interactivity, such as tutorials and games, or customized routines, such as a calculator or a stopwatch, require authoring applications with programming capability.

Programming in authoring applications is either "script" or "icon" based. A **script** is a series of commands specifying the properties or behavior of a specific element in a multimedia application. A button script may cause the button to change appearance or produce the sound of a click when a mouse button is depressed. Scripts are a form of *high level programming language* because they use English-like phrasing to write commands. Script commands are *interpreted*, that is they are translated to machine language, and executed one at a time. This makes it easier for developers to test and debug their scripts.

Some scripting languages exist only within an authoring environment. Lingo, for example, is a language that operates only within Director. Other scripting languages, such as JavaScript, can be written outside the authoring environment using a common text editor. They can then be embedded in multimedia projects such as web pages or Flash files.

Scripting languages add functionality to a multimedia project. The developer can program scripts to control animations, play video, launch external applications, and control interactivity. The possibilities are limitless. The first scripting language was HyperTalk. Introduced in 1987, it was bundled in the HyperCard authoring environment and launched a cult of programmers writing HyperCard routines that were widely popular in the early days of multimedia development. Director's scripting language, Lingo, is very similar to HyperTalk. Flash relies on ActionScript, a variant of Javascript, which is a language commonly used to program web page features (Table 10.1).

Icon programming is a type of visual programming. Icons are arranged in the application window and the developer defines the parameters for the specific icon's use. For example, a sound icon will require parameters to define the sound's name and the length of time it should play. The advantage of icon programming is that it does not require knowledge of programming rules. The developer only needs to know how to define the parameters of each icon to best control the application. Authorware and IconAuthor offer extensive control of application development using the icon programming approach.

> **How Scripts Work**
>
> Scripting languages are similar to object-oriented programming. Objects contain program modules that are reused, modified, and executed based on events that occur within the application.
>
> The script consists of a "message handler" and a series of commands that are attached to an object. The object can be a button, image, portion of text, a screen or frame, even an entire sequence of screens. Each object has the possibility of containing a sequence of code. For example, a button may contain this script:
>
> ```
> On MouseDown
>   Beep 2
>   Go Next
> End MouseDown
> ```
>
> When a user holds the mouse down on that button, the computer will beep twice and go to the next screen. The "event," MouseDown, launches the code stored in the button object.
>
> Events trigger messages in an object-oriented environment. The event of holding down the mouse sends a message to the system. The first object to have an appropriate handler (*On MouseDown*) grabs the message and executes the code. If the button doesn't contain an appropriate handler, the message is passed up a hierarchy of objects, each time checking for a handler to grab the message. The hierarchy of objects is defined within the authoring system. The message could pass through the button, to the image, to the screen, to the background, to the project before it finds a handler to intercept the "MouseDown" message.

Database Support

Multimedia projects may require access to a database. A **database** is a collection of related files that share a common field of data. Multimedia tutorials might require a database to record the student's name and performance on various lesson segments. The questions are retrieved from one database file and the answers are recorded to another database file. If the student returns at a later time to complete the lesson, the application will load the previous responses and append additional responses to the database file based on the student's name and/or password. Authorware and Director have specific tools to read and write to databases.

Table 10.1 **Sample Scripts**

Script to play a series of notes four times when a card opens. (HyperTalk in HyperCard)	Script for a frame to play one of two random sounds when the play head moves into a frame on the time-line. (Lingo in Director)	Script for a button to play a sound when mouse is released on an object. (ActionScript in Flash)

On openCard
  Repeat 4 times
Play "harpsichord" tempo 150
  "g4e f g eb g d g"
  End repeat
End openCard
	On enterFrame
	If random(2) = 1 then
	  sound playFile "ocean"
	else
	  sound playFile "wind"
	End if
	end
		On {release} {
		mySound = new Sound ();
		mySound.attachSound ("ocean");
		mysound.start;
		}

Previewing, Testing, and Debugging

Previewing, testing, and debugging are important components in the development of more complex multimedia projects. The elements of a project are often assembled in a *development mode*, such as PowerPoint's outline view, Flash's timeline, or Authorware's flowline. These approaches improve the efficiency of multimedia creation but they do not present screen content as it will appear in the final product. *Preview* controls allow developers to view the application as it will appear to the user. A common technique is to provide a player controller similar to a VCR pad with play, rewind, and stop as common buttons. Activating the player allows the developer to preview screen layouts and test navigation and other user interactions.

Applications that directly support programming also generally include debugging capability. A **debugger** is a utility that tracks the execution of program code to assist developers in locating coding errors.

Project Delivery

To deliver a product to users, developers must "publish" their applications in a form that will play outside the authoring environment. There are two main approaches to this process. In the first, a separate small program called a **player** is used to present the multimedia application on the user's computer. Some multimedia players must be licensed for distribution with applications; others are free. QuickTime player, for example, often resides on a user's computer ready to play back any multimedia application that is published in QuickTime format. Other common players include Flash Player, Windows MediaPlayer, and RealPlayer.

The second approach to publishing embeds or bundles a player directly in the mul-timedia project. In this case, the player is no longer separate; it becomes part of the application file. This increases application file size, but it has the advantage of producing a stand-alone file for easy distribution. PowerPoint's "Package for CD" feature embeds the PowerPoint Viewer into the presentation. Users do not have to own PowerPoint to view the file nor do they need a separate player, the application "stands alone." Similarly, a project created in Flash may be published as a stand-alone "projector" file. This embeds the Flash Player, producing an application that will play without the use of a browser.

Developers also consider the delivery platform as they make publishing decisions. One of the advantages of web-based applications is that they can be viewed on a wide range of computers. Pages may display quite differently, however, on different platforms. Authoring applications for the Web often contain features to ensure effective display on different types of computers. These include "web-safe" color palettes and utilities to make font adjustments between different platforms.

More significant adjustments are needed for applications destined for the desktop. In order to reach the widest possible audience, a project created in Director or Authorware is usually published twice: once in a format compatible with PCs, and once for the Macintosh platform. To support multi-platform publishing, authoring applications may have the ability to adjust file characteristics and formats to be compatible with a variety of computer platforms.

10.3 Choosing an Authoring Application

No single authoring tool is suitable for all multimedia projects. Multimedia developers select authoring applications by matching the requirements of specific projects to the features available in a given authoring product. The following guidelines identify some of the major considerations in this process.

1. **Consider the Subject.**

   Is the content mainly static (not changing over time, such as photos or text) or dynamic (sound, animation, video)? Card-based applications will be easier to use and very effective for most static content. Dynamic media may require timeline-based applications.

   Will the content require specialized features? If so, these should be directly matched to capabilities of the authoring application. For instance:

   - capturing, storing and retrieving user responses
   - extensive hyperlinks
   - external database support

2. **Consider the Media**.

   Are the file formats of the graphics, audio, animations, and video for the project directly supported in the authoring application? If not, can they be readily converted?

3. **Consider Delivery.**

   Where will the application be used?

   Desktop applications are often delivered on CD- or DVD-ROMs with high storage capacities. This permits ready delivery of large, media-rich projects developed in applications such as Director.

   Network delivery often requires applications optimized for small file sizes, such as Flash.

4. **Consider Maintenance.**

Is the application widely used and supported? If so, expertise is more likely to be available for future revision.

Will the project require frequent updates? If so, choose an application that simplifies this process.

- Some applications store individual media once, referencing each with an alias for repeated use. Changing an element such as a logo may mean simply replacing one graphic with a new one—all the references to that one image are automatically updated.

- Some applications can import external files at the time of playback. Updating the application may be as easy as replacing one of the files. This is particularly useful in projects that rely on timely data such as catalogs or advertisements.

10.4 Summary

Authoring applications are used to *assemble* and *synchronize* media elements, develop the user *interface*, and provide *interactivity*. Authoring applications are based on different development *metaphors*. One readily grasped metaphor organizes the content on a sequence of *cards*, *pages*, or *slides*. An *icon* metaphor organizes media on a *flowline*, and the *timeline* metaphor presents the content in a sequence of *frames* with multiple *layers* of media elements. Authoring applications have a range of tools for *importing*, *creating*, and *editing* media elements. In addition, many applications support some form of *programming* to control navigation, playback, and interaction with the media. Because these applications vary in their features and uses, multimedia developers may employ different authoring products for different projects. They make their choices by matching project requirements to the metaphor and features of the authoring application.

Key Terms

Authoring	Icon
Authoring application	Icon metaphor
Background layer	Icon programming
Card metaphor	Image map
Conditional	Linear
Database	Metaphor
Debugger	Networked
Flowline	Player
Foreground layer	Programming
Frame	Script
Hierarchical	Storyboard
Hyperlink	Timeline metaphor

Review Questions

1. What is an authoring application?
2. What is the benefit of an authoring application over programming languages to develop a project?
3. What is a metaphor?
4. What is the purpose of authoring metaphors?
5. What are the three common authoring metaphors for project development?
6. What are the two layers on a card?
7. What are the benefits of using a background layer in the card metaphor?
8. How does the icon metaphor organize media content?
9. What type of media content is most appropriate for a timeline metaphor?
10. What is a storyboard? What is its function in the authoring process?
11. Identify and explain the four basic navigation structures.
12. What is an image map and how is it used to create a navigation structure?
13. What navigational structure would make use of hyperlinks?
14. How do scripting languages add functionality to a multimedia project?
15. What is a debugger?

Discussion Questions

1. What is the most appropriate authoring metaphor to develop an application that displays the motion of the planets? Explain your choice.
2. What is the most appropriate authoring metaphor for developing an interactive tutorial on safe driving? Explain your choice.
3. List the main components of the timeline metaphor and identify the purpose of each.
4. Identify the interrelated tasks in multimedia authoring and evaluate either PowerPoint or Flash in terms of their ability to complete these tasks.
5. What are the two approaches to publishing a project for distribution? What are the advantages or disadvantages of each approach?
6. As the project manager for a multimedia presentation on student campus life at your college, identify the four criteria for selecting an authoring application and explain how each criterion will apply to that project.

Chapter 11

Multimedia Development

Topics you will explore include:

Multimedia permeates all areas of modern communication and entertainment. From advertising and marketing to games, training, and education, multimedia is producing new products and transforming the creation of old ones. Print publications increasingly use the Web to distribute words and images, to add late-breaking developments, and to more fully engage their readers with audio and video. Television uses the tools of digital multimedia to produce traditional commercials and programming and to add new forms of interactivity using a wide variety of websites. Few educational publishers—and virtually no marketing campaigns—ignore the potential contributions of multimedia to their products.

This wide range of products gives rise to a variety of approaches to multimedia development. Print publishers, filmmakers, game producers, corporate trainers, and educators all approach their work differently. But all share common challenges and opportunities dictated by the nature of multimedia technology. As a result, multimedia developers share a common set of essential tasks and procedures. In this chapter, we explore the elements of multimedia development common to the production of the majority of advanced applications.

After completing this chapter you should understand:

- The skills and functions of the members of a typical multimedia development team: project manager, project designer, content experts, writers, media specialists, programmers, acquisitions specialist
- The three stages of a multimedia development plan: definition, design, and production
- The objectives and products of each stage: preliminary proposal, storyboard, functional specification; media creation, interface design, prototype; alpha version, beta version, gold master

11.1 The Development Team

Effective multimedia is developed by small groups and even by individuals, but successful commercial products are the result of teams of professionals following a carefully planned development process. A team is important for two reasons. First, different specialists are needed to produce high quality media. A person skilled in graphics, for example, is seldom equally skilled in sound. Second, a multimedia project is usually shaped, and reshaped, by the interactions of team members. Multimedia development is both *interactive* and *iterative*. It is **interactive** in the sense that team members often contribute to the development of components outside their immediate area of expertise. It is **iterative** in that further product development and testing often leads to changes to earlier work. The best products are the result of a creative team dynamic that fosters the sharing of ideas and a willingness to revise.

Multimedia development also requires leadership and planning. The same qualities that can lead to exceptional results can also spell disaster without effective coordination and direction. Enthusiastic team members can easily expand content and features well beyond the practical limits of budgets and delivery schedules. To keep the efforts of the team on track, a systematic development plan, with clearly articulated steps and outcomes, is also essential.

No one team and no particular set of steps is used for all multimedia development. Teams, and the organization of the work they do, vary by industry and even by project. The teams that create multimedia products relating to film often include "producers" and "directors." Projects originating in the computer industry may include "project managers" and "software engineers." One project may employ several video specialists while another makes no use of that medium at all. But nearly all development projects must tap certain types of expertise and complete a common set of major tasks. Understanding these tasks, and the contributions of different specialists, is essential for all members of the multimedia team, even for the ambitious "team" of one.

11.2 Team Members

Among the essential members of a multimedia team are the *project manager*, the *project designer*, *content experts*, *writers*, *media specialists*, *programmers*, and *acquisitions specialists*.

Project Manager

Commercial multimedia productions are complex and expensive. Projects often take many months to complete and companies take significant economic risks funding their development. The **project manager** is the person with ultimate responsibility for assuring that the product is delivered with the promised features, on time, and on budget. The project manager oversees the business aspects of multimedia development.

The work of the project manager includes:

- contract negotiations with the client
- hiring and evaluation of team members
- creating and monitoring a production schedule
- budgeting
- monitoring client review and approval
- coordinating testing and revision
- assuring product delivery
- overseeing product documentation and the archiving of project materials.

Successful project managers have an understanding of the multimedia market and current technologies. They are well organized, focused, and task-oriented.

Project Designer

The **project designer** is responsible for the overall structure of the product's content and for the look, feel, and functionality of the user interface. The designer must understand the ways in which each of the media can most effectively convey project content. Above all, the designer must understand what is new in "New Media." This includes a thorough understanding of the strengths and weaknesses of text, graphics, sound, animation, and video in a computer environment. The heart of new media, however, is interactivity. The designer must be aware of the potential to engage users in novel ways by shifting the focus from the project's contents to the user's interactions with that content. Depending on the project, interactions might include: navigation options; contextual help screens and audio; customizing options such as setting difficulty levels; queries, challenges or reinforcements tied to user performance; and immersive, virtual reality experiences.

One person may carry out project design but it may also be a shared responsibility. In some educational and training products, for instance, instructional designers are responsible for content structure while a graphics designer shapes the appearance of the interface. Instructional designers are trained to identify specific educational outcomes and strategies. They also have expertise in evaluating the results of educational products. Graphics designers are skilled in the principles governing the creation and effective use of graphic elements such as color, line, shape, and spatial organization.

The work of the project designer includes:

- organizing information by topic and structuring content
- establishing the look and feel of the product (formal, playful, etc.)
- determining the metaphor for the user interface
- creating the navigational structure
- supervising the work of media specialists and writers.

Content Experts

Content experts have a detailed understanding of the topic presented in the multimedia application. The need for content experts varies significantly with different applications. An application designed to assist diabetes patients with management of their disease requires very specific, current, and accurate information from a specialist. A basic business website may not require a content expert as a team member though it will, of course, demand careful consultation with the business owner and/or employees.

The work of the content expert includes:

- identifying facts, theories, procedures, processes or other information to be presented
- assuring the accuracy of all product content
- assisting in product testing and revision
- identifying other, specialized content experts as required.

The content expert should have a thorough working knowledge of his or her specialty. This includes basic subject content as well as the latest research and sources of additional expertise. It is helpful if the expert also has an understanding of the essentials of multimedia technology and the ways in which it may be effectively applied to the presentation of the topic.

Writers

The development of a multimedia product requires a variety of written documents. **Writers** are the individuals responsible for producing these documents. In some cases, the product itself is focused on writing. Multimedia children's books, for instance, have specific stories as their focus. Here, the writer is at the very heart of the project and his or her creativity is central to its success. In applications that are not centered on a written text, such as retail marketing sites or action games, writing still plays an essential role.

In these and other projects, writers may be called upon to produce:

- a product proposal for a potential client
- a detailed product specification
- scripts for dialog and action to guide animators, actors, or programmers
- bug and testing reports
- release notes and manuals
- help screens.

Writing is often the responsibility of more than one person, particularly when the project calls for creative as well as technical writing. Multimedia writers benefit from a knowledge of the development process. They also need an understanding of the specific limitations and possibilities of the written word in multimedia applications.

Media Specialists: Graphics, Sound, Animation, and Video

Media specialists are responsible for the preparation of the individual elements in a multimedia application. As members of the team, they also interact with others, sharing ideas for product features both within and beyond their specialties.

Graphics   Graphics are an important component of nearly every multimedia product. Graphics capture the eye and the attention of the user, they establish a product's mood, they convey information; and they are critical guides for effective navigation and user interactions. Multimedia graphics specialists are artists skilled in design principles and in the most current digital technology. They understand the principles of color, line, and image composition as well as the workings of draw, paint, and illustration software.

The graphics specialist is a required member of most multimedia production teams. He or she may be called on to:

- choose the graphics software used to create the product
- design screen layouts
- select stock graphics from clip art, photo houses, and other sources
- edit existing graphics
- perform conversions between different graphics file formats
- produce original artwork such as logos, drawings, and buttons
- assure consistent graphics display across different computer platforms.

Sound   Producing high-quality sound requires both expertise and specialized equipment. The sound specialist for a multimedia project is trained in traditional sound production and has a thorough working knowledge of the sound studio. He or she is also familiar with the latest digital tools for creating and editing sounds of all types from narrations, to music, to sound effects. As part of the multimedia team, this person must also understand both the limits and potential of sound delivered via computer. The sound professional will be the best judge of the most effective strategies for assuring high quality sound within the limitations of the delivery options available. As an important contributor to the development process, he or she also often affects design decisions by suggesting ways in which different types of sound—background music, ambient sounds, sound transitions, auditory cues, and reinforcement—may improve the multimedia product. Often these suggestions will be based on experience in radio, television, film, or theater.

The sound specialist may be asked to:

- identify existing sources for required sound elements
- conduct recording sessions for narration, music, sound effects
- edit sounds—adjust and correct sound segments for length, pitch, amplitude; mix sound tracks; add special effects
- digitize analog sound sources
- select and implement appropriate sound sample rates and compression strategies
- select and convert sounds to appropriate digital file formats
- evaluate proposed uses of sound.

Animation   Animation can be one of the most labor-intensive, and expensive, aspects of multimedia production. The computer makes it possible to generate the individual frames of an animation much more rapidly than traditional techniques, but animation still requires the artist to envision and create a large number of individual frames. Animators typically are skilled artists who understand the principles of composition and color and can quickly produce drawings. In addition to these skills, they must understand the elements of motion and be able to envision sequences of actions. Multimedia animators must combine these abilities with a thorough working knowledge of computer animation programs and techniques. Projects using significant amounts of animation will require the services of the computer animator very early. This team member's expertise will be critical to determining the type and amount of animation to be included. Development time and hardware or software needs must be identified early. Advanced 3-D animation, for instance, may require software and/or computers that exceed the time and budget resources of the proposed project.

In addition to creating various animation sequences, the tasks of the animator include:

- identifying animation software and hardware for the project
- storyboarding—creating sketches of the project screens
- drawing characters, objects, background scenes
- supervising the work of other artists.

Video   High quality video is the result of a combination of skills. Accomplished videographers, like photographers, must understand composition, light, focus, color, and exposure. They must also understand the principles and procedures for capturing and editing sound. Like the writer, they must know how to develop character and plot to tell a story. In addition to these skills, video also demands a command of the special techniques of film—framing, camera angles, shot variations, transitions. To these skills, the video specialist on a multimedia team must add knowledge of digital video production and editing.

Typical responsibilities of this member of the multimedia team include:

- identifying appropriate screen sizes, frame rates, and lengths of video segments
- locating sources of required video
- digitizing and editing of analog video sources
- shooting and editing digital video
- selection of codecs and compression settings for completed video.

Programmer   The **programmer** is responsible for the computer code that unites the media elements and provides the product's functionality. In simpler projects, these tasks may be performed using authoring applications that require little or no independent code writing. Most advanced projects, however, will require the creation of programmed routines for specialized functions. In some instances these may be written in the built-in programming language of the authoring application, such as Lingo in Macromedia's Director. Other routines may be produced using independent programming languages such as C++. In either case, the multimedia programmer needs familiarity with the language to be used as well as experience in creating a range of features and user interactions.

The multimedia programmer may be called on to:

- provide user navigation—buttons, image maps, conditional branching
- develop various forms of user interaction—text boxes, speech recognition, touch-screen controls
- create specialized controls or functions—moveable objects, video controllers, calculators, interactive calendars, driving, flying or fighting controls
- support project development—tools to automate tasks such as quickly renaming, updating or distributing a group of files
- debugging—identifying, correcting, and documenting application bugs.

Acquisitions Specialist   Securing copyright permissions can be complicated and time-consuming. In many instances, the content of a project will be determined by the costs involved in this process—content that developers might ideally choose to use may simply be unavailable or prohibitively expensive. The **acquisitions specialist** is knowledgeable about the sources for copyright-protected content and the process of securing permissions. His or her efforts are critical to protecting developers from liability for copyright infringement (see Chapter 12 for discussion of copyright law).

The acquisitions specialist can also play a role in another important copyright issue—the protection of the creative work of the project developers. Explicit written agreements should be made between the developer and the client regarding the ownership of copyright for the original content of the product. Particularly important are elements the developer may wish to re-use on future products such as interface designs or programming routines for special functions. Often, these represent major investments that can significantly lower development costs for future projects.

In simpler cases, another team member, such as the project manager, may fill the role of the acquisitions specialist. Advanced projects often require a position dedicated to this function.

The acquisitions specialist typically will:

- research availability and costs of copyright permissions for projected content
- complete copyright agreements for selected content
- maintain documentation of copyright permissions
- write copyright agreements between team members and the developer
- write copyright agreements between the client and the developer.

11.3 The Development Plan

Like most creative undertakings, multimedia development is a balancing act. The flow of ideas between team members determines the form and even "personality" of the product but it often leads to a "blue-sky" profusion of features that must be balanced against the need to produce a marketable product on time and on budget. The development plan is both tightrope and safety net—it must stimulate the creative energies of the team while also clearly defining the product and the steps that will lead to its successful completion.

Development plans take many different forms but each must address three essential tasks: *definition*, *design*, and *production*. Progress markers, sometimes referred to as *rewards*, are identified for each stage. Often the rewards are *deliverables*, documents or elements of the application that are delivered to the client as the product takes shape. Payment schedules are often tied to deliverables. Each stage depends on its predecessors but the results of previous stages are often modified as a result of later work. Obstacles to preparing or licensing a particular video segment, for example, may result in a redefinition of the product. As noted previously, multimedia development is usually *iterative*—earlier stages are re-shaped or reformulated as development progresses.

Stage 1: Definition

Something must justify the time, energy, and other resources demanded by multimedia development. The most important question in the development process is: "What is the purpose of the product?" The second most important is: "Why should we use multimedia to achieve it?"

The product's purpose is defined through its goal or goals. A product goal is not simply a description of its features. "Produce a web-based music store with recording samples, critics' reviews, and videos of the latest concerts" is not a goal. "Increase sales of *Rolling Stone* CDs to female purchasers aged 20 to 32 by at least twenty percent" *is* a goal. The product goal clearly states what the application should accomplish.

Identifying the goal also involves identifying the audience. Who are the intended users? What are their ages, gender, class, and nationality? What access do they have to computers? Both content and the way in which it is presented need to be tailored to the user.

With goal and audience in mind, a third set of questions is posed about the application itself. What are the advantages of multimedia for accomplishing the goal? What media elements will it require? What forms of interactivity will be provided? How will it be delivered? Will it need to be regularly updated? What are the rough costs of development?

Product definition then proceeds in stages based on the results of increasingly specific formulations. There are often three key documents in this process: *preliminary proposal*, *storyboard*, and *functional specification*.

Preliminary Proposal   The **preliminary proposal** is a short one- to three-page description of the proposed application. It is used to begin the process of developer-client negotiations. The proposal:

- identifies the goal
- specifies the need and the audience
- outlines projected outcomes and benefits
- briefly describes projected media content
- describes types and uses of interactivity, and
- provides a preliminary cost estimate.

The preliminary proposal often includes a flowchart. A **flowchart** is a simple box diagram with brief descriptions of product contents. Lines or arrows are often used to connect these boxes to identify navigational paths. The flowchart is a broad overview, sketch, or outline of the product. Figure 11.1 shows a sample flowchart for an application created by the authors.

Storyboard   The product is further defined through the storyboard. A **storyboard** is a series of sketches of major screens. Rough drawings of media elements such as photos, animations or videos are sketched in. Buttons and other navigational objects such as pull-down menus are also sketched and their functions are briefly described (see Figure 11.2). Storyboards may be produced with pencil and pen, on paper or white boards, or with a computer. General-purpose presentation programs such as PowerPoint are often used for storyboarding. More powerful authoring applications are often appropriate for

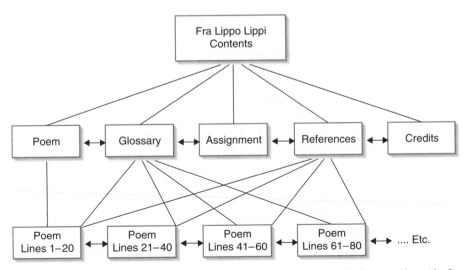

Figure 11.1 A flowchart—Main application elements identified (Exploring *Fra Lippo Lippi*).

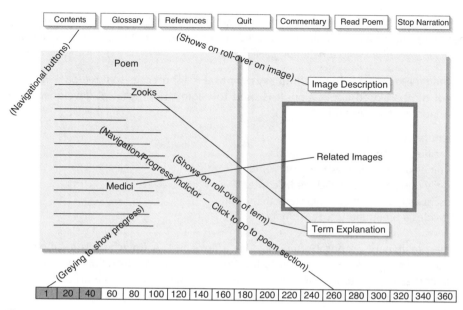

Figure 11.2 A storyboard—Screen content and basic functions sketched (Exploring *Fra Lippo Lippi*).

storyboarding as well. These have the advantage of allowing developers to readily add more advanced features to the storyboard as they further define the product.

Storyboards are very helpful in communications with clients during product definition. They make it possible to easily visualize ideas for content and features. This allows developers to test their proposed creations with clients before committing time and other resources. Storyboards also continue to be important during later stages because they make it easier to communicate project goals and requirements to all members of the development team.

Functional Specification   The **functional specification** is a detailed description of the elements and the performance of the multimedia product. What media components—drawings, photos, sound segments, animation or video sequences—will be created? What types of user interactions—navigation options, queries, suggestions, reinforcements, on-line ordering—will be supported?

The functional specification is often the basis of a detailed business contract. Such contracts are critical to the success of the development process. The novelty and potential complexity of multimedia products provide fertile ground for misunderstanding and disappointment. Costs and delivery schedules can easily get out of hand as additions and changes are made to the project. Both the developer and the client must understand exactly what has been promised and the procedures to be followed if either party wishes to change the specifications.

Stage 2: Design

The definition stage specifies what the product is to be. The objective of the *design phase* is the creation of an incomplete working model of the product called a **prototype**.

During product design, the first media elements are created, the interface is designed, and these elements are combined to create the prototype.

Media Creation   Media creation involves several tasks. The first is identifying required media. A detailed listing, called a **content inventory list**, is developed. This document lists each media element or "asset," the party responsible for its creation, and whether or not it has been completed.

The content inventory list is important because it serves as an early reality check. Can the required media be produced in a timely and cost-effective manner? This list will be further refined as the design process continues and media elements are modified, eliminated, or added to the product. It will also guide the work of team members during the production phase of the project.

Other tasks in media creation include *preproduction*, *production*, and *postproduction*. **Preproduction** is the process of preparing media for editing—scanning photos or other graphics, digitizing an analog sound or video source, or performing file conversions. In the **production** phase the asset is edited using the software that has been selected for that medium (Photoshop, Sound Forge, Final Cut, etc.). In **postproduction**, media is edited using other software to achieve desired effects. Adobe After Effects, for example, is often used to add animated text and special effects, such as sparkles, smoke, or fire, to video.

Interface Design   The **user interface** is the content of the application as the user experiences it on screen. This includes the presentation of media elements and the resources—buttons, menus, hints, specialized controls—that allow the user to interact with the application. In the design stage this interface is carefully specified.

The goal of interface design is to engage the user. In linear, non-interactive products, such as a simple information kiosk, this may simply mean holding the user's interest and attention. In fully developed interactive applications, the interface may need to anticipate choices, provide hints or reinforcements, or present new interactions based on previous user responses, as in games or tutorials. Whatever the application, the user interface must present media elements and user interactions in a way that supports the product's goals and matches the expectations and abilities of its audience. Figure 11.3 presents one element of an interface design.

The user interface should establish an appropriate tone. The tone of the application is determined by the style of its media elements and controls. Virtually any tone may be created—playful, humorous, casual, formal, dignified, serious, businesslike, and so on. Cartoon-like images, bright primary colors, and large animated buttons help to set a playful and welcoming tone for a children's animated story. Sounds, fonts, and video clips would similarly be chosen to appeal to children and support the entertainment or educational goals of the product.

Figure 11.3 Interface Design. *Exploring Fra Lippo Lippi* uses an interactive progress indicator to locate the reader's position in the poem. Grayed sections indicate progress through the poem. Clicking on a line number jumps the user to that section.

A user interface should also be *intuitive, consistent, predictable,* and *reliable.* An **intuitive interface** is one that is immediately understood by its user. A common strategy for creating intuitive interfaces is the use of metaphors. A **metaphor** is a widely understood or familiar symbol or procedure that is used to represent something new or unfamiliar. Common metaphors in multimedia interfaces include desktops, notepads, books, and VCR controls (Figure 11.4). These familiar images and processes make it easier for users to understand and interact with applications. One of the more important considerations for ensuring an intuitive interface is clear and effective navigation. Familiar navigational icons—arrows, buttons, or underlined text—are quickly understood and show users how to move within the application. Graphic overviews of the application showing current location and progress indicators help to readily orient users to where they are and where they can go.

Figure 11.4 Metaphor. Flash uses the VCR metaphor to control progress through animation frames.

Ease of use is also very dependent on the *consistency* of an interface design. A small number of basic screen designs, each with common background elements and consistent locations of user controls, make it easier for users to anticipate and control product content. Designers carefully consider factors such as the relative sizes and locations of interface elements. Larger or more prominently placed buttons or text, for instance, will be perceived as more important by the user.

An interface is *predictable* and *reliable* when similar actions produce similar results and identical actions can be repeated with identical results. Of course, the meaning and implementation of predictability and even reliability varies with different products. A multimedia roulette wheel probably should not reliably produce the same result on each spin—but the spin button should reliably produce a rotation and a stop with some outcome clearly displayed.

Prototype   The prototype, an incomplete working model of the final product, is the goal of the design phase. Prototypes serve three important functions: *refining the definition* of the product, *testing* proposed features, and *guiding the further work* of team members.

The prototype is built using the authoring software and/or programming languages that will produce the final product. It includes some finished media components and as many of the product's projected major functions as possible. As the first opportunity to see how the product will actually work, both the developer and the client can use it to further define content and functions. Different media may be selected. The navigational options may be changed. Specialized functions may be added or eliminated.

Testing is important in all phases of multimedia development but takes on special significance once the prototype has been developed. The prototype is the first look at the product itself and the first opportunity to fully test the proposals and assumptions of the definition and design stages. Testing often includes both in-house and external product review. Designers, programmers, and media specialists test the prototype to determine if it performs as anticipated and if the complete product can be developed within the time and budget constraints of the project. External testers are often used to confirm the assumptions and projections of the project team. Do the test users understand the product's purpose? Are they able to navigate and use other functions easily and effectively?

Problems or limitations discovered in this stage can avoid client dissatisfaction and save many hours of development time.

Once the prototype is reviewed and tested, it also serves as an important resource in the next phase of the multimedia project. Team members use the prototype to guide their individual work on the production of the media and software routines needed to complete the product.

Stage 3: Production

In the production stage, all remaining elements of the product are created and integrated into the application (see Figure 11.5). Content, media, and acquisitions specialists continue the work of identifying, securing, creating, and editing media elements. Programmers complete needed software routines and integrate media with the user interface. In many projects, designers continue to refine the interface itself. This is particularly true in highly interactive and imaginative applications such as games, which are often significantly redesigned, or "tweaked," during the production stage.

Production also includes regular quality assurance testing, complete with bug reports and documentation of corrective measures. Pre-release versions of the product are often created to facilitate both in-house and external testing. An **alpha** version includes most of the media elements but many bugs. As bugs are identified and corrected and the remaining media elements added, a **beta** version is created. The beta version includes all media but is not yet free of all bugs. Successive revisions of beta eventually produce the complete, bug-free application, ready for distribution. This is sometimes called the "gold master." Production also includes the completion of several other tasks essential

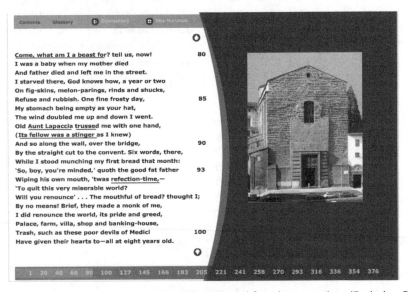

Figure 11.5 A production screen—All media and functions complete (Exploring *Fra Lippo Lippi*). See Color Plate 28.

to product delivery and distribution such as the preparation of release notes, manuals, and packaging.

Finally, many multimedia developers stress the importance of *systematic archiving* of project materials as the development process is completed. Archiving is important for several reasons: disputes may arise between the various parties in the development process; the project may need to be revised or updated in the future; and materials for which the developer has retained copyright may be needed for future products.

11.4 Summary

Advanced multimedia development is a *team effort* that is guided by a *development plan*. The composition of development teams and the steps they follow vary according to industry and project. Most multimedia development teams include a *project manager*, a *project designer*, *content experts*, *writers*, *media specialists*, *programmers*, and *acquisitions specialists*.

The development plan is centered on three major stages: *product definition*, *design*, and *production*. The *preliminary proposal*, *flowchart*, and *storyboard* lead to a *functional specification* defining the product. This stage often concludes with the writing of a business contract specifying the legally binding agreements between client and developer. In the design phase, an incomplete working model of the product called a *prototype* is built. The prototype includes some completed media elements and most of the functionality of the proposed product. The prototype is used to test and refine the design. Testing of the prototype may lead to revisions to the proposed product and to adjustments in projected development schedules and costs.

The prototype is also used to guide the further development of the product in the production phase. *Production* completes media development and the programming of all product functions. This phase is often marked by preliminary releases of the product called *alpha* and *beta* versions. Frequent testing is done, bugs are identified and corrected, and the final product is created. The production phase concludes with the creation of supporting documentation such as manuals and release notes, the preparation of packaging for product distribution, and the systematic archiving of project materials.

Key Terms

Acquisitions specialist
Alpha
Beta
Content experts
Content inventory list
Development plan
Flowchart
Functional specification
Interactive
Intuitive interface
Iterative
Media specialists

Metaphor
Postproduction
Preliminary proposal
Preproduction
Production
Programmer
Project designer
Project manager
Prototype
Storyboard
User interface
Writer

Review Questions

1. What is the main function of a project manager?
2. Why should a project designer know the potential of "new media"?
3. Identify three documents that would be the work of a multimedia writer. Do you think the same person would be responsible for writing all three of the documents? Explain.
4. Why are graphics an important component of most multimedia projects?
5. Why is a sound specialist an important member of a multimedia production team?
6. Why could animation be the most expensive and labor-intensive component of a multimedia application?
7. What are three skills required of accomplished videographers?
8. Why is a programmer an important member of a development team?
9. What are the main responsibilities of the acquisitions specialist?
10. What are the three essential tasks that are addressed in the development plan?
11. What are the three key documents that are created in the definition stage?
12. What is the main objective of the design phase of the development plan?
13. What is a content inventory list and why is it important in the design phase?
14. What are three common tasks in media creation? Which task(s) might use paint or draw applications?
15. What is the goal of interface design?
16. What is a common strategy for creating an intuitive interface?
17. What is a prototype? What three functions does it serve in the development plan?

Discussion Questions

1. Why is multimedia development both interactive and iterative?
2. Why is it important to have a development team and plan to produce successful multimedia products?
3. Does the project manager or the project designer need to know more detail about creating effective multimedia applications? Defend your selection.
4. Should the content expert be the client who has contracted the multimedia application or not? Explain your choice.
5. What is a project goal? Explain the role and importance of goals in the development plan.
6. What is the importance of a storyboard in the development process?
7. Locate your college website and evaluate the interface based on consistency and predictability. Base your comments on analysis of two separate pages.
8. Identify and explain the versions of an application that are used in the quality-testing phase.
9. Why is systematic archiving necessary in the development process?

Chapter 12

Professional Issues in Multimedia Development

Topics you will explore include:

- The Definition of a Profession
- Codes of Professional Ethics
- Copyright
  - Traditional Rights
  - Digital Challenges
- Digital Rights Management

This chapter considers the meaning of professional responsibility and explores some of its implications for multimedia development. Multimedia applications are often, perhaps usually, designed and developed with little attention to issues of professional responsibility. As in other areas of life, multimedia development often follows well-traveled paths with relatively clear goals and expectations; and most of the time those habitual practices themselves suggest the right thing to do. But a little reflection suggests that the success of a multimedia project hinges nearly as much on the professionalism of those involved as it does on the technical skills they bring to their work. Professional responsibility includes taking responsibility for learning and applying the most current knowledge available. It also includes respecting and encouraging the independent work of colleagues. These and other professional guidelines become very important indeed when they are *not* followed, when, for instance, the team must contend with an incompetent person in a key position or a supervisor who is more interested in his own advancement than the well-being of his subordinates.

Competence, collegiality, and respect for the work of subordinates are values common to many professions, as are a number of the other guidelines we will consider. But multimedia development also raises more specific concerns and issues, some of which relate to the nature of digital media itself. Following a discussion of the meaning of "profession" and the elements of professional ethics, this chapter turns to the professional issues raised by two topics directly related to the digital revolution: *copyright* and *digital rights management*.

After completing this chapter you should understand:

- Definition of a profession
- Main elements in a professional code of ethics
- Definition, rights, and remedies of copyright
- Challenges and revisions to copyright law created by the digital revolution
- Meaning, challenges, and opportunities of Digital Rights Management (DRM)

12.1 Professions and Professional Responsibility

In Leicester, England, in 2004, fourteen-year-old Stefan Pakeerah was murdered by a young acquaintance, Warren Leblanc. Leblanc lured Pakeerah to a park where he attacked the boy from behind with a knife and a claw hammer. While police concluded that Leblanc's motive for the murder was robbery (he was apparently in debt to drug dealers), Pakeerah's parents came to believe that a video game, *Manhunt*, distributed by Rockstar Games, played a role in the crime. *Manhunt*, a third-person shooter game, graphically portrayed violent killings, sometimes using weapons like those wielded by Leblanc. Learning from his friends that Leblanc had been "obsessed" by *Manhunt*, the Pakeerahs spoke out publicly against the game. "[T]he way Warren committed the murder is how the game is set out," they said. They insisted that "there is some connection between the game and what he has done" ("Video game 'sparked hammer murder' 2004"). These charges were widely reported in the press, contributing to growing public concern over the possible anti-social effects of violent video games.

What responsibility, if any, do the developers and distributors of *Manhunt* have for this brutal murder?

Few would claim that they have any *legal* responsibilities. The police seem to have dismissed the suggestion that the game provided the attacker's motive and certainly *Manhunt*'s developers had no intent to cause harm to the victim. But it is also clear that societies, and professionals too, do not function solely on the basis of legal obligation; not everything that we *may* legally do is something that we *should* do. Professional ethics takes us beyond the legally compulsory to ask what people should and should not do within the context of their work and careers. The developers of *Manhunt* promoted their product as a "sado-masochistic" game. One early review commented: "'Manhunt' raises the bar for video game violence and gore. It's not just part of the game, it is the game" ("Video game 'sparked hammer murder' 2004"). The media elements and interactions that the developers included were conscious choices. Did they have a *professional* responsibility to think about the possible consequences of those choices?

To answer questions such as this, we need to answer another: What is the meaning of "profession" and "professional responsibility"?

What is a Profession?

A **profession** is an occupation that requires specialized education and training. Preparation for a profession usually includes formal education, often through an accredited program of study. In order to continue in practice, professionals must continue to learn. Professional associations, established to advance the interests of the profession, sometimes establish standards for this continuing education. They also promote both education and research through conferences, institutes, and journals.

Professional associations often formulate codes of ethics for their members. The specialized skills of many professionals (such as physicians, lawyers, engineers, and teachers) are essential to the performance of socially important tasks. As a result, professionals have obligations to the individuals they serve and to society at large. As members of the association and representatives of their profession, they also have obligations to one another and to the profession as a whole. The active role of professional associations in stating, encouraging, and enforcing these obligations illustrates another defining feature of professions: professions are largely autonomous and self-regulating.

Multimedia development includes many of the defining properties of a profession. Multimedia developers employ specialized knowledge and require continuing education and training. Members of development teams, such as graphics designers, sound engineers, and writers, often belong to professional associations that represent their specialties. Professional associations dedicated to multimedia development itself are also emerging. Educational standards are developing as the field matures and colleges and universities define their curricula. Finally, as evidenced in the *Manhunt* case, the work of the multimedia developer may have significant social consequences. Like other professionals, multimedia developers have an interest in regulating their own actions. They may eventually define their professional obligations through a formal code of ethics.

Professional Responsibility and Codes of Ethics

A professional code of ethics is a statement of obligations. These obligations are directed to individuals, to laws, to society, and to the profession itself. A **code of ethics** is a statement of the standards and obligations that define a practitioner's professional responsibilities.

As an emerging profession, multimedia development is not yet guided by a common set of professional standards. To get a sense of the shape of a possible code of ethics for multimedia developers, consider The Software Engineering Code of Ethics and Professional Practice jointly developed by the Association for Computing Machinery (ACM) and the Institute for Electrical and Electronics Engineers (IEEE). This code relates quite directly to the work of a multimedia programmer, and offers guidance to other members of a development team as well.

The Software Engineering Code of Ethics   The code is organized as eight "principles" with a set of specific obligations for each of these. The principles are major obligations: general courses of action that software professionals should undertake. The specific obligations for each principle identify the ways in which they are fulfilled in the course of a professional's daily work. Although the principles sometimes overlap, in general they suggest that professionals have obligations in several different areas—to society at large, to the laws that govern their practice, to clients and employers, to colleagues and subordinates, and to the profession itself. The following summary identifies the principles and highlights a number of obligations in the ACM/IEEE code that are relevant to the work of multimedia developers. For the complete code, see Appendix C.

1. The "Public" Principle: *"Software engineers shall act consistently with the public interest."*

   Professionals are obligated to consider the broader, public consequences of their work. The code specifically notes the need to develop and approve software that is "safe, meets specifications, passes appropriate tests, and does not diminish quality of life, diminish privacy or harm the environment." They are also expected to consider the ways in which physical disabilities, economic disadvantage, and other factors might limit access to the software they develop. Finally, the code contends that professionals should also serve the public interest by volunteering their professional skills to public causes.

   Each of these injunctions has a more or less obvious application to the work of multimedia developers. They, too, need to consider the ways in which their products impact society as a whole, whether they function properly, are safe, and accessible to disadvantaged segments of the population.

2. The "Client and Employer" Principle: *"Software engineers shall act in a manner that is in the best interests of their client and employer, consistent with the public interest."*

   In addition to their public responsibilities, professionals have specific obligations to their clients and employers. For instance, the code requires them to:

   • work within their areas of competence and honestly acknowledge limitations of experience or education

   • use the property of clients or employers only as authorized and appropriate

- preserve the confidentiality of client/employer information
- promptly disclose major problems with a project
- decline outside work that may interfere with completing the client/employer's project.

In the course of their work, multimedia developers often have access to information that must be treated confidentially as well as to equipment and other resources that should consistently be used in the interests of the client, provided that it does not conflict with other legal or ethical requirements. They must represent their abilities honestly and avoid other work commitments that interfere with their primary obligations.

3. The "Product" Principle: *"Software engineers shall ensure that their products and related modifications meet the highest professional standards possible."*

   Professionals also have obligations to create products that are:
   - of high quality, produced at reasonable cost, and on schedule
   - free of "ethical, economic, cultural, legal and environmental" concerns
   - systematically tested and debugged
   - well documented.

   Again, these requirements are clearly mirrored in the responsibilities of multimedia developers, whose products must also meet each of these standards.

4. The "Judgment" Principle: *"Software engineers shall maintain integrity and independence in their professional judgment."*

   Professionals directly consider the ways in which they make the various decisions in their work and they maintain high standards of integrity in those decisions. For example, the code requires that software engineers:
   - be objective and unbiased in the assessment of software
   - avoid unethical or illegal financial practices such as bribery or double-billing
   - refuse to use unlicensed software
   - avoid conflicts of interest.

   While the specific judgments of multimedia developers vary widely with their different roles in a project, the requirement to maintain independence and integrity in professional decisions applies throughout.

5. The "Management" Principle: *"Software engineering managers and leaders shall subscribe to and promote an ethical approach to the management of software development and maintenance."*

   Professionals must often guide the completion of projects and manage the work of others. The ACM/IEEE code includes several corresponding obligations. For example, software engineers should:
   - develop procedures to promote quality and reduce risk in project development
   - provide fair remuneration
   - fully disclose employment conditions

- create fair agreements for ownership of intellectual property developed during the project
- assign work consistent with the employee's knowledge and experience.

Within the context of a typical commercial multimedia project, these guidelines have clear applications to the work of the project director and to any team member supervising the work of others.

6. The "Profession" Principle: *"Software engineers shall advance the integrity and reputation of the profession consistent with the public interest."*

Professionals typically identify with their professions and take steps to advance its development. The ACM/IEEE code reflects this by noting responsibilities to:

- participate in professional associations and meetings
- advance public knowledge of the profession
- place the interest of the profession or the public over their own interest
- support and defend the profession's code of ethics.

Because of the variety of functions they fulfill, the different members of a development team serve different professional interests. Writers, for example, have a different set of professional commitments than sound engineers. In the context of multimedia, however, many of these individuals can serve another important professional function: participating in an on-going public discussion of the nature and implications of the multimedia applications they have helped to create. For instance, many professionals active in video game development have provided interviews to the press, written articles or blogs themselves, or participated in television broadcasts devoted to examining this aspect of multimedia development.

7. The "Colleagues" Principle: *"Software engineers shall be fair to and supportive of their colleagues."*

Professionals in all fields are expected to value their colleagues. In the ACM/IEEE code, this appears in the requirements to:

- support the professional development of colleagues
- be fair and objective in assessing the work of colleagues
- properly credit the work of others.

These guidelines are significant in any working group. As noted in Chapter 11, the multimedia development process is both interactive and iterative: individuals often contribute to one another's work and earlier work is often revised in light of later decisions. Effective collegial relationships are particularly important to the creative exchanges, the give and take, of this process.

8. The "Self" Principle: *"Software engineers shall participate in lifelong learning regarding the practice of their profession and shall promote an ethical approach to the practice of the profession."*

Professionals assume personal responsibility for maintaining the knowledge and skills essential to the effective practice of their professions. The ACM/IEEE code requires software engineers to:

- continually develop their knowledge and skills

- design, test, develop, and maintain high-quality, reliable software
- provide accurate, clear documentation
- understand the environment in which their products are used.

The importance of this principle to multimedia development would be difficult to overstate. Multimedia is directly affected by the continual evolution of digital technology and by the rapid development of new products and services. Maintaining currency with recent developments in their respective fields is critical to the work of all multimedia professionals.

The ACM/IEEE code effectively suggests a wide range of guidelines for the professional practice of software engineering. Many of these also apply to professional multimedia development. The need for ethical guidance is often felt most strongly in areas in which the profession encounters novel challenges to well-established understandings and practices. In medicine, for instance, the development of advanced technologies to sustain life led to a range of challenging questions about the rights of patients and the responsibilities of physicians. New practices, procedures, and legal instruments, such as living wills, were developed in the context of a broad public discussion with economic, political, religious, and ethical components. Multimedia developers similarly must respond to significant changes and challenges. Today, the creation and protection of intellectual property, especially the many forms of creative expression covered by copyright, produce important challenges for multimedia developers.

Copyright is embodied in laws. Those laws create both important protections and equally important restrictions for multimedia development. No multimedia professional can function effectively without a basic understanding of copyright. Knowledge of copyright thus clearly falls under the professional injunction that developers know and follow the laws governing their work; but a multimedia professional's relationship to copyright goes beyond this simple injunction. Copyright is currently a focal point in a major contest between different cultural interests and values, and multimedia developers are in the middle of the fray. The practices that they develop and follow, as well as the technologies and products they help to create, will affect, and be affected by, a continuing copyright debate. To understand the professional issues raised by copyright, multimedia developers must first consider its traditional formulation and the specific protections it affords to content creators.

12.2 The Copyright Tradition: Rights, Remedies, and Exceptions

One reason that understanding copyright is important to multimedia developers is to guard against intentional or unintentional violations of the rights of others. The relative ease of digital editing, copying, storage, and transmission greatly increase the potential for copyright infringement by any member of a development team. In addition, the wide range of media that may be included in multimedia products often requires copyright permission from many different individuals or organizations. Another reason to become familiar with copyright is that developers need to protect their own work by retaining rights to elements such as interface designs that may be useful on other projects. This in turn requires that developers understand how to organize and define the work of their teams and consultants. Developers may also need to frame agreements with their clients to specify copyright ownership for specific elements in a multimedia product. Each of these activities requires an understanding of what copyright is, the protections it affords, and how it is enforced.

Copyright Defined

Copyright is a form of legal protection given to creators of "original works of authorship." The primary purpose of copyright protection is cultural advancement—people are more likely to undertake creative work if they can enjoy the economic benefits of their efforts.

Copyright differs from another common protection of creative effort, *patents*. Copyright applies to original or creative *expression*, but not to the facts, processes, theories or ideas that are expressed. The "Better Mousetrap" is not protected by copyright, but the words used to describe it in trade publications and advertisements are. Patents, on the other hand, do protect mousetraps and other inventions. A **patent** is a grant of rights to the creator of an original, useful invention. The holder of a patent is given an exclusive right to make, use, and sell their invention for a certain period of time.

U.S. copyright law protects virtually any form of original expression—literature, music, drama, pantomimes, choreography, pictures, graphics, sculptures, motion pictures, sound recordings, architecture. The only requirement is that the expression be in a **fixed form**, a form in which it can be preserved and from which it can subsequently be "perceived, reproduced or otherwise communicated" (United States 2007, 2). A dance routine performed on a street corner is not protected unless it is also in a fixed form, perhaps as a set of notations on a page, or as a video recording. But once it is fixed, original expression is automatically protected. The work does not need to be registered and, since 1989, no notice of copyright needs to be given. Computer programs are treated as "literary works" and are also covered by copyright, although there is much discussion of the advisability of treating them instead as inventions subject to the protections of patents. For the multimedia developer, this broad understanding of "works of original authorship" combined with the automatic coverage of works in fixed form means that virtually any content created by another party is potentially covered by copyright.

Copyright Protections   The owner of a copyright has five major rights:

- to reproduce the copyrighted work
- to produce derivative works (for instance, a film version of a novel)
- to distribute copies to the public (by sale, rental, lease or lending)
- to perform the work publicly
- to display the work publicly.

The creator retains these rights unless they are specifically transferred to another party. For instance, the purchaser of a painting does not own the right to reproduce it as a postcard unless the right to produce derivative works has been transferred to the new owner. Agreements with content providers should specify the rights being transferred. Similarly, client contracts should specify the rights to any multimedia content, such as screen designs, that the developer wishes to retain.

Copyright infringement occurs when someone makes any of the above-noted protected uses of a copyrighted work without authorization from the rights holder. Infringement can lead to a variety of sanctions. Injunctions may be issued prohibiting the further production or distribution of a product. Infringing copies may be impounded or destroyed. Compensation may be awarded to the copyright holder for actual monetary damages plus the infringer's profits. Statutory damages and criminal sanctions may also be imposed. While registration is not necessary for a work to be protected by copyright, it is generally required before a lawsuit can be brought against an infringer. Registration is also usually a requirement for the collection of statutory damages and attorneys' fees. Multimedia developers are well advised to register their works. Registration is inexpensive, provides important evidence of copyright claim, and establishes a basis for legal enforcement should such action be necessary.

The rights granted to copyright holders are for a specified period of time. Currently in the United States, works created after 1978 are protected for the life of the creator plus 70 years. If the creator is not an individual (e.g., a corporation) protection is afforded for 95 years from the date of publication or 120 years from creation (whichever comes first).

Exceptions to Copyright Protection Original expression is not always protected by copyright. Works for which copyright has expired, or to which copyright never applied (e.g. those not in fixed form or most publications of the U.S. federal government), are said to be "in the **public domain**" and may be freely used by anyone. In addition, limited use may be made of copyright protected works under the doctrine of *fair use*.

- Fair Use
  The **fair use** doctrine is intended to advance important social goals such as a free and open press, education, research, and scholarship by providing users with a defense against claims of copyright infringement. The conditions of fair use are described in section 107 of the U.S. Copyright Act. These include "reproduction in copies . . . for purposes such as criticism, comment, news reporting, teaching (including multiple copies for classroom use), scholarship, or research . . . " (United States 2007, 19).

  Fair use does not give educators, researchers or others unlimited access to copyright protected works. In determining whether or not a particular use is fair, four criteria are usually considered: the *purpose and character* of the use, the *nature* of the copyrighted work, the *amount and significance* of the portion used, and the *effect* of the use on the value of the work. The determination of fair use in any given case will depend on factors specific to that case and on the precedents established by previous court decisions. In general, fair use is more likely to be found for uses that:
  - are non-profit rather than commercial
  - are factual rather than creative, and published rather than unpublished (creators should have the first opportunity for publication)
  - use small amounts of the work
  - have little or no effect on the value or potential market for the work.
- Works for Hire
  Ordinarily, the owner of copyright is the creator of the work, but works produced under the specific direction of an employer and with the use of the employer's resources are

likely to be regarded as **works for hire**. In these cases, an employer may own the copyright for works created by an employee. As in determining fair use, however, there are many ambiguities and uncertainties involved in identifying works for hire. Developers and their employees will be well served by explicit, written agreements detailing copyright ownership for the content workers produce.

Copyright laws seek to define and balance interests, rights, and obligations among individuals and between individuals and society at large. Fair Use, for instance, seeks a balance between the property rights of individual creators and the interests of society in an open press and unfettered education. This balancing process has always been fluid and, at its borders, marked by uncertainty. Rather than being a set of specific directives etched in stone, copyright law is, instead, a set of general principles whose application to specific cases ranges from clear and definite to highly debatable and uncertain. For instance, how much of a work can a journalist quote in a book review?

A few properly cited sentences clearly seem to be allowed under fair use; the whole book clearly would not be. What about approximately 300 words from an unpublished manuscript of some 200,000 words? The answer depends on the application of the criteria for fair use and here even the courts themselves may disagree. In 1979, Harper & Row Publishers entered into an agreement with *Time* magazine that allowed *Time* to publish portions of President Gerald Ford's memoirs. The memoirs were soon to be released in book form by Harper & Row. Prior to *Time*'s publication, another magazine, *The Nation*, surreptitiously acquired a copy of Ford's manuscript and published an article that used approximately 300 words directly from that source. Following this "scoop" by *The Nation*, *Time* refused to make its final payment to Harper & Row, which then brought suit against *The Nation* for copyright infringement. A lower court originally found in favor of Harper & Row but on appeal this decision was reversed: the appeals court ruled that *The Nation*'s publication of quotations from Ford's manuscript was a fair use. In 1985, the Supreme Court reversed the appeals court ruling, finding that *The Nation* had in fact infringed Harper & Row's copyright. In part, the court argued that the small portion of Ford's manuscript taken by *The Nation*, which dealt with his pardon of former President Nixon, was "essentially the heart of the book" and was therefore "qualitatively substantial" even though it was a tiny fraction of the original source (O'Connor 1985, IV).

As this case illustrates, uncertainties in the application of copyright law have long been a fact of life for publishers, journalists, and others. The development of digital media has complicated matters even more.

12.3 Copyright in the Age of Digital Media

The relative ease of copying, editing, and transmitting digital media poses serious challenges to traditional copyright protections. Copyright law developed in the age of analog media and the rights that it established were defensible largely because of the nature of the media itself. Paintings, books, photographs, music, and films, for instance, are much more difficult to copy and distribute in analog form. Few individuals had the resources to do so, and those organizations that chose to ignore copyright could be readily identified and prosecuted. Digital versions of these media, on the other hand, can be copied and transmitted by anyone with a computer, inexpensive software, and an Internet connection. Analog copies are also usually inferior to originals, especially as copies are made of previous copies, a process known as "generation decay." In contrast, each version of a copied digital file potentially preserves all the quality of an original. Similarly, the process of creating derivative works from analog originals is more difficult to accomplish and easier to detect. In the world of digital media, editing tools for images, sounds or video make it very easy to produce, and disguise, "new" creations based on others' work. Performance and public display rights are similarly threatened as Web technologies evolve to readily support uploading and public display or performance of images, sounds, animations, and videos.

One reaction to the disruptive effects of digital media has been to strengthen and improve the enforcement of existing legal protections. Thus, for instance, major stakeholders in copyright ownership, such as the film and music industries, have tried to strengthen existing copyright provisions and improve the enforcement of existing law (see the following discussion of the Digital Millennium Copyright Act). Another reaction has been to develop and exploit new opportunities inherent in the change itself. Digital technology alters the fundamental conditions of media itself, leading to new models for its development, use, and distribution (for instance, online music distribution through Napster, eMusic, or iTunes). Both responses, enhanced protection of traditional interests and implementation of new media models, are represented in the broad set of initiatives known as Digital Rights Management.

12.4 Digital Rights Management

Digital Rights Management (DRM) is the application of digital technologies to the management of intellectual property (IP). DRM has been applied to many forms of IP, including patents and sensitive corporate reports and communications (Enterprise-DRM), but the main focus of the technology is creative works, "works of original authorship," traditionally covered by copyright. Electronic books, music, videos, and photographs are prominent examples of digital media to which DRM has been applied. While multimedia developers are most often concerned with digital formats, it should be noted that DRM applies to all forms of intellectual property including analog "legacy media" such as printed books and analog photographs. As one researcher insists, "DRM is the 'digital management of rights' and not the 'management of digital rights' " (Iannella 2001, 1).

It is also important to note that creative works can be protected by contract law as well as by copyright law. While copyright law establishes automatic protections for creators, it also limits enforcement of their claims through provisions such as fair use, discussed previously, and the "First Sale Doctrine." First Sale limits a creator's rights to the first exchange of his or her work. For instance, a copyright holder controls the first sale of a printed book, but the book owner may freely lend or sell it to another person and may alter it by removing or marking pages and so on. Later owners can similarly dispose of the book as they like without the permission of the copyright holder. The rights holder, in short, has no further control over *that copy* of the work. Owners of creative content can eliminate these and other limitations on their rights through contracts with users. Instead of selling a user a copy of a work, the owner sells a license to use the product in certain ways specified in a contract. Such agreements, called **end user license agree-ments** (EULAs) are very common for software programs and they are becoming more common for digital content such as electronic books. Users who casually click through the "Agree" buttons on first use of an e-book may have, quite unknowingly, surrendered their traditional fair use privileges. DRM can be used to protect contract rights just as it can protect copyright.

Many applications of DRM have focused on defending the rights of content owners. In effect, this involves using digital technology to try to solve problems created by the digital revolution itself. If a computer can be programmed to readily copy a file, it can also be programmed to copy-protect that file or otherwise limit a user's access. If copyrighted digital media is readily edited and transmitted, so, too, can digital techniques be used to permanently mark its original identity and track its subsequent uses.

The use of DRM to limit media piracy by controlling user copying and access is perhaps the most visible and controversial area of the technology. In fact, many popular accounts identify DRM exclusively with these controls, and some critics have quipped that DRM really stands for Digital *Restrictions* Management (Free Software Foundation 2006). Copy and/or access restrictions to media have taken many forms and have often generated both consumer dissatisfaction and persistent efforts to defeat the DRM safeguards. For example:

- Adobe, the developer of the popular PDF format for text documents, also markets electronic books called "eBooks." eBooks use a DRM-enabled form of PDF. Various controls can be set through Adobe DRM to limit copying, sharing, and reading of purchased or loaned texts. Libraries, for instance, can loan eBooks for a specified period of time. After the loan period expires, the eBooks become unreadable. Adobe's rationale for including DRM was the need to protect the copyright interests of creators by forestalling mass duplication of digital copies. Critics have noted, however, that Adobe has published eBooks that are actually in the public domain. In these instances, DRM effectively blocks perfectly legal copying of the public domain content in the work (at least from a copyright point of view; a license agreement may legally prohibit this use) (Lessig 2004, 151). A Russian company, Elcomsoft, developed software they called the Advanced eBook Processor that allowed a user to convert eBooks into a DRM-free PDF format, thereby removing copy and access limitations. In 2001, one of Elcom's programmers, Russian citizen Dmitry Sklyarov, was arrested by the FBI in Las Vegas, Nevada, where he was attending a professional conference. Sklyarov was charged with distributing a product intended to circumvent electronic copyright protection measures. Though charges against him were ultimately dropped, Skylarov spent several weeks in U.S. jails and was required to remain in the U.S. for several months as legal proceedings against Elcomsoft continued.

- **Content Scrambling System** (CSS) is the form of encryption used by the motion picture industry to protect DVDs from digital piracy. CSS scrambles the contents of a DVD, which can then be viewed only through a player licensed to use corresponding descrambling algorithms. This frustrated both legal (for instance, copying selected portions of a movie for discussion in film classes) and illegal uses of the medium. In addition, it was initially not possible to view DVDs on computers running the Linux operating system because licensed DVD players were not available for Linux. In 1999,

Jon Lech Johansen and unidentified associates developed a program commonly known as DeCSS that defeated CSS encryption, allowing direct access to the disc's digital video. Johansen was charged with violation of Norwegian "economic crime" laws. He was eventually acquitted and went on to develop and post software to circumvent Apple Computer's FairPlay DRM for online music, becoming a controversial symbol of resistance to DRM control technology.

- Audio CDs initially had no copy protection. As technology for "ripping" CDs and transferring music to computers became commonplace, some music publishers turned to DRM to prevent widespread copying and redistribution. One such company was Sony BMG. In 2005, Sony began adding DRM to its music CDs to control playback of their music on Windows PCs. Sony's CDs installed software to the PC, sometimes without a user's consent or knowledge. When Sony's DRM was found to interfere with the operation of some other programs and to open user's computers to potential security breaches, a series of legal challenges arose that included class action lawsuits and actions by individual states alleging violations of laws banning the deployment of "spyware." Sony's attempts to remove the software from affected machines exacerbated the problem when it was reported that their initial uninstall program did not remove the offending software and may have further compromised computer security. Sony ultimately recalled all CDs on which the DRM software (XCP/Mediamax) had been installed and offered refunds to consumers. Sony has since abandoned efforts to protect its CDs with DRM and, as of this writing, no other major distributor is using DRM on its audio CDs.

- DRM was applied to the sale of music on the Internet. Microsoft, for instance, embedded DRM in the Windows Media Audio (WMA) format used for playback of downloaded music on its Zune players and Windows PCs. Sony developed a proprietary format for its music, as did Apple for the music provided through its popular iTunes store. Apple's DRM format, known as FairPlay, limited users' ability to copy purchased music to five computers though it could be copied to an unlimited number of iPods. In contrast to open standards such as Advanced Audio Coding (AAC) or MP3, the proprietary formats of Microsoft, Sony, Apple, and others are not interoperable: music files that play on one device generally do not play on others. This generated consumer dissatisfaction, spawned attempts to crack the DRM, and encouraged other vendors, such as eMusic, to provide music in an open format.

The application of DRM copy/access controls to digital media, as these examples suggest, has often produced unhappy consumers. Such restrictions sometimes interfere with legitimate uses of media and, worse, may degrade the performance of the user's computer. It has been estimated that the presence of DRM controls creates processing overhead that "can cut the battery life of MP3 players by 25 percent" (Center for Democracy and Technology 2006, 20). Even in the absence of these effects, such restrictions frustrate the expectation of flexibility in copying, editing, and remixing media that have become hallmarks of the digital revolution. People realize that such flexibility in all forms of digital media is possible and they resent and resist restrictions on these freedoms.

On the other hand, digital "freedoms" clearly do not imply a right to freely appropriate copyrighted media. As copyright owners continue to press for effective ways to protect their property, they face a fundamental challenge: it is extremely difficult to develop and maintain a system of DRM that is free from attack by determined "crackers." As Apple CEO Steve Jobs commented in an open letter on the subject, "there are many smart people in the world, some with a lot of time on their hands, who love to discover [DRM] secrets and publish a way for everyone to get free (and stolen) music" (Jobs 2007). These challenges spurred another attempt to defend traditional copyright protections, the Digital Millennium Copyright Act.

The Digital Millennium Copyright Act

The **Digital Millennium Copyright Act** (DMCA) is an extension to U.S. copyright law enacted in 1998. The act responded to rights holder's concerns about media piracy and also implemented provisions of the 1996 World Intellectual Property Organization (WIPO) treaty that required revisions in the copyright laws of signatory nations, including the United States. The DMCA contains a number of provisions that directly affect the work of digital media professionals: it clarified the permitted copying of digital media by libraries, archives, and educational institutions; it limited the liability of Internet service providers (ISPs) for copyright infringement by those who use their services; it criminalized the circumvention of DRM control measures even if no other violation of copyright protections occurred; and it outlawed the creation and distribution of any "technology, service or device" intended to circumvent a "technological measure that effectively controls access to a work protected by [copyright]" even if such devices were not actually used to violate copyright (United States 2007, 237).

The DMCA is controversial. In fact, the act is a virtual case study in the clash of traditional interests, rights, and legislation with the challenges posed by a revolutionary technology. Stakeholders in media, such as the software, entertainment, and publishing industries, have welcomed the law, while many librarians, researchers, and public advocacy groups have opposed it (UCLA Online Institute for Cyberspace Law and Policy 2001). The various provisions of the DMCA raise practical issues of direct concern to multimedia developers in their daily work as well as professionally significant social and legal issues. Among these are the following:

- **Potential Abuse of Copyright Claims**—ISPs have a strong incentive to immediately remove media from websites they host as soon as a copyright holder notifies them of an alleged violation. This is because their exemption from liability for copyright infringement under the provisions of the DMCA depends on acting "expeditiously to remove, or disable access to" the offending material as soon as they are notified of a copyright infraction (United States 2007, 155). The notification process is usually simple and no independent determination of the legitimacy of the claim is required for the ISP to take action. This provides media creators and other owners of copyright with a straightforward, practical way to respond to violations of their rights. On the other hand, a website may be disabled simply because an infraction of copyright has been alleged, whether the allegation is true or not. Although the act also provides for a counter-notification denying that the media is being displayed in violation of copyright, many ISPs will follow the safer course of removing disputed material. This opens the door to frivolous or malicious attacks on websites and other multimedia applications where no copyright violation has actually occurred.

- **Fair Use**—The framers of the DMCA were concerned with balancing copyright protections with the exemptions embodied in Fair Use. They explicitly indicated that nothing in the act was to affect "limitations, or defenses to copyright infringement, including fair use" (United States 2007, 238). However, many critics have alleged that the law undermines legitimate fair uses of media by essentially allowing copyright holders to place an unbreakable lock on their content. Under the DMCA, it is illegal to circumvent an electronic protection. Thus media that otherwise could be copied for such fair use purposes as research, criticism, or news reporting, could be rendered inaccessible through DRM. In anticipation of this problem, the act also defined a process for granting exemptions from the circumvention prohibition. An exemption made in 2006, for instance, permitted educational libraries and media studies departments to circumvent DRM protections of audiovisual works for educational purposes. Critics note, however, that such specific exemptions fail to address other potentially fair uses of content that has been protected by DRM. Fair use has always been an ambiguous area of the law and its practical meaning has been determined by court decisions. DRM, enforced through the DMCA, may effectively curtail this process of testing and revising understandings of acceptable uses because it precludes the presumptive fair use in the first place. For instance, a music critic could not make a potential fair use of a small portion of a DRM-protected song without violating the DMCA. Thus, legitimate challenges to fair use restrictions may never make it to court. In *Free Culture*, Lawrence Lessig argued that this amounts to substituting computer code and the "judgment" of a machine for law and the reasoned analysis of a judge (Lessig 2004, 148, 152). Further, he pointed out that DRM software, created under the direction of media companies, may regulate users, and limit their creativity, in ways that have nothing to do with copyright at all. He notes, for instance, limitations on the use of eBooks by Adobe, including denying permission to copy, lend, or give away works that are actually in the public domain (Lessig 2004, 148–153).
- **Research**—The DMCA prohibits circumventions of the electronic protection measures designed to prevent violations of copyright. Thus it is illegal to disable such protections even if no illegal use is actually made of the media they protect. While the law does provide exemptions to this prohibition for research purposes, critics have argued that those exemptions are so narrowly defined that they hamper both research and freedom of expression. The arrest of Dmitry Sklyarov and the prosecution of Elcomsoft, discussed previously, are often cited as instances of the chilling effects of the DMCA on research. In a number of other cases, faculty and students have been threatened with prosecution under DMCA for publicizing the results of their research on DRM. At least one textbook suffered a delay in publication because of fear of prosecution under the DMCA (Electronic Frontier Foundation 2006).
- **Creative Expression**—As we have seen throughout our study of modern multimedia, the digital computer has transformed the conditions of creating and using media. Easily learned media-specific software enables individuals to readily express themselves through text, sound, images, videos, and animations. Authoring software

makes it possible for nearly anyone to combine media and add various forms of interactivity. These capabilities have opened new fields for creative expression, and a generation of computer users is emerging that expects to fully express itself using these tools. As a study by the Center for Democracy and Technology has commented: "Digital technologies and open computer architectures can empower individual consumers to be much more than passive consumers of media . . . . In a world in which people increasingly express themselves through rich media, they will want the ability to quote, comment, and editorialize on and through all kinds of media in the same way they have historically been able to do with text" (2006, 17). While acknowledging the continuing importance of copyright protections, some critics have warned that measures like the DMCA are tipping the balance against creativity. Lawrence Lessig, for instance, argues that the digital technology that underlies new creative possibilities can also support unprecedented forms of stifling controls. Digital restrictions, embodied in DRM, can be combined with automatic monitoring of millions of websites to effectively enforce ever-stricter interpretations of copyright. The widely reported, aggressive enforcement activities of organizations such as the Recording Industry Association of America (RIAA) make it clear that an individual's use of media can already be effectively monitored. This may well have a chilling effect on creative expression. As Lessig notes: "We're building a technology that takes the magic of Kodak, mixes moving images and sound, and adds a space for commentary and an opportunity to spread that creativity everywhere. But we're building the law to close down that technology" (Lessig 2004, 47). These new conditions of creative expression, and potential repression, will require a continuing dialogue about both the limits of fair use and the implementation of DRM. The work of multimedia developers, both amateur and professional, will continue to help shape, and be shaped by, this crucial debate.

The continuing controversy surrounding the DCMA reflects the fundamental challenges implicit in DRM as an access/copy control technology. On the one hand, it appeals to copyright holders as a defense against digital piracy. On the other, it potentially undermines fundamental individual rights and social interests. And, perhaps most significantly, it may be unworkable in a world in which digital technology provides not only the tools to create locks for copyrighted media, but also the keys to the locks. It is still very difficult to prevent determined crackers from disabling DRM. A combination of social, legal, and market forces will determine the future of this aspect of digital rights management. Restrictions on the use of digital media may always be a necessary component of copyright protection. But this form of DRM has been described as just its "first generation" (Iannella 2001; Jamkhedar and Heilman 2005), and whatever the fate of copy/access control, this is only half the story of digital rights management. Implicit in the use of digital technology to manage intellectual property rights is another strategy and another generation of DRM. This second generation of DRM will still be concerned with protecting the rights of creators, but it may also support a freer flow of copyrighted media and new opportunities for both creators and users to benefit from a wider distribution of copyrighted work. Digital watermarking is one of the DRM technologies offering evidence of these possibilities.

DRM and Digital Watermarks

Digital watermarks are alterations to a media file that encode information about the file. This information typically includes identification of copyright ownership, but many other types of information such as a creator's identity, a purchaser's identity, a record of copyright transfers, and even the chain of distribution of media such as images, music, or video broadcasts can be included. Digital watermarking takes its name from the background images traditionally added to stationary, paper money, and printed documents to identify the producer or deter counterfeiting. Unlike their traditional namesakes, digital watermarks are usually hidden from users. The basic strategy is to add digital data to image or audio files in ways that cannot be readily altered and do not impact the display or performance of the media itself. Special-purpose hardware or software is then used to reconstruct the hidden information. Basic watermarking is readily available in image editing programs such as Photoshop, which can read or add watermarks. Creators can also watermark image, audio, and video files, as well as PDF documents, using a growing array of commercial and home-use applications.

Watermarking is often used for copyright enforcement. According to the Digital Watermarking Alliance, watermarks are now found on "billions of audio, video, image and print objects and hundreds of millions of watermarked enabled applications" (2006–2008, 1). Digital watermarks can be preserved through unlimited copies and can even persist through conversion from analog to digital form. They can also be distributed ("wallpapered") through media in ways that preserve information for parts of the original, making it possible to identify the origins of details or crops from images or sounds. Web crawlers can be used to search for illegal use of images and other media on the Internet. This information can then be used in legal proceedings to recover lost revenue and deter further violations. In these respects, watermarking is similar in purpose to DRM copy/access controls, but watermarking does not usually compromise the performance of the media, introduce surreptitious software on the user's machine, or limit the uses that may be made of the media. Of course, watermarking alone also fails to directly prevent unauthorized uses.

In addition to its role in the defense of traditional copyright, however, digital watermarking can also serve as a component in a broader form of DRM in which the management of copyright can lead to new models for the use of digital media. The key to this broader application of watermarking lies in the use of embedded information to trigger other actions. For instance, the reading of a watermark may trigger an update to a database that tracks media usage or it may trigger activation of a link to related content or services. This "second generation" of DRM is not yet fully developed. Its elements, partially implemented in a number of independent applications, have been variously described (Iannella 2001; Van Tassel 2006). The general functions of those elements include the following:

- **Rights Description, Validation, and Record Keeping**—A system, ideally in a standardized, interoperable, and open language, to describe the rights associated with a given media item. There should also be a way to validate the claim of copyright (for example, by access to centralized rights databases) and maintain its currency.

Information encoded through digital watermarks could also help to resolve the problem of "orphan copyrights," protected works whose owner's identities have been lost. Since the watermark can be a permanent feature of the media, subsequent conversions and editing would not result in loss of the identity of the rightful copyright holder. And, because a watermark can be preserved throughout the process of conversion from digital to analog and from analog back to digital, it also offers a solution to the problem of the "**analog hole.**" The analog hole is the vulnerability to copying and piracy that occurs because digital images and sounds must be converted to analog format to be experienced by humans. These unprotected signals can then be sampled to produce a new digital file that is free of original copy/access controls. Files with digital watermarks, however, will preserve the identity of the rightful copyright owner.

- **Media Access**—A system supporting identification and access to relevant available media. This may be thought of as a "virtual repository" through which media available for use by others and stored on widely dispersed computers could be accessed through standardized, interoperable procedures.
- **Trading**—A means of exchanging payment for specific rights to use media items. Once identified through an access system, a photo, for instance, would have an associated listing of rights holders, rights available for purchase, and perhaps related information such as the number of times it has been licensed for use. Different rights (to display or make a derivative work, for instance) and different conditions of use (profit, non-profit, low-resolution, high-resolution, etc.) may be tied to a variable pricing structure. Users can then select their options and make payments automatically to rights holders (as well as to others, such as the providers of the permissions services). Proponents of digital watermarking also note that watermarks can serve as links to related content, thus adding to the functionality and value of the media element.
- **Implementing/Monitoring Rights Usage**—A system to ensure that purchased rights are delivered and that uses are consistent with the conditions of purchase. For example, media may be encrypted or otherwise "wrapped" to permit delivery only under certain conditions such as playback on designated software, time limits for availability of the media, or limits on the number of times it may be used. Uses may be monitored to assure compliance with specific rights transferred.
- **Tracking**—A means of determining and recording actual conditions of use for purposes of providing strategic information to others. For instance, a TV broadcast network may want information on the actual use of feeds to subsidiaries to better plan its marketing strategies.

The Benefits of "Second Generation" DRM   First generation DRM focuses on the use of digital technology to *prevent* copyright violations. It seeks to *protect* traditional rights and practices by limiting the very capabilities that define the digital revolution: the ease of copying, editing, recombining, linking, and transmitting media of all kinds. This "prevent and protect" strategy is very likely to fail. It attempts to forestall the full implementation of the most significant revolution in publishing, and in communications generally, since the printing press. The digital revolution threatens to roll right over first generation DRM: crackers worldwide will continue their assaults on electronic protections and grandmothers worldwide will continue to add clips of their favorite music to slideshows of their grandchildren—and post it all to the Web. These facts do not condone violations of copyright, especially those thefts of the creative work of others intended to bring profit to perpetrators. But they do suggest the need for a different approach to copyright in the age of digital media.

Second generation DRM suggests a different course, one that may move the technology of digital rights management beyond the emphasis on "prevent and protect" to something closer to "respect and promote." Experiments in new models of publishing music, for instance, have produced some surprising results. Magnatunes is a publisher of electronic music that distributes works by independent artists. The artists receive 50% of the selling price. Albums have a suggested price and a minimum price. The buyer decides what to pay. In an interview with *USA Today*, founder John Buckman reported that the average amount paid exceeded both the minimum and the suggested price.

Buckman concluded that consumers were willing to pay more for music that they liked when they knew that artists were benefiting significantly from the sale (Maney). But Buckman has taken this new approach to distributing music further. Magnatunes encourages distribution of its music to a limited number of friends, allows royalty-free use of some music for non-commercial podcasts, and provides links to quickly purchase licenses for other purposes.

Another experiment in new ways of distributing music took advantage of the very Peer to Peer (P2P) networks targeted in many enforcement actions by the music industry. A distribution service called Weed encouraged customers to download its music and pass it along to others. On this model, copyright owners submit their work to an Independent Content Provider (ICP) who verifies copyright ownership and then has the material packaged using Weed's proprietary DRM encryption. A consumer downloads the file and can play it three times. On the fourth attempted play, the consumer is given the option to purchase the file. Those who do make a purchase can then copy the file to a limited number of computers and also burn a copy to CD. The novel element is that they also can share the file with anyone. Individuals who receive the file can then play it three times, at which point they, too, may purchase the file. Every purchase results in a 50% payment to the copyright holder. But each previous purchaser also receives a percentage of the purchase price. This provides a financial incentive for sharing music with those who are likely to purchase it.

As of 2008, Weed had suspended operations after approximately four years in business. Company officials cited incompatibilities with new versions of the Windows operating system (Vista) and Windows Media Player. They indicated that operations might resume if they were able to "rebuild using a more open media format that will be playable on all computer platforms: PCs, Macs, portable devices, and cell phones" (Beezer 2007). The Weed experiment thus demonstrates both the innovative models that can be supported by DRM and also the importance of open standards and interoperability to the successful deployment of these new models.

Successful development of second-generation DRM systems will require addressing issues such as open standards for DRM-enabled media access. Many other challenges, both technical and legal, will undoubtedly need to be overcome. But the potential benefits of the technology are significant. Today, it is often very difficult and expensive to secure copyright permissions to use existing media in new multimedia applications. In many cases, the owner or owners of copyright are not easily identified. When multiple owners are involved, it is time-consuming and expensive to negotiate costs with each party. Often, holders of copyright demand large payments for relatively modest uses of their media. And recent extensions in the period for which works are protected by copyright and other changes in copyright law have further limited access to media. In 1973, the average time for which a work was protected by copyright was 32.5 years. After that time it entered the public domain and was available for use by other creators. Today, the average period of copyright protection has nearly tripled to 95 years, making it more important than ever before to find efficient and economical ways to use copyrighted media (Lessig 2004, 135). A system for managing rights to media that provides ready identification of owners, a searchable database of available content, flexible permission and licensing options, automated secure payment to copyright holders, and a means of automatically monitoring and tracking media use is likely to benefit creators, copyright holders, and the innovators who develop new models and methods for the exchange of creative content.

Given the character of digital media and the capabilities of computers, the expansion of Digital Rights Management is nearly inevitable. Keeping up with the transformations in the definition, uses, and protection of copyrighted media will remain an important professional concern for multimedia developers for some time to come. The various ways in which developers interact with the issues of copyright also illustrate key elements of professional responsibility. For instance, the "Self Principle" of the ACM/IEEE code implies the need for professionals to stay informed of changes in copyright law and practice. The "Colleagues Principle," to be "fair to and supportive of," colleagues suggests the importance of clearly defining copyright ownership for work produced in the course of a project. The "Product" and "Management" principles both suggest the need to seek and properly document copyright permissions. Finally, developers' obligations to the profession and to the public imply a professional responsibility to increase awareness of copyright issues affecting not only the practice of multimedia development but also society at large.

12.5 Conclusion

This chapter examined the meaning of professional responsibility and explored a specific issue, copyright, that is central to the work of virtually all multimedia developers. But the range of potential professional issues extends far beyond copyright. One clear indication of the importance of considering these issues is the attention given to multimedia development by *other* professionals, individuals who, in the course of exercising their own professional responsibilities, have directed their attention to multimedia products.

As noted at the beginning of the chapter, one way of highlighting the need to consider professional issues in multimedia development is the public controversy surrounding video games. In the United States, both the American Psychological Association and the American Medical Association have issued reports on the behavioral and health implications of video games. Psychologists and physicians have raised concerns about a variety of health effects. These include specific physical symptoms such as epileptic seizures and "musculoskeletal disorders of the upper extremities and increased metabolic rate" (Kahn 2007, 3). More frequently, however, the concerns focus on possible psychosocial and behavioral effects including video game overuse or addiction, social isolation, and increased violence and aggression. Parents, religious leaders, and legislators have raised similar issues. The development of a rating system for video games was one effect of these widespread public concerns.

On the other hand, professionals and others have often noted the potential benefits of video games. In addition to their role in providing entertainment and diversion, games have been lauded for a range of other benefits. They have been used for military training, health education, and the treatment of phobias. One study found a positive effect of game playing on the development of surgeon's skills (Dobnik 2004); other studies have noted the social engagement and bonding provided by multiplayer online games (Taylor 2006). Some have argued that playing violent games actually has the positive effect of releasing tension and aggressive emotions. And many educators are convinced that the immersive, interactive characteristics of video games hold great promise for learning (Gee 2007; Glazer 2006).

The video game controversy, like the issues surrounding copyright, will be with us for some time; advocates and detractors alike insist on the need for further long-term experience and study. Whatever the outcome of debates such as these, one thing is clear: the revolutionary technologies of modern multimedia will continue to generate significant social effects and widespread public interest. It is important that the voices of those who are creating multimedia products be a part of the discussion. As participants in an emerging profession, developers must define the codes of professional responsibility that lend authority to their voices. Professional values begin with individual competence and integrity, widen to supportive, respectful relationships with colleagues, then widen further to include obligations to the profession itself and to the well-being of society as a whole. The early pioneers of multimedia envisioned a world made better through a remarkable technology. Modern multimedia developers now wield the creative tools that their predecessors could only imagine.

What kind of a world will they build?

Key Terms

Analog hole	End User License Agreement (EULA)
Code of ethics	Fair use
Content Scrambling System (CSS)	Fixed form
Copyright	Patent
Digital Millennium Copyright Act (DMCA)	Profession
Digital Rights Management (DRM)	Public domain
Digital watermark	Works for hire

References

Beezer, John. "Weedshare will suspend operations on April 9!" *CD Baby Talkback*, April 3, 2007. http://cdbaby.org/stories/07/04/03/6098077.html (accessed January 8, 2008).

Center for Democracy and Technology. "Evaluating DRM: Building a Marketplace for the Convergent World." 1.0. 2006. http://www.cdt.org/copyright/20060907drm.pdf (accessed November 28, 2007).

Digital Watermarking Alliance. *Glossary.* http://digitalwatermarkingalliance.org/glossary.asp (accessed January 3, 2008).

Dobnik, Verena. "Surgeons may err less by playing video games." *MSNBC*, April 7, 2004. http://www.msnbc.msn.com/id/4685909 (accessed January 25, 2008).

Electronic Frontier Foundation. "Unintended Consequences: Seven Years under the DMCA," vol 4. 2006. http://www.eff.org/files/DMCA_unintended_v4.pdf (accessed January 25, 2008).

Free Software Foundation. "Digital Restrictions Management and Treacherous Computing." 2006. http://www.fsf.org/campaigns/drm.html (accessed January 25, 2008).

Gee, James. *What Video Games Have to Teach Us about Learning and Literacy.* New York: Palgrave Macmillan, 2007.

Glazer, Sarah. "Video Games: Abstract." *C Q Researcher*, November 10, 2006. http://library.cqpress.com/cqresearcher/document.php?id=cqresrre2006111000 (accessed November 16, 2007).

Iannella, Renato. "Digital Rights Management (DRM) Architectures." *D-Lib Magazine*, June 2001. http://www.dlib.org/dlib/june01/iannella/06iannella.html (accessed January 6, 2008).

Jamkhedkar, Pramod A., and Gregory L. Heileman. "The Role of Architecture in DRM Vendor Economics." 2005. http://infosecon.net/workshop/pdf/12.pdf (accessed November 28, 2007).

Jobs, Steve. "Thoughts on Music." *Apple*, February 6, 2007. http://www.apple.com/hotnews/thoughtsonmusic/ (accessed January 4, 2008).

Kahn, Mohamed. "Emotional and Behavioral Effects, Including Addictive Potential, of Video Games." 2007. http://www.eapassn.org/public/articles/ama0707.pdf (accessed January 25, 2008).

Lessig, Lawrence. *Free Culture.* New York: Penguin, 2004.

Maney, Kevin. "Apple's iTunes may not be the only answer to ending piracy." *USA Today.* http://www.magnatunes.com/info/press/coverage/usa_today (accessed December 30, 2007).

O'Connor, Sandra Day. "Harper & Row, Publishers, Inc. et al. v. Nation Enterprises et al.," May 20, 1985. U.S. Supreme Court. http://digital-law-online.info/cases/225PQ1073.htm (accessed January 25, 2008).

"Software Engineering Code of Ethics and Professional Practice." *Association for Computing Machinery*, vol 5.2. http://www.acm.org/about/se-code#full (accessed November 18, 2007).

Taylor, T. L. *Play Between Worlds: Exploring Online Game Culture.* Cambridge, MA: MIT Press, 2006.

UCLA Online Institute for Cyberspace Law and Policy. "The Digital Millennium Copyright Act," February 8, 2001. http://www.gseis.ucla.edu/iclp/dmca1.htm (accessed December 7, 2007).

United States. *Circular 92: Copyright Law of the United States and Related Laws Contained in Title 17 of the United States Code. The Library of Congress*, October 2007. http://www.copyright.gov/title17/circ92.pdf (accessed January 25, 2008).

Van Tassel, Joan. *Digital Rights Management: Protecting and Monetizing Content.* Burlington, MA: Focal, 2006.

"Video game 'sparked hammer murder,' " CNN.com, July 29, 2004. http://www.cnn.com/2004/WORLD/europe/07/29/uk.manhunt/index.html (accessed November 21, 2007).

Review Questions

1. What constitutes a profession? Identify members of a multimedia development team who may already have professional codes to guide them.
2. What is a professional code of ethics? Identify and briefly explain three elements of the ACM/IEEE code of ethics for software engineers that apply to the work of a multimedia developer.
3. Why must multimedia professionals be knowledgeable about copyright law?
4. What is the basic requirement for content to receive copyright protection?
5. What are the five major rights of a copyright holder?
6. How long does copyright protection last?
7. What is the distinction between copyright and patent? Would a multimedia product be patented? Explain your answer.
8. What is the distinction between "fair use" and "public domain" as exceptions to copyright protection?
9. What is digital rights management? Why did Sony feel it was necessary to use a DRM technology?
10. What are the main provisions of the Digital Millennium Copyright Act?
11. Identify and explain two practical issues raised by the DMCA for multimedia development.
12. How can digital watermarking solve the problem of the "analog hole" when it comes to copying and distributing portions of a DVD?
13. Explain the basic distinction between first and second generation DRM.

Discussion Questions

1. Research a current computer game such as Manhunt or EverQuest. If you were a key member of the development team that created that game, what specific principles of professional ethics would guide decision making for you as a graphic artist, an interface designer, or a project manager?
2. Study the ACM/IEEE code of ethics and identify the principle or principles that would address the following situations. What would be the "right" decision regarding each situation?
    a. Your project manager tells you not to create interface controls that allow the deaf and blind to use the multimedia application since they won't be part of the target market.
    b. Your project manager wants all math tutorials to have equal representation of males and females in the animation sequences.
    c. As a new hire, you misrepresent your ability to write programming sequences for an instructional application in order to get an increase in pay.
    d. As a multimedia writer, you develop a dialog for an online video game that includes suggestive and offensive language.
    e. You download Adobe's Creative Suite from BitTorrent for a staff of three because your graphics department didn't budget for upgrading the software.

f. As the product manager, you loosely manage the timeline for completing a project so you can charge the client more for the application.

g. You use your lunch hours to manage your avatar on Second Life and develop a virtual store that sells sportswear on your employer's network.

h. You program the code for a game that gives extra points for shooting young women.

i. You use the employer's Internet connection to send previews of a new game interface you are developing to your friends.

j. As videographer, you film aggressive behavior toward children for a video action game.

k. You attend the SIGGRAPH conference every year to identify new trends in multimedia applications.

l. As an animation specialist, you frequently give guest lectures at the area Community College's art program.

m. You freely use the drawings from a graphic artist in your animation series without her approval.

n. You are the audio specialist for a new instructional application during the day and call in sick every Friday morning so you can work at your friend's startup web company as their sound engineer.

o. You write the dialog for a new first person shooter game that is directed at identifying and shooting police officers in a large city.

3. If you are hired to create original graphics for a multimedia project, can you use those graphics on your personal consulting projects? Explain your answer.

4. Multimedia development is a global enterprise. Research the laws governing intellectual property in a foreign country of your choice. Report your findings and relate them to the basic protections of U.S. copyright law.

5. Research the CopyLeft movement (http://www.gnu.org/copyleft/). Report the basic principle of this movement. Do you think this could be an alternative to DRM? Explain your position.

6. Your friends want you to join in the production of a home video to showcase your snowboarding ability. The background music will be a popular rap song. Can you incorporate the entire song, or any portion of the song, in this video that will be uploaded to YouTube for public viewing? Explain your response.

7. If the "First Sale Doctrine" applies to the textbook you purchase at the bookstore, why doesn't it apply to the eBook you purchase at Amazon?

8. Research and report on the current status of DeCSS strategies. Take a position on the use of such techniques to gain access to video content on a DVD.

9. Critics of DMCA report that the act effectively undermines the Doctrine of Fair Use. Explain why they might feel this way. Do you agree with this assessment?

10. Research and report the purpose of Creative Commons (http://creativecommons.org/). Do you think the Creative Commons licensing program is a solution to any of the problems that critics identify with DRM?

11. Adobe Photoshop provides a means to "digitally watermark" your image creations. Research and report other software applications that offer the same watermarking capability.

12. If you digitally watermark the home video you created in Question 6 to showcase your snowboarding skills, what benefits might you receive once the video is posted on YouTube?

13. Some would argue that the age of copy protection for intellectual property is over. Copyright in the digital age can't be enforced, lacks strength, isn't respected internationally, and restricts creativity. As a multimedia developer and creative artist, take a position on the status of copyright law in the digital age.

14. Research and develop a position on a social issue that you think multimedia developers will need to address to secure the future of their work. Relate your position to the code of ethics presented in the chapter and appendix and current developments in multimedia applications.

CD Data Format and Disc Standards

CD Data Format

Compact discs use a special format to encode digital data. There is not a direct correlation between a "bit" and a "pit" in optical storage. Optical drive optics are not sufficiently precise to read and interpret each individual "pit" as a bit. Laser beams are focused into a spot of about 1 micron in diameter so they can miss pits that are .83 microns wide. The solution was to devise a coding scheme that bundles user data with error correction and synchronization data into a symbol called a *channel bit*. Laser beams read transitions between these symbols. CD drives include code to interpret these channel bits on playback. The coding scheme for CD-ROM data is called *EFM* (Eight-to-Fourteen Modulation). Each channel bit groups an 8-bit character into a 14-bit symbol. EFM codes include 267 symbols, sufficient for the 256 possible combinations of ones and zeros in a byte. EFM decoders built into every CD-ROM player convert light modulations produced by the symbols into a binary data stream and discard extraneous bits to report only the actual 8-bit data item within the 14-bit symbol. The transition between symbols could still be difficult to perceive by the laser so three additional *merge bits* are added to insure that the laser can focus on transitions between closely positioned channel bit symbols. The final result is that twice as many bits are needed to report a byte of data. This may seem like a waste of potential storage space, however CDs record 43,000 bits per inch, so ample bits exist to package 8-bit data with 9 extra bits of wrapping.

Optical Data Format Summary
Group of 14 bits forms a "channel bit" symbol.
Symbols are separated with 3 "merge bits."
Group of 588 channel bits form a frame.
Group of 98 frames form a sector.

A Brief History of CD Standards

Before the full potential of optical storage could be realized, standards for the physical disc, data formats, and specialized optical drives were needed so all computers could address and display data uniformly. Current computer optical storage technologies derive from standards first established by the music CD industry. This brief history shows how technology borrows from existing science, adapts it for the needs at the time, and creates standards to promote its widespread use.

Industry standards are articulated in a series of "books" that are known as the Color Book Standards because each book has a different color cover. Philips and Sony defined many elements of the first standard when they created the audio CD. These include:

- Disc size fixed at 120mm with a 15mm center hole and 1.2mm thickness. This physical standard has not changed and allows all CDs to fit into any drive.
- Data recording method in a long continuous spiral track.
- Data read method at a constant transfer rate (CLV).
- Data formats to insure high fidelity and accuracy. A unique form of encoding data added extra bits to the data string for error checking and correction if the surface of the CD was damaged.
- CD storage capacity. The disc could hold 74 minutes of digital music at 44.1kHz sample rate and 16-bit sample size.

These standards were formally adopted in the *Red Book*, which continues to define CD-Digital Audio (CD-DA) formats.

Philips and Sony soon recognized that the CD was ideal for recording and distributing growing volumes of computerized data. In 1984, the *Yellow Book* standard defined new formats for recording data. Data is alphanumeric and organized in frames and sectors with more stringent error correction code. This additional code was necessary because if even one bit of data is lost due to surface damage, the entire data item is compromised. The Yellow Book standard required additional error detection/correction code to preserve data integrity. It also included standards for adding audio and video to the disc by defining two modes for storing different types of data. *Mode 1* contains more error correction code for the alphanumeric data and executable files. *Mode 2* requires less error correction code for graphics, video, and audio data. The Yellow Book standard introduced the possibility of including different types of media on a CD.

The *Green Book* standard defined a proprietary disc known as *CD-I* (Compact Disc Interactive). Philips designed the CD-I standard in 1986 as an extension of the Yellow Book but added proprietary hardware and software to play back interactive multimedia applications. The disc not only contained multimedia data, but also the software required to view the application. CD-I filled a gap in microcomputer development. PCs did not have operating systems or hardware capable of playing true multimedia applications in the 1980s. Today, CD-I technology is no longer necessary; however, several important advancements were articulated by the Green Book standard. In particular, CD-I allowed data tracks to be *interleaved* so the computer can play a unified multimedia application. Interleaving alternated audio and graphics data to facilitate their integration in animation and video playback.

Philips and Sony established the *Orange Book* in 1992. These standards transformed the CD from a read only format to a write once, read many format. The Orange Book defined the multi-session CD. Rather than record the entire CD in one session, a CD now contains blocks of data written at different times, each with its own separate track table of contents (TTOC). The Orange Book also defined the physical structure of the recordable-CD as well as how the data areas on the disc are used.

Additional standards appeared in the form of Blue and White Books. The *Blue Book* was published in 1995 to require the first track of a multi-session disc to be CD-Audio format and the second track to hold computer data. The *White Book* defined a specialized disc that contains the CD-I application and video CD for playback on CD-I players.

The "Color Book" history is not unique; it reminds us that our current multimedia developments derived from industry-specific efforts to capture and record digital media. The CD-DA set the foundation for optical storage of digital music. Future developments added interactive multimedia and the ability to write our own multi-session CDs. Without these standards, we could not play music CDs in every player or use a CD-R disc in any computer.

Appendix B

The Scanning Process

Scanning typically involves six major steps: selecting the part of the image to be scanned, setting color mode, setting spatial resolution, specifying output dimensions, making adjustments to image quality, and executing the scan.

Step One: Selecting the Image Area

Scanning software includes a "preview mode" in which the scanner makes a rapid pass over the image and creates a low-resolution preview. Once the preview is on screen, the user outlines the area to be scanned by dragging a rectangle around it. This is the only part of the image that will be captured when the scan command is given.

Step Two: Select Color Mode

Color mode is the type of image to be produced. Typical options are "line art" or "black and white bitmap," "grayscale," and "color." Selecting a color mode sets the color resolution of the image (the number of bits assigned to each pixel). Line art images use one bit; grayscale images use eight bits. The bit depth available in color mode varies with the capability of the scanner (24-, 30-, 42-, or 48-bit, for instance).

The flatbed scanner is the type most often used in multimedia production. These are similar to copy machines. Images or objects are placed on a glass surface. A light and scan head move beneath the glass and the reflected light produces the different voltages used to encode the image as a digital file. Flatbed scanners often include adapters to capture transparent media such as 35 mm slides. Additional scanner software settings include:

- Exposure adjustments to reduce shadows or introduce highlights.
- Halftone patterns to apply to line art images. As in traditional printing, computers create line art images through different combinations of black and white

dots. Different image effects can be achieved with different patterns (fine dots, vertical lines, horizontal lines, diffused patterns etc.).

- Descreening is an image adjustment that compensates for scans that pick up the linescreen pattern of a printed image. The interaction of the scanner and the original linescreen may produce a wavy or rippled effect sometimes called a *moire* pattern.

Step Three: Set Spatial Resolution

Spatial resolution is the number of pixels that will be created for each square inch of the image (ppi). This is usually called *resolution* in scanning software.

In general, resolution should be set to match the intended output device. Images to be displayed on monitors might be set to 72 ppi while a resolution of 300 ppi or more would be used for printing.

Step Four: Set Output Dimensions (Scaling)

Scanning software allows users to scale the output dimensions of images to produce either larger or smaller versions of the original. Scaling is important because an enlargement made at the time an image is scanned is usually better than one made after scanning. In effect, the scanner can do better enlargements because it has the original image at hand. Trying to enlarge the image after a scan will either spread the existing pixels or require *resampling*, a process in which the editing software interpolates values for new pixels. Either approach can significantly distort the image.

Step Five: Make Image Adjustments

A variety of image adjustments are usually available. These include position changes (rotate right, rotate left, mirror), sharpening, changing color ranges, adjusting exposure, setting different halftone patterns, and descreening. Sharpening accentuates divisions between different colors and helps to reduce the blurriness of scanned images. Use sharpening with care; too much sharpening distorts images. Changing color ranges allows users to shift the amounts of particular colors in the image. These shifts are sometimes used to correct defects in the original (for instance, a "yellowed" photo) or for artistic effect.

Step Six: The Scan

Once the selection, color mode, resolution, output dimensions, and adjustments have been determined, the image is ready to be scanned. Giving the scan command causes the scanner to make a much slower pass or, in some models, a series of passes over the selected area to create the higher resolution final image.

This step often includes options for the destination of the final scan—scan to an open application, to a particular location on the hard drive, or to CD, for instance.

Scanning Tips

The following suggestions can improve the efficiency and effectiveness of scanning.

- Clean the glass. Dust produces speckles on scanned images.
- Use high quality originals. Store originals carefully.
- Scan at the highest spatial resolution you will need (for instance, 300 ppi for printing). Bitmapped images can be reduced in size ("downsampled") without loss of quality, but adding pixels ("upsampling") will degrade the image.
- To produce a larger image than the original, scale during scanning. The scanner will do a better job enlarging an image than an image editing program can do later.
- Avoid grayscale scanning of line art and *printed* grayscale images. The crisp edges of line art are often blurred by grayscale scanning. Printed grayscales, unlike black and white photos, are not contone images. They are actually halftones, made up of pure black and white dots. They, too, can be blurred in grayscale mode.
- Avoid enlargements of line art and *printed* grayscale images. Unlike a contone image, line art and printed grayscales do not have continuous areas of color to sample—enlarging increases the distances between individual lines and dots, degrading the image.
- Save and organize files of original image scans. These will contain the greatest amount of information for later editing.

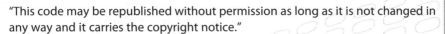

Appendix C

Software Engineering Code of Ethics and Professional Practice

Short Version: Preamble

The short version of the code summarizes aspirations at a high level of abstraction. The clauses that are included in the full version give examples and details of how these aspirations change the way we act as software engineering professionals. Without the aspirations, the details can become legalistic and tedious; without the details, the aspirations can become high-sounding but empty; together, the aspirations and the details form a cohesive code.

Software engineers shall commit themselves to making the analysis, specification, design, development, testing, and maintenance of software a beneficial and respected profession. In accordance with their commitment to the health, safety, and welfare of the public, software engineers shall adhere to the following eight Principles:

1. Public. Software engineers shall act consistently with the public interest.
2. Client and employer. Software engineers shall act in a manner that is in the best interests of their client and employer, consistent with the public interest.
3. Product. Software engineers shall ensure that their products and related modifications meet the highest professional standards possible.
4. Judgment. Software engineers shall maintain integrity and independence in their professional judgment.

5. Management. Software engineering managers and leaders shall subscribe to and promote an ethical approach to the management of software development and maintenance.

6. Profession. Software engineers shall advance the integrity and reputation of the profession consistent with the public interest.

7. Colleagues. Software engineers shall be fair to and supportive of their colleagues.

8. Self. Software engineers shall participate in lifelong learning regarding the practice of their profession and shall promote an ethical approach to the practice of the profession.

Full Version: Preamble

Computers have a central and growing role in commerce, industry, government, medicine, education, entertainment, and society at large. Software engineers are those who contribute, by direct participation or by teaching, to the analysis, specification, design, development, certification, maintenance, and testing of software systems. Because of their roles in developing software systems, software engineers have significant opportunities to do good or cause harm, to enable others to do good or cause harm, or to influence others to do good or cause harm. To ensure, as much as possible, that their efforts will be used for good, software engineers must commit themselves to making software engineering a beneficial and respected profession. In accordance with that commitment, software engineers shall adhere to the following Code of Ethics and Professional Practice.

The Code contains eight Principles related to the behavior of and decisions made by professional software engineers, including practitioners, educators, managers, supervisors, and policy makers, as well as trainees and students of the profession. The Principles identify the ethically responsible relationships in which individuals, groups, and organizations participate and the primary obligations within these relationships. The Clauses of each Principle are illustrations of some of the obligations included in these relationships. These obligations are founded in the software engineer's humanity, in special care owed to people affected by the work of software engineers, and in the unique elements of the practice of software engineering. The Code prescribes these as obligations of anyone claiming to be or aspiring to be a software engineer.

It is not intended that the individual parts of the Code be used in isolation to justify errors of omission or commission. The list of Principles and Clauses is not exhaustive. The Clauses should not be read as separating the acceptable from the unacceptable in professional conduct in all practical situations. The Code is not a simple ethical algorithm that generates ethical decisions. In some situations, standards may be in tension with each other or with standards from other sources. These situations require the software engineer to use ethical judgment to act in a manner that is most consistent with the spirit of the Code of Ethics and Professional Practice, given the circumstances.

Ethical tensions can best be addressed by thoughtful consideration of fundamental principles, rather than blind reliance on detailed regulations. These Principles should influence software engineers to consider broadly who is affected by their work; to examine if they and their colleagues are treating other human beings with due respect;

to consider how the public, if reasonably well informed, would view their decisions; to analyze how the least empowered will be affected by their decisions; and to consider whether their acts would be judged worthy of the ideal professional working as a software engineer. In all these judgments concern for the health, safety and welfare of the public is primary; that is, the "Public Interest" is central to this Code.

The dynamic and demanding context of software engineering requires a code that is adaptable and relevant to new situations as they occur. However, even in this generality, the Code provides support for software engineers and managers of software engineers who need to take positive action in a specific case by documenting the ethical stance of the profession. The Code provides an ethical foundation to which individuals within teams and the team as a whole can appeal. The Code helps to define those actions that are ethically improper to request of a software engineer or teams of software engineers.

The Code is not simply for adjudicating the nature of questionable acts; it also has an important educational function. As this Code expresses the consensus of the profession on ethical issues, it is a means to educate both the public and aspiring professionals about the ethical obligations of all software engineers.

Principles

Principle 1: Public

Software engineers shall act consistently with the public interest. In particular, software engineers shall, as appropriate:

1.01. Accept full responsibility for their own work.

1.02. Moderate the interests of the software engineer, the employer, the client, and the users with the public good.

1.03. Approve software only if they have a well-founded belief that it is safe, meets specifications, passes appropriate tests, and does not diminish quality of life, diminish privacy, or harm the environment. The ultimate effect of the work should be to the public good.

1.04. Disclose to appropriate persons or authorities any actual or potential danger to the user, the public, or the environment, that they reasonably believe to be associated with software or related documents.

1.05. Cooperate in efforts to address matters of grave public concern caused by software, its installation, maintenance, support, or documentation.

1.06. Be fair and avoid deception in all statements, particularly public ones, concerning software or related documents, methods, and tools.

1.07. Consider issues of physical disabilities, allocation of resources, economic disadvantage, and other factors that can diminish access to the benefits of software.

1.08. Be encouraged to volunteer professional skills to good causes and to contribute to public education concerning the discipline.

Principle 2: Client and employer

Software engineers shall act in a manner that is in the best interests of their client and employer, consistent with the public interest. In particular, software engineers shall, as appropriate:

2.01. Provide service in their areas of competence, being honest and forthright about any limitations of their experience and education.

2.02. Not knowingly use software that is obtained or retained either illegally or unethically.

2.03. Use the property of a client or employer only in ways properly authorized, and with the client's or employer's knowledge and consent.

2.04. Ensure that any document upon which they rely has been approved, when required, by someone authorized to approve it.

2.05. Keep private any confidential information gained in their professional work, where such confidentiality is consistent with the public interest and consistent with the law.

2.06. Identify, document, collect evidence, and report to the client or the employer promptly if, in their opinion, a project is likely to fail, to prove too expensive, to violate intellectual property law, or otherwise to be problematic.

2.07. Identify, document, and report significant issues of social concern, of which they are aware, in software or related documents, to the employer or the client.

2.08. Accept no outside work detrimental to the work they perform for their primary employer.

2.09. Promote no interest adverse to their employer or client, unless a higher ethical concern is being compromised; in that case, inform the employer or another appropriate authority of the ethical concern.

Principle 3: Product

Software engineers shall ensure that their products and related modifications meet the highest professional standards possible. In particular, software engineers shall, as appropriate:

3.01. Strive for high quality, acceptable cost, and a reasonable schedule, ensuring significant tradeoffs are clear to and accepted by the employer and the client, and are available for consideration by the user and the public.

3.02. Ensure proper and achievable goals and objectives for any project on which they work or propose.

3.03. Identify, define, and address ethical, economic, cultural, legal, and environmental issues related to work projects.

3.04. Ensure that they are qualified for any project on which they work or propose to work, by an appropriate combination of education, training, and experience.

3.05.   Ensure that an appropriate method is used for any project on which they work or propose to work.

3.06.   Work to follow professional standards, when available, that are most appropriate for the task at hand, departing from these only when ethically or technically justified.

3.07.   Strive to fully understand the specifications for software on which they work.

3.08.   Ensure that specifications for software on which they work have been well documented, satisfy the user's requirements, and have the appropriate approvals.

3.09.   Ensure realistic quantitative estimates of cost, scheduling, personnel, quality, and outcomes on any project on which they work or propose to work and provide an uncertainty assessment of these estimates.

3.10.   Ensure adequate testing, debugging, and review of software and related documents on which they work.

3.11.   Ensure adequate documentation, including significant problems discovered and solutions adopted, for any project on which they work.

3.12.   Work to develop software and related documents that respect the privacy of those who will be affected by that software.

3.13.   Be careful to use only accurate data derived by ethical and lawful means, and use it only in ways properly authorized.

3.14.   Maintain the integrity of data, being sensitive to outdated or flawed occurrences.

3.15.   Treat all forms of software maintenance with the same professionalism as new development.

Principle 4: Judgment

Software engineers shall maintain integrity and independence in their professional judgment. In particular, software engineers shall, as appropriate:

4.01.   Temper all technical judgments by the need to support and maintain human values.

4.02.   Only endorse documents either prepared under their supervision or within their areas of competence and with which they are in agreement.

4.03.   Maintain professional objectivity with respect to any software or related documents they are asked to evaluate.

4.04.   Not engage in deceptive financial practices such as bribery, double billing, or other improper financial practices.

4.05.   Disclose to all concerned parties those conflicts of interest that cannot reasonably be avoided or escaped.

4.06.   Refuse to participate, as members or advisors, in a private, governmental, or professional body concerned with software-related issues in which they, their employers, or their clients have undisclosed potential conflicts of interest.

Principle 5: Management

Software engineering managers and leaders shall subscribe to and promote an ethical approach to the management of software development and maintenance. In particular, those managing or leading software engineers shall, as appropriate:

5.01. Ensure good management for any project on which they work, including effective procedures for promotion of quality and reduction of risk.

5.02. Ensure that software engineers are informed of standards before being held to them.

5.03. Ensure that software engineers know the employer's policies and procedures for protecting passwords, files, and information that is confidential to the employer or confidential to others.

5.04. Assign work only after taking into account appropriate contributions of education and experience tempered with a desire to further that education and experience.

5.05. Ensure realistic quantitative estimates of cost, scheduling, personnel, quality, and outcomes on any project on which they work or propose to work, and provide an uncertainty assessment of these estimates.

5.06. Attract potential software engineers only by full and accurate description of the conditions of employment.

5.07. Offer fair and just remuneration.

5.08. Not unjustly prevent someone from taking a position for which that person is suitably qualified.

5.09. Ensure that there is a fair agreement concerning ownership of any software, processes, research, writing, or other intellectual property to which a software engineer has contributed.

5.10. Provide for due process in hearing charges of violation of an employer's policy or of this Code.

5.11. Not ask a software engineer to do anything inconsistent with this Code.

5.12. Not punish anyone for expressing ethical concerns about a project.

Principle 6: Profession

Software engineers shall advance the integrity and reputation of the profession consistent with the public interest. In particular, software engineers shall, as appropriate:

6.01. Help develop an organizational environment favorable to acting ethically.

6.02. Promote public knowledge of software engineering.

6.03. Extend software engineering knowledge by appropriate participation in professional organizations, meetings, and publications.

6.04. Support, as members of a profession, other software engineers striving to follow this Code.

6.05. Not promote their own interest at the expense of the profession, client, or employer.

6.06. Obey all laws governing their work, unless, in exceptional circumstances, such compliance is inconsistent with the public interest.

6.07. Be accurate in stating the characteristics of software on which they work, avoiding not only false claims but also claims that might reasonably be supposed to be speculative, vacuous, deceptive, misleading, or doubtful.

6.08. Take responsibility for detecting, correcting, and reporting errors in software and associated documents on which they work.

6.09. Ensure that clients, employers, and supervisors know of the software engineer's commitment to this Code of Ethics, and the subsequent ramifications of such commitment.

6.10. Avoid associations with businesses and organizations which are in conflict with this Code.

6.11. Recognize that violations of this Code are inconsistent with being a professional software engineer.

6.12. Express concerns to the people involved when significant violations of this Code are detected unless this is impossible, counterproductive, or dangerous.

6.13. Report significant violations of this Code to appropriate authorities when it is clear that consultation with people involved in these significant violations is impossible, counterproductive, or dangerous.

Principle 7: Colleagues

Software engineers shall be fair to and supportive of their colleagues. In particular, software engineers shall, as appropriate:

7.01. Encourage colleagues to adhere to this Code.

7.02. Assist colleagues in professional development.

7.03. Credit fully the work of others and refrain from taking undue credit.

7.04. Review the work of others in an objective, candid, and properly-documented way.

7.05. Give a fair hearing to the opinions, concerns, or complaints of a colleague.

7.06. Assist colleagues in being fully aware of current standard work practices including policies and procedures for protecting passwords, files, and other confidential information, and security measures in general.

7.07. Not unfairly intervene in the career of any colleague; however, concern for the employer, the client, or public interest may compel software engineers, in good faith, to question the competence of a colleague.

7.08. In situations outside of their own areas of competence, call upon the opinions of other professionals who have competence in those areas.

Principle 8: Self

Software engineers shall participate in lifelong learning regarding the practice of their profession and shall promote an ethical approach to the practice of the profession. In particular, software engineers shall continually endeavor to:

8.01. Further their knowledge of developments in the analysis, specification, design, development, maintenance, and testing of software and related documents, together with the management of the development process.

8.02. Improve their ability to create safe, reliable, and useful quality software at reasonable cost and within a reasonable time.

8.03. Improve their ability to produce accurate, informative, and well-written documentation.

8.04. Improve their understanding of the software and related documents on which they work and of the environment in which they will be used.

8.05. Improve their knowledge of relevant standards and the law governing the software and related documents on which they work.

8.06. Improve their knowledge of this Code, its interpretation, and its application to their work.

8.07. Not give unfair treatment to anyone because of any irrelevant prejudices.

8.08. Not influence others to undertake any action that involves a breach of this Code.

8.09. Recognize that personal violations of this Code are inconsistent with being a professional software engineer.

Digital Multimedia Timeline

The Vision:

1843   Ada Byron (Lady Lovelace) predicted that the calculating machine proposed by Charles Babbage (Analytical Engine) might be used to compose music and produce graphics as well as be utilized in scientific inquiry. [www.ideafinder.com/history/inventors/lovelace.htm]

1914   Winsor McCay introduces *Gertie the Dinosaur,* an animated film consisting of 10,300 separate drawings. It was the first film animation to be created using keyframe animation techniques.

1915   Max Fleischer invented rotoscoping, an animation technique where the artist traces over live-action film movement, frame by frame. Computers have replaced the work of the artist in tracing over the live action.

1915   The first modern film is released by D.W. Griffith. *The Birth of a Nation* introduced moving shots and close-ups to movie production.

1928   The first cartoon with synchronized sound is released by Disney. *Steamboat Willie* gave birth to Mickey Mouse on November 18th.

1936   Alan Turing conceives the Universal Turing Machine, an abstract machine that could complete the tasks of any other information processing machine. Turing's work established the theoretical foundation of modern general-purpose computers.

1940   *Pat the Bunny* by Dorothy Kunhardt uses multimedia and interactivity to promote love of reading and learning in young children. The book includes rabbit fur, flowers to smell, mirrors, and a peek-a-boo blanket to generate interactivity with the story. (Random House Golden Books)

1945   Vannevar Bush publishes "As We May Think" in the *Atlantic Monthly*. In the article, Bush proposes a new way to organize information "as we think" and manage that information using multimedia input/output to the "Memex." The system he proposed would have microfilm, screen viewers, cameras, a vocoder, and electromechanical controls. This and a subsequent article predicted the technologies of hypertext, personal computers, speech recognition, expert systems, online encyclopedias, and the Internet.

1960s	NLS, or oNLine System, was designed by Douglas Engelbart at Stanford Research Institute. NLS was the first practical use of hypertext, the mouse, raster-scan video monitors, screen windowing, and presentation programs. These developments pre-dated the personal computer, but contributed to modern graphical computer applications. (www.wikipedia.org, NLS computer system)
1960	J.C.R. Licklider published "Man Computer Symbiosis" where he proposed that computers should be developed with the goal of "enabling men and computers to cooperate in making decisions and controlling complex situations without inflexible dependence on predetermined programs" (Packer & Jordan 2001, 56).
1963	Ivan Southerland created Sketchpad, a computer program that is considered the ancestor to modern computer-aided drafting programs and a breakthrough in computer graphics. The Graphical User Interface is developed from Sketchpad. (www.wikipedia.org, Sketchpad)
1966	Ivan Sutherland invented a head-mounted display to immerse the viewer in a visually simulated 3-D environment. He describes his "ultimate display" as a "room within which the computer can control the existence of matter" (Packer & Jordan 2001, 256).
1967	Ted Nelson invented the word "hypertext" for his non-sequential method of writing. Later he called the quest for relating all things Project Xanadu. His work continues as XanaduSpace, free software that allows the user to work with parallel documents. (www.xanadu.com/)
1970s	Alan Kay and Adele Goldberg reveal the prototype for the Dynabook. The precursor of the multimedia laptop computer, it was conceived as "a dynamic medium for creative thought," capable of synthesizing all media—pictures, animation, sound, and text—through a personal computer. They also developed "Smalltalk," an object-oriented software language that led to the invention of the GUI (Packer & Jordan 2001, 170).
1970s	The Aspen Movie Map project allowed the viewer to navigate through an interactive video-disc view of Aspen, Colorado. Developed by Scott Fisher, this type of "surrogate travel" suggests the current notion of virtual reality (Packer & Jordan 2001, 260).
1972	PONG, the first commercial video game, was released by Atari. The Magnavox Odyssey, the first home video game system was released as well.
1974	The Intel 8080 microprocessor was released. MITS released the first successful personal computer, the Altair 8800, with one KB of memory and available by mail for $397.
1975	Bill Gates founds Microsoft as a software publishing enterprise.

Multimedia Matures

1976	Steven Jobs and Steve Wozniak launch Apple Computing. The Apple II in 1977 is the first to use color graphics.
1977	Myron Krueger explores the computer as a component in interactive art. In his "responsive environments" the artist is a composer of intelligent real-time computer media spaces.
1979	Richard Bolt creates a "Spatial Data Management" system where the user is engaged with data in forms of vision, sound, and touch. Working at the MIT Arch-MAC group with Negroponte, his spatial data-management system was the first hypermedia system to organize information in a 3-D virtual environment he called "dataland" (Packer & Jordan 2001, 186).
1981	IBM releases the first PC which runs the new MS-DOS operating system.

1983	Compact Disc Technology is introduced in the U.S. The standard was proposed by Philips & Sony in 1980.
1984	Apple introduces the Macintosh computer with a GUI operating system, mouse, 128KB RAM, and 3.5 disk drive for $2495.
1985	Commodore Amiga combines advanced graphics, sound, and video capability to create the first true multimedia computer.
1988	Macromedia Director is released as the authoring software to produce desktop multimedia applications.
1991	Tim Berners-Lee distributes the first web browser and publishes the HTTP and HTML standards. His software was initially developed to unite research, documents, programs, laboratories, and scientists in an open hypermedia environment at CERN Switzerland (Packer & Jordan 2001, 209).
1991	The MP3 digital audio compression format is invented.
1992	Text-based Virtual Realities create social phenomena called Mudding. A Multi-User Dungeon is a software program that accepts networked connections and gives each user real time access to a shared database of "rooms," "exits," and other objects to manipulate in the telling of a shared adventure. LambdaMOO was the first popular MUD (Packer & Jordan 2001, 353).
1993	CAVE (Cave Automatic Virtual Environment) is an environment that combines interactive, computer-generated imagery, and 3-D audio with physical space. Constructed by Sandin, DeFanti, and Cruz-Neira, the CAVE frees the user from the Head Mounted Display and dataglove of earlier environments (Packer & Jordan 2001, 287).
1993	Broderbund releases Myst, the first successful interactive computer game.
1995	*Toy Story* is released by Disney and Pixar. It is the first feature length movie developed solely from digital animation techniques. The 77 minute film took 4 years to make and over 800,000 hours to render.

Multimedia Lifestyle

1994–96	Digital cameras become affordable and widely available. Apple QuickTake was the first digital camera for the consumer marketed to work with a home computer through a serial cable. Kodak, Casio, and Sony soon followed.
1995	DVD specifications are finalized for DVD-Movie player and DVD-ROM computer applications.
2000	Play Station 2 video game console is developed by Sony.
2001	*Shrek* released by Dreamworks. Over 275 artists, computer animators, and engineers spent three years completing the film which was the most visually rich and technically challenging computer animated film of the day.
2001	Steve Jobs stuns MacWorld in Oct. 2001 with the first iPod. The original 5GB model could store 1,000 tunes in your pocket. The iPod also came with iTunes, and a new way of buying music by the song.
2003	Linden Research, Inc. introduces an Internet-based virtual world named Second Life. Users adopt avatars and interact with each other in a type of meta-verse where they own land, create, and trade items and services with each other.

2005	YouTube changes the landscape for film production. Videos can be uploaded, viewed, and shared from this website. News, entertainment, and personal expression are published by amateur videographers and professionals alike. Founded by three former PayPal employees, it was sold to Google in 2006.
2006	Nintendo introduces the Wii, a new game console that features a wireless controller used as a pointing device. The Wii Remote can detect acceleration in three dimensions. The Wii introduces new forms of interactivity directed to a single game experience.
2007	Google introduces Street View, a feature of Google Maps that provides 360° panoramic street level views of selected neighborhoods. Street View collects photos taken from a car that travels the streets of selected cities. Users can navigate from any direction and a variety of angles.
2007	Steve Jobs introduces the iPhone at January MacWorld. The iPhone combines a mobile phone, widescreen iPod with touch controls, and Internet communications. New interface software includes cover flow, multi-touch display and a predictive keyboard.

References

Ament, Phil. "Ada Lovelace." Nov. 23, 2005. The Great Idea Finder. Dec.13, 2007 http://www.ideafinder.com.

Barabash, Craig and Janice Kyllo. "History of Multimedia." Dec. 13, 2007. http://www.ucalgary.ca/~edtech/688/hist.htm.

Butzgy, Mike. "Writing for Multimedia: Great Moments in Multimedia History." 2004. Dec. 14, 2007 http://writing.atomicmartinis.com/moments.htm.

Montgomery, Tim. "The Unofficial DreamWorks Animation Archive." Jan. 16, 2007. Dec. 14, 2007 http://animationarchive.net/.

Packer, Randall, and Ken Jordan, editors. Multimedia from Wagner to Virtual Reality. 2001, New York: W.W. Norton & Company.

Wikipedia. "SketchPad." Nov. 16, 2007. Dec. 14, 2007 http://wikipedia.com.

Wikipedia. "NLS (computer system)." Jan. 8, 2008. Dec. 14, 2007 http://wikipedia.com.

Zakon, R.H. "Hobbes' Internet Timeline v8.2." 1998. Dec.13, 2007 http://www.zakon.org/robert/intyernet/timeline/.

Glossary

3-D imaging program: Software used to model 3-D objects, define surfaces, compose scenes, and render a completed image.

8mm: An analog tape format used in lightweight video cameras that supports a screen resolution of 230 lines.

Access point: A central transmitter and receiver of radio signals on a wireless LAN.

Access time: The time to locate and load data from a disk surface. Measured in milliseconds (ms), access time includes the seek time—moving the arm over the appropriate track, and rotational delay—the time to spin the disk under the read/write head to the correct sector location.

Acquisitions specialist: A member of a multimedia team who secures appropriate permissions to use copyright-protected content in a project.

Active matrix: A type of LCD display in which a single transistor controls each liquid crystal cell to produce a faster display rate on the screen. Also called TFTs (thin film transistors).

Adaptive indexing: The process of selecting colors in an indexed color palette based on an analysis of the dominant colors in an image.

ADB (Apple Desktop Bus): A serial transmission interface for keyboard, printer, and mouse on older Apple computers.

ADC (Analog to Digital Converter): An electronic device that converts an analog data stream into digital data.

Additive color: Color produced by combining varying amounts of differently colored light. The color on computer monitors and television displays is additive color produced by combining red, green, and blue light. See also *subtractive color*.

Address bus: Electronic pathway that carries information about memory locations of data. Bus size, measured in bits, determines how much memory the processor can address.

AIFF (Audio Interchange File Format): A digital audio file format from Apple used by Macintosh computers.

Aliasing: An inaccurate or "false" representation of data. As used in text, aliasing is the appearance of ragged letter edges, especially on diagonal lines. As used in sound, aliasing is the false representation of a high frequency as a low frequency as the result of an inadequate sample rate.

Alignment: In text display, the position of lines of text relative to the margins. Common alignments include left, right, and centered.

Alpha: In multimedia development, an initial test version of an application that typically contains most media elements but may have many bugs.

Alpha tweening: Animation technique that creates the illusion of motion by altering the color or opacity of an object from one frame to another.

ALU (Arithmetic Logic Unit): A component of the CPU that performs mathematical and logical calculations on data.

Amplitude: A measure of sound pressure; the amount of energy associated with the sound. Different amplitudes are perceived as variations in loudness.

Analog data: Data that varies continuously such as temperature, voltage, or pressure.

Analog hole: A loophole to avoid compliance with the protections on digital media. Playing a digital file and capturing the analog signal to a recording device will circumvent the digital protective measures.

Animated GIF: A file of .gif images that repeat in sequential order to produce a simple animation. A waving flag could be produced in an animated gif file format.

Animating with physics: A method of animation that specifies motions based on the properties of objects and the laws of physics.

Animation: The technique of rapidly displaying a series of still images to produce the appearance of motion. This illusion of motion is possible due to a phenomenon known as "persistence of vision."

Anti-aliasing: In text display, a method used to produce characters with smooth edges by blending the color of the text with the background color of the screen or page.

Application: Software that performs a specific task, such as word processing or image editing.

Artificial intelligence: The branch of computer science that explores methods to mimic human decision-making in computer software and hardware. The term was first used by John McCarthy in 1956 at MIT. Examples of applications that use AI are computer games, expert systems, and robotics applications.

Ascender: The portion of a letter written above the normal text body. Letters such as *h*, *k*, and *t* have ascenders.

ASCII (American Standard Code for Information Interchange): A code to represent letters, symbols, and numbers in binary format. It was originally developed in 1965 as a 7-bit code for 128 characters that were compatible with all data processors. In 1981, IBM introduced an eight-bit code with 256 unique characters for its personal computers. Today's standard is 8-bit or "extended ASCII."

Aspect ratio: The relationship between width and height on a computer monitor, television display, or movie screen. The aspect ratio of NTSC video is 4:3, while HDTV is 16:9.

Assembler: Software to convert abbreviated commands in assembly programming languages to machine code. Like the language itself, assemblers are dependent on the specific machine instruction set used by the computer.

Assembly language: A low-level programming language that uses symbolic instruction codes to define instructions for the computer to execute. The codes are machine dependent, developed for one specific type of processor. Assembly language requires an assembler, a program to convert the abbreviated codes to machine language for program execution.

AU: AUdio file format developed by Sun that is used on the Internet for transmission of relatively low-quality sound files.

Authoring: The process of integrating media and creating the user interface for a multimedia application.

Authoring application: Programs especially designed to facilitate the development of multimedia products. This software supports integration of various digital media and ability to create interactivity.

Autotracing: The process of converting a bitmapped image to a vector image by identifying image areas that can be treated as shapes. These shapes are then defined by mathematical formulas to complete the conversion to vector format.

Background layer: In multimedia authoring, an area that holds media elements shared across multiple screens.

Backward compatibility: The ability of more recent hardware or software to use data from an earlier product (for example CD discs are readable in CD/RW drives).

Bandwidth: The amount of data that can be transmitted over a communications medium, or band.

Basic interactivity: User control of multimedia information through common navigation techniques like buttons, menus, navigation bars, or VCR-like controls.

Beta: In multimedia development, an advanced test version of an application that usually contains all media components and few bugs.

Binary code: The coding system consisting of two digits, 0 and 1. Binary code is the universal language of computers.

Bit: A binary digit used to encode digital data (*0* or *1*).

Bit depth: The number of bits used to represent a data sample.

Bitmap: A computer graphic with 1-bit color depth resulting in the possibility of two colors, generally black and white. See also *line art*.

Bitmapped font: A technique for displaying text through a monitor or printer. Each pixel of a letter is described by a binary code of one or more bits creating a bitmap of the letter.

Bitmapped image: A graphic represented as a grid of rows and columns of dots in memory. The value of each dot (or picture element) is stored as one or more bits of data. The density of dots (spatial resolution) determines the sharpness of the displayed image. The number of bits for each dot determines the color resolution for each dot.

Bitmapping: The process of defining an image as an array of individual pixels.

Block: The smallest addressable unit of CD audio data storage. A block consists of 58 frame units of data.

Bluetooth: Standardized as 802.15, Bluetooth provides wireless networking of data and/or voice devices in a small area (up to 30 ft). Bluetooth supports a basic data rate of 1Mbps and is intended for wireless data exchange between a computer and local peripherals such as a printer, keyboard, or PDA.

BMP: A Windows bitmapped image file format.

Browser (web): A software application that resides on a client computer to process and display documents transmitted by the HTTP protocols. Web browsers became popular in 1993 when Marc Andreessen developed Mosaic as the first graphical browser. Mosaic became the "killer application" of the Internet because its graphical interface provided easy navigation to pages that could display text and images on the client computer.

Bump map: An image of a textured surface produced by creating a pattern of lighter and darker shades of color. Lighter shades appear higher and darker shades appear lower.

Bus: An electronic channel or path that carries bits within the circuitry of a computer system.

Bus width: The number of bits a bus can transfer at one time. Wider bus size means more data can be transferred faster. A 32-bit bus can move twice the data than a 16-bit bus.

Bush, Vannevar: (1890—1974) A scientist and professor at MIT, Bush constructed the Differential Analyzer. He was also a visionary of modern multimedia. In "As We May Think" (*Atlantic Monthly*, 1945), he introduced the concept of "Memex," an interactive hypertext system for organizing information.

Byte: A group of 8-bits.

Cache: High-speed electronic storage that holds recently accessed data. Cache is designed to increase the speed of processing by keeping a copy of frequently read data closer to the processor, thus saving the time that would be required to fetch it from main memory.

Card metaphor: A common metaphor for authoring applications that organizes media content in sequential order where each point of information is placed on a card or displayed on a screen.

Cartridge disk: A portable magnetic storage medium where the disk is a rigid platter contained in a sealed plastic case. The most popular form of cartridge disk is the Zip disk, which offers higher storage capacities and faster access times than floppy disk storage.

Case: A typographical characteristic of letters. Capital letters are called upper case; small letters are designated as lower case. The term is derived from the manual typesetting industry. As early as 1588, blocks of letters were organized in wooden cases. The capital letters were in drawers above (upper case) and the small letters were below (lower case).

CAV (Constant Angular Velocity): In optical storage, a method to locate and access data where the disc is rotated at a constant speed, similar to hard drives.

CBR (Constant bit rate encoding): A method of encoding digital video or sound that assigns the same number of bits per second to all parts of the video or sound. See also *VBR.*

CCD (Charge-Coupled Device): An electronic device used in scanners and digital cameras to capture an image as a set of voltages that are then sent to an ADC where they are translated into binary data.

CD-DA (Compact Disc Digital Audio): Optical storage standard developed by Philips/Sony in 1982 to hold 74 minutes of high fidelity digital audio. Some later audio CDs can store 80 minutes of music depending on the configuration of the track.

CD-R (Compact Disc-Recordable): A standard for discs that can be written to by a computer. CD-R discs are coated with a layer of photo-reactive dye. A laser light in the drive alters the molecular structure of the dye to store data. CD-R discs can support multi-session recording, but cannot be erased to store new data.

CD-ROM (Compact Disc Read Only Memory): An optical disc standard for the storage of computer data. Developed in 1984, CD-ROM holds approximately 650–680MB of data stored in pits and lands.

CD-RW (Compact Disc-ReWritable): A compact disc that can be read, erased, and recorded. CD-RW requires a disc with a special layer of "phase-change" substance that alters its crystalline structure when heated by a laser light. The CD-RW drive has two intensities of laser light. A stronger light beam will erase and write data. A less intense light is used to read the data.

CD video (CDV): An audio/video format introduced in 1987 that delivered 20 minutes of audio information and 5 minutes of analog video on a standard CD size disc. Format was popular with music videos, but disappeared from the commercial market in 1991.

Cel: An abbreviation of *celluloid*, a thin sheet of transparent acetate on which images for animation were drawn and painted. The cels were layered to build up a scene in traditional animation. This technique is simulated in digital animation applications to create multiple layers in one frame of animation.

Chrominance: Color hue. Chrominance is mixed with luminance in the composite NTSC signal.

Client: The client part of a client/server network architecture. Clients are PCs or workstations that rely on servers for resources such as data or devices. Clients process the data locally using client applications such as a browser or email applications.

Client/server: A network structure where one or more computers act as servers to distribute data, commands, or applications. The client computer processes the data or runs the applications locally. This distributed network model is efficient since all processing occurs at the local level. It is most commonly used by the WWW protocols.

Clip art: Collections of images made available for use by others (usually by purchase).

Clipping: A form of sound distortion that occurs when the amplitude of a sampled sound exceeds the range of digital values available to encode it. The familiar "testing, one, two, three" is carried out to make certain that sound amplitude falls within recordable range.

Clock speed: Also called *clock rate*, clock speed is the time required for the microprocessor to perform a single instruction. Clock speed is measured in Mhz or Ghz.

Cluster: A logical unit of storage defined by the operating system. Clusters may consist of two to eight contiguous sectors depending on the operating system.

CLUT (Color Look-Up Table): A CLUT defines the set of colors available to generate an image on a computer. Each available color is listed in the table.

CLV (Constant Linear Velocity): A method to locate and access data in optical storage. Data is stored in a single spiral. The drive motor varies the speed of the disc, rotating faster at the center and slower at the outside edge to guarantee a constant data transfer rate.

CMYK: A color model used in printing. Colors are created by combining varying amounts of cyan, magenta, yellow and a key color, which is usually black.

Code of ethics: A statement of professional responsibilities. Codes outline rules and procedures of professional conduct.

Codec: A program designed to compress and decompress digital data.

Color banding: The disruption of the continuous transitions between shades of color as a result of quantization. The smooth gradation of a color is replaced by noticeable boundaries between separate shades.

Color gamut: The range of available colors.

Color indexing: The process of defining a color palette based on an analysis of the colors in an image and/or the conditions of human perception.

Color palette: The set of colors available to a computer at any given time.

Color resolution: A measure of the number of different colors that can be represented by an individual pixel. Color resolution is determined by bit depth.

Command line interface: A method for users to interact with an operating system by entering commands based on a specific syntax. MS-DOS and UNIX are common operating systems that have a command line interface.

Command-based: A method of encoding digital media that uses program instructions to recreate the media. MIDI is an example of command-based media encoding. See also *description-based*.

Compact Disc (CD): Optical storage media first developed in early 1980s to hold high fidelity sound. The CD standard was subsequently extended to include computer data and became an important distribution medium for multimedia applications and other software.

Compiler: Software that converts the entire source code (high-level program) into a machine level program. The result is an executable file that runs on a specific computer system.

Component color: A technique for producing color in which each color component, red, green, and blue, is represented in a separate color channel.

Composite color: A technique for producing color in which luminance (brightness) and chrominance (color hue) are mixed and transmitted in a single signal.

Compression: A process of re-encoding data to reduce storage or transmission requirements. See also *lossless* and *lossy*.

Computer platform: A category of computer defined by the combination of CPU and operating system used. Applications are written for specific platforms such as Windows/ PC or Macintosh.

Computer system: An integrated set of hardware and software designed to process data and produce a meaningful result.

Condensed text: Text in which the width of all characters is narrowed.

Conditional: A navigational structure in a multimedia application that is based on the user's responses or progress in the application.

Content expert: A person who knows the subject matter of the multimedia project. The content expert is frequently the client. Responsibilities include: determining the project objectives, targeting audience and user needs; providing the content materials; providing additional resources; and providing feedback on content, design and interactivity development in relation to the subject matter.

Content inventory list: A document that identifies the required media for a multimedia project.

Content Scrambling System (CSS): A form of encryption used by the motion picture industry to protect DVDs from digital piracy.

Contone (Continuous tone): An image made up of continuous areas of color such as an analog photograph.

Control Unit (CU): The set of transistors in the CPU that directs the flow of data and instructions within the processor and electronic memory.

Convention: Standard or agreed upon procedures.

Copyright: A form of legal protection given to creators of original works.

CPU (Central Processing Unit): A complex set of transistors that execute program instructions and manipulate data.

Cross-platform compatibility: The ability of an application to run on different hardware and operating systems

CRT (Cathode Ray Tube): A monitor that displays output by scanning the back of a phosphor-coated screen with an electron beam. CRTs are used in television as well as computing.

Cycle: A series of images that can be reused to extend repetitive action in traditional animation.

D1: A high resolution component color format used in expensive cameras and editing systems for the production of broadcast quality TV using 19mm tape.

D2: Digital video file format for composite color used in TV production. It uses 19 mm tape and records up to 208 minutes on a single cassette.

D3: An uncompressed composite digital video file format using ½" tape cassettes for recording PAL or NTSC signals sampled at 8 bits. Cassettes can record up to 245 minutes.

DAC: See digital analog converter.

Data: Facts that can be organized and grouped in meaningful collections.

Data bus: Electronic pathway that carries data between memory and the CPU.

Data file: See *file*.

Database: A collection of integrated and related files.

Debugger: A utility to track the execution of program code and assist developers in locating coding errors.

Decibel: A measure of sound amplitude. Each 10 dB increase roughly doubles the perceived volume of a sound.

Descender: The portion of a letter written below the line. Letters such as **p**, **g**, and **j** have descenders.

Description-based: A method of encoding digital media that stores a digital representation of the media element. A bitmapped image stores each picture element in the image. See also *command-based*.

Development plan: A structured procedure to create a multimedia project that includes all the steps that will lead to successful completion of the product. Development plans address three essential tasks: definition, design, and production.

Device driver: A program that works with the operating system to communicate with peripheral devices. Drivers are often provided with the hardware and may also be available as downloads from the manufacturer's website.

Device-dependent: A type of digital data in which the dimensions of output depend on the device being used. Bitmapped graphics are device-dependent because the dimensions of the output from a given file vary between devices such as printers and monitors.

Device-independent: A type of digital data in which the dimensions of output do not depend on the device being used. Vector graphics files are device-independent.

Digital: A description of data represented in discrete units. Derived from *digit*, meaning *finger*. In computer language, these numbers are 0 and 1 or binary digits. The opposite of analog.

Digital Analog Converter (DAC): An electronic device that converts a series of discrete digital values to an analog signal.

Digital data: Data represented as discrete units such as numbers.

Digital encoding: The process of assigning bits to a data item.

Digital Millennium Copyright Act (DMCA): An extension to U.S. copyright law enacted in 1998. The act responded to rights holder's concerns about media piracy and also implemented provisions of the 1996 WIPO (World Intellectual Property Organization) treaty that required revisions in the copyright laws of signatory nations, including the United States.

Digital Rights Management (DRM): The application of digital technologies to the management of intellectual property. DRM has centered around digital music but also applies to any controls to copy/access digital media.

Digital Signal Processor (DSP): A chip that converts analog signals into digital data and in some cases performs adjustments to the original data before storing it in digital format.

Digital Television (DTV): A standard replacing NTSC analog television. It provides movie quality image and sound as well as interactivity.

Digital watermark: Alterations to a media file that encode information about the file. This information typically includes identification of copyright ownership and is used for copyright enforcement.

Digital zoom: A technique that simulates the effect of telephoto lens on a digital camera by digitally enlarging and cropping an image.

Digitization: The process of converting analog data into digital or discrete data.

Directory: A common label for collections of files, often called a *folder* in GUI operating systems.

Dithering: The process of combining pixels of different colors to produce another color that is not available in the current color palette.

Dot matrix printer: An impact printer that forms characters by striking a paper. Commonly used for multi-part forms.

Downloaded audio: Sound files transferred from the server to a client computer before they start playing.

Downsampling: Reducing the sample rate (sound) or spatial resolution (images).

DPI (Dots Per Inch): A measure of spatial resolution for printed output.

Draw program: Software to create vector graphics. The program uses mathematical formulas to define lines that can be scaled and resized without distortion.

Dual-core processor: Central processing unit that contains two execution cores on a single integrated circuit. These processors are better suited to multitasking computing tasks because each core can execute a separate task. The operating system can address each core in parallel, which improves overall multitasking events.

DV (Digital Video): A file format for relatively high quality digital video. DV has a screen resolution of 720 × 480 pixels and uses M-JPEG compression. Because M-JPEG does not use inter-frame compression, the DV format is often preferred for digital video editing. Other formats, such as DVD video, are more widely used for video distribution.

DVD (Digital Versatile Disc): An optical storage standard introduced in 1997 that holds up to 17GB of data. Originally developed to distribute digital video, it is also used for any type of media, thus the name "versatile." Disc capacity is increased due to developments in shorter laser wavelength, smaller pits, denser track pitch, and more efficient channel encoding. The disc is also manufactured with four layers of potential storage at 4.7GB per layer.

DVD video: A video standard for delivery on DVD optical discs. Screen resolution is 720 $\times$ 480 pixels. DVD video uses MPEG-2, a codec that produces both intra-frame and inter-frame compression. DVD video is a widely adopted format for the delivery of previously edited video.

DVD-RAM: A read-write optical disc standard for high capacity storage of digital data on a computer. It is manufactured with a special "phase change" substance that supports reading, writing, and erasing of data, but the capacity is reduced to 2.6GB. DVD-RAM discs have limited compatibility with computer drives and DVD players.

DVD-ROM: A high capacity read-only optical storage standard for any type of computer data. It is equivalent in transfer rate to an 8X CD-ROM but has seven times more capacity.

DVD-Video: A high capacity read-only optical disc format used for interactive playback of movies or games and playback of movies or audio using the MPEG-2 video compression format. Designed to play on a DVD player or computer equipped with a special hardware decoder and supporting software.

Dye sublimation: A method for printing high quality color using color dyes stored on a cellophane ribbon. Once heated, the color turns to gas and diffuses on the print surface where it dries.

Dynabook: An early multimedia "personal" computer proposed by Alan Kay at Xerox PARC in the late 1960s. The Dynabook included many features that would later be common on multimedia computers, including a GUI, keyboard, mouse, and painting and music composition programs.

Ease-in/Ease-out: A gradual increase or decrease in the rate of motion to simulate (and often exaggerate) the effect of gravity or force in animation.

Editable text: Computer text that can be altered by a word processing application.

Effective code: A code that represents each desired data item with a unique combination of symbols. An effective binary code to represent each of the seven days of the week would use three bits and have 2^3 or eight unique combinations of 0s and 1s.

Effective procedure: A step-by-step process guaranteed to produce a particular result. Computer programs are effective procedures. Also called an *algorithm*.

Efficient code: A code that represents each desired data item without wasting storage, processing, or transmission resources.

Encapsulated PostScript (EPS): A file format to deliver graphic images between software programs and computer platforms.

Encoding: The process of assigning bits to a data item.

End User License Agreement (EULA): A license to use the product in certain ways specified in a contract. Commonly used in software programs and becoming a common means to control the uses of digital media.

Engelbart, Doug: A scientist at the Stanford Research Institute (SRI) where he proposed *computer-human interaction* as a research project. His team developed hypertext, the first mouse, the GUI interface, and researched the power of computer networks. At SRI, Engelbart was instrumental in ARPAnet, the precursor of the Internet.

ENIAC: Electronic Numerical Integrator and Computer. The first general purpose electronic computer. Built in 1943–1945 for over $500,000, it was used to calculate military firing tables.

Ethernet: A popular network protocol for local area networks first developed at Xerox PARC in 1976.

Expert systems: A form of artificial intelligence (AI). Expert systems are software applications that utilize a knowledge base to make decisions from "rules" stored in an "inference engine."

Extended ASCII: An addition to 7-bit ASCII standard made by using 8 bits to generate 256 characters, thus increasing the range of letters, symbols, diacritics, and special characters.

Extended text: Text in which the width of all characters is increased.

Extrusion: The process of generating a 3-D shape by extending the lines of a two-dimensional object through space. For example, a 2-D rectangle extended vertically produces a cube.

Fair use: An exception to copyright protection intended to support important social goals such as a free and open press, education, research, and scholarship.

Field: In video, the partial image created by scanning every other line of a TV screen. Two fields are combined to form a complete video frame.

File: A container for data and programs.

File allocation table (FAT): An index to each file name and cluster location on a storage device.

File compatibility: Describes the interoperability of data and program files between operating systems and/or applications.

File conversion: The process of changing a file format from one convention to another. A common example is to convert a Photoshop file format into a JPEG file format using the *Save As* option.

File extension: One or more letters following the filename separated by a period. The extension may designate the program that created the file (.psd is Photoshop) or the type of file (.html is a web page).

File format: The convention that specifies how instructions and data are encoded in a computer file. Formats are often designated by the file extension. A .txt file stores the data in ASCII format.

File system: A method of storing and organizing files such that the operating system can locate and randomly access the data and instructions on secondary storage devices. Common disk file systems are FAT, NTFS, and HFS.

FireWire: Apple Computer's designation for the IEEE 1394 standard for a high-speed serial interface. FireWire ports support up to 63 devices in daisy-chain format. Each device is "hot-swappable." Transmission speeds vary from 100Mbs to 800Mbs depending on the version of FireWire.

Fixed form: A requirement for copyright protection. The original or creative expression must be in a form in which it can be preserved. For example, a speech is not in fixed form unless it is preserved in writing, on audiotape, or in another tangible medium.

Flash drive: A storage module made of flash memory chips. This solid-state storage has no movable components, is lightweight, and can store gigabytes of data. It is also known as a USB drive, thumb drive, jump drive, or pen drive.

Flash memory: Solid-state storage made of a grid of cells, each with two transistors where data is electronically stored and erased. This non-volatile storage is found in USB "thumb" drives and memory cards for digital cameras.

Flipbook: An early animation technique that presents individual images on a succession of pages and "plays back" the motion sequence by flipping the pages in rapid succession.

Floppy disk (or diskette): A thin plastic Mylar film material coated with a substance that holds binary data in magnetic form. The Mylar disk is loosely protected by a paper or plastic case that keeps dust and fingerprints from reaching the magnetic material. Storage capacity is limited to just over a megabyte of data.

Flowchart: A simple box diagram to give a broad overview of a multimedia product's content. Generally introduced in the definition stage of a multimedia development plan.

Flowline: A graphical representation of the relationships between the components of a multimedia application used in icon-based authoring applications.

Font: A complete set of letters in a specific typeface, style, and size. For example, Times Bold 10 point is a font.

Font technologies: Techniques for displaying text on a monitor or printer. Two basic font technologies are bitmapped and outline fonts.

Foreground layer: In multimedia authoring, an area that holds media elements that will change frequently on successive screens. See also *background layer*.

Formatting: An operating system process that prepares a disk to accept data by defining tracks, sectors, clusters, and a file system on the disk surface.

Formula modeling: A 3-D graphics technique to create objects by specifying mathematical formulas that are subsequently drawn by the computer.

Forward kinematics: A type of 3-D modeling in which objects are adjusted by the animator as collections of separate elements. See also *kinematics* and *inverse kinematics*.

Frame (animation, film, video): The individual images that are rapidly displayed to produce the illusion of motion.

Frame (authoring application): One instance of content in a timeline-based authoring application. Each frame contains all the media for a single unit of time in the animated sequence, as in frames per second.

Frame (CD storage): The basic unit of information on a CD. Frames define the physical format of data.

Frame-by-frame animation: An animation technique that requires each individual frame to be created manually.

Frame rate: The speed at which frames are displayed in animation, film, and video.

Frequency: The rate at which a sound wave completes a cycle from lowest to highest amplitude. Different frequencies are perceived as variations in pitch.

Frequency modulation: In synthesized sound, a method for producing audio output from a synthesizer. FM synthesis produces different sounds by using one signal to modulate the frequency of another signal.

Functional specification: A document in a multimedia development plan that specifies the media elements and performance of the multimedia project.

Generation decay: In analog media reproduction, the degradation in the quality of sound or video recordings as copies are made from previous copies.

GIF (Graphics Interchange File): A cross-platform file format for graphics frequently used for images on the Web. GIF images use lossless compression and are limited to 8-bit color resolution.

Gigabyte: Approximately a billion bytes. More precisely 2^{30} or 1,073,741,824 bytes.

Graphical user interface (GUI): A method of controlling operating system functions through display of intuitive icons that the user manipulates using a pointing device such as a mouse or trackball. Initially suggested by Douglas Engelbart at SRI and further developed by Xerox, the GUI was first made popular by Apple Computer in 1984 with the introduction of the Macintosh computer.

Graphics tablet: An input device that facilitates freehand image creation using a flat surface and a stylus pen.

Graphics text: Letters and symbols created in a graphics application as an image. This method is widely used for creating artistic logos or word images designed for visual impact.

Grayscale: A digital image composed of pixels representing white, black, and shades of gray.

Halftone: A print image composed of dots of black or white.

Handles: Control points on vector graphic images that can be moved to produce changes in shape.

Hard disk: Rigid platters mounted on a spindle in a sealed container. Hard disk locations are addressed by tracks, sectors, and cylinders.

Hard drive: A non-volatile storage device that records data in magnetic format on rapidly rotating hard disk platters. First introduced by IBM in the mid-1950s, the platters were 24″ in diameter. Since then the disks and drives have been reduced to less than an inch. Toshiba introduced the first .85″ drive that holds 4GB of storage.

Hardware interface: A connection between the circuitry of the computer system board and peripheral devices. USB and FireWire are common interfaces for peripheral devices.

HDTV (High Definition TV): A digital television standard that increases the screen resolution to produce higher quality images. There are two major options within HDTV: 1280 × 720 pixels or 1920 × 1080 pixels.

Hertz: A unit of frequency measurement, one cycle per second. Microprocessor clock speed is measured in cycles of *gigahertz*, or billions of Hertz. As it applies to sound, one hertz is one repetition of a waveform in one second of time. Sound is sampled at *kilohertz* rates, or thousands of times per second.

Hi8: An analog videocassette format for NTSC television systems introduced by Sony for the camcorder industry. Higher-grade tape and recording heads captured greater picture detail and increased screen resolution to 400 horizontal lines. Image quality was further improved by the use of Y/C color.

Hierarchical: A navigational structure that organizes the content from most general to specific.

High-level language: Programming code that is independent of a specific computer's machine instruction set. The programs written in these languages are more English-like and easier to code; but they must be converted to a machine code before they can be executed. High-level language programs are often called "source" code.

Holds: In animation, a sequence of identical drawings that express a particular state or action. For example, to show one second of surprise, a traditional animation artist will *hold* or repeat the facial expression for 24 frames.

HTML (HyperText Markup Language): A standard set of commands to define the format for text and multimedia file display. The commands are interpreted by browser software to display the formatted document. HTML was first developed in the early 1990s at CERN to share research documents on a network. Soon after, it became the language of the World Wide Web.

HyperCard: An authoring application developed at Apple Computer. It used a card metaphor to organize and connect information.

Hyperlink: A connection between two data items in the same document or in an external file. Popularized on the Web where a word or image is clicked to bring up another related set of text or multimedia data.

Hypermedia: An extension of hypertext that includes interconnected media to form an organized structure of information.

Hypertext: An organized structure of interconnected terms. Introduced by Theodore Nelson in 1965, hypertext is the foundation for hyperlinked terms on the Web.

Icon: A graphic symbol. In operating systems, icons, such as trash cans, folders, and drives, are the foundation of GUIs.

Icon metaphor: In multimedia authoring, a method of organizing media and sequencing events that uses icons to define media and forms of interactivity. See also *flowline*.

Icon programming: A type of visual programming whereby icons are arranged in the application window and the developer defines the parameters for the specific icon's use.

IEEE 1394: See FireWire.

Illegal colors: In NTSC video, colors that cannot be properly displayed through the composite color signal of analog TV.

Image map (3-D graphics)**:** Photos, drawings, or other images that are transferred or "mapped" to an object surface.

Image map (navigation)**:** In interactive navigation, a set of images used to designate navigation options in a multimedia application.

In-between frames: A series of animated objects between a start and end key frame. Traditional animators drew each in-between frame in the animated sequence. Digital animation software can automatically interpolate these in-between frames.

Incompatible (data formats)**:** Encodings that work with one type of hardware or software but do not work with others.

Information: Useful data; data interpreted and organized to produce understanding.

Ink jet printer: A non-impact printer that sprays ink onto a page one line at a time.

Inkers: Artists in traditional animation who apply the lines of the image to one side of a celluloid sheet.

Instruction set: A set of instructions that the processor can carry out.

Intellimedia: Multimedia applications that demonstrate aspects of intelligence as they interact with the user.

Interactive multimedia: Applications that give users control of the flow of information.

Interface port: The electronic circuit on computer system board that connects to peripheral devices. Serial, parallel, FireWire, and USB are common interface ports.

Inter-frame compression: A form of digital video compression that eliminates some frames completely, saving only the changes between them.

Interlacing (graphics)**:** In web display of graphics, the technique of progressively displaying an incomplete, low-resolution image that is "filled in" as the download continues.

Interlacing (monitor)**:** In monitor display, the technique of generating an image by scanning alternate image lines on successive passes.

Internet: A network of networks. First developed by ARPA in 1969 to share research data and computers across the United States, the Internet evolved into a worldwide information resource.

Interpreter: Software that translates high-level languages into machine code by converting one line, executing that line, then moving to the next line in the program to repeat the process.

Intra-frame compression: A form of digital video compression that re-encodes information within frames but preserves all the individual frames of the video.

Intuitive interface: A method of interacting with the content on the screen that is immediately understood by the user.

Inverse kinematics (IK): An animation technique in which the motion of one body part produces related motions in other body parts. IK presupposes basic anatomical knowledge. See also *kinematics* and *forward kinematics*.

Iterative: Repetitive or recurrent. The multimedia development plan is an iterative process in which earlier stages are re-shaped or reformulated as the development progresses.

Jaggies: The stair-step effect on the rounded edges and diagonal lines of letters, numbers, and other images displayed on a monitor or printer. A common method to reduce jaggies is anti-aliasing.

Jobs, Steve: Cofounder and CEO of Apple Computer. In the early 1980s Jobs recognized the future of multimedia computing and incorporated the mouse, GUI, and built-in audio in the Macintosh computer.

JPEG (Joint Photographics Experts Group): A file format for photo-quality bitmapped images. JPEG provides varying degrees of lossy compression and supports 24-bit color. Widely used on the Web and in digital cameras.

Justification: Adjusting lines of text to produce straight edges at the left and right margin. Often, extra space is added between words or letters to stretch the line out evenly to the right margin.

Kay, Alan: Computer scientist who developed the concept computer called the Dynabook, which resembles today's laptop. He was one of the founders of object-oriented programming language and a key developer of the GUI environment.

Kerning: Adjusting the space between specific pairs of letters. The appearance of paired letters such as *A* and *W* benefits from kerning because it produces a spacing that is more consistent with other letters.

Key frames: The images drawn by principal artists in traditional animation, usually the start and finish of an animated sequence. Other artists would create the frames between these two major points. Digital applications define the parameters and attributes of a start and end key frame. The software automatically creates subsequent frames by interpolating changes to the image between these frames. See also *in-between frames*.

Kilo: 2^{10} or 1024, i.e. *approximately* one thousand.

Kilobit (Kb): 2^{10} or 1024 bits, i.e. *approximately* 1000 bits.

Kilobyte (KB): 2^{10} or 1024 bytes, i.e. *approximately* 1000 bytes.

Kinematics: The study of how the parts of bodies move in relation to each. For example, the motion of an arm generates related motion in the shoulder, elbow, wrist, and fingers.

Kiosk: A freestanding multimedia information system. Frequently has a touch screen for user input.

LAN (Local Area Network): A series of computers connected within an organization. The communication links are maintained by the organization.

Land: The flat surface on an optical disc that directly reflects light to a light-sensing diode in a CD or DVD drive.

Laser (Light Amplification by Stimulated Emission of Radiation): An amplified light focused into a single wavelength.

Laser printer: A non-impact printer that uses copier-like technology to fuse an image to the paper.

Lathing: In 3-D graphics, the process of generating a 3-D object by rotating a 2-D line on an axis. For example, lathing can rotate the profile of half a bowl through 360 degrees to "sweep out" the full 3-D shape.

Layers: In graphics, the planes on which different parts of an image are drawn. Layers can be thought of as stacks of image elements, each of which can be separately edited. Combining layers, called *grouping*, locks elements together, while *flattening* merges layers to a single plane.

LCD (Liquid Crystal Display): A display technology used on small portable devices, computers, and televisions. Lightweight and requiring little power, LCDs contain liquid crystal molecules that are controlled by transistors. When the molecule is altered to let light through, a pixel of the image is displayed.

Leading: The spacing between lines of text. The term derives from the practice of adding strips of lead beneath the characters on a printing press to increase line height.

Lee, Tim Berners: The inventor of the World Wide Web.

Leica reel: A working draft of the complete animation used in filmed animation production. A leica reel includes preliminary animated stills arranged with recorded audio. Derived from a German camera called a Leica originally used to develop these filmed storyboards.

Line art: An image drawn only as lines without color filling or shading. Line art uses 1-bit color depth to produce just two colors (usually black and white). See also *contone*.

Linear: A navigational structure that organizes the content for the user along a sequential path.

Lines per inch (lpi): A measure of spatial resolution for print images.

Linescreen: The print resolution (in lpi) used for a particular graphic. For example, newspapers use a coarser linescreen (approximately 85 lpi) while magazines use a finer linescreen (150 lpi or more).

Link anchor: In hyperlinking, the point of departure leading to related media.

Link marker: The method used to identify a link anchor. Web documents often use underlined style with blue text color as the link marker.

Lossless compression: A form of file compression that preserves all the information in the original file.

Lossy compression: A form of file compression that does not preserve all the information in the original file.

Low-level language: A class of programming languages that are dependent on the specific computer. Programs developed in machine code or assembly language are not portable to another computer since these are low-level languages.

Luminance: The brightness of a light source.

Machine code: A programming language using binary digits to code commands for specific computer systems. All software must be converted to machine code before a computer can execute it. Often called "object code."

Machine cycle: The basic steps the processor carries out for each instruction: fetch, decode, execute, and store.

Macintosh: Mac for short, the first commercially successful personal computer with a GUI interface. Introduced in January 1984 by Apple Computer.

Magnetic storage: A technique that utilizes magnetic properties of materials to store data. The storage media may be disk, tape, or drum. The most common are disks that are coated with an iron oxide material that holds magnetism if exposed to a magnetic field from a read/write head. This results in non-volatile storage for binary data.

Mainframe computer: The first electronic computers. Today's mainframe computers process billions of instructions, support multiuser systems, and store terabytes of data. They are used by organizations to process and store large volumes of data in complex databases.

Markup language: A set of rules that define the layout, format, or structure of media within a document.

Master video: The sequence of video clips as they are being developed in the editing environment.

Matrix: In graphics, the rectangular grid of rows and columns used to store pixel descriptions for bitmapped images.

Media specialists: The members of a multimedia development team who prepare the media content such as graphics, animation, audio, and video.

Media utilities: Programs, generally free or shareware, that support a specific function in creating or editing media. For example, utility programs can provide visual effects, color management, compression, image screen grab, or font creation.

Media-specific application: Software used to create and edit a specific media type such as sound, video, or images.

Mega: 2^{20} or 1,048,576, i.e. *approximately* one million.

Megabyte: 2^{20} or 1,048,576 bytes, approximately a million bytes.

Megapixel: A measure of spatial resolution of digital imaging devices such as a scanner or camera. Approximately one million pixels.

Memex: A theoretical information-processing machine described by Vannevar Bush. The Memex would store large volumes of multimedia data and organize that data based on associations created by the user.

Memex II: A theoretical machine envisioned by Vannevar Bush that built on features first defined in the Memex. Based on new technology, the Memex II would store data on magnetic tape and combine with a digital computer to efficiently organize the growing mass of information.

Memory card: A solid-state storage device for digital cameras, cell phones, game consoles, and portable data storage.

Message: In synthesized sound, a MIDI command.

Metaball modeling: A 3-D modeling technique that creates objects by combining elements called blobs. Building an object with metaballs is similar to working with lumps of clay. This technique is useful for creating objects with soft edges.

Metafile: A file format that can encode both bitmapped and vector graphics.

Metamedium: A term Alan Kay used to describe the Dynabook. This concept computer was to embody any medium; thus the Dynabook itself was a metamedium.

Metaphor: The use of one thing to represent or suggest another. In multimedia authoring, metaphors are often used to relate unfamiliar content or processes to familiar objects or operations, as in the use of VCR-like controls to play and pause animations.

Microcode: A programming technique for implementing the instruction set of a processor.

Microcomputer: A computer based on a microprocessor and designed to support a single user. Microcomputers appeared in the early 1970s after the introduction of the 4004, the first commercial microprocessor by Intel.

Microelectronics: Miniature integrated circuits often found on silicon chips.

Microprocessor: A single silicon chip that contains all the elements of a Central Processing Unit. Its development in the early 1970s by Intel led to the microcomputer revolution.

MIDI (Musical Instrument Digital Interface): A standard method of connecting and playing musical instruments, synthesizers, and other digital devices.

Mixing: The process of combining two or more audio signals into a single sound track.

M-JPEG (Motion-JPEG): A video codec based on JPEG image compression. M-JPEG uses intra-frame but not inter-frame compression.

Modeler: In 3-D graphics, software that creates shapes directly rather than building them from more basic objects. Common types of modelers include polygon, spline, metaball, and formula.

Modeless: An ideal computing environment advocated by Alan Kay where the user could switch easily from one mode of activity to another.

Modeling: The process of specifying the shape of objects in 3-D graphics.

Monospaced font: A typeface that assigns the same space to all letters. Courier is a mono-spaced typeface.

Morphing: An animation technique that transforms one shape into another over time.

Motion capture: The animation technique of recording the motions of actual objects and mapping these motions to a computer-generated animated character.

Motion tween: A digital animation procedure that interpolates the position of an object from one location on the scene to another based on the position of the start and end key frame.

MP3 (MPEG1 audio layer 3): A lossy codec that maintains near CD-quality sound files.

MP3 player: Originally created to store and play MP3 compressed music files, some players can also store data files. Players may use flash memory or have mini-hard drives to hold music and data.

MPEG (Motion Picture Experts Group): A codec specifically designed for video that uses both intra-frame and inter-frame compression to produce small files.

Multi-core: Technology to describe two or more CPU's working together on a single chip. See *dual-core processor*.

Multi-core processors: CPU chip architecture that combines two or more logic cores on a single integrated circuit to execute more tasks and improve overall system performance.

Multifunction printer (MFP): An output device that combines printer, fax, copier, scanner, and often a memory card reader in one unit. This combination of peripheral devices conserves the desk space that would be used by multiple devices.

Multimedia: The development, integration, and delivery of any combination of text, graphics, animation, sound or video through a computer.

Multi-processing: Combining multiple processors to execute instructions simultaneously. Apple's G5 computer has dual processor capability; many PCs have a math or video co-processor.

Multitasking: A method controlled by the operating system to share the computer processor with more than one program. Each program is allotted its own space in RAM and its own peripherals but share the processor concurrently. Often called "event driven" because processor sharing is based on events that take place in the program.

Multitimbral: Capable of playing multiple instruments at the same time. MIDI systems are multitimbral—they simultaneously process the information for multiple instruments in different channels.

Nanotechnology: An industry focused on shrinking the size of microelectronic components to nanometer size. A nanometer is one billionth of a meter. Nanotechnology will dramatically reduce the size and increase the speed of processors by working with components that are the size of individual atoms.

Native file format: Coding conventions used by specific applications for their data files. For instance, .psd is the native file format for Photoshop.

Nelson, Ted: Early multimedia theorist who coined the term "hypertext" in 1963. Nelson conceived Project Xanadu, a large information base connected by networks with a simple user interface. While Xanadu never succeeded, it is considered the inspiration for the Web.

Network: A collection of computers connected through a communication link to share hardware, data, and applications.

Networked: A navigational structure that allows the user to freely explore content often based on hyperlinks to related material.

Nodes: In hypertext and hypermedia, the content items that are linked together.

Non-interactive: A form of multimedia that integrates digital media into a single application but does not give the user control over the sequence or display of the information.

Notepad: An ASCII text editor, provided as a utility program in the Windows operating system.

NTSC (National Television Standards Committee): The analog TV standard developed for the U.S. in 1952.

NURB (Non-Uniform Rational B-spline): A technique for defining the shape of a 3-D object. A NURB defines an image using mathematical formulas that can be adjusted to vary its size and shape.

Object-oriented programming language (OOP): A language that uses self-contained elements (objects). Each object holds the data and instructions related to that element. Objects interact with each other by passing messages or commands to various components. Since each object does not require recoding each time it is used, this language is generally more efficient than traditional procedural languages.

OCR (Optical Character Recognition): The process of converting printed text into digital files that can be edited in a word processing application. Requires a scanner and specialized OCR software.

Onionskinning: An animation technique to draw an image in reference to the previous one. Using thin paper or a light table, the traditional animation artist could reference the preceding images to locate and draw the current image. Digital applications simulate onionskinning by displaying grayed-out preceding frames in the animated sequence.

Opaquers: In traditional animation, opaquers are the artists who apply the colors to the drawn image on a celluloid sheet.

Operating System (OS): Software that manages the user interface and computer hardware, and controls program execution.

Optical photo conductor (OPC): The light sensitive coating on the surface of the drum in a laser printer.

Optical storage: A method to store binary data using laser technology. Data is represented through various techniques that either reflect or absorb light emitted from a laser diode.

OS utility program: Software that provides tools to optimize the basic functions of an operating system. Disk management tools, accessibility options, and text editors are examples of OS utilities.

Outline font: A technique for displaying text through a monitor or printer by storing a description of the letter shape. Outline fonts such as TrueType are scaled by changing the dimensions of the basic description to produce an accurate display of the re-sized character.

Output resolution: The screen resolution that matches the capabilities of the output medium. A developer can reduce the output resolution of a video window to improve the color and motion of the video as it is displayed on less powerful computers or on lower bandwidth networks.

Oversampling: In sampled sound, recording at a higher sample rate than that required to capture the desired frequency range. Oversampling is often done to avoid sound aliasing. Once captured, oversampled sounds are often downsampled to reduce file size.

Overscanning: Producing a screen image that is larger than the display device. NTSC TV uses overscanning. This assures that the televised image will completely fill a TV screen.

Over-the-shoulder shot: An angle for shooting video that includes the subject as well as others observing the subject.

Paint program: An application used to produce bitmapped images. Paint programs can create original bitmapped images or they can be used to edit existing images, including digital photographs.

PAL (Phase Alternate Line): A standard for analog television broadcast used in England and much of Europe.

Palette flashing: A brief display of inaccurate color as a computer shifts from one color palette to another.

Parallel data transmission: The simultaneous transmission of a set of bits; each bit has its own wire or path.

Parallel processing: A technique of linking multiple processors to operate at the same time on a single task.

Parametric primitive: In 3-D graphics, a basic 3-D object (e.g. cube, pyramid, cone, sphere) that can be scaled and otherwise transformed by specifying parameters such as a sphere's radius.

Parity: A technique to determine if any errors in digital data were introduced during transmission.

Parity bit: A binary digit appended to an array of bits to make the sum an even or odd value. Used in error checking schemes.

Passive matrix: A type of LCD display with fewer transistors to control the position of the liquid crystals. Best used for black and white displays of text.

Patent: Rights given to the creator of an original, useful invention.

Path-based animation: A digital animation procedure that interpolates the position of an object along a defined path on the scene. The object is evenly distributed along the path from the start key frame to the end key frame.

PDA (Personal Digital Assistant): A small handheld computer that embeds input and display functions in the system unit for portable usage.

PDF (Portable Document Format): A cross-platform standard developed by Adobe to preserve the original formatting of text documents. PDF files are created using Adobe Acrobat and viewed through a free, widely distributed reader program.

Pencil test: A stage of traditional cel animation in which a series of simple sketches are photographed and projected to test the design of an animated sequence.

Perceptual indexing: The technique of selecting colors for an indexed color palette based on the conditions of human perception.

Peripheral device: Any device that supports the system unit. Generally, peripherals are external to the system unit and connected via interface ports such as USB, parallel, or FireWire ports. Common peripheral devices include keyboards, mice, and disk drives.

Persistence of vision: A physiological phenomenon whereby the retina of the human eye retains an image for a brief moment. Animators rely on this visual memory of one image to the next to achieve the illusion of motion.

Personal computer (PC): A system that uses a microprocessor to provide computing for a single user. Other labels include *microcomputer*, *desktop computer*, and *laptop computer*. In popular usage, PC also designates an "IBM" compatible microcomputer using the Windows operating system.

Photo printer: A color printer especially designed to produce photos.

Pica: A standard unit of text measurement predominately found on typewriters. A pica is 12 points; six picas equal one inch.

PICT: An image file format developed by Apple and widely used in Macintosh graphics applications. PICT is a metafile format; it can store both bitmapped and vector graphics.

Pipelining: A method of increasing processor speed by processing data in a sequence of stages, each stage providing input to the next task prior to the completion of the full fetch/execute cycle.

Pit: An indentation on an optical disc that scatters reflected light, thus reducing the reflection detected by a light sensing diode in a CD or DVD drive.

Pitch: The psychological perception of sound frequency.

Pixel: A digital picture element.

Pixels per inch (ppi): A measure of spatial resolution for the display of computer graphics.

Platform: The combination of computer hardware and the operating system.

Player: A small program used to present media on a computer. Players include general purpose programs such as the QuickTime player or RealPlayer that display a category of media (graphics, audio, video) as well as specialized programs such as the Flash player that present content developed through a specific authoring application.

Plug and Play (PnP): A feature of modern operating systems that automatically identifies and installs peripheral devices.

PNG (Portable Network Graphic): A bitmapped graphics file format developed to replace GIF. PNG supports 48-bit color and provides lossless compression.

Point: A measure of the size of type from the ascender to the descender of the letter. One point is approximately 1/72 of an inch; 12 points is 1/6 of an inch.

Polygon modeling: The process of creating a 3-D graphic shape as a combination of straight line figures, usually triangles or quadrilaterals.

Polyphonic: Capable of playing more than one note simultaneously.

Postproduction: A phase in media creation for a multimedia project where content is edited using specialized software to achieve desired effects.

PPI: See pixels per inch.

Preemptive multitasking: The operating system controls program access to the CPU by assigning "time slices" for each task in a multitasking environment. This process replaced program control of the CPU which often led to system crashes when a program would not release sufficient "time slices" for other running tasks.

Preliminary proposal: In multimedia development, a short description of the proposed application. The preliminary proposal is part of the definition stage and generally includes the application's goals, audience, projected outcomes, and a preliminary cost estimate.

Preproduction: The step in media creation for a multimedia project that prepares media for editing such as scanning photos, digitizing analog sound or capturing video footage.

Primary memory: Electronic storage locations on the system board directly addressed by the CPU.

Primitives: In 3-D modeling, basic 3-D shapes, such as cubes, cones, or spheres, that can be combined to create more complex shapes. The term has also been extended to include other basic elements of 3-D scenes as in *environmental primitives* such as fog or fire.

Production: The third stage in multimedia development in which all remaining elements of the product are created and integrated into the application.

Profession: An occupation that requires specialized education and training such as a computer programmer.

Program: A set of instructions that can be carried out by the computer. Programs are written in a programming language and converted to binary code for the computer to execute the instructions.

Program file: Contains instructions for the computer to execute. Applications such as Word and Photoshop are program files.

Programmed animation: A computer animation technique in which motion is produced through coded commands.

Programmer: A member of a multimedia team who uses a programming language or authoring tool to add functionality to a project.

Programming: The process of writing instructions for a computer using a script or icon in authoring applications. More generally refers to writing instructions using a programming language for computer execution.

Programming language: A defined system of syntax and semantics to write computer software.

Progressive download: In sound, a method of transferring a file to a client over the Internet. As the sound is downloaded to the hard disk, it is buffered in main memory and begins to play. This shortens the delay from the initial access to when the user hears the audio file.

Progressive scan: The technique of producing a screen image by scanning each line on each pass, rather than every other line as in an interlaced scan. Progressive scanning is used on computer monitors and in some HDTV formats.

Project designer: A member of a multimedia team who is responsible for the overall structure of the project's content as well as the look and feel of the user interface.

Project manager: The person responsible for planning and managing all the human and technological elements of a multimedia project, from concept to completion. The responsibilities include: meeting with the content expert or client; planning budgeting and preparation; managing concept design and user research; overseeing the content, creative and technical development; supervising site testing, release and evaluation; bringing the project to completion within the time frame and budget; and trouble-shooting.

Proportional font: A typeface that adjusts the width between letters based on letter shape. For example, Times New Roman typeface allows less space for the *i* and more for the *o* shape.

Protocol: A set of rules or conventions that govern the exchange of data between computers. Common protocols include TCP, IP, FTP, MIME, and HTTP.

Prototype: An incomplete working model of the final multimedia project. It includes some finished media and many of the major functions for the operation of the application.

Public domain: The status of creative products (works of "original authorship") that are not protected under copyright.

Pure tones: Tones (such as the notes produced by tuning forks) that can be represented as simple waves that regularly repeat a smooth transition from high to low pressure (a sine wave).

Quantization: The process of rounding off a sample to the closest available value in the digital code being used. May produce distortion of the original data.

QuickTime: A cross-platform file format principally intended for dynamic data (animation, sound, and video) developed by Apple Computer. QuickTime uses the .mov extension.

Random access: A method of locating data or programs in which all items can be accessed in an equivalent amount of time. The opposite of sequential access in which the time required to access data depends on its location on the medium. Videotape, for example, is sequential access.

Random Access Memory (RAM): A component of primary memory consisting of addressable storage locations for data and instructions in electronic format. RAM is volatile storage—when power is interrupted, all contents are cleared from memory.

Raster scan (graphics): An image stored as an array of uniform horizontal and vertical pixels. Bitmapped graphics are raster scanned.

Raster scan (monitor): The process that creates an image on a CRT by illuminating a grid of picture elements (pixels) with an electron-scanning beam. The beam draws the display horizontally across the screen one parallel line at a time.

Rasterize: The process of converting text or images into a matrix of pixels, or bitmap, for display on a screen or printed page.

Ray tracing: Advanced technique used in computer-generated graphics to create image properties that are controlled by light sources (rays) such as shadow, color, and shading. Ray tracing requires large amounts of CPU processing time.

Read-only Memory (ROM): Nonvolatile storage on the system board that contains critical programs and settings that manage the initial configuration and booting of the operating system. The contents of ROM can be read, but not altered or erased.

RealAudio: A streaming audio technology for the Internet from RealNetworks. Released in 1995, the .ra file format is used by many Internet radio programs.

RealVideo: A file format for streaming video developed by RealNetworks.

Registers: High-speed electronic memory locations on the CPU. Registers support the basic fetch/execute function of the CPU by storing data, instructions, and addresses for immediate access by the Control Unit or ALU.

Rendering: In 3-D graphics, animation, and video, the process through which the computer generates the finished images as specified by the artist or editor through modeling, surface definition, and scene composition.

Resampling: The process of increasing or decreasing the number of samples described in the file. See also *downsampling* and *upsampling*.

Resolution: The number of addressable pixels that can be illuminated in a CRT, LCD, or other display device. Settings in the operating system can alter the resolution of a monitor from 800 × 600, for example, to 1024 × 768 pixels.

RGB: Red, Green, Blue color model for computer displays. Each color is represented separately, which generates a nearly limitless range of pure colors.

RISC (Reduced Instruction Set Computing): A processor design strategy to make the CPU more efficient by using a smaller and simpler set of instructions and executing them faster.

RLE (Run Length Encoding): A form of lossless compression. RLE replaces sequences of repeated data with a single description for the length of the run. RLE is useful in images with large areas having the same color.

Rotoscoping: The process of producing traditional animation by tracing the individual frames of a film or video. Rotoscoping can also be carried out using a digital draw or paint program.

Router: A network device to route (or transfer) data packets from one location to another along a network using IP addressing.

RS232C: An industry standard for serial data communication between devices such as printers, terminals, and modems. Often abbreviated as COM on the interface port.

RTF (Rich Text Format): A text file format developed by Microsoft for cross-platform, cross-application compatibility. RTF includes ASCII text code and additional code to define the formatting characteristics of the text.

Rule of thirds: A widely used guideline for framing a video shot by dividing the camera into thirds both horizontally and vertically. Designed to avoid a cramped or cropped image and to effectively suggest direction of motion in a frame.

Safe action area: The portion of a computer monitor that will be displayed to a TV screen when converted to the NTSC format. This is approximately 90% of the screen surface of the computer monitor.

Safe title area: The portion of a computer monitor that will provide adequate screen margins (top, sides, and bottom) for text display when converted to the NTSC format. This is approximately 80% of the screen surface of the computer monitor.

Sample rate: In sampled sound, the frequency with which samples of analog sound are collected. Sample rate is measured in kHz, thousands of samples per second.

Sample resolution: The number of bits used to represent a digital sample. Generally more bits means improved sample quality.

Sampled sound: A digital recording of previously existing analog sound waves. A sampled sound file contains digital values for many thousands of individual amplitude samples.

Sampling: The process of measuring an analog signal and converting it to digital code.

Sans serif: A typeface that lacks decorative lines at the end of a letter's stroke. *Sans* means *without* in French.

Scalable compression: A compression technique that allows the user to adjust media quality by varying the amount or type of compression. JPEG is a popular scalable compression option.

Scanner: A peripheral input device that samples a source and produces a corresponding digital graphic. Sources can include printed pages, artwork, photos, film and three-dimensional objects. Scanners can be flatbed, sheet-fed, or handheld devices.

Scene composition: One of the main stages of 3-D graphic development. Objects are arranged, backgrounds are introduced, environmental effects are added, and lighting is established.

Scratch track: A draft of an animation's audio track.

Screen grab: A bitmapped image created by capturing the graphics displayed on a computer monitor.

Screen resolution (analog video)**:** The number of lines used to recreate an image on an analog video screen. NTSC established the maximum resolution of 525 lines to produce each frame. PAL and SECAM use 625 lines on the screen.

Screen resolution (digital video)**:** The number of horizontal and vertical pixels used to present the video image.

Script: A series of commands specifying the properties or behavior of an element of a multimedia application.

SCSI (Small Computer System Interface): A parallel interface between the system board and peripheral devices. Introduced by Apple Computer in 1984, SCSI ports can support between 7 to 15 devices daisy chained together.

SDTV: The standard definition for digital television broadcast that provides a screen resolution of 704 $\times$ 480 pixels and supports either interlacing (480i) or progressive scan (480p). See also *HDTV*.

SECAM (*Sequential Couleur Avec Memoire*): An analog television standard used in France, Russia, and some other countries.

Secondary storage: The media that holds data and instructions outside the system unit for long periods of time. Early media included paper and magnetic tape. Current storage media include magnetic disks, flash media, and optical discs.

Sector: A logical unit of data on secondary storage media. On magnetic storage media, the sector is a pie-shaped division of a track that holds a specific number of bytes.

Sequencer: In synthesized sound, a device to control the flow, or "sequencing" of MIDI data.

Serial data transmission: The transmission of data as a single stream of bits.

Serif: A typeface with a decorative line to finish a letter's stroke.

Server: A host computer that may distribute data, manage email, or store web pages or applications on a network. See also *client/server.*

Session: A single recorded segment on a CD. It may consist of multiple tracks and contain multiple data types. Each session has an index of contents. Multisession discs can record many different sessions, each with its own table of contents.

Shader: A collection of surface characteristics and shading techniques that are applied to an object during the rendering process. The basic surface characteristics contained in most shaders include reflectivity, color, texture, and transparency.

Shooting on twos: A traditional animation technique to reduce the number of required images to generate motion. Each image is filmed twice so a series of 12 images would produce 24 frames (images) per second, the standard playback rate of analog films.

Shooting to edit: A videographer captures source footage concentrating on a variety of sequences that will later be trimmed, re-ordered, and blended to communicate a message.

Shooting to record: A videographer attempts to capture the complete video sequence in one session without consideration of editing and reorganizing clips. Professional video projects are rarely captured in this manner.

Sine waves: A periodic wave that regularly repeats a smooth transition from high to low pressure.

Size-tweening: A digital animation procedure that interpolates the size of an object over a series of frames. The initial size is defined in the start key frame and the resulting size is defined in the end frame.

Software: The collection of computer programs that govern the operation of a computer.

Solid-state storage: Method that uses non-volatile, electronic flash memory to store data. Does not have movable parts as found on hard or optical drives.

Source video: Captured clips of raw video that have been transferred from the camera to the computer editing application.

Spatial resolution: The density of pixels in a bitmapped graphic. Spatial resolution is measured in pixels per inch (ppi).

Speech recognition: The ability of a computer system to process spoken commands or data. Operating system utilities and special applications capture the spoken word, convert it to digital format, and process the command or data.

Speech synthesis: An output process that produces spoken words from digital data. Computer synthesizers form the human-like sounds based on stored recordings of words, or by storing the phonetic sounds of letters and combining them to read back the text using a synthetic voice.

Spline modeling: In 3-D graphics, a curve-based technique for creating three-dimensional shapes.

Splitting: The editing process of dividing a digital video clip into multiple parts.

Stamping: The process of creating a CD or DVD by pressing pits into a plastic base.

Storage capacity: A measure of the maximum amount of data a secondary memory device (such as a hard disk, DVD or Flash drive) can contain. Storage capacity is given in units of bytes. Most storage media can hold millions of bytes (MB) or billions of bytes (GB). Large hard drives are capable of holding trillions, or terabytes, of digital content.

Storyboard: A series of sketches outlining screen content and action used to guide the development of film, video, animation, or multimedia productions.

Streaming audio: A one-way audio transmission over a network. Streaming technology allows the client computer to begin playing a sound while it is being downloaded from the server. Sound segments are buffered as they are downloaded. Once played, the sound is not saved on the secondary storage of the client computer unlike downloaded audio that is first saved then played.

Stretch / Squash: A traditional animator's technique of drawing that distorts objects to simulate (and often exaggerate) motion. A bouncing ball will begin as a circle and be *squashed* into an ellipse as it hits the floor.

Style: A text characteristic that defines a distinct set of characters within a typeface. Styles are readily recognized variations in the appearance of characters that allow users to adapt the typeface to specific purposes. Bold, italic, and underline are common styles.

Subtractive color: Color produced as a result of pigments absorbing portions of the spectrum of light, i.e. *subtracting* some colors and leaving others to reach the eye. Color produced in the natural world and in printing is subtractive color. See also *additive color*.

Supercomputer: Designates the fastest, most powerful computer of the day. The first supercomputers were developed by Seymour Cray. The Cray-1 in 1976 processed at 167 megaflops (millions of floating point operations per second). Today's fastest supercomputers run at speeds in the hundreds of teraflops (trillions of floating point operations per second).

Surface definition: The stage in 3-D graphics that specifies the textures that are applied to the model's surface.

S-VHS (Super VHS (Video Home System)**):** An enhanced version of VHS that provides greater screen resolution and improved color.

S-Video (Separated Video): An analog video standard that uses separate signals to transmit luminance and chrominance information. This technique, known as Y/C, is a variant of component color that results in an improved TV signal as compared to the composite signal used in NTSC transmission.

SVG (Scalable Vector Graphics): The newest of the general-purpose vector formats. SVG is a language for describing two-dimensional graphics and graphical applications in XML.

Symbol: A representation of something else.

Synthesis: The combination of separate elements to form a whole. Sound synthesis occurs when computer software sends commands to generate notes from a synthesizer. Speech synthesis occurs when the computer software sends commands to form spoken words based on written text.

Synthesized sound: Sound generated (or synthesized, "put together") by the computer. A file for synthesized sound contains instructions that the computer uses to produce a sound.

Synthesizer: A device that creates sounds electronically based on commands, most commonly MIDI instructions.

System board: The main circuit board on a microcomputer. The system board provides the bottom plane of circuitry to connect other component parts to one another. Also known as the motherboard.

System bus: The electronic pathway between the CPU and memory.

System unit: Contains the electronic components to process and store data. This includes CPU, electronic memory, system board circuitry, expansion slots, and all the interface ports on a microcomputer. Often is used to refer to the "box" that contains these components and other peripheral devices.

TCP/IP (Transmission Control Protocol/Internet Protocol): A series of standards that controls data transmission between network computers as a series of addressed data packets. The TCP standard breaks sending data into packets, adds error detection, and reassembles packets at the destination host. The IP standard delivers the data packets to various network systems through routers that direct the packets to the correct host computer based on an IP address. The protocols were originally developed in the 1970s by ARPA (Advanced Research Projects Agency) to create a fault-tolerant network system in the U.S.

Terabyte: Approximately a trillion bytes. More precisely 2^{40} or 1,099,511,627,776 bytes.

Thin film transistor (TFT): Flat panel display technology in which each pixel is controlled by one to four separate transistors. Most expensive, but provides the best resolution quality for flat panel computer screens.

TIFF (Tagged Image File Format): A cross-platform bitmapped format often used in scanning and for wide distribution of images.

Time code: In video, a record of the time when each frame is shot. Time code is stored on each frame in the form of hours: minutes: seconds: frames. The time code serves as the frame's address.

Timeline (video editing software): Place to assemble video clips that shows the duration of the video. A timeline displays multiple tracks for both motion and audio components of the video.

Timeline metaphor: A multimedia authoring metaphor that organizes media content and interactivity as sequences of frames. This metaphor is appropriate for dynamic media such as video or sound that change over time.

Timesharing: A method controlled by the operating system to share the computer processor with multiple users simultaneously. Each user is given a slice of the processor's cycle for program execution. Sometimes referred to as a "multi-user" system since more than one person is using the computer for different tasks.

Track: A path on disk storage where data is stored and accessed. Tracks on a hard or floppy disk are concentric bands, while on an optical disc the tracks form a spiral from the inside of the disc to the outside edge.

Track Table of Contents (TTOC): An index of every track and its contents on a CD disc. Single session CDs have one TTOC, while multisession discs have a separate index for each session.

Tracking: A technique to adjust the spacing between all letters in a text passage. Tracking is distinct from kerning, which adjusts spacing only between specific pairs of letters.

Transfer rate: The speed at which data moves from secondary storage into RAM or from RAM onto secondary storage. Transfer rates are measured in bytes/second.

Transitions: Video effects used to move into or out of a clip. Cut, fades, and dissolves are common transitions applied to video sequences.

Trimming: The process of removing unwanted frames from the beginning and/or end of a video clip.

TrueType: Outline font technology developed in 1991 by Microsoft and Apple and incorporated in all Macintosh and PC computers. It displaced Postscript outline technology for microcomputer use.

Turing machine: A theoretical device envisioned by Alan Turing to carry out an effective procedure. In 1936, Turing demonstrated that a particular type of Turing machine, called a *Universal Turing Machine*, could carry out any effective procedure. This was a theoretical model of the modern computer.

Turing test: An exercise proposed by Alan Turing to demonstrate that a computer can think. Proposed in a 1950 paper, "Computing Machinery and Intelligence," the test consists of an interrogator communicating via teletype with a person in one room and with a computer in another. If the interrogator cannot determine which of his interlocutors is the person and which is the computer, the computer is said to be thinking.

Tween animation: A computer animation technique in which the animator creates key frames and the computer automatically generates the tweens. See also *tweens*.

Tweens: In traditional cel animation, a sequence of drawings to represent an object's change of position between one extreme and another extreme. Tweens were frequently drawn by apprentice animators, while the extremes were created by accomplished artists. See also *keyframe*.

Typeface: A family of letters that share the same design. Common categories include serif, sans serif, and script. Typeface includes all the styles, cases, and sizes of each letter. New York, Times, and Courier are examples of typefaces.

Underscan: The technique of producing a display image that is smaller than the screen of the display device. This assures that all screen content will appear on the display screen.

Unicode: A binary coding scheme using 16 bits to encode text from any alphabet system. The first 128 characters of Unicode are identical to ASCII coded data.

Upsampling: Adding samples to increase the spatial resolution of a bitmapped graphic file. Upsampling usually degrades the quality of the image.

URL (Uniform Resource Locator): The address scheme used in WWW protocols to hyperlink from one resource (web page or data file) to another. The URL syntax contains the HTTP protocol, the host computer name, domain, and a path to a particular resource on the Internet such as: http://yahoo.com/animation.html.

USB (Universal Serial Bus): An input/output bus standard published in 1996 to connect peripheral devices to the system board. USB supports 127 devices daisy chained together to one system port. Each device is "hot swappable" so they can be connected and disconnected randomly without interrupting service to other devices.

User interface (authoring application): The content of a multimedia application as the user experiences it on the screen. The interface should establish an appropriate tone, be intuitive, consistent, predictable, and reliable.

User interface (operating system): The software that facilitates interaction with computer programs. Early software used a command line interface. Current operating systems and applications rely on a graphical interface (GUI) for user interactivity.

VBR (Variable Bit Rate): An encoding technique that varies bit resolutions according to the complexity of the data to be encoded. This maximizes quality of audio or video while minimizing overall file size.

Vector: A line defined by length, curvature, and direction.

Vector drawing: A technique for creating digital graphics that defines images as a set of drawing commands. The commands produce lines and shapes such as circles, triangles, and quadrilaterals.

Vector graphics: Images composed of lines that are mathematically defined to form shapes, such as rectangles, circles, and polygons.

VHS (Video Home System): A standard for recording and playing videocassettes. VHS originally stood for Vertical Helical Scan, the technique used to read and record its magnetic tapes.

Video CD: A CD standard that uses MPEG-1 compression to store low-resolution video on a CD disc.

Video for Windows: A file format developed by Microsoft for the Windows operating system. Video for Windows uses the .avi (audio video interleave) extension.

Virtual memory: A method used by the operating system to extend the amount of physical memory (RAM, cache). Virtual memory is an alternate set of memory addresses set up on a hard drive. Programs open in memory may be allocated virtual memory addresses until the code is executed at which time it is "swapped" into main memory by the operating system.

Virtual reality (VR): An immersive form of multimedia that simulates a real world experience. May involve a data glove or suit to interact with 3-D image projections.

Visual programming: A category of programming languages that provides graphic elements to build the application rather than text commands. Program components such as buttons, boxes, and arrows are arranged on the screen where properties are defined for each graphic unit of the application.

Volume: The perception of a sound's amplitude or loudness. See also *amplitude*.

WAN (Wide Area Network): A network that connects computers over a wide geographic region. The users lease the communication link from a service provider such as a telephone or cable company.

WAV: The native digital audio file format for Windows. WAV supports 8- and 16-bit samples and rates of 11,025 Hz to 44,100 Hz.

Wavetable synthesis: The creation of synthesized digital sound through combinations of very short samples of naturally produced sounds.

Web-safe color palette: A set of colors selected to maximize the color compatibility of images displayed on different web browsers and on different computer platforms.

Weight: In text, weight is the width of the lines that form a character. Wider lines produce a heavy weight similar to bold style while narrower lines produce lighter weight text.

Wi-Fi (Wireless-Fidelity): The most popular form of wireless networking protocol, otherwise known as 802.11b. Wi-Fi provides standards for wireless LANs.

Word size: The group of bits that a processor can manipulate as a unit in one machine cycle.

Works for hire: In multimedia development, works produced under the specific direction of an employer and using the employer's resources. The copyright for works for hire generally belongs to the employer, rather than the employee.

Writer: In multimedia development, the team member who creates the written material for a project such as the project proposal, scripts for scenes, and help screens.

WWW (World Wide Web): A distributed information system developed by Tim Berners-Lee. Utilizes HTTP protocols to deliver information in a client/server environment.

Xanadu: A proposed worldwide resource of interconnected knowledge bases defined by Theodore Nelson in the early 1970s. The WWW embraces several principles first defined by Nelson in the Xanadu project, most notably a non-linear means of accessing information.

XHTML (eXtensible Hypertext Markup Language): The current version of the codes used to define and format the elements of a web page. Many of the basic codes or "tags" are similar to HTML, originally used by Tim Berners-Lee to form web documents. XHTML is based on XML, which provides the tools to extend the ability of web developers to create their own syntax for data types and complex web page formation.

XML (eXtensible Markup Language): A set of standardized tools that can be used to create new markup languages. This open standard provides a structure for defining custom elements that fit the needs of the data to be displayed. XHTML is one language based on these standards.

Y/C (Luminance/Chrominance): A variant of component color that transmits video as separate luminance (brightness) and chrominance (color hue) signals. See also *S-Video*.

Zip disk: A cartridge storage medium made popular by Iomega. Zip drives support cartridges of 100, 250, or 750MB capacity.

Index